A Practitioner's Guide to the City
Code on Takeovers and Mergers
2014/2015

A Practitioner's Guide to the City Code on Takeovers and Mergers 2014/2015

Introduced by

Philip Robert-Tissot
Director General
The Panel on Takeovers and Mergers

SWEET & MAXWELL

 THOMSON REUTERS

Published in 2014 by Thomson Reuters (Professional) UK Limited trading as Sweet & Maxwell, Friars House, 160 Blackfriars Road, London, SE1 8EZ (Registered in England & Wales, Company No 1679046.
Registered Office and address for service: 2nd floor, Aldgate House, 33 Aldgate High Street, London EC3N 1DL)

For further information on our products and services, visit *http://www.sweetandmaxwell.co.uk.*

Typeset by Letterpart Limited, Caterham on the Hill, Surrey CR3 5XL

Printed and bound in Great Britain by CPI Antony Rowe, Chippenham, Wiltshire

No natural forests were destroyed to make this product: only farmed timber was used and replanted.

A CIP catalogue record of this book is available from the British Library.

ISBN: 978-0-414-03403-7

Thomson Reuters and the Thomson Reuters Logo are trademarks of Thomson Reuters. Sweet & Maxwell ® is a registered trademark of Thomson Reuters (Professional) UK Limited.

Crown copyright material is reproduced with the permission of the Controller of HMSO and the Queen's Printer for Scotland.

Biographies

Philip Robert-Tissot is Director General of The Panel on Takeovers and Mergers, a position that he took up on April 1, 2013 for a period of two years, on secondment from Citi. Philip graduated from Birmingham University in 1983, worked for four years for Rio Tinto Zinc and received an MBA from Cranfield School of Management. In 1989, Philip joined Schroders in its UK Investment Banking team, which was acquired by Citi in 2000. Prior to his secondment to the Panel, Philip was a Managing Director and Chairman of Citi's EMEA M&A business, having formerly been Head of UK Banking & Broking.

Piers Prichard Jones is a partner in Freshfields' London office. He focuses on domestic and cross-border mergers and acquisitions and has advised on a number of significant UK public transactions in recent years, including Xstrata's merger with Glencore, BAE Systems' proposed merger with EADS and CKI's acquisition of Northumbrian Water. He also advised the consortia which took private BAA and Kelda (Yorkshire Water). Piers is a regular speaker at conferences, and a regular contributor to publications, on UK takeovers.

Andy Ryde became a Partner at Slaughter and May in 1996. He is Head of the Corporate practice and works on UK and international corporate and M&A deals and securities offerings.

Roland Turnill became a Partner at Slaughter and May in 2004. He specialises in public takeovers and mergers, private acquisitions and disposals, and securities offerings.

Christopher Pearson is a Partner at Norton Rose Fulbright LLP. He qualified as a solicitor in 1984 and joined Norton Rose in 1986. From 1988 to 1991 he practised in Hong Kong. He became a partner of Norton Rose in 1992 and specialises in public company work. In recent years he has worked on a number of high-profile transactions including the Guinness/GrandMet merger; Mannesmann/Orange; Texas Utilities/The Energy Group; Ciba Specialty Chemicals/Allied Colloids; Trinity/Mirror Group; Deutsche Börse/London Stock Exchange; Brascan/Canary Wharf; and Carlsberg/Heineken/Scottish & Newcastle.

Nick Adams is a Partner at Norton Rose Fulbright LLP, specialising in corporate finance. Nick has extensive experience of public company takeovers. Deals Nick has worked on include Mannesmann/Orange; Mannesmann/Vodafone; Texas Utilities/The Energy Group; Trinity/Mirror Group; Siemens Financial Services/Broadcastle; Mechel/Oriel Resources; and BA/Iberia. During 2000, Nick spent a year working as an investment banker at Citigroup.

Mark Gearing is a Partner at Allen & Overy LLP. He has been a Partner in the Corporate Department since 1992. His practice covers all types of corporate and commercial transactions, including domestic and international corporate finance and securities work. He has particular experience of public company takeovers and was joint Secretary of the Takeover Panel between 1992 and 1994.

Carlton Evans has been a Corporate Partner at Linklaters since 1997 and was a Senior Executive at the Takeover Panel for the two years ending June 1998. He is an M&A and private equity expert, including having advised on deals such as: the £7.6 billion merger of Siebe and BTR to form Invensys; the £17 billion break-up takeover of Cable & Wireless Communications by Cable & Wireless and ntl; the P2P offer by TPG for GlobeOp; P2Ps of LA Fitness by MidOcean, of Caffè Nero by its founder Gerry Ford and Paladin, and of Willis Corroon by KKR; sales by Apax/Nordic Capital/Capio of Capio UK and Capio Spain; the $1.8 billion investment in BTG Pactual by a consortium including GIC and Ontario Teachers; and the EUR 2.5 billion takeover to redomicile New World Resources in the UK.

David Pudge is a Partner in the Corporate Finance practice at Clifford Chance LLP. He specialises in domestic and cross-border mergers and acquisitions, corporate finance transactions and public company advisory work, with a particular focus on public takeover offers. Significant transactions include advising: International Power Plc on its combination by way of reverse takeover with the international power business of GDF Suez and the subsequent scheme of arrangement whereby GDF Suez acquired the shares it did not already own in International Power; Man Group plc on its acquisition of NYSE listed alternative investment manager GLG Partners Inc; BPB on its defence against the unsolicited offer from Saint-Gobain; and Banco Santander on the acquisition of Abbey National Plc by way of a scheme of arrangement. David also advised GKN Plc on the demerger of its support services activities and their combination with Brambles Industries Limited of Australia by way of a dual listed companies structure.

Lee Coney became a partner in the Corporate Finance practice at Clifford Chance LLP in 2007. Lee advises UK and international companies, private equity houses and investment banks on a range of corporate finance transactions and has extensive experience in public company takeovers. Significant transactions include advising EADS on its proposed combination with BAE Systems, Babcock International on its acquisition of VT Group, George Wimpey on its merger with Taylor Woodrow, Kraft Foods on its acquisition of Cadbury, Banco Santander on its acquisition of Abbey National, and Eurasian Resources Group on its £3 billion offer for Eurasian Resources Corporation Plc. Lee spent 12 months in one of the UK M&A teams at Citigroup in 2001.

Ursula Newton is a Partner in the Capital Markets Group at PricewaterhouseCoopers LLP where she specialises in advising on listing and public company transactions particularly in the London Market. She regularly lectures on the Listing Rules and City Code reporting issues.

Mark Bardell is a partner at Herbert Smith Freehills LLP. He has a particular focus on domestic and cross-border, corporate finance and M&A, including public takeovers. He is recommended in Legal 500 for M&A premium deals and noted for his public takeover expertise. In September 2011, he completed a two-year secondment as Secretary to the Takeover Panel. He is a contributor to leading practitioner's texts on topics including market abuse, schemes of arrangement and takeovers. He regularly lectures at Cambridge University to postgraduate students as part of the Deals Course on the MCL.

Contents

2 The Approach, Announcements and Independent Advice

Piers Prichard Jones

Partner

Freshfields Bruckhaus Deringer LLP

3 Share Dealings and Holdings—Restrictions and Disclosure Requirements

Andy Ryde

Partner

Slaughter and May

Roland Turnill

Partner

Slaughter and May

7   Conduct During the Offer; Timing and Revision; and Restrictions Following Offers

David Pudge
Partner
Clifford Chance LLP

Lee Coney
Partner
Clifford Chance LLP

Chapter 1

The Panel on Takeovers and Mergers

Philip Robert-Tissot

Director General

The Panel on Takeovers and Mergers

1.1   Introduction

The Panel on Takeovers and Mergers (the Panel) is an independent body whose main functions are to issue and administer the Takeover Code (the Code) and to supervise and regulate takeovers and other matters to which the Code applies.

The Panel was established in 1968, since when its composition and powers have evolved as circumstances have changed. On May 20, 2006, the Panel was designated by the Secretary of State for Trade and Industry as the supervisory authority to carry out certain regulatory functions in relation to takeovers pursuant to the European Directive on Takeover Bids (the Directive). Its statutory functions are set out in Pt 28 of the Companies Act 2006 (the Act), which, among other things, implemented the Directive. The Rules set out in the Code also have statutory effect in the Isle of Man, Jersey and Guernsey by virtue of legislation applying in those jurisdictions.

The Code is designed principally to ensure that shareholders in an offeree company are treated fairly and are not denied the opportunity to decide on the merits of a takeover, and that shareholders in the offeree company of the same class are afforded equivalent treatment by an offeror. The Code also provides an orderly framework within which takeovers are conducted. In addition, it is designed to promote, in conjunction with other regulatory regimes, the integrity of the financial markets.

The Code is not concerned with the financial or commercial advantages or disadvantages of takeovers. These are matters for the companies concerned and their shareholders. In addition, it is not the purpose of the Code either to facilitate or to impede takeovers. Nor is the Code concerned with matters of public interest, such as competition policy, which are the responsibility of Government and other bodies such as the Competition Commission, the Office of Fair Trading and the European Commission.

The Code has been developed since 1968 to reflect the collective opinion of those professionally involved in the field of takeovers as to appropriate business standards and as to how fairness to offeree company shareholders and an orderly framework for takeovers can be achieved.

The Code applies to all offers for companies which have their registered offices in the United Kingdom, the Channel Islands and the Isle of Man, if any of their securities are admitted to trading on a regulated market or multilateral trading facility (each as defined) in the United Kingdom or on any stock exchange in the Channel Islands or the Isle of Man. The Code also applies to offers for other public companies and certain private companies which have their registered offices in the United Kingdom, the Channel Islands or the Isle of Man and which are considered by the Panel to have their place of central management and control in one of those jurisdictions (the residency test). In addition, under the Directive, the Panel has shared jurisdiction with regulators in other Member States of the European Economic Area in certain circumstances.

The Code comprises six General Principles, 38 Rules, the accompanying Notes on these Rules and seven Appendices, as well as the Introduction and Definitions section. The six General Principles (which are taken directly from the Directive) apply to takeovers and other matters to which the Code applies. The General Principles are expressed in broad terms and the Code does not define the precise extent of, or limitations on, their application. They are applied in accordance with their spirit in order to achieve their underlying purpose. The General Principles are as follows.

1. All holders of the securities of an offeree company of the same class must be afforded equivalent treatment; moreover, if a person acquires control of a company, the other holders of securities must be protected.
2. The holders of the securities of an offeree company must have sufficient time and information to enable them to reach a properly informed decision on the bid; where it advises the holders of securities, the board of the offeree company must give its views on the effects of implementation of the bid on employment, conditions of employment and the locations of the company's places of business.
3. The board of an offeree company must act in the interests of the company as a whole and must not deny the holders of securities the opportunity to decide on the merits of the bid.
4. False markets must not be created in the securities of the offeree company, of the offeror company or of any other company concerned by the bid in such a way that the rise or fall of the prices of the securities becomes artificial and the normal functioning of the markets is distorted.
5. An offeror must announce a bid only after ensuring that he/she can fulfil in full any cash consideration, if such consideration is offered, and after taking all reasonable measures to secure the implementation of any other type of consideration.
6. An offeree company must not be hindered in the conduct of its affairs for longer than is reasonable by a bid for its securities.

These General Principles, which are essentially statements of standards of commercial behaviour, encapsulate the spirit of the Code and form the foundation upon which the Rules and the accompanying Notes are based.

1.2 Key characteristics of the Panel: application of the Code according to the underlying purpose

The essential characteristics of the Panel are flexibility, certainty and speed, enabling the parties to an offer to know where they stand under the Code in a timely fashion. These characteristics are important in order to avoid over-rigidity of the Rules and the risk of takeovers becoming delayed by litigation of a tactical nature, which may frustrate the ability of shareholders to decide the outcome of an offer. Central to this approach is the concept that it is the spirit of the Code which must be observed as well as the letter.

Situations frequently arise in takeovers which could not reasonably have been envisaged and the Panel Executive (the Executive) is able to respond to such situations by applying the General Principles and the Rules in accordance with their spirit in order to achieve their underlying purpose in the particular circumstances. The Panel is able to derogate or grant a waiver to a person from the application of a Rule, provided that, in the case of a transaction and Rule subject to the requirements of the Directive, the General Principles are respected.

When a person or its advisers are in any doubt whatsoever as to whether a proposed course of conduct is in accordance with the General Principles or the Rules, or whenever a waiver or derogation from the application of the provisions of the Code is sought, that person or its advisers must consult the Executive in advance. To take legal or other professional advice on the interpretation, application or effect of the Code is not an appropriate alternative to obtaining a ruling from the Executive.

1.3   Some key Rules

Most of the individual Rules of the Code are accompanied by Notes which provide guidance on the application of the Rules in certain given circumstances. In addition, as more particularly referred to below, the Executive from time to time issues Practice Statements which provide guidance as to how the Executive normally interprets and applies relevant Rules in particular circumstances.

In this Chapter, some particular Rules of the Code which reflect the General Principles are highlighted; later chapters deal with some of the specific Rules in more detail.

As will be noted, a number of these Rules refer to the concept of "acting in concert". Under the Code, persons acting in concert comprise persons who, pursuant to an agreement or understanding (whether formal or informal), co-operate to obtain or consolidate control (see 1.3.1 below) of a company or to frustrate the successful outcome of an offer for a company. Without prejudice to the general application of this definition, persons who fall within certain prescribed categories are presumed under the Code to be acting in concert with each other unless the contrary is established. These categories include, broadly, companies within the same corporate group, companies with their directors and pension funds, fund managers with any funds that they manage on a discretionary basis, and financial advisers and corporate brokers with any parties to an offer that they are advising in relation to the offer. In practice, given the importance of this definition to the application of a number of Rules, the Executive is frequently consulted on the composition of so-called "concert parties".

1.3.1   *General Principle 1: equivalent treatment and protection of non-controlling shareholders*

Perhaps the best known Rule of the Code is Rule 9, which prescribes the circumstances in which a mandatory offer must be made, the terms on which it must be made and the person who is primarily responsible for making it. The mandatory

5

offer Rule reflects the requirement for equivalent treatment of all shareholders and seeks to ensure that de facto control of a company cannot be bought by a person paying a premium price to one or more shareholders, whilst at the same time leaving the remaining shareholders behind with a new controller and no opportunity to exit at the same premium price. For the purposes of the Code, shares carrying 30 per cent or more of the voting rights of a company are regarded as conferring control.

The requirement under Rule 9 for a person to make a mandatory offer arises in circumstances where:

1. that person acquires (whether by a series of transactions over a period of time or not) an interest in shares which, taken together with shares in which persons acting in concert with him are interested, carry 30 per cent or more of the voting rights of a company; or
2. that person, together with persons acting in concert with him, is interested in shares which in aggregate carry not less than 30 per cent of the voting rights of a company, but does not hold shares carrying more than 50 per cent of such voting rights, and that person, or any person acting in concert with him, acquires an interest in any other shares which increases the percentage of shares carrying voting rights in which he is interested.

A mandatory offer under Rule 9 must be made in cash, or include a full cash alternative, at a price not less than the highest price paid by the person who is subject to the mandatory offer requirement (or anyone acting in concert with him) for any interest in shares in the offeree company during the 12 months prior to the announcement of the offer. In addition, the offer can be conditional only upon the receipt of sufficient acceptances so as to result in the offeror and persons acting in concert with him holding shares carrying more than 50 per cent of the voting rights in the offeree company.

Rule 11 is also based on the requirement that shareholders should be afforded equivalent treatment, specifically in relation to the type of consideration that they receive from an offeror. Broadly speaking, Rule 11 requires an offer to be in cash or accompanied by a full cash alternative whenever an offeror or any person acting in concert with him acquires, for cash, any interest in shares in the offeree company during the offer period. Further, it provides that where an offeror or any person acting in concert with him acquires, for cash, interests in shares in the offeree company carrying 10 per cent or more of the total voting rights in the offeree company during the offer period and within 12 months prior to its commencement, the offer must be in cash or accompanied by a cash alternative at not less than the highest price paid by the offeror (or any person acting in concert with him) during the offer period and within 12 months prior to its commencement.

Rule 6 relates to the value of the consideration that shareholders receive from an offeror, and provides that where an offeror or any person acting in concert with him acquires an interest in shares in the offeree company either during the offer period or in the three month period prior to its commencement, the offer to shareholders must be on no less favourable terms.

In addition, favourable deals between an offeror and particular shareholders and other persons interested in shares in the offeree company, which are not made available to all shareholders, are generally prohibited under Rule 16.

1.3.2 *General Principle 2: sufficiency of time, information and advice*

Rule 31.1 requires an offer to be open for at least 21 days following the date on which the offer document is published. Once an offer has become or is declared unconditional as to acceptances (other than an offer which is unconditional from the outset), the offer must, under Rule 31.4, then remain open for not less than 14 days after the date on which it would otherwise have expired. Rule 32.1 requires that, if an offer is revised, the offer must be kept open for at least 14 days following the date on which the revised offer document is published. In addition, Appendix 7 sets out similar timetable requirements in relation to offers being effected by means of a scheme of arrangement, including the requirement that the shareholder meetings required in order to implement the scheme must be held on not less than 21 days' notice, and that any revision of the terms of the scheme should normally be made by no later than 14 days prior to the date of those meetings.

Rule 23 requires shareholders to be given sufficient information and advice to enable them to arrive, in good time, at a properly informed decision regarding the offer. The obligation under Rule 23 is reinforced by the requirements of Rule 3 and also Rules 24 and 25.

Under Rule 3, the board of the offeree company must obtain financial advice from a competent independent adviser. The substance of that advice must be made known to all shareholders. As a result, shareholders in the offeree company have the benefit of that adviser's views, as well as the opinion of the directors.

Rule 24 requires an offeror to send an offer document to shareholders in the offeree company and persons with information rights as well as making it readily available to the pension scheme trustees and employee representatives (or the employees themselves, if they have no representatives). Rule 25 requires the board of the offeree company to send a circular to shareholders in the offeree company and persons with information rights as well as making it readily available to pension scheme trustees and employees/employee representatives. The circular must set out the board's opinion on the offer and its reasons for forming its opinion. Rules 24 and 25 also set out detailed requirements as to the contents of these documents, which may be combined into a single document in a recommended offer. These include a requirement that the offeror states its intentions with regard to the future business of the offeree company (including its strategic plans and their likely repercussions on employment and the locations of the offeree company's places of business), and explains the long-term commercial justification for the offer, and a corresponding requirement that the board of the offeree company sets out its views on these matters. In addition, both the offeror and the offeree company must disclose certain financial information in relation to themselves, including, in relation to the offeror, details of the way in which it is financing the offer. Since September 2011 (see 1.4.1.1 below) it has also been a requirement that the offeror and offeree company disclose details of the fees and expenses expected to be incurred by them in relation to the offer.

Rule 20.1 requires information about companies involved in an offer to be made equally available to all offeree company shareholders as nearly as possible at the same time and in the same manner.

Rule 19.1 requires that each document published, or statement made, during the course of an offer must be prepared with the highest standards of care and accuracy and that the information given must be adequately and fairly presented. If any such statement made by a party to an offer relates to any particular course of action that it intends to take or not take after the end of the offer period, that party will be held to its statement for a period of 12 months from the date on which the offer period ends, or such other period of time as is specified in the statement, unless there has been a material change of circumstances.

Other Rules also set out the consequences of making certain specific statements during an offer period, for example Rule 2.8 ("no intention to bid" statements), Rule 31.5 ("no extension" statements) and Rule 32.2 ("no increase" statements). In summary, a party which makes a statement during an offer period will, generally speaking, be bound by it.

1.3.3   General Principle 3: shareholders to be given an opportunity to decide on the merits of a bid

Rule 21.1 provides that during the course of an offer, or even before the date of the offer if the board of the offeree company has reason to believe that a bona fide offer might be imminent, the board must not, without the approval of shareholders in general meeting, take any action which may result in any offer or bona fide possible offer being frustrated or in shareholders being denied the opportunity to decide on its merits. However, shareholder approval may not be required where:

1.   the proposed action is in pursuance of a pre-existing contract or other pre-existing obligation; or
2.   a decision to take the proposed course of action had been taken before the date on which the offeree company was first approached or, if earlier, the date on which the offeree company had reason to believe that a bona fide offer might be imminent, and the proposed course of action had either been partly or fully implemented before such date or is otherwise in the ordinary course of the offeree company's business.

Under Rule 21.2, except with the consent of the Panel, neither the offeree company nor any person acting in concert with it is permitted to enter into any offer-related arrangement (as defined) with either the offeror or any person acting in concert with it during an offer period or when an offer is reasonably in contemplation. This is because offer-related arrangements between one offeror and the offeree company (for example inducement fee agreements, implementation agreements or other "deal protections") might have the object or effect of deterring another offeror or offerors, thereby denying offeree company shareholders the possibility of deciding on the merits of a competing bid or bids.

On January 17, 2014, the Executive published Practice Statement No.27 in order to clarify the way in which the Executive interprets and applies Rule 21.2 in relation to irrevocable commitments and letters of intent given by offeree company shareholders who are also directors of the offeree company. The Practice Statement states that, while such persons are permitted to enter into irrevocable commitments and letters of intent, they must be limited to a commitment or intention to accept the offer (or to vote in favour of a scheme of arrangement). Irrevocable commitments and letters or intent given by offeree company directors must not extend to other matters, for example commitments not to solicit a competing offer or to provide due diligence information to an offeror. These commitments would be regarded by the Executive as having been entered into in the individual's capacity as a director of the offeree company (being a person acting in concert with the offeree company) and therefore would be in breach of Rule 21.2.

1.3.4 *General Principle 4: avoidance of false markets*

Transparency and disclosure are fundamental to the way in which the Panel seeks to avoid false markets in the securities of companies subject to bids. The importance of secrecy prior to the announcement of an offer or possible offer is paramount and Rule 2.2 of the Code provides that prior to any such announcement only a very restricted number of people (typically comprising not more than six outside parties) should have knowledge of a possible offer.

If a potential offeror is actively considering an offer or has entered into talks with the offeree company, and the offeree company is the subject of rumour or speculation or there is an untoward movement in the offeree company's share price, an announcement will typically be required in order to avoid a false market developing in the offeree company's shares. The obligation to make such an announcement will rest with the potential offeror if it has yet to approach the offeree company regarding its possible offer but will pass to the offeree company after the making of such an approach—provided the approach is not unequivocally rejected.

The announcement of a possible offer in relation to an offeree company will commence what is called an "offer period" (not

11

to be confused with the formal offer timetable, as mentioned in 1.3.2 above and 1.3.6 below), during which time a number of Rules in the Code will come into effect. One of these is Rule 8, which requires prompt disclosure of positions and dealings (which includes, in the case of the latter, the entering into of options and derivatives) in relevant securities by the parties to an offer and any person who is interested (directly or indirectly) in one per cent or more of any class of relevant securities of either the offeree company or any offeror that is offering its own shares as consideration under the offer.

1.3.5 General Principle 5: certainty of bid funding

Rule 2.7 provides that an offeror should announce a firm intention to make an offer only when that offeror has every reason to believe that it can and will continue to be able to implement the offer.

Rule 2.7 also requires that when the offer is for cash or includes an element of cash, the announcement must include confirmation by an appropriate third party (usually the offeror's financial adviser) that resources are available to the offeror sufficient to satisfy full acceptance of the offer. Rule 24.8 contains a similar "cash confirmation" requirement in respect of the offer document itself.

1.3.6 General Principle 6: offeree company not to be hindered in its affairs for longer than is reasonable

The Code contains detailed Rules relating to the timetable within which a potential offeror that has been publicly identified must confirm its intentions, and also within which an offer must be implemented. These Rules seek to prevent the offeree company from being the subject of an extended period of unwelcome "siege" as a result of an offer period continuing for longer than is reasonable, as well as to provide an orderly framework within which takeovers may be conducted.

Rules 2.4 and 2.6 set out the so-called "put up or shut up" regime which is designed principally to protect offeree companies against a protracted "virtual bid" period (i.e. a situation where a potential offeror announces that it is considering making an offer, often setting out indicative terms, but without formally committing itself to doing so).

Rule 2.4 requires that an announcement by the offeree company which commences an offer period must identify any potential offeror with which the offeree company is in talks or from which an approach has been received (and not unequivocally rejected). Further, any subsequent announcement by the offeree company which refers to the existence of a new potential offeror must identify that potential offeror, except where the announcement is made after an offeror has announced a firm intention to make an offer for the offeree company under Rule 2.7.

Rule 2.6 requires that an identified potential offeror must (subject to certain exceptions), by not later than 17.00 on the 28th day following the date of the announcement in which it is first identified, either:

1. announce a firm intention to make an offer (i.e. "put up"); or
2. announce that it does not intend to make an offer (i.e. "shut up"), in which case the potential offeror will normally be restricted from making an offer for the offeree company for a period of six months,

unless the Panel has consented to an extension of the deadline.

The Panel will normally consent to an extension of a "put up or shut up" deadline at the request of the board of the offeree company and after taking into account all relevant factors. The requirement for an identified potential offeror to make one of the announcements referred to above by the "put up or shut up" deadline will cease to apply if another offeror has already announced, or subsequently announces (prior to the relevant deadline), a firm intention to make an offer for the offeree company under Rule 2.7.

1.4 Code amendment

The Panel, through the Code Committee, is responsible for keeping the Code under review and for proposing, consulting on, making and issuing amendments to the Code. Matters leading to possible amendments to the Code might arise from a number of sources, including specific cases which the Panel has considered, market developments, and representations from third parties (such as shareholders). The Committee welcomes both suggestions from interested parties for possible amendments to the Code and the valuable responses to consultations which it receives.

In the ordinary course of events, once it has been agreed that a particular matter is to be pursued, the Committee will, with the assistance of the Executive, prepare and publish a Public Consultation Paper (PCP) seeking the views of interested parties on the proposals and setting out the background to, reasons for and (where applicable) full text of the proposed amendments. Consultation periods in relation to PCPs vary depending on the complexity of the subject but will usually be between one and two months. It is the Committee's policy to publish written responses it receives to a PCP, unless the respondent requests otherwise. Following the end of the consultation period, and once it has considered the responses received, the Committee will, with the assistance of the Executive, publish its conclusions on the proposed amendments, together with the final text of the Code amendments (if any), in a Response Statement (RS).

In certain exceptional cases, the Committee might consider it necessary to amend the Code on an expedited basis, for example because a particular market development appears to the Committee to require that the proposed amendment be made more quickly than the usual public consultation process would permit. In such cases, the Committee will publish the amendment with immediate effect, together with a public statement explaining the rationale for the amendment and its effect but without prior formal consultation. Publication of a Code amendment on such an expedited basis will be followed in due course by a PCP seeking views on the amendment, which might be modified as a result, or removed altogether, depending on the Committee's conclusions following the consultation process.

Where, in the opinion of the Committee, any proposed amendment to the Code either does not materially alter the effect of the provision in question or is a consequence of changes to relevant legislation or regulatory requirements, the Committee may publish the text of the amendment without any formal consultation process. The amendment will, however, be made public before the date on which it comes into effect, wherever practicable.

1.4.1 Recent Code Committee publications

1.4.1.1 Review of the September 2011 Amendments

In July 2011, the Committee published RS 2011/1 which proposed a number of amendments to the Code following the wide ranging consultation on certain aspects of the regulation of takeover bids that had followed the takeover of Cadbury Plc by Kraft Foods Inc. These amendments (the September 2011 Amendments) came into effect in September 2011. In RS 2011/1, the Committee had stated that, given the significance of the September 2011 Amendments, it intended to undertake a review of their operation by reference to a period of not less than 12 months following their implementation. The Committee published the conclusions of its review in November 2012 in Panel Statement 2012/8. The main conclusions were that:

1. the Rule changes designed to increase the protection for offeree companies against protracted "virtual bid" periods, notably the codification of the "put up or shut up" regime (see 1.3.6 above) had worked well and that there was no evidence of offeree companies having been put under siege for protracted periods in the period reviewed;
2. the general prohibition on "deal protection measures" and inducement fees (see 1.3.3 above) had generally achieved its objectives of reducing the tactical advantages which

15

offerors had previously been able to obtain over offeree companies and of redressing the balance in favour of offeree companies;

3.	the new Rules which require offerors and offeree companies to disclose in offer documents and offeree board circulars details of the fees and expenses expected to be incurred in relation to an offer had improved transparency with regard to offer-related fees and expenses;

4.	the Rule changes in relation to the financial and other information required to be disclosed by an offeror, including in relation to the financing of the offer, had worked well;

5.	there had been an improvement in the quality and detail of disclosures by offerors of their intentions with regard to the offeree company and its employees (see 1.3.2 above)—although the Committee was disappointed that, in many cases, disclosures had not been sufficiently specific; and

6.	the September 2011 Amendments appeared to have gone a considerable way towards achieving their objectives of improving communications between offeree companies and their employee representatives, and of enabling employee representatives to be more effective in providing their opinion on the effects of an offer on employment.

### 1.4.1.2	*Profit Forecasts, Quantified Financial Benefits Statements and Material Changes in Information*

In July 2012 the Code Committee published PCP 2012/1, which proposed a number of amendments to the Code in relation to its treatment of profit forecasts and quantified financial benefit statements made by the parties to an offer, as well as a number of changes to the Rules in relation to material changes to certain information previously published in connection with an offer.

The Committee published RS 2012/1 on July 24, 2013. Having considered the responses to the consultation, the Committee adopted most of the amendments to the Code proposed in PCP 2012/1, although some of the new provisions were introduced in a modified form. The principal aim of these changes was to liberalise and update the regime for profit forecasts, removing the requirement for a company to publish reports from accountants and financial advisers where the profit forecast is made before the offer approach to the offeree company, where it relates to a period ending more than 15 months from the date on which it is published or where it is an "ordinary course" profit forecast which is made either before the commencement of the offer period or, if the other parties to the offer agree, during the offer period. The rule changes were made by Instrument 2013/4 and came into effect on September 30, 2013. (The new regime is described in further detail in Chapter 8.)

1.4.1.3 Pension Scheme Trustees

Also in July 2012, the Code Committee published PCP 2012/2, which related to pension scheme trustee issues. Broadly, the amendments proposed in PCP 2012/2 were designed to afford to the trustees of an offeree company's pension scheme similar rights to those afforded under the Code to an offeree company's employee representatives. The Committee's intention was to create a framework within which the effects of an offer on an offeree company's pension scheme could become a debating point during the course of the offer and a point on which the parties to the offer and the trustees of the pension scheme could have an opportunity to express their views.

Following consideration of the comments received from respondents and discussions held with the Pensions Regulator by the Executive on the Committee's behalf, the Committee adopted the proposed amendments, in slightly modified form, in RS 2012/2, which was published on April 22, 2013. The Rule changes, which were made by Instrument 2013/2, came into effect on May 20, 2013.

1.4.1.4 Companies Subject to the Code

The third and final consultation published by the Committee in July 2012 was PCP 2012/3, which proposed the removal from the Code of the "residency test", i.e. the requirement for a company which is registered in the United Kingdom, the

Channel Islands or the Isle of Man, and whose securities are not admitted to trading on a UK regulated market, to have its place of central management and control in the United Kingdom, the Channel Islands or the Isle of Man in order for the company to be subject to the jurisdiction of the Code (see 1.1 above). The Committee had proposed the removal of the residency test with respect to all companies to which it applied, being companies whose securities are admitted to trading on a multilateral trading facility in the United Kingdom, companies whose securities are admitted to trading on an overseas market and companies whose securities are not admitted to trading on a public market.

In the light of responses received, however, the Committee concluded in RS 2012/3, which was published on May 15, 2013, that the residency test should be removed only with respect to the United Kingdom, Channel Islands and Isle of Man companies whose securities are admitted to trading on a multilateral trading facility in the United Kingdom. The changes to the Panel's jurisdiction, which were made by Instrument 2013/3, came into effect on September 30, 2013.

1.4.1.5 *Replacement of the Office of Fair Trading and the Competition Commission by the Competition and Markets Authority*

On March 4, 2014, the Committee published Instrument 2014/1, which made various minor amendments to the Code in order to reflect the replacement of the Office of Fair Trading and the Competition Commission by the Competition and Markets Authority. These amendments took effect on April 1, 2014. As the amendments were made either as a consequence of changes to legislation or did not materially alter the effect of the provisions in question, they were approved by the Committee without public consultation.

1.4.1.6 *PCP 2014/1 – Miscellaneous amendments*

On July 16, 2014, the Committee published PCP 2014/1, which proposed a number of miscellaneous amendments to the Code.

The proposed amendments set out in PCP 2014/1 included, amongst other matters, the following:

(a) A change to the deadline for a potential competing offeror to clarify its position from a flexible date set by the Panel on a case-by-case basis to a fixed date, being the 53rd day after the publication of the first offeror's offer document.
(b) An amendment to Note 2 on Rule 2.8 which provides that, where a potential competing offeror makes a "no intention to bid" statement but nevertheless acquires interests in shares in the offeree company after "Day 53", the former potential offeror will forfeit the ability to set aside its no intention to bid statement with the agreement of the offeree company board.
(c) Changes to Note 4 on Rule 2.2 which provide that, where a potential offeror has been granted a dispensation from having to make an announcement under Rule 2.2, that potential offeror is restricted from doing any of the things set out in Rules 2.8(a) to (e) for a period of six months from the date on which the dispensation is granted and, in addition, from actively considering making an offer, making an approach to the offeree company board or acquiring any interests in shares in the offeree company for a period of three months from the date on which the dispensation is granted.
(d) Modifications to the default auction procedure which the Panel would normally impose in order to resolve a competitive situation which continues to exist on "Day 46" of the second offeror's offer timetable and the incorporation of the default auction procedure into the Code as a new Appendix 8.
(e) The introduction of a requirement that, where a potential new controller is granted a "whitewash" waiver under Note 1 of the Notes on Dispensations from Rule 9, the shareholder circular must explain that the potential new controller will not be restricted from making an offer for the company following the approval of the proposals at the shareholders' meeting unless it has entered into a standstill agreement or has made a statement that it does not intend to make an offer.

(f) Certain minor changes to the rules on "no increase" and "no extension" statements.

(g) Changes relating to the disclosure of irrevocable commitments, letters of intent and interests in relevant securities.

(h) Amendments to Rule 3 which clarify the distinction between the role of an independent adviser appointed under Rule 3.1 to provide financial advice on the offer to the board of the offeree company and the role of the offeree company board to give its opinion on the offer to offeree company shareholders.

The implementation of the proposed amendments is subject to the outcome of the consultation.

1.5 Practice Statements

The Executive, from time to time, publishes Practice Statements in order to provide informal guidance to companies involved in takeovers and practitioners as to how the Executive normally interprets and applies relevant provisions of the Code in particular circumstances. Practice Statements do not form part of the Code and, accordingly, are not binding on the Executive or the Panel and are not a substitute for consulting the Executive to establish how the Code applies in a particular case. Practice Statements are periodically reviewed by the Executive and are amended or withdrawn, as necessary. All current Practice Statements can be found on the Panel's website (*http://www.thetakeoverpanel.org.uk*) [Accessed July 14, 2014].

1.6 The Panel and its Committees

A brief description of the membership, functions, responsibilities and general activities of the Panel and certain of its Committees is set out below.

1.6.1 The Panel

The Panel assumes overall responsibility for the policy, financing and administration of the Panel's functions and for the functioning and operation of the Code. The Panel operates through a number of Committees and is directly responsible for those matters which are not dealt with through one of its Committees.

The Panel comprises up to 35 members:

1. the Chairman, who is appointed by the Panel;
2. up to three Deputy Chairmen, who are appointed by the Panel;
3. up to 20 other members, who are appointed by the Panel; and
4. individuals appointed by each of the following bodies:
    (a) the Association for Financial Markets in Europe (with separate representation also for its Corporate Finance Committee and Securities Trading Committee);
    (b) the Association of British Insurers;
    (c) the Association of Investment Companies;
    (d) the British Bankers' Association;
    (e) the Confederation of British Industry;
    (f) the Institute of Chartered Accountants in England and Wales;
    (g) the Investment Management Association;
    (h) the National Association of Pension Funds; and
    (i) the Wealth Management Association.

The Chairman and the Deputy Chairmen are designated as members of the Hearings Committee. Each other member appointed by the Panel under para.(3) above is designated upon appointment to act as a member of either the Panel's Code Committee or its Hearings Committee. The members appointed by the bodies under para.(4) above become members of the Hearings Committee without further designation by the Panel. In performing their functions on the Hearings Committee and the Panel, such members act independently of the body which has appointed them and not as that body's agent or delegate, and exercise their own judgment as to how to perform their functions and how to vote.

No member of the Code Committee may simultaneously or subsequently be a member of the Hearings Committee.

1.6.2 The Code Committee

The Code Committee represents a spread of shareholder, corporate, practitioner and other interests within the Panel's regulated community. Up to 12 members of the Panel are designated as members of the Code Committee.

As noted above, the Committee carries out the rule-making functions of the Panel and is solely responsible for keeping the Code (other than certain matters set out in the Introduction, which are the responsibility of the Panel itself) under review and for proposing, consulting on, making and issuing amendments to the Code.

The Terms of Reference of the Committee and the procedures it has adopted for amending the Code can be found on the Panel's website.

1.6.3 The Hearings Committee

The Hearings Committee comprises the Chairman, the Deputy Chairmen, up to eight other members designated by the Panel and the individuals appointed by the bodies listed at para.1.6.1(4) above.

The principal function of the Committee is to review, on application, rulings of the Executive. The Committee also hears disciplinary proceedings instituted by the Executive when the Executive considers that there has been a breach of the Code or of a ruling of the Executive or the Panel. The Committee may also be convened for hearings in certain other circumstances.

The Terms of Reference and Rules of Procedure of the Committee can be found on the Panel's website.

Rulings of the Committee are binding on the parties to the proceedings and on those invited to participate in those proceedings unless and until overturned by the Takeover Appeal Board (see 1.8 below).

1.7 The Executive

The day-to-day work of takeover supervision and regulation is carried out by the Executive. This includes, either on its own initiative or at the instigation of third parties, the conduct of investigations, the monitoring of relevant dealings in connection with the Code and the giving of guidance and rulings on the interpretation, application or effect of the Code. The Executive is available both for consultation and also the giving of rulings on the interpretation, application or effect of the Code before, during and, where appropriate, after takeovers or other relevant transactions. In carrying out these functions, the Executive operates independently of the Panel.

The Executive is staffed by a mixture of employees and secondees from law firms, accountancy firms, investment banks and other organisations. It is headed by the Director General, usually an investment banker on secondment, who is an officer of the Panel. The Director General is assisted by Deputy Directors General (who are permanent), Secretaries (including one or more solicitors on secondment from prominent law firms) and other members of the Executive's permanent and seconded staff (including a number of secondee Assistant Secretaries). In performing their functions, the secondees act wholly independently of the firms which have seconded them.

The Assistant Secretaries are primarily responsible for dealing with casework and the daily volume of general enquiries. They have the main responsibility for communicating with practitioners and parties to bids. They receive the initial enquiries and they disseminate the Executive's responses and rulings.

The nature of the Executive's rulings will depend on whether or not the Executive is able to hear the views of the other parties involved. If the Executive is not able to hear the views of other parties involved, it may give a conditional ruling (on an ex parte basis) which may be varied or set aside when any views of the other parties have been heard; if the Executive is able to hear the views of other parties involved, it may give an unconditional ruling. An unconditional ruling is binding on those who are made aware of it unless and until overturned by the Hearings Committee or the Takeover Appeal Board. In addition, such persons must comply with any conditional ruling given by the Executive for the purpose of preserving the status quo pending the unconditional ruling.

The Executive keeps under review and carries out research into issues which might require a Code amendment and, if appropriate, recommends Code changes to the Code Committee. Most changes to the Code are subject to public consultation (as described in 1.4 above) and the Executive manages the consultation process, including the preparation of PCPs and RSs.

The Executive also monitors market dealings in shares of companies which are either in an offer period or which the Executive has been informed might go into an offer period. The Executive focuses on enforcing compliance with the disclosure requirements of the Code (in particular, Rule 8), monitoring for abuses of the "exempt" status of the principal trading and fund management divisions of financial institutions, and of recognised intermediary status, and checking for breaches of the Code through dealings by parties to a takeover on the various trading platforms. Securities firms and market operators regularly receive enquiries from the Executive as to the identities of their clients, why transactions have not been disclosed and, occasionally, requests for a more detailed account of the reasons for a particular transaction. The Executive also seeks to identify transactions which might require an announcement under Rule 2 of the Code where there is evidence of speculation or informed dealing in the market but where no announcement has been made of an offer or possible offer.

1.8 Takeover Appeal Board

The Takeover Appeal Board (the Board) is an independent body which hears appeals against rulings of the Hearings Committee. The Chairman and Deputy Chairmen of the Board will usually have held high judicial office and are appointed by the Master of the Rolls. Other members, who will usually have relevant knowledge and experience of takeovers and the Code, are appointed by the Chairman (or, failing that, the Deputy Chairmen) of the Board. The names of the members of the Board are available on the Board's website (*http://www. thetakeoverappealboard.org.uk*) [Accessed July 14, 2014].

Any party to a hearing before the Hearings Committee (or any person denied permission to be a party to a hearing before the Hearings Committee) may appeal to the Board against any ruling of the Hearings Committee or the Chairman of the hearing (including in respect of procedural directions).

Proceedings before the Board are generally conducted in a similar way to those before the Hearings Committee, using the procedure set out in the Board's Rules which are available on its website. The Board may confirm, vary, set aside, annul or replace the contested ruling of the Hearings Committee.

1.9 Relationship between the Panel and the courts

The proceedings of the Panel are, in the same way as other bodies performing public functions, open to judicial review by the courts. There have been very few instances in which leave to apply for judicial review has been sought. One example was the Datafin case, which related to rival bids for McCorquodale in December 1986 (*R. v Panel on Takeovers and Mergers Ex p.*

Datafin Plc [1987] Q.B. 815; (1987) 3 B.C.C. 10 CA). The Master of the Rolls, Lord Donaldson, held that:

"... in the light of the special nature of the Panel, its functions, the market in which it is operating, the time scales which are inherent in that market and the need to safeguard the position of third parties, who may be numbered in thousands, all of whom are entitled to continue to trade upon an assumption of the validity of the Panel's Rules and decisions, unless and until they are quashed by the court, I should expect the relationship between the Panel and the court to be historic rather than contemporaneous. I should expect the court to allow contemporary decisions to take their course, considering the complaint and intervening, if at all, later and in retrospect by declaratory orders which would enable the Panel not to repeat any error and would relieve individuals of the disciplinary consequences of any erroneous finding of breach of the Rules."

The Guinness/Distillers case was the subject of a Court of Appeal judgment in July 1988 (*R. v Panel on Take-overs and Mergers Ex p. Guinness Plc* [1990] 1 Q.B. 146; [1989] 1 All E. R. 509). In this case the Court also indicated its reluctance to interfere in the Panel's decisions. Lord Diplock held that there was a public interest in the Panel acting to enforce the Code and, since no injustice had been done by the Panel's refusal to adjourn its case against Guinness, there was no case for judicial review.

The Court of Appeal's approach was confirmed in late 1988, when Grand Metropolitan sought judicial review of the Panel's decision not to require any remedy for breaches of the Code that the Panel held had been committed by Irish Distillers and Pernod Ricard, when the latter was gathering irrevocable undertakings to support its successful offer. The High Court refused to grant Grand Metropolitan an expedited order for the judicial review hearing on the grounds that the Court of Appeal had made it plain that such proceedings were not intended to reverse Panel decisions taken in the course of takeovers. As a result, the proceedings were discontinued. Judgments such as these demonstrate the courts' support for the Panel and thereby lend authority to its decisions.

The Court of Appeal's decision in the *Datafin* case underlies the approach taken at the time of the implementation of the Directive. For example, following implementation, rulings of the Panel have a binding effect; parties to a takeover are not able to sue each other for breach of a Rule-based requirement, and a transaction, once completed, may not be unpicked (see ss.945 and 956 of the Act).

The support of the court for the Panel, and the Rules contained in the Code, in establishing a framework for the conduct of public offers, was reinforced in connection with the *Expro* case in June 2008 (*Re Expro International Group Plc* [2008] EWHC 1543 (Ch); [2010] 2 B.C.L.C. 514). In that case, certain shareholders submitted to the court that the decision of the directors of Expro to reject a proposal from a competing offeror was wrong and, therefore, the court should not sanction the proposed scheme of arrangement being used to implement the initial offer in order to permit the competing offeror to make its proposal to Expro's shareholders. As part of his judgment rejecting the shareholders' arguments, Richards J. concluded that there should, if possible, be a common approach to bids whether they are structured as an offer or a scheme of arrangement and that it would not be desirable if the court procedures involved in a scheme of arrangement should introduce a level of uncertainty which the provisions of the Code had successfully eliminated or reduced in the course of contractual offers.

1.10 Enforcement of the Code

The Panel focuses on the consequences of breaches of the Code, rather than simply on disciplinary action, with the aim of providing appropriate redress. In certain circumstances the Panel may issue rulings to restrain a person from acting in breach of Rules or from following a particular course of action pending a Panel ruling on whether that action would be in breach of the Code. Furthermore, in respect of certain breaches of the Code, disciplinary action may be appropriate (see 1.11). Following implementation of the Directive, the Panel has certain statutory enforcement powers, further details of which are set out below.

1.10.1   Compliance rulings

If the Panel is satisfied that:

1.   there is a reasonable likelihood that a person will contravene a requirement imposed by or under Rules; or
2.   a person has contravened a requirement imposed by or under Rules,

the Panel may give any direction that appears to it to be necessary in order:

(a)   to restrain a person from acting (or continuing to act) in breach of Rules; or
(b)   to restrain a person from doing (or continuing to do) a particular thing, pending determination of whether that or any other conduct of his is or would be a breach of Rules; or
(c)   otherwise to secure compliance with Rules.

1.10.2   Compensation rulings

Where a person has breached any of the Rules of the Code requiring the payment of a certain level of consideration, for example, Rules 6, 9 and 11, the Panel may make a ruling requiring the person concerned to pay, within such period as it specifies, to the holders, or former holders, of securities of the offeree company, such amount as it thinks just and reasonable so as to ensure that such holders receive what they would have been entitled to receive if the relevant Rule had been complied with.

1.10.3   Enforcement by the courts

Under s.955 of the Act, the Panel has the power in certain circumstances to seek enforcement by the courts. If the court is satisfied that:

1. there is a reasonable likelihood that a person will contravene a requirement imposed by or under Rules; or
2. a person has contravened a requirement imposed by or under Rules or a requirement imposed under s.947 of the Act,

the court may make any order it thinks fit to secure compliance with the requirement. Any failure to comply with a resulting court order may be a contempt of court.

1.10.4   Power to require information and documents

The Panel expects any person dealing with it to do so in an open and co-operative way. It also expects prompt co-operation and assistance from persons dealing with it and those to whom enquiries and other requests are directed. Under s.947 of the Act the Panel has the power to require documents and information where they are reasonably required in connection with the exercise of its functions. A document describing how the Executive will exercise this power on behalf of the Panel is available on the Panel's website.

1.11   Disciplinary powers

The disciplinary Rules of the Panel in connection with breaches and alleged breaches of the Code are as follows:

1.11.1   Disciplinary action

The Executive may itself deal with a disciplinary matter where the person who is to be subject to the disciplinary action agrees the facts and the action proposed by the Executive. In any other case, where it considers that there has been a breach of the Code, the Executive may commence disciplinary proceedings before the Hearings Committee. A note setting out the factors that the Executive will take into account when deciding whether to initiate disciplinary action and in proposing the appropriate sanction to the Hearings Committee is available on the Panel's website.

1.11.2 Sanctions or other remedies for breach of the Code

If the Hearings Committee finds a breach of the Code or of a ruling of the Panel, it may:

1. issue a private statement of censure;
2. issue a public statement of censure;
3. suspend or withdraw any exemption, approval or other special status which the Panel has granted to a person, or impose conditions on the continuing enjoyment of such exemption, approval or special status, in respect of all or part of the activities to which such exemption, approval or special status relates;
4. report the offender's conduct to a United Kingdom or overseas regulatory authority or professional body (most notably the FCA) so that that authority or body can consider whether to take disciplinary or enforcement action (for example, the FCA has power to take certain actions against an authorised person or an approved person who fails to observe proper standards of market conduct, including the power to fine); or
5. publish a Panel Statement indicating that the offender is someone who, in the Hearings Committee's opinion, is not likely to comply with the Code. The Panel Statement will normally indicate that this sanction will remain effective for only a specified period. The "cold-shouldering" Rules of the FCA and certain professional bodies would then apply such that persons authorised by the FCA and members of those professional bodies would be obliged, in certain circumstances, not to act for the person in question in a transaction subject to the Code, including any dealing

in relevant securities requiring disclosure under Rule 8, for the duration of the relevant period.

1.12 Confidentiality, information sharing and co-operation

The Panel has always been scrupulous about ensuring that confidential information provided to it in the course of applying the Code is kept confidential. The Panel has a statutory duty of confidentiality so that information received by the Panel in connection with the exercise of its statutory functions may not be disclosed without the consent of the individual or business to which it relates, except as permitted by the Act.

Under the Act, the Panel must, to the extent it has power to do so, take such steps as it considers appropriate to co-operate with a number of other UK and international regulators including the FCA, the Prudential Regulation Authority, the Bank of England and other EU supervisory authorities designated for the purposes of the Directive, including by the sharing of information which the Panel is permitted to disclose under the Act. It may also exercise its powers to require documents and information for this purpose. In particular, the Panel works closely with the FCA in relation to insider dealing and market abuse.

Chapter 2

The Approach, Announcements and Independent Advice

Piers Prichard Jones

Partner

Freshfields Bruckhaus Deringer LLP

2.1 General considerations

This Chapter identifies the companies and transactions to which the Code applies. These Rules are set out in s.3 of the Introduction to the Code which was substantially revised in 2006 to reflect the implementation of the EU Directive on Takeover Bids (the Takeover Directive). One of the main changes to the Introduction was to the scope of the Panel's jurisdiction. The Panel is required by the Takeover Directive to take jurisdiction over a number of companies that were not previously covered by the Code. Its jurisdiction has since been further expanded with the removal of the "residency test" (explained further below) for certain companies following the amendments to the Code set out in RS 2012/3 which came into effect on September 30, 2013.

This Chapter also deals with Section D of the Code: Rules 1 to 3. These Rules are concerned with the crucial "pre-bid" period. The importance of this period cannot be over-emphasised. The commercial and tactical aspects—including the fundamental decision whether or not to proceed with the bid—can assume paramount importance, especially following the Code amendments effective from September 19, 2011 following the consultation in PCP 2011/1, the results of which are set out in RS 2011/1. The success or failure of the bid may hang on decisions taken at this stage. The pressures on all those involved can be enormous. Speed is critical and the whole enterprise can take on a momentum of its own. Once the formal "firm intention" press announcement is released the die is irretrievably cast. The Panel reiterated in its 2003 Annual Report that notwithstanding the time pressure on decisions taken in the "pre-bid" period, it is essential that the Executive is consulted under s.6(b) of the Introduction to the Code where there is any doubt whatsoever as to whether a proposed course of action is in accordance with the General Principles or the Rules of the Code.

The Panel has placed increasing emphasis on the special duty which advisers have to ensure that their clients are aware of their responsibilities under the Code. It is often the advisers who will be criticised by the Panel when things go wrong (for example, the criticism of the financial advisers to Transcomm Plc in the Panel's ruling in March 2004, referred to in 2.6.1 below). The Introduction to the Code states that financial advisers have a particular responsibility to comply with the Code and to ensure, so far as they are reasonably able, that their client and its directors are aware of their responsibilities under the Code and will comply with them, and that the Panel is consulted whenever appropriate (s.3(f)). However, it is not only financial advisers that the Panel will consider to have responsibility for their clients' compliance with the Code.

The Panel is also determined to ensure that all members of a board of directors—not just those entrusted with the day-to-day conduct of a bid—share responsibility for compliance with the Code. Appendix 3 to the Code spells out in detail the obligation to keep all directors fully informed and the responsibility of all directors to monitor the conduct of a bid.

The Code is made up of six General Principles (these are the six General Principles set out in the Takeover Directive which replaced the Code's previous 10 General Principles) and 38 detailed Rules (as well as seven further Appendices). The General Principles are relevant to interpreting the Rules—they are "applied in accordance with their spirit in order to achieve their underlying purpose" (see s.2(b) of the Introduction). The following are particularly relevant to Section D of the Code.

General Principle 4:

"False markets must not be created in the securities of the offeree company, of the offeror company or of any other company concerned by the bid in such a way that the rise or fall of the prices of the securities becomes artificial and the normal functioning of the markets is distorted."

General Principle 5:

"An offeror must announce a bid only after ensuring that he/she can fulfil in full any cash consideration, if such is offered, and after taking all reasonable measures to secure the implementation of any other type of consideration."

General Principle 6:

"An offeree company must not be hindered in the conduct of its affairs for longer than is reasonable by a bid for its securities."

One more "General Principle" should be added: for all intents and purposes, a press announcement is every bit as important as the offer document itself. This Chapter will consider a variety of press announcements ranging from the "talks are in progress" or "we are considering making an offer" kind to the formal announcement of the takeover. Whatever the type, all press announcements in the takeover context are designed to achieve the same purpose: to provide information which the market is entitled to rely upon and, where appropriate, to provide information needed to avoid the creation of a false market. In either case, press announcements must be prepared to the highest standards of care and accuracy. Once statements are made in a press announcement, the Panel will invariably expect the parties to adhere to them. In effect, there is little to distinguish the press announcement from the formal offer or defence documents which follow.

2.2 Companies and transactions to which the Code applies

Section 3 of the Introduction to the Code identifies the companies and transactions to which the Code applies. As explained above, it was substantially amended in May 2006 to reflect the implementation of the Takeover Directive. The Takeover Directive determines the minimum scope of the jurisdiction of the competent authority in any EU Member State by reference to the location of the registered office of the offeree company and the regulated market on which its securities are traded. The Code's jurisdiction is, however, wider than the minimum required by the Takeover Directive.

In 2012, the Code Committee published a consultation paper (PCP 2012/3) proposing certain changes in this area and, in May 2013, a response to that consultation (RS 2012/3) setting out the amendments to be made to the Code following the consultation. Those amendments to the Code came into effect on September 30, 2013.

2.2.1 *United Kingdom, Channel Islands and Isle of Man registered and traded companies*

The Code applies to offers for companies and Societas Europaea which have their registered offices in the United Kingdom, the Channel Islands or the Isle of Man, and which have any of their securities admitted to trading on a regulated market (which includes the London Stock Exchange's main market, and the ISDX Main Board) in the United Kingdom or on a multilateral trading facility (which includes AIM and also the ISDX Growth Market) in the United Kingdom or on a stock exchange in the Channel Islands or the Isle of Man (other than those companies which are covered by shared jurisdiction arrangements, see 2.2.3 below). These companies already fell within the Code prior to the implementation of the Takeover Directive (or, in respect of those companies admitted to trading on a multilateral trading facility but not a regulated market, prior to the amendments to the Code set out in RS2012/3 coming into effect), but only if they satisfied the Panel's residency test. This would be the case if the Panel considered that they had their place of central management and control in the United Kingdom, the Channel Islands or the Isle of Man. The residency test no longer applies in respect of any of these companies. Therefore, for example, the current position is that if a company is registered in the United Kingdom and has its shares admitted to trading on the main market of the London Stock Exchange, it is covered by the Code even if its place of central management and control is overseas. Similarly, a company registered in the United Kingdom that has its shares admitted to trading on AIM is also now (as a result of the amendments to the Code brought into force by RS2012/3) automatically covered by the Code even if its place of central management and control is overseas.

2.2.2 Other companies

The Code also applies to all offers (not falling within 2.2.1 above or 2.2.3 below) for other public and certain private companies and Societas Europaea that have their registered offices in the United Kingdom, the Channel Islands or the Isle of Man, but only if they are considered by the Panel to have their place of central management and control in these territories. When considering where a company is resident, the Panel will look at the structure of the board, the functions of the directors and where they are resident. Sometimes the Panel may also look at other relevant major influences on the management of the company, for example, in the case of an investment trust, the identity and location of the investment manager.

The residency test is therefore still applicable to a company that has its registered office in the United Kingdom, the Channel Islands or the Isle of Man if it is (a) a public company whose securities are either (i) not admitted to trading on any public market or (ii) admitted to trading on a public market but not one that is either a regulated market (in the United Kingdom or another EEA (European Economic Area) member state (a Member State)), a multilateral trading facility in the United Kingdom or a stock exchange in the Channel Islands or the Isle of Man—for example, a public company whose shares are only traded on the New York Stock Exchange—or (b) a private company.

Even if the directors of a target company not meeting the residency test volunteer to the Panel to subject themselves to the Code or incorporate a reference to the Code in the company's articles of association, the Panel will normally refuse to accept jurisdiction.

Offers for private companies satisfying the residency test are only subject to the Code (a) if any of their securities have been admitted to trading on any regulated market or multilateral trading facility in the United Kingdom or on any stock exchange in the Channel Islands or the Isle of Man within the past 10 years (which is a broadening of the scope of the equivalent test for private companies prior to the amendments to the Code contained in RS2012/3, when the only relevant market was the Official List, and now mirrors the test in s.3(a)(i) of the Introduction to the Code), or (b) if dealings and/or bid offer prices for their securities have been regularly published for at least six months within the past 10 years, whether via a newspaper, electronic price quotation system (such as the PLUS-quoted market) or otherwise, or (c) if any of their securities have been subject to a marketing arrangement within the past 10 years, or (d) if they have filed a prospectus (and, in the case of a filing with a relevant authority outside the United Kingdom, the Channel Islands or the Isle of Man, only if such filed prospectus is public) for the issue, offer or admission to trading of securities within the past 10 years (which is a narrowing of the scope of the equivalent test for private companies prior to the amendments to the Code contained in RS2012/3, which turned on whether a prospectus was *required* to be filed rather than *actually* filed). The

Introduction to the Code acknowledges that the provisions of the Code may not be appropriate to all such private companies and the Panel may therefore apply the Code with a degree of flexibility in suitable cases.

In its 2002 Annual Report, the Panel commented on the practice of re-registering a public company as a private company, with the result that the Code does not then apply to any offer for that company provided it does not fall within one of the categories described in the previous paragraph. The Panel advised that it would expect the circular convening the general meeting to effect the conversion to explain that one of the consequences of re-registration would be to take the company outside the ambit of the Code. The Panel should be consulted in advance in order to ensure that the circular contains an explanation of the Code and the implications for shareholders of re-registration. This is now reflected in s.3(e) of the Introduction to the Code, under which early consultation with the Panel is advised before re-registration if the relevant company has more than one shareholder so that guidance can be given by the Panel on the appropriate disclosure to be made regarding the loss of Code protection.

2.2.3 *Shared jurisdiction*

Section 3(a)(iii) of the Introduction to the Code deals with matters necessary to implement art.4.2(b), (c) and (e) of the Takeover Directive relating to shared jurisdiction in cases involving certain UK and other EEA registered and traded companies.

The Panel will share the regulation of an offer with a relevant competent authority in another Member State when the offeree company is:

1. a company which has its registered office in the United Kingdom and its securities are not admitted to trading on a UK regulated market but are admitted to trading on a regulated market in one or more other Member States;

2. a company registered in another Member State whose securities are admitted to trading only on a UK regulated market (and not, therefore, on a regulated market in any other Member State); or

3. a company registered in another Member State whose securities are admitted to trading on regulated markets in more than one Member State including the United Kingdom (but not on a regulated market in the Member State in which it has its registered office) if:

    (a) the company's securities were first admitted to trading on a UK regulated market; or

    (b) the company's securities were admitted to trading simultaneously on more than one regulated market on or after May 20, 2006 and the company notified the Panel and the other relevant regulatory authorities on the first day of trading that it had chosen the Panel to regulate it; or

    (c) the company's securities were admitted to trading on more than one regulated market before May 20, 2006 and were admitted simultaneously, and either the competent authorities of the relevant Member States agreed before June 19, 2006 that the Panel should be the regulator or, failing that, the company chose on June 19, 2006 to be regulated by the Panel.

In any case falling within (3)(b) or (3)(c), the company will have to notify a Regulatory Information Service of the selection of the Panel as the relevant regulator without delay.

On the basis set out in art.4.2(e) of the Takeover Directive, the Panel will be responsible under (2) and (3) above for regulating matters relating to the consideration offered, in particular the price, and matters relating to the "bid procedure" (for example announcements of offers and the contents of the offer document) and under (1) above for matters relating to the information to be provided to employees of the offeree company and matters relating to "company law" (for example fixing the control threshold for a mandatory offer, any derogation from the obligation to launch a mandatory offer and provisions relating to frustrating action). In each case, the supervisory authority in another Member State will be responsible for those matters not regulated by the Panel.

Section 3(d) of the Introduction to the Code states that early consultation with the Panel is advised in shared jurisdiction cases so that guidance can be given on how any conflicts between the relevant Rules may be resolved and, where relevant, which provisions of the Code apply pursuant to art.4.2(e) of the Takeover Directive.

2.2.4 *Transactions*

The Code has always applied to a wider range of transactions than those covered by the Takeover Directive—the Takeover Directive applies only to public, control-seeking offers. Except in relation to cases covered by the shared jurisdiction arrangements (see 2.2.3 above), the Code applies to takeover bids and mergers however effected (including by means of statutory merger or court-approved scheme of arrangement) and also to other transactions which are used to obtain or consolidate control of a relevant company ("control" for these purposes as defined in the Code). This includes, for example, the acquisition of control pursuant to the exercise of "drag along" rights contained in a company's articles of association (see the Panel's 2001 Annual Report). The transaction in question need not involve the acquisition of a controlling interest: the Code will also apply to partial offers and offers by a parent for the minority in its subsidiary. In the case of statutory mergers under the Companies (Cross-Border Mergers) Regulations 2007, the Executive confirmed in Practice Statement No.18 that the Code will apply to a "merger by absorption" where the transferor company is a Code company and will normally apply to a "merger by formation of a new company" where one or more of the transferor companies is a Code company (unless the Panel is satisfied that the substance of the transaction is the acquisition by the Code company of a non-Code company).

In the case of a target company that is subject to the shared jurisdiction arrangements, the Code will apply only to offers that fall within the narrow, Takeover Directive-based definition of an offer (coming from art.2.1(a) of the Takeover Directive), which covers only public, control-seeking offers (whether mandatory or voluntary). This would not capture, for example, a scheme of arrangement under Pt 26 of the Companies Act 2006.

For the avoidance of doubt, it is clear that the Code applies to all relevant transactions at any stage of their implementation, including, for example, when an offer is in contemplation but has not been announced.

2.2.5 *Dual holding companies and newco structures*

Since August 2002, the Code has applied to the establishment of a dual holding company structure involving a UK-resident Plc. These are corporate groups with dual holding companies, typically listed on different exchanges but having identical boards, which operate as a single economic enterprise. The Code therefore applies (subject to the considerations in the following paragraph) to a dual holding company transaction involving a UK company with shares admitted to trading on a regulated market in the United Kingdom or on a multilateral trading facility in the United Kingdom or on a stock exchange in the Channel Islands or the Isle of Man and any other public UK company (and certain private UK companies) which the Panel considers to be resident in the United Kingdom, the Channel Islands or the Isle of Man. A dual holding company transaction involving a company falling within the shared jurisdiction provisions referred to in 2.2.3 above will not, however, be subject to the Code as these only apply to transactions falling within the narrow, Takeover Directive-based definition of an offer.

Where the Code applies, the company subject to the Code will usually be treated as the offeree company and the offer regarded as a securities exchange offer for the purposes of the Code. Whilst the normal Code Rules would then apply, the Panel indicated in the consultation paper on dual listed company transactions issued in April 2002 (PCP 11) that certain

Rules, principally those relating to the offer timetable and acceptances, would be applied flexibly having regard to the particular circumstances. Nevertheless, there may be cases where there is no doubt that the substance of a dual holding company transaction is the acquisition by a Code company of a non-Code company. In such circumstances, the Panel may be willing to agree that the Code should not apply. The public consultation paper referred to above also contains guidance on how the Code will be applied to newco structures (where a new holding company acquires both parties) and, as referred to above, although the Code will normally apply to a "merger by formation of a new company" under the Companies (Cross-Border Mergers) Regulations 2007 where one or more of the transferor companies is a Code company, if the Panel is satisfied that the substance of the transaction is the acquisition by the Code company of a non-Code company, it may agree that the transaction should not be subject to the Code.

2.2.6 Dual jurisdiction

A company which is subject to the Code may also be subject to the jurisdiction of other overseas regulators. In such circumstances, the Panel recommends early consultation so that guidance can be given on how any conflicts between the relevant requirements may be resolved.

It is now common for offers to be structured to comply with both the Code and the "tender offer" rules of the United States Securities and Exchange Act of 1934. Areas of particular conflict between the United States and United Kingdom rules may include market purchases, the timing of the first closing date and, in circumstances where the target is listed in the United States, withdrawal rights and disclosure requirements. In addition, where share (or other security) consideration is offered, the bidder may need to comply with the registration requirements of the United States Securities Act of 1933. Certain exemptions to the US tender offer rules and registration requirements are available. The extent of relief provided by these exemptions depends on the size of a non-US offeree's US shareholder base. If US-resident beneficial shareholders hold 10 per cent or less of the shares of a non-US offeree (as calculated in accordance with the relevant Rules), the bid qualifies for the "Tier I" exemption and the bidder is able to conduct its bid in accordance with "home country" rules (i.e. the Code in the case of a bid for a company in respect of which the Panel has jurisdiction) and certain additional (largely procedural) requirements stipulated in the exemption. If US-resident beneficial shareholders hold more than 10 per cent but not more than 40 per cent of the shares of a non-US offeree, the bid qualifies for the "Tier II" exemption, which provides more limited exemptive relief. The cross-border exemptions do not exempt bidders from US securities law liability for misleading statements and omissions and fraudulent or manipulative acts in connection with such transactions.

Where the offeree company has a number of shareholders in any overseas jurisdiction, appropriate advice should be taken at an early stage as documentation is now required to be circulated to all shareholders unless a dispensation is available (see Rule 23.2).

2.3 The approach

Rule 1 deals with the "approach".

2.3.1 Notifying the offeree company

Rule 1(a) requires that an offeror (or its advisers) must notify a firm intention to make an offer in the first instance to the offeree board or to its advisers. The degree of contact will, in practice, vary according to the nature of the bid. Where the bid is unilateral or "hostile", pre-announcement contact is likely to be minimal. In some cases, it may take the form of a telephone call to the chairman to say that a press announcement will be released in five minutes. Many hours can be spent planning how to get hold of the chairman to receive such a call.

2.3.2 *Identity*

The importance of the identity of the offeror is emphasised by Rule 1(b): where an approach to the offeree company with regard to a possible offer is not made by the offeror or potential offeror, its identity must be disclosed to the board of the offeree company at the outset. This applies even in the case of a cash bid, where it might be assumed that identity is not important. The provision is reflected also in Rule 2.7(c), which requires the offeror to be identified in the formal press announcement.

Occasionally, it may not be clear who is to be regarded as the "offeror"—for example, where the offer is made by a subsidiary or a special bid vehicle, or where the bidding company is controlled by a consortium. In such circumstances, the Panel should be consulted and may be expected, in appropriate cases, to apply a "look-through" principle to the parent or "quasi" parent requiring the identity of that "parent" or controller to be disclosed.

2.4 Announcing the offer

The Code places a very strict obligation on offerors and their financial advisers to exercise due care before formally announcing an offer. This is on the basis that the announcement of a firm intention to make an offer will inevitably have a profound effect on the offeree company and the market price of its shares. While investors in a company which is the subject of an offer appreciate that it may fail due to lack of acceptances or regulatory problems, they expect that the offer will only be withdrawn for other reasons in a small minority of cases.

There are two particularly important Code provisions to note in this respect.

General Principle 5:

"An offeror must announce a bid only after ensuring that he/she can fulfil in full any cash consideration, if such is offered, and after taking all reasonable measures to secure the implementation of any other type of consideration."

Rule 2.7(a):

"An offeror should announce a firm intention to make an offer only after the most careful and responsible consideration and when the offeror has every reason to believe that it can and will continue to be able to implement the offer. Responsibility in this connection also rests on the financial adviser to the offeror."

General Principle 5 relates to the steps a bidder should take, before announcing the offer, to ensure that the offer consideration will be available. The announcement of an offer that includes cash must also include a confirmation by the financial adviser, or by another appropriate third party, that resources are available to the offeror sufficient to satisfy full acceptance of the offer (see Rule 2.7(d)). Rule 24.8 requires an equivalent confirmation to be given in the offer document. Although Rule 2.7(a) makes it clear that a financial adviser shares responsibility for ensuring the offeror will be able to implement the offer, under Rule 2.7(d) and Rule 24.8 it is clear that the person giving the cash confirmation will not be expected to produce the cash itself provided "it acted responsibly and took all reasonable steps to assure itself that the cash was available".

An example of the application of these responsibilities was the proposed offer by Luirc for Merlin Properties. The offeror was a newly incorporated British Virgin Islands company with a nominal capital. When the bid was announced the offeror had received a comfort letter that funds were available, but no formal loan agreement had been negotiated or signed. The Panel ruled that no announcement of the bid should have been made before the offeror had received an irrevocable commitment to provide the funds. The Panel's ruling stated that

"compliance with [General Principle 5 and Rule 2.7(a)] is of great importance. The announcement of an offer is always highly significant for the offeree company and will usually affect its share price. If the offer is subsequently withdrawn, at the very least a false market in the shares in the offeree company is likely to have been created.

The Executive's view is that, when a financial adviser is acting for a newly created offeror, such as an off-the-shelf overseas company, the standard of care required under [General Principle 5 and Rule 2.7(a)] clearly has an additional dimension. In short, the only way in which such an offeror and its financial adviser can be sure that funds will be available is to have an irrevocable commitment from a party upon whom reliance can reasonably be placed, for example a bank, at the time of the announcement of the offer."

As referred to above, if it did not act responsibly and take all reasonable steps as referred to in Rules 2.7(d) and 24.8, the financial adviser or other third party giving the cash confirmation may be required to come up with the cash itself. The following extract from the Panel's 1991 Annual Report is a salutary lesson:

"In a cash offer [Rule 24.8] requires the offer document to contain confirmation, normally by the offeror's bank or financial adviser, that there are resources available to the offeror sufficient to satisfy full acceptance of the offer. If accepting shareholders are not paid and the Panel considers that the party giving the cash confirmation did not act responsibly and did not take all reasonable steps to assure itself that the cash was available, the Panel may look to the party giving the confirmation to produce the cash itself.

It is a matter of judgment in each case for the party giving the cash confirmation to satisfy itself that there will be funds available to meet the offer. In making that judgment, the party giving the cash confirmation will be influenced by a variety of matters such as the standing of the offeror, the extent and nature of its relationship with the offeror and the size of the offer. In the rare event of cash not subsequently being made available to accepting share-holders, the Executive will investigate what steps were taken by the party giving the cash confirmation.

In a recent case an offeror failed to pay certain of the accepting shareholders and the Executive found that the adviser that gave the cash confirmation in the offer document had not exercised adequate care in ensuring that cash would be available to the offeror. The Executive ruled that the adviser concerned should pay the considera-tion that was due under the offer and the outstanding payments were duly made."

In April 2005, the Executive issued Practice Statement No.10 relating to cash offers financed by the issue of offeror securities. The Executive noted that

"if an offer, which was to be financed by the issue of offeror securities, lapses or is withdrawn owing to a failure to fulfil a condition relating to the issue, the Executive will wish to be satisfied that [General Principle 5 and Rule 2.7(a)] were complied with (so that, on announcement, the offeror and its financial adviser had had every reason to believe that the offer could and would be implemented)."

The Executive also thought that

"in order to satisfy [General Principle 5, Rule 2.7(a) and Rule 24.8], it was the responsibility of the party giving the cash confirmation and the offeror (and, if it is not the cash confirmer, the offeror's financial adviser) to take all reasonable steps, before the announcement of the offer, to satisfy themselves that the issue of new securities will be successful, and that the offeror will have the necessary cash available to finance the full acceptance of the offer."

Rule 2.7(a) requires the offeror's pre-announcement due diligence exercise to cover all aspects of implementing the offer, not just ensuring the availability of consideration. The Panel's statement in August 1989 dealing with Wm Low's lapsed bid for Budgens is still required reading in this area. Following the announcement of its bid, Wm Low discovered details about Budgens' working capital and borrowings which led it to conclude that the offer no longer made financial sense. Since the bid was conditional on Wm Low's shareholders' approval, the Panel agreed to it being withdrawn on the basis that, with the directors of Wm Low changing their earlier recommendation to vote in favour, shareholders would inevitably withhold their approval. But, in the inquest that followed, the Panel had some strong words of criticism to say about Wm Low's financial advisers and about what was then General Principle 3 (now part of Rule 2.7(a)), including the following:

> "Compliance with this principle is of great importance. The announcement of an offer inevitably has a profound effect upon the market. The share price of the offeree company will be affected and, in consequence, if the offer is subsequently withdrawn—for whatever reason—many people may have dealt on the basis of expectations which are not fulfilled. Against this background, [Rule 2.7(a)] attempts to reduce to a minimum the number of offers which are withdrawn by placing upon potential offerors and their advisers an obligation to exercise due care before making an offer. This Code duty is of a standard similar to that which the law imposes upon professional people or indeed anyone who purports to possess some special skill.
>
> It is a duty to display that standard of skill and care which would ordinarily be expected of someone exercising or professing to exercise the particular skill in question. The Panel stresses that [Rule 2.7(a)] is designed to protect shareholders of the offeree company and those who might deal or consider dealing in the shares of the offeree company. Accordingly, to the extent that it is practically possible to exercise care, the Code duty arising under [Rule 2.7(a)] cannot be limited simply to setting out conditions to which a particular offer is subject.

The practical content of the Code duty to exercise appropriate care will inevitably depend upon all the circumstances of the case. Where there is a unilateral offer, it may be very difficult for the offeror to obtain reliable detailed information concerning the business of the offeree company. The issue of what is reasonable in each case turns in part upon the likely reaction of the offeror to unanticipated developments or revelations following the announcement of an offer. If, for example, a very large company were proposing to take over a small company just to obtain a particular product, it might be perfectly reasonable for it not to investigate the profitability or borrowings of the target, because subsequent revelations relating to those aspects of the target's business would not be relevant to the offeror. But, on the other hand, in the case of a proposed merger of companies of similar size, the offeror is likely to be much more sensitive to the precise financial position of the offeree. In such a situation, which existed in the present case, it is necessary for the offeror, where it has the opportunity to do so, to take greater care to investigate that position in advance."

In April 2005, the Executive issued Practice Statement No.11 relating to working capital requirements in cash and securities exchange offers and it stated that the Executive's practice in this area was that in the event of an offer lapsing as a result of working capital concerns, the Executive would wish to be satisfied that the offeror and its financial adviser had, at the time of announcement of the offer, complied with what are now General Principle 5 and Rule 2.7(a).

In its 1997 Annual Report, the Panel commented as follows:

"Subject to the need to maintain secrecy, parties and their advisers should... seek to address all potential concerns in relation to the offeree company before issuing an announcement of a firm intention to make an offer. To the extent that this is possible, these concerns should be identified in advance by undertaking appropriate due diligence. However, the scope for doing so will depend upon, in particular, whether or not the offeror has the co-operation of the offeree board."

A further aspect of the obligation in Rule 2.7(a) is to ensure that the offeror has obtained all necessary consents and approvals to the making of the offer before it is announced, other than those which cannot be obtained in advance and can be included as conditions or pre-conditions to the offer in accordance with Rule 13. This was illustrated in the pre-conditional, recommended offer by ONGC Videsh Limited (OVL) for Imperial Energy Plc. After announcement of the offer and satisfaction of the stated regulatory pre-conditions, OVL sought further time before posting its offer document in order for it to be approved by the Indian Government (which controlled 74 per cent of OVL). In dismissing OVL's appeal for an extension, the Hearings Committee of the Panel stated in Panel Statement 2008/46:

"The Committee wishes to reiterate the importance of treating a [Rule 2.7] announcement as a firm commitment to make an offer in accordance with the terms of the announcement and to follow the Code timetable unless and to the extent that the Panel modifies such obligations, something which all concerned would rightly expect to happen only in exceptional circumstances and with the consent of the offeree, at least in the event, as here, of a recommended offer. After a [Rule 2.7] announcement, to attempt to introduce unilaterally a pre-condition to the offer is manifestly unacceptable (subject to the very limited exceptions in Rule 32.4 of the Code).

The issue at the hearing seemed to the Committee… to be not whether the Government of India had other more pressing priorities and/or was unable or unwilling until some later date to decide whether or not to approve the posting of the offer document. Rather, the prior question was whether to allow to be imposed on OVL and Imperial Energy a pre-condition enabling the Government of India to grant or withhold such approval. This is a question of principle, not one requiring detailed exploration of such matters as why the Government of India asserts such a right or of whether it has already had sufficient time to reach a decision on the point."

2.5 Secrecy

2.5.1 *The basic obligation*

Rule 2.1(a) imposes an obligation on all persons privy to confidential information concerning a possible offer to treat the information as secret prior to the announcement of the offer or possible offer, and requires such persons to conduct themselves so as to minimise the chances of a leak of the information. For example, confidential information should only be passed to another person if it is necessary to do so and if that person is made aware of the need for secrecy. A party to an offer and its advisers should consider at the outset what controls they are going to put in place to maintain secrecy (including by reference to the FSA's *Market Watch* issues No.21 (July 2007) and No.27 (June 2008)—"Thematic review of controls over insider information relating to public takeovers"), and this is something the Panel may well investigate if there is a leak.

These obligations are closely linked to the requirement in Rule 2.2(e) that where more than a very small number of people (essentially those who need to know in the companies concerned and their immediate advisers) are included in pre-bid discussions, the Panel should be consulted and an announcement may need to be made.

2.5.2 *Financial advisers' obligations*

In turn, Rule 2.1(b) places financial advisers under a specific obligation to warn clients about the requirement for secrecy and, indeed, about their responsibilities under the Code in general. In the Executive's view, it is unlikely to be sufficient simply to send a standard form memorandum to the client, so financial advisers should take steps to talk senior executives of the client through these issues in order to discharge their responsibilities under this Note.

2.5.3 Employee consultation

Although the Code never did prohibit communications with employees, in Panel Statement 2010/22 the Code Committee concluded that the Code should be amended to improve communication between the board of the offeree company and its employees and to make it clear that the Code does not prevent the passing of information in confidence during the offer period to employee representatives.

Accordingly, following the consultation in PCP 2011/1, a new Note 6 on Rule 20.1 was introduced which states that, subject to the basic secrecy obligations contained in Rule 2.1, the Code does not prevent the passing of information in confidence by an offeror or the offeree company to its own employees or employee representatives, or by an offeror to the employees or employee representatives of the offeree company (provided the employees or employee representatives are acting as such and not as shareholders). And the final paragraph of Note 6 exempts meetings with employees or employee representatives from the usual requirements of Note 3 on Rule 20.1 (although the Panel should be consulted if employees are interested in a significant number of shares). Therefore, any necessary or desired employee consultation can take place both before and during a bid, subject to the confidentiality requirements of Rule 2.1.

2.6 Pre-bid announcements

2.6.1 When an announcement is required

Rules 2.2 to 2.6 deal with the difficult issue of announcements made before the formal offer announcement (historically referred to as "possible offer announcements" or "Rule 2.4 announcements"). The first issue to consider is when a possible offer announcement must be made, and here the Panel's paramount concern is to avoid the creation of a false market: see General Principle 4. The difficulty is to strike the balance between achieving this objective and protecting the legitimate commercial interests of potential offerors (who in the whole would not want to reveal their hands until they have dotted the "i's" and crossed the "t's").

An excellent explanation of the background to this perennial of topical issues is to be found in the Panel's 1988 Annual Report. In it, the Panel dealt firmly with the reluctant offeror as follows:

> "An area that has caused the Executive some concern over the last year relates to the timing and quality of information released relating to an offer. It is amongst the more important tasks of the Panel to ensure that information is made available equally to all shareholders, and also that the parties to an offer use every endeavour to prevent the creation of a false market in the securities of the companies concerned throughout the offer. Accordingly, although this is not a new problem and was the subject of a Panel Statement last September, its importance is such that it is worth repeating here.
>
> There has on several occasions been a considerable amount of speculation concerning a possible offer; in some cases it has been well founded but in others it has not. But, whenever there is such speculation, the companies and their advisers must consider whether an announcement is required under Rule 2.2 of the Code.
>
> In particular, Rule 2.2(d) imposes an obligation on the potential offeror to make an announcement when, before an approach has been made, the offeree company is the subject of rumour and speculation, or there is an untoward movement in its share price, and there are reasonable grounds for concluding that it is the potential offeror's actions which have led to the situation.

The Rule can sometimes pose difficulties for an offeror, particularly when he is in the process of finalising his plans. So there may be a reluctance to make an announcement, leading the offeror to accept, perhaps too readily, alternative explanations as to why there is speculation or an untoward price movement, rather than the most likely one, which is that his security is inadequate. But the Code requires that where there is speculation or an untoward price movement, but the offeror and his advisers do not propose to make an immediate announcement, the Panel should be consulted."

The Panel further emphasised its position in its 1996 Annual Report where, having stressed the need for secrecy pre-announcement and the necessity of "prior and full consultation with [the Executive] in respect of the announcement obligations under Rule 2", the Panel went on to state:

"The Executive also wishes to emphasise that a requirement on a potential offeror to make an announcement of its interest under Rule 2.2(d) can, and often does, arise prior to any decision being made to proceed with such an offer, or prior to the funding needed for such an offer being finalised. The Executive takes the view that if there is rumour and speculation relating to a particular offeree company or there is an untoward movement in its share price and there are reasonable grounds for concluding that this is as a result of the potential offeror's actions, then, even if the potential offeror has not yet decided to proceed with an offer, an announcement of its possible interest is required."

And again, in Practice Statement No.20 (issued in March 2008, revised in March 2009, and re-issued in September 2011—and required reading on the subject of Rule 2), the Executive explained that

"on occasion, it is argued that to require an announcement referring to the possibility of an offer when the offer preparations are at a preliminary stage might, of itself, lead to the creation of a false market in the offeree company's securities. The Executive does not find this argument persuasive. In the Executive's opinion, if it appears that details of the possible offer may have leaked, leading to rumour and speculation or an untoward movement in the offeree company's share price, the overriding requirement is that an announcement should be made immediately and the fact that the offer preparations are at a preliminary stage may be made clear in the announcement."

There are a number of limbs to when an announcement may be required under Rule 2.2. Rules 2.2(a) and (b) are straightforward, requiring an announcement when a firm intention to bid is notified to the offeree board by or on behalf of an offeror or when the offeror triggers a mandatory offer obligation under Rule 9.1.

Rules 2.2(c), (d) and (f)(i) all apply when there is rumour and speculation concerning the offeree company, or an "untoward" movement in its share price. Paragraph (c) covers the position after an approach by or on behalf of a potential offeror to the board of the offeree company has been made. Paragraph (d) applies after a potential offeror first actively considers an offer but before an approach if there are reasonable grounds for concluding that the rumour and speculation or movement in the share price resulted from some action of the offeror— through inadequate security or otherwise. Paragraph (f) applies when a purchaser is being sought for an interest, or interests, in shares carrying in aggregate 30 per cent or more of the voting rights of a company, or when the board of a company is seeking potential offerors. Prior to September 19, 2011, the Panel was generally significantly less likely to require an announcement if the offeree company was already in an offer period, on the basis that after there had already been one announcement of a possible offer it would be understood that additional potential offerors may emerge. However, since that date and the introduction of Note 3 on Rule 2.2, it is now the case that if rumour and speculation specifically identifies a potential offeror whose identity has not previously been announced, the Panel will now normally require an announcement, either (according to Rule 2.3—see below) by the potential offeror or by the offeree company identifying the potential offeror, even if an offer period has already commenced.

Note 1 on Rule 2.2 makes it clear that whether or not a movement is "untoward" is for the Panel to determine, on the following basis:

> "The question will be considered in the light of all relevant facts and not solely by reference to the absolute percentage movement in the price. Facts which may be considered to be relevant in determining whether a price movement is untoward for the purposes of Rules 2.2(c), (d) and (f)(i) include general market and sector movements, publicly available information relating to the company, trading activity in the company's securities and the time period over which the price movement has occurred. This list is purely illustrative and the Panel will take account of such other factors as it considers appropriate."

After an approach to the board of the offeree company (in the case of Rule 2.2(c)), or after an offer is first actively considered by a potential offeror (in the case of Rule 2.2(d)), or after the board starts to seek one or more potential offerors (in the case of Rule 2.2(f)(i)), there is an obligation to consult the Panel at the latest when the offeree company becomes the subject of any rumour and speculation relating to a possible offer for the offeree company (regardless of whether the rumour and speculation is specific to the possible transaction under consideration or the manner in which, or medium by which, it has been disseminated) or where there is a price movement of 10 per cent or more above the lowest share price since the time of the approach etc. An abrupt price rise of a smaller percentage (for example a rise of five per cent in the course of a single day) could also be regarded as untoward and accordingly the Panel should be consulted in such circumstances.

This obligation of consultation with the Executive is viewed by it as being of crucial importance in the application of Rule 2.2

although, as the Executive was keen to stress in Practice Statement No.20, "consultation will not necessarily lead to a requirement to make an announcement; this will depend on all the relevant circumstances". That Practice Statement also gives guidance on when, for the purposes of Rule 2.2(d) and Note 1, an offer will be treated as "first actively considered". The Executive will take various factors into account when determining whether and when an offer is "first actively considered", including whether the possible offer has been considered by the board, investment committee or senior management of the offeror, whether work is being undertaken by external advisers and whether external parties (e.g. potential lenders etc) have been approached. The Panel's Annual Report for 2003 also states that notwithstanding the requirement to consult "the parties should not delay an announcement in order to consult the Panel if it is clear that an announcement is required".

Practice Statement No.6 of 2004 outlines how the Executive interprets Rule 2 in the context of a company announcing a strategic review of its business. Often in these circumstances an offer is one of a number of options under review and it is not always clear whether a strategic review announcement will trigger the commencement of an offer period. If the announcement does refer to an offer as being an option under consideration this will automatically start an offer period (this mirrors the definition of "offer period" as covering a "proposed or possible offer"). If the review later concludes that the offer will not be pursued then the company must make a public announcement in order for the offer period to end.

If the announcement does not refer to an offer, the Panel will make direct enquiries of the board. If an offer is one option actively under consideration and there is subsequently either rumour about the offer or an untoward movement in the company's share price, the Panel will then require the company to make an announcement. At this point the offer period will commence. If the review subsequently concludes not to pursue the offer, a further public announcement is required to end the offer period. Companies are encouraged to consult with the Executive prior to making any strategic review announcements in order to avoid any misunderstanding.

An announcement may also be required under Rule 2.2(e) when more than a very restricted number of people (outside those who need to know in the parties concerned and their immediate advisers) are to be approached in relation to a possible offer. This would include potential providers of finance (whether equity or debt), shareholders in the offeror or the offeree company, the offeree company's pension fund trustees, potential management candidates, significant customers of, or suppliers to, the offeree company or potential purchasers of assets. Rule 2.2(f)(ii) has a similar requirement where para.(f) applies and the number of potential purchasers or offerors approached is about to be increased to include more than a very restricted number of people.

In the case of Rule 2.2(e), the Executive regards a "very restricted number" of people to be six. However, it may be prepared to consent to more than six external parties being approached without an announcement being made, provided it is consulted in advance. In considering whether to allow a wider group to be approached, the Executive will want to be satisfied that secrecy will be maintained and, like any other person privy to price-sensitive information concerning an offer, the external parties approached must, as required by Rule 2.1, keep the discussions secret and must not themselves approach additional third parties without consulting the Panel. As required by Note 1 on Rule 2.2, in the case of Rule 2.2(f)(ii), the consent of the Executive should be obtained before more than one potential purchaser or offeror is sought.

Rule 2.3 establishes a clear demarcation of responsibility for making pre-bid announcements. Before a potential offeror approaches the offeree board, the obligation is that of the potential offeror. As a result, and as advised in Practice Statement No.20, the offeror and its financial adviser will need to establish a system that tracks the offeree company's share price on a real time basis and at all times during market hours in order to monitor whether there is an untoward share price movement, and will need to monitor the press, newswires, trade publications and internet bulletin boards for any rumour and speculation. The offeror is also responsible for making the announcement when an obligation to make a mandatory offer under Rule 9.1 is incurred.

Once an approach has been made to the board of the offeree company, responsibility for making any possible offer announcement will move to the offeree company and it and its financial advisers will then need to establish the same monitoring systems. And where a purchaser is being sought for an interest in shares carrying 30 per cent or more of the voting rights but without the involvement of the offeree company, responsibility will rest with the potential seller.

Rule 2.3(d) also includes a reminder that the potential offeror should not resort to any "strong-arm tactics" in an attempt to prevent the offeree company board from making an announcement relating to the possible offer or publicly identifying the potential offeror at any time it considers appropriate. The Panel also advised in its Annual Report for 2003 and in Practice Statement No.20 that if the offeror's approach is rejected by the offeree company, the announcement obligation will normally revert to the offeror as only the offeror will then know whether it intends to proceed with the offer.

A key issue in applying Rule 2.3 is what amounts to an "approach", which the Executive dealt with in Practice Statement No.20 as follows:

> "For these purposes, the Executive interprets the term 'approach' broadly. Each case will turn on its own facts, but the Executive normally considers an approach to have been received when a director or representative of, or an adviser to, an offeree company is informed by, or on behalf of, a potential offeror that it is considering the possibility of making an offer for the company. This may be at a very preliminary stage in the offeror's preparations and the manner of the approach may be informal and no more

than broadly indicative. For example, there is no requirement for an approach to be made in writing, or for an
indicative offer price (or any terms or conditions) to be
specified, and it could be made as part of a conversation
on unrelated matters...

In order to avoid confusion, the parties should agree
which of the offeror and the offeree company has
responsibility for making an announcement at any particular time following the initial approach. If the parties
are unable to reach agreement as to where the responsibility rests, or if there is any doubt as to whether there has
been an unequivocal rejection of an approach, the Executive should be consulted."

Except as outlined in 2.6.2 below, once a possible offer
announcement obligation has arisen under Rule 2.2, the Panel
will expect that it is made within a matter of minutes. As
referred to in 2.6.3 below, a brief announcement of the
possibility of an offer being made and identifying the potential
offeror or offerors is all that is required, and so the Panel will
not be sympathetic to delays as a result of drafting changes
being made or parties wishing to include additional information in the announcement (a further announcement can always
be made if wanted). This will also mean that in practice, and as
advised in Practice Statement No.20, an offeror or offeree
company, and its financial adviser, will want to have an
appropriate draft announcement prepared at an early stage in
any bid preparations and have a procedure in place to ensure
the prompt release of the announcement if required.

There have been many instances of parties and their advisers
being criticised for a failure to make a timely announcement or
to consult the Panel as to whether an announcement is
required, and it is worth referring to a few to highlight the
Panel's approach. In February 1992, the Panel ruled that Rule
2.2(c), (d) and (e) had been breached prior to the Petrocon bid
for James Wilkes. On this occasion, the share price of Wilkes
had increased by some 26 per cent before an announcement
was made. Apart from share purchases, the bidder's advisers

approached institutional shareholders in confidence to establish the likely reaction to a bid without the consent of the Panel. On both counts, the advisers were criticised. The responsibility then passed to James Wilkes and its advisers when the approach was made over the weekend, and they were criticised for failing to insist on an announcement.

In February 1996, in connection with Rentokil's unilateral offer for BET, the Panel concluded that Rentokil's financial advisers should have been more alert to the need to consult the Panel under Rule 2 of the Code. In that case, there was market speculation and the Panel took the view that, given the market rumour and the fact that Rentokil was at an advanced stage of preparation for a possible offer, the Panel should have been consulted immediately upon such rumours commencing. The Panel also emphasised that, as part of such consultation, there is an obligation on the financial adviser to provide the Panel with background information in order for the Panel to make a full assessment of the situation, and went on to underline the importance of prior and full consultation with the Panel in respect of the announcement obligation under Rule 2 of the Code, particularly in the context of a possible unilateral offer. The Executive similarly criticised the financial adviser to Transcomm Plc in March 2004 for its failure to consult the Executive as required by Note 1 on Rule 2.2. Transcomm had been in discussions with British Telecommunications Plc for a number of months before making an announcement that it was in talks that might lead to an offer for the company. During the period prior to the announcement, although the share price moved from 11p per share to 14.5p per share, Transcomm's financial adviser determined, without consulting the Executive, that no announcement was required. In its statement the Executive emphasised the importance which the Panel attaches to Rule 2.2 and to the making of timely announcements.

It is worth noting that since the introduction of the market abuse regime in the Financial Services and Markets Act 2000 (FSMA), failure to make an announcement where there is a regulatory obligation to do so can amount to market abuse.

The Financial Services Authority's Disclosure and Transparency Rules also contain announcement obligations for companies on the London Stock Exchange's main market. In addition, for a company whose home Member State is the United Kingdom and which has its shares admitted to a securities market in the United Kingdom, a dishonest omission from, or dishonest delay in publishing, an announcement may also give rise to liability under the issuer liability regime now contained in s.90A and Sch.10A of FSMA.

2.6.2 *Avoiding a possible offer announcement*

Under Note 4 on Rule 2.2, where an obligation to make a possible offer announcement would normally arise as a result of rumour and speculation or an untoward movement in the offeree company's share price, the Panel may nevertheless agree that no announcement is required provided it is satisfied that the potential offeror has ceased to actively consider making an offer. The potential offeror will therefore normally have a choice between an announcement being made that it is considering making an offer or privately or publicly "downing tools" and walking away from the transaction. If it chooses to down tools privately, the potential offeror will be prevented under the current version of Note 4 on Rule 2.2 from actively considering making an offer for the offeree company for a period of six months. In a consultation paper published in July 2014 (PCP 2014/1), the Code Committee has proposed reducing this period to three months with other restrictions applying in a further period of three months (see further below).

The current six month lock-out period may be set aside, however, (1) where a third party announces a firm bid (not just a possible offer announcement), (2) if the offeree company announces a whitewash or a reverse takeover, (3) if the Panel determines there has been a material change of circumstances or (4) at the request of the offeree company (although this limb will not normally apply in the first three months).

If the potential offeror decides to down tools publicly it will have to make an announcement that it has no intention to bid under Rule 2.8. A party making such an announcement will be subject to a similar six month lock-out period for a private downing of tools. However, there are differences between the two six months lock-out regimes which mean that a potential offeror might prefer to make a public announcement that it does not intend to make an offer (despite the publicity that will attract) than to accept a private down tools. For example, in a private down tools the potential offeror is prohibited from any active consideration of the transaction during the lock-out period, while following a public no-bid announcement the potential offeror is permitted to continue preparations for an offer to be made at the end of the lock-out period, provided knowledge of the possible offer is not extended outside those who need to know in the potential offer and its immediate advisers.

Notwithstanding that a dispensation from making a possible offer announcement may have been granted in the case of a private down tools, an announcement may still be required by the Panel if any rumour and speculation is repeated or the Panel otherwise considers it necessary to prevent the creation of a false market.

It should be noted that the Code Committee published a consultation paper (PCP 2014/1) in July 2014 which includes various proposed changes to the private down tools require-ments in Note 4 on Rule 2.2. These changes, which at the time of writing have yet to come into effect, include reducing the period in which the potential offeror is prohibited from any active consideration of the transaction from six months to three months, with other restrictions applying for a further three month period. These other restrictions would mirror those that apply under Rule 2.8 where a potential offeror has publicly downed tools and could be set aside in any of the four circumstances described in the second paragraph of this section on p.61. The restriction on active consideration in the first three month period could be set aside in the same circumstances (other than at the request of the offeree company).

2.6.3 Possible offer announcements

When a possible offer announcement obligation is triggered by Rule 2.2, a brief announcement that talks are taking place or that a potential offeror is considering making an offer will be sufficient. However, since September 19, 2011 and the amendments to the Code following the consultation in PCP 2011/1, any possible offer announcement by the offeree company must identify any potential offeror or offerors (unless previously publicly identified) with which the offeree company is in talks or from which an approach has been received (that has not been withdrawn or unequivocally rejected)—see Rule 2.4. In addition, any subsequent announcement by the offeree company that refers to the existence of a possible white knight must identify that new potential offeror.

The only exceptions to these obligations to name potential offerors are if another offeror has already announced a firm intention to make an offer for the offeree company or if the offeree company has already announced that it is seeking one or more potential offerors by means of a formal sale process as referred to in Note 2 on Rule 2.6.

The above requirements to identify potential offerors in announcements made by the offeree company were part of a package of changes introduced following the consultation in PCP 2011/1 designed to increase the protection for offeree companies against protracted "virtual bid" periods—i.e. a lengthy period of speculation, and sometimes "assault", following a possible offer announcement and before a firm offer announcement was made or the potential offeror withdrew.

Any possible offer announcement by a potential offeror or by an offeree company which first identifies a potential offeror must include a summary of the provisions of Rule 8 and specify the "put up or shut up" deadline referred to in 2.6.4 that will apply in respect of that potential offeror.

Provided it complies with these minimum content requirements, a possible offer announcement may go further and include whatever additional information about the possible offer or situation that the potential offeror or the offeree company, as the case may be, wishes to include. Indeed, there have been examples of possible offer announcements looking as full as a firm intention offer announcement, but making clear that the actual making of the formal offer was subject to the satisfaction of certain stated pre-conditions.

Where a possible offer announcement does go further, Rule 2.5 deals with any statements as to proposed offer terms that are made in the announcement and the regime requires that the Panel be consulted in advance of any statement relating to the proposed terms of a possible offer. Where a potential offeror makes an unqualified statement about the terms of a possible offer, for example if it specifies a price or says that the terms of the possible offer are "final", it will be bound by those terms if it does proceed to make an offer, except in wholly exceptional circumstances (see in this regard Panel Statement 2011/11 relating to the possible offer for Kalahari Plc). As this applies equally to formal and informal statements there will consequently need to be strict public relations controls in place.

Proposed terms can, within limits, be expressly qualified so long as any qualification is capable of objective determination. For example, a bidder may specify a possible offer price but reserve the right to bid at a lower level of consideration in certain circumstances. A subsequent bid at a lower price will then be permitted where the specific circumstances of the particular qualification have arisen. Qualifications that will always be permitted are a target board's recommendation and a firm offer by a third party (whereas the satisfactory outcome of a due diligence exercise will not be permitted). Where the terms refer to an anticipated price range, an approximate price, or a relative price, prior consultation with the Panel will be required.

With the consent of the Panel, a possible offer announcement can include pre-conditions and these can be subjective in nature (see 2.7.2 below for further details). If so, the announcement must make it clear whether these pre-conditions are waivable and must also emphasise that there is no certainty an offer will be made (even if the pre-conditions are satisfied or waived).

2.6.4 *"Put up or shut up" deadlines*

For a number of years the Panel has operated a "put up or shut up" regime following a possible offer announcement aimed at preventing an offeree company from suffering from a protracted period of speculation before a firm offer announcement is made or a potential offeror issues a "no intention to bid" statement—and which therefore reflects General Principle 6. In its 2001 Annual Report, the Panel clarified its general approach at the time in this regard:

> "Following [a possible offer announcement] there is no fixed deadline in the Code by which a potential offeror must clarify his intentions. The timing of any subsequent announcements will depend, inter alia, on the reaction of the offeree board to the potential offeror and the state of preparedness of the potential offeror.
>
> Where the offeree board is prepared to enter into a dialogue with the potential offeror, many months may pass before an offer is finally made. Provided the target company is content for the uncertainty to continue, the Executive would not normally seek to intervene in the process. However, in certain circumstances, usually where the potential offeror is unwelcome, the target company may request the Executive to intervene by imposing a deadline by which the potential offeror must clarify his intentions, i.e. 'put up or shut up'.
>
> In this regard, 'put up' is communicated by way of a … firm offer announcement and 'shut up' by way of a no intention to bid statement.

Requests by the target company for the offeror to be required to 'put up or shut up' are generally made at the early stages of an offer period. In such cases, the Executive endeavours to balance the interests of shareholders in not being deprived of the opportunity to consider the possibility of an offer against potential damage to the target company's business arising from the uncertainty surrounding the company and the distraction for management. In this regard, the Executive's normal approach is to seek clarification by the potential offeror within six to eight weeks from the original announcement of the possible offer. If a request is made at a later stage, the Executive will consider the circumstances at that time.

If the potential offeror clarifies his intentions by way of a no intention to bid statement, this statement will be governed by Rule 2.8 and the potential offeror will normally be prevented from making an offer for the company for a period of six months (unless there is a material change of circumstances and subject to any specific reservations set out in the statement). However, if the Executive considers that the offeree company has suffered excessive siege as a result of the potential offeror's actions, it may impose the restrictions contained within Rule 35.1(b) and prevent the potential offeror from making an offer for a period of 12 months."

This concept was formally incorporated into the Code for the first time in 2004. However, the regime was substantially altered on September 19, 2011, following the consultation in PCP 2011/1, and is now contained in Rule 2.6. Under the new regime, whenever a potential offeror makes a possible offer announcement or an offeree company announces the identity of a potential offeror in accordance with the requirements of Rule 2.4 (or otherwise), an automatic 28 day "put up or shut up" deadline will apply—so, it will no longer be necessary for the offeree company to request a deadline be set and the deadline will no longer be a matter to be negotiated between the offeree company, the potential offeror and the Panel (and will be shorter than the 6–8 weeks that previously applied).

The only exceptions to this automatic imposition of a 28 day deadline will be if a third party has already announced a firm intention to make an offer for the offeree company (or does so subsequently, in which case the deadline will cease to apply) or if the offeree company has already announced that it is seeking one or more potential offerors for the offeree company by means of a formal sales process as envisaged by Note 2 on Rule 2.6.

Where the 28 day deadline applies, the potential offeror must by 17.00 on the relevant "put up or shut up" date (or any extension to it) either announce a firm intention to make an offer for the offeree company in accordance with Rule 2.7 or announce that it does not intend to make an offer for the offeree company (a "no intention to bid statement" or "Rule 2.8 statement"), or secure the Panel's consent to an extension to the deadline. An extension to the deadline will only be granted at the request of the board of the offeree company (and normally only shortly before the deadline is due to expire), and in considering whether to grant its consent the Panel will take into account, among other matters, the status of negotiations between the parties and the anticipated timetable to reach a recommended deal. If extended, the offeree company must promptly announce the new "put up or shut up" deadline and must comment in the announcement on the above factors. Once extended, the same regime applies to the new deadline.

Where there is more than one potential offeror subject to "put up or shut up" deadlines, Note 1 on Rule 2.6 makes clear that the offeree company may request different deadline extensions for different potential offerors and may request a deadline extension for one potential offeror, but not others.

2.6.5 *"No intention to bid" statements*

Where a potential offeror "shuts up" at the end of (or before) a "put up or shut up" deadline, under Rule 2.8 it and any concert party (and any person that subsequently acts in concert with either of them) will be prevented from announcing an offer or possible offer for the offeree company for six months from the date of the statement. However, an announcement of an offer or possible offer can be made prior to the end of the six month period (i.e. the Rule 2.8 restrictions will cease to apply) if: (1) the Panel determines there has been a material change of circumstances; (2) a third party announces a firm bid for the offeree company (not just a possible offer announcement); (3) the offeree company announces a whitewash or reverse takeover; or (4) the board of the offeree company agrees to the no intention to bid statement being set aside (although, if the statement was made after a third party had made a formal offer announcement, this limb will normally only apply if that other offer has been withdrawn or lapsed). If the potential offeror wishes to approach the offeree company to seek its agreement to the statement being set aside it must first get the Panel's consent to the approach being made. If no such agreement is forthcoming, no further approach is permitted within the six month lock-out period.

Since September 19, 2011, it is no longer necessary to set out the above reservations in any no intention to bid statement.

A person may also make a Rule 2.8 announcement or statement during an offer period even though it has not been publicly identified as a potential offeror—and on occasion no intention to bid statements are made even though no offer period has commenced (for example by a person responding to unfounded speculation about its intentions in relation to a potential competitor). Rule 2.8 applies to such statements in the same way as if made during an offer period and in response to a "put up or shut up" deadline, except that where the no intention to bid statement is made in relation to a company that is not in an offer period, the person may also include in the statement other specific events (reservations) following which the restrictions in Rule 2.8 would cease to apply (in addition to those that apply automatically as above).

The Panel should be consulted before any no intention to bid statement is issued, particularly if it is intended to include specific reservations to set aside the statement (Note 1 on Rule 2.8).

Note that the Panel applies this Rule 2.8 not only to formal public statements, but also to informal or private comments which are subsequently publicly reported. It also takes the view that a simple denial of speculation as to the person's intention to make a bid, even though falling short of an explicit statement that the person does not intend to make a bid, will still be caught. So Rule 2.8 contains traps for the unwary.

2.6.6 *Statement of interest by potential competing bidder*

The Code also deals with holding statements by potential rival offerors. During the battle for control of National Westminster Bank Plc (NatWest) the Executive (and, on appeal, the Panel) refused to impose a "put up or shut up" timetable on the Royal Bank of Scotland (RBS) in the early stages of the offer period. The Bank of Scotland (BOS) had announced a firm intention to bid for NatWest and RBS had announced, following press speculation, that it had been considering and would continue to consider its position. BOS requested that the Panel impose a deadline on RBS to clarify its position as the announcement had, in BOS's view, created market uncertainty and had allowed RBS to obtain an unfair advantage over BOS. RBS submitted that it had done nothing to create or increase market uncertainty. The Panel refused to set a firm deadline for RBS to clarify its intentions but indicated that Day 50 appeared to the Panel to be the latest day for clarification of RBS's position— although the Panel reserved the right to specify an earlier or later date depending upon developments.

This principle is now enshrined in the Code in Rule 2.6(d) and (e), together with Note 3 on Rule 2.6. Rule 2.6(d) deals with a potential offeror that has made a possible offer announcement where another party has made a formal offer announcement (whether before or after the possible offer announcement). The Rule provides that, by a date "in the later stages of the offer period", the potential offeror must either announce a firm offer in accordance with Rule 2.7 or make a Rule 2.8 statement.

Similarly, where, as permitted by the exception in Rule 2.4(b), the offeree company has announced that it is in discussions with a white knight but without revealing its identity, the Rule provides that the white knight must either announce a firm offer or confirm to the offeree company that it does not intend to make an offer—which the offeree company must then announce—again, by a date "in the later stages of the offer period".

The Note makes clear that the phrase "in the later stages of the offer period" means on or around 10 days before the end of the acceptance period for the firm offer (i.e. normally around day 50)—or in the case of a scheme, on or around 10 days before the shareholder meetings.

On the MSREF offer for Canary Wharf, Brascan (a potential rival offeror) was required to clarify its intentions 10 days before a target shareholder meeting to approve the transaction (equivalent to Day 50 of a conventional offer timetable) and a potential rival bidder for Ask Central was given until Day 53 to clarify its intention. The Panel's concern is that target shareholders have sufficient time to accept the first offer if the rival bidder decides not to bid (i.e. "shuts up").

2.7 Bid announcements

2.7.1 *Announcement of a firm intention to make an offer*

As referred to above, the provisions of Rule 2.7(a) require that a firm intention to make a bid should only be announced when the offeror has every reason to believe that it can and will be able to implement the offer. In citing the Executive's submission in the Panel's decision on the OVL offer for Imperial Energy, the Panel noted that

"[The Executive] pointed to the distinction in the Code between an announcement of a firm intention to make an offer under [Rule 2.7] and an announcement of a possible offer under Rule 2.4. The former represents a formal commitment to proceed with an offer and, as such, will almost inevitably have a profound effect upon the offeree company and the market price of its shares—hence the need for care on the part of both an offeror and its financial adviser ..."

The required contents of an announcement of a firm intention to make an offer (as opposed to a Rule 2.4 announcement) are specified in Rule 2.7(c). In particular, the announcement must:

1. set out the terms of the offer—detailed terms will be included, although a number of "further terms" are postponed until the offer document;
2. identify the offeror—the questions mentioned above about who is the offeror (see 2.3.2 above) will again need to be considered;
3. include all conditions or pre-conditions to which the offer or the making of it is subject;
4. give details of any agreements or arrangements to which the offeror is a party which relate to the circumstances in which it may or may not invoke or seek to invoke a pre-condition or a condition to its offer and the conse-quences of its doing so, including details of any break fees payable as a result (see Rule 2.7(c)(iv));
5. give details of any arrangements in relation to relevant securities within Note 11 on the definition of acting in concert (see Ch. 3);
6. include a summary of the provisions of Rule 8 (the Rule requiring disclosure of dealings during an offer period);
7. include a summary of any offer-related arrangement permitted under, or excluded from, Rule 21.2;
8. include confirmation that the offeror is on the same day disclosing or has previously disclosed the details required under Rule 8.1(a); and
9. include a list of the documents on display in accordance with Rule 26.1 (and a website address where these documents are published).

As explained in 2.4, the offer announcement must also include confirmation from the financial adviser that resources are available to the offeror sufficient to satisfy full acceptance of the offer where it is a cash offer (Rule 2.7(d)).

Two points on the Notes to Rule 2.7 are worth mentioning:

1. a reminder is given that the language used in the announcement should clearly and concisely reflect the position being described. This reflects the general require-ment that press announcements be prepared with a standard of care and accuracy effectively equivalent to that imposed on the formal offer document; and
2. there is a warning that the Panel should be consulted before (a) any condition is included which is not entirely objective, (b) any condition relating to financing is included or (c) it is intended to make a pre-conditional Rule 2.7 announcement.

2.7.2 Pre-conditional offer announcements

Over the years, there have been a number of pre-conditional offers (i.e. an offer where the offer document will only be posted if certain pre-conditions are satisfied). The most common pre-conditions relate to regulatory clearances where these are unlikely to be obtained in the usual Code timetable. Some examples include Carnival Corporation's initially hostile offer for P&O Princess Cruises, the proposed merger between Granada and Carlton, E.ON's bid for Powergen, which was subject to nine regulatory pre-conditions, and BHP Billiton's hostile bid for Rio Tinto which was subsequently withdrawn when one of the regulatory pre-conditions was invoked. Carnival Corporation's first offer for P&O Princess Cruises was also subject to a financing pre-condition in respect of the cash element of the offer (later reformulated as a pre-condition to a partial cash alternative). Lafarge's hostile offer for Blue Circle likewise included a financing pre-condition (that funding for the offer was arranged on terms satisfactory to it).

In the light of increasing use of pre-conditions, the Code Committee of the Panel issued Consultation Paper 2004/4 and Response Statement 2004/4 in which it reviewed its previous approach to pre-conditions. Changes were made to the Code in April 2005. The Code Committee considered it necessary to look separately at pre-conditional possible offer announcements made under Rule 2.5 (as it is now) and pre-conditional firm offer announcements made under Rule 2.7 (as it is now). The inclusion of pre-conditions in either type of announcement requires prior consultation with the Panel (see Rule 2.5(c) and Note 2 on Rule 2.7 respectively). The Panel takes a strict approach to permitted pre-conditions in firm offer announcements on the basis that the announcement of a pre-conditional offer under Rule 2.7 is intended and required to provide a high level of certainty—as with any Rule 2.7 firm offer announcement.

Rule 13.3 sets out the pre-conditions that will be acceptable to the Panel in a Rule 2.7 announcement. Except with the consent of the Panel, an offer must not be announced subject to a pre-condition unless the pre-condition concerned:

1. relates to OFT/Competition Commission or European Commission clearance; or
2. involves another material official authorisation or regulatory clearance relating to the offer and either the offer is publicly recommended by the offeree company board or the Panel is satisfied that it is likely to prove impossible to obtain the authorisation or clearance within the Code timetable.

Also, the degree of subjectivity permitted in pre-conditions included in a Rule 2.7 announcement is now the same as that permitted for conventional offer conditions (Rule 13.1), and the test for invoking pre-conditions is now basically the same as that for conventional conditions (Rules 13.2 and 13.4(a)). The Code Committee decided against allowing greater flexibility. Although many different types of pre-conditions had been used in the past, from April 2005 an offeror has only been allowed to include the pre-conditions described above and the Panel will no longer allow wide and/or subjective pre-conditions in Rule 2.7 announcements. According to the Code Committee in RS 2004/4, the circumstances in which the Panel should be prepared to consider exercising its discretion to allow pre-conditions outside the permitted categories are likely to be very limited, for example if it relates to a matter concerning the offeree company that is likely to be incapable of resolution within the normal offer timetable and is a matter without which it would be unreasonable to expect the offeror to make the offer at all.

As referred to above, pre-conditional Rule 2.7 announcements have sometimes contained a pre-condition in relation to financing (i.e. that the offeror will have the facilities in place to finance the cash element of a bid) or in relation to the adequacy of working capital for the enlarged group. In PCP 2004/4 and in RS 2004/4, the Code Committee proposed that the same prohibition on financing conditions in offers should normally also apply to financing pre-conditions.

However, as set out in the Note on Rules 13.1 and 13.3, in exceptional cases the Panel may be prepared to accept a pre-condition related to financing either in addition to another pre-condition permitted by Rule 13.3 or otherwise; for example where, due to the likely period required to obtain any necessary material official authorisation or regulatory clearance, it is not reasonable for the offeror to maintain committed financing throughout the offer period, in which case:

1.   the financing pre-condition must be satisfied (or waived), or the offer must be withdrawn, within 21 days after the satisfaction (or waiver) of any other pre-condition(s) permitted by Rule 13.3; and
2.   the offeror and its financial adviser must confirm in writing to the Panel before announcement of the offer that they are not aware of any reason why the offeror would be unable to satisfy the financing pre-condition within that 21 day period.

It is clear from PCP 2004/4 and RS 2004/4 that the Panel has adopted the same approach to working capital conditions. However, the Panel exercised its discretion to allow the pre-conditional offer by Boots for Unichem in October 2005, for example, to include a pre-condition that the two companies be reasonably satisfied for the purposes of the requirements of the

FSA and the UKLA that the necessary financing facilities would be available on reasonable market terms, following completion of their merger, to provide for the working capital requirements of the group.

As regards possible offer announcements, subjective pre-conditions can be included and do not have to be confined to anti-trust clearances etc. This is on the basis that, since the making of the offer still remains within the discretion of the potential offeror even where the pre-conditions are satisfied, neither shareholders nor the market can gain any more certainty from a requirement that only objective pre-conditions will be permissible. Therefore, a possible offer can be pre-conditional on, for example, offeree board recommendation, satisfactory due diligence or arranging financing. However, in order to avoid false market concerns, it must be clear from the wording of any possible offer announcement whether or not the pre-conditions must be satisfied before an offer can be made or whether they are waivable (see Rule 2.5(c)). If a pre-condition is not stated to be waivable, the potential offeror would not normally be permitted to make an offer unless the pre-condition was clearly satisfied.

In order to ensure that shareholders and the market are not confused as to whether a potential offeror is committed to proceed if the pre-conditions are satisfied, a pre-conditional possible offer announcement should include a prominent warning to the effect that the announcement does not amount to a firm intention to make an offer and that, accordingly, there can be no certainty that any offer will be made even if the pre-conditions are satisfied or waived.

2.7.3 Disclosure in the offer announcement of side agreements relating to pre-conditions and conditions

In December 2001, the Code was amended to impose an obligation to disclose side agreements (whether formal or informal) relating to offer pre-conditions and conditions. When a firm intention to make an offer is announced, that announcement must include details of any agreements or arrangements to which the offeror is party which relate to the circumstances in which it may or may not invoke or seek to invoke a pre-condition or a condition to its offer and the consequences of its doing so, including details of any break fees payable as a result. This requirement has been incorporated as Rule 2.7(c)(iv).

It should be noted that this obligation extends to agreements in relation to the acceptance condition, for example if a bidder undertakes to a lending bank that it will not declare the offer unconditional as to acceptances unless at least 75 per cent acceptances are achieved.

This obligation should not generally extend to a disclosure letter entered into between an offeror and an offeree company where one or more of the conditions to the offer contains an explicit carve out for information disclosed in writing by the offeree company to the offeror—although this should be confirmed with the Panel on a case-by-case basis.

The Panel stated that, in exceptional circumstances, it would be prepared to grant a dispensation from this obligation in respect of agreements which are commercially sensitive and/or do not have a bearing on the offer. Furthermore, in the context of regulatory side agreements, the Panel may be prepared to grant a dispensation from the obligation of disclosure where the offeree company and its advisers confirm in writing that disclosure would be likely to prejudice negotiations with the relevant regulatory authority to an extent which is material in the context of the offer.

Under the normal principles of the Code, parties are required to behave in a manner which is consistent with what has been publicly disclosed. However, the Panel has acknowledged that where parties had good commercial reasons to amend the terms of a side agreement once they had been publicly disclosed, the Panel could grant them dispensation to do so.

2.7.4 Circulation of announcement

Under Rule 2.12, whenever an offer period commences (except where the offer period begins with a Rule 2.7 announcement), the offeree company is required to circulate the relevant announcement to its shareholders and certain other persons (including option-holders), and to make it readily available to its employee representatives or the employees themselves. It also has to circulate any firm Rule 2.7 firm offer announcement. Also, both the offeror and the offeree company have to make the Rule 2.7 announcement, or a summary, readily available to their employee representatives or, where there are no such representatives, to the employees themselves. This rule also imposes a requirement on the offeror and offeree company, where necessary, to explain the implications of the announcement. Also, where the offeree company is sending any announcement or summary to its employee representatives or employees, it must also inform them of the employee representatives' rights under Rule 25.9. Following RS 2004/3 and RS 2008/3, there are additional requirements to include both a summary of the provisions of Rule 8 in any Rule 2.12 circular and a statement that offeree company shareholders' address details may be provided to the offeror as required under Section 4 of Appendix 4 of the Code.

When the bid is hostile, this obligation on the offeree company is often rather grudgingly discharged: a repudiatory letter from the offeree board dismissing the bid is accompanied by an Appendix with the detailed terms and conditions of the offer set out in tiny type designed to discourage all but the most persistent readers!

2.7.5 Consequences of announcement

Following an announcement of a firm intention to make an offer, the offeror must normally proceed with the offer unless, in accordance with the provisions of Rule 13, the offeror is permitted to invoke a pre-condition to the posting of the offer or would be permitted to invoke a condition to the offer if the offer were made. An exception to this obligation in Rule 2.7(b) is that with the consent of the Panel an offeror can be released from the obligation to proceed if a competitor has already announced a firm intention to make a higher offer.

2.7.6 Announcement of numbers of relevant securities in issue

The Panel explained in PCP 14 issued in April 2003 that there had been cases where a party had failed to comply with the dealing disclosure obligations in Rule 8 because it had been unaware either of the exact number of relevant securities in issue or that holdings or dealings in certain lines of stock were disclosable. The sources on which firms often rely for the relevant information were not always up to date or accurate and a company's issued share capital can alter frequently. Therefore the Panel considered it would be in the interests of the market generally for every company whose securities are subject to the dealing disclosure regime in Rule 8 to announce the exact number of the relevant securities in issue and keep the market updated of any subsequent changes.

Accordingly, in July 2003, Rule 2.10 was introduced which requires the offeree company, when an offer period begins, to announce, as soon as possible and in any case by 09.00 on the next business day, details of all classes of relevant securities issued by the offeree company, together with the numbers of such securities in issue. An offeror or potential offeror must also announce the same details relating to its relevant securities by 09.00 on the business day following any announcement identifying it as an offeror or potential offeror, unless it has stated that its offer is likely to be solely in cash. The announcement should include, where relevant, the International Securities Identification Number for each relevant security. If the information included in an announcement made under Rule 2.10 changes during the offer period, a revised announcement must be made as soon as possible. Note 1 on Rule 2.10 (introduced by RS 2005/2) states that, for the purposes of that Rule, options to subscribe for new securities in the offeree company or an offeror are not to be treated as a class of relevant securities. Note 2 on Rule 2.10 makes it clear that only relevant securities which are held and in issue outside treasury should be included in the announcement.

2.8 Independent advice

2.8.1 Offeree

Under Rule 3.1, the board of an offeree company must obtain competent independent advice and make the substance of that advice known to its shareholders. The Panel has been at pains to stress the importance of the adviser's role in assisting the board in presenting its views, and in ensuring that full information, and the board's reasoned arguments, are circulated to shareholders.

The Notes on Rule 3.1 amplify the basic Rule, and cover:

1. management buyouts and offers by controlling shareholders (stressing the importance of the independence of the advice obtained in these circumstances);
2. the situation where there is uncertainty about the financial information in the offeree company's most recently published financial results—important factors must be highlighted by the board and the independent adviser; and
3. the situation where the financial adviser is unable to express a view on the merits of an offer. In these circumstances, an explanation must be given and the arguments in favour and against acceptance of the offer should be clearly set out. The Panel should also be consulted in such cases.

2.8.2 Offeror company

The offeror board (where the offeror is a company which would be subject to the Code if it was the offeree company) is under a similar obligation to seek independent advice where the offer is a reverse takeover (i.e. where the offeror may need to increase its existing issued voting equity share capital by more than 100 per cent) or where the directors have a conflict of interest. Examples of a conflict of interest given in Note 2 on Rule 3.2 include where there are significant cross-shareholdings between an offeror and the offeree company, a number of directors common to both companies or when a person has a substantial interest in both companies.

Advice obtained under Rule 3.2 should be obtained by the offeror board before the offer is made and should address the question of whether the offer is in the shareholders' interests. The offeror shareholders must be given sufficient time to consider this advice before any meeting is held at which a vote is to be taken on the offer.

2.8.3 The financial adviser

Rule 3.3 (and Appendix 3) reinforces the requirement that financial advice must be independent. If one part of a multi-service organisation acts for the offeror, another part of it may well not be permitted to act for the offeree company. In addition, those with a significant interest in, or financial connection with, either the offeror or offeree company will normally be disqualified. For example, if the investment management arm of a bank advises an investment trust, the corporate finance arm will not normally be able to act for that trust in a bid as an independent Rule 3 adviser.

In its 1995 Annual Report, the Panel emphasised the importance of independent advice, stating:

> "The Panel has always regarded it as of paramount importance that the adviser should be sufficiently independent so that its advice should be objective beyond question.
>
> A prospective adviser to an offeree company might not be considered sufficiently independent, for example, if it has had a recent advisory role with the offeror or has a very close advisory relationship with a large shareholder in the offeree company. The precise circumstances of every case

will be different, links may be economic or advisory and sometimes quite a fine judgment will have to be made. The views of the offeree company's board will always be an important factor. The Panel strongly recommends early consultation with the Executive in any case where the independence of an adviser could be in doubt."

This is echoed in Note 1 to Rule 3.3. An example of the application of this Note 1 was the role of Dresdner Kleinwort Benson in relation to the offer by Abbey National for Cater Allen (as reflected in Panel Statement 1997/9). In that case, the Panel upheld a ruling by the Executive that Dresdner Kleinwort Benson would not be an appropriate person under Note 1 on Rule 3.3 to give independent advice to Cater Allen in relation to the recommended offer by Abbey National. This was due to Kleinwort Benson's "close, recent and continuing" advisory relationship with Abbey National; Kleinworts had been one of Abbey's advisers since flotation. The Panel emphasised the importance of the adviser not only being, but being viewed objectively as being, independent. Cater Allen therefore had to appoint another adviser to give advice under Rule 3.1.

Specifically in relation to broking relationships, in its 2002 Annual Report, in reference to Rule 3.1, the Panel stated:

"Financial advisers within groups which have an advisory relationship with an offeror are not normally regarded as appropriate persons to give advice to the offeree board on an offer. In this context, broking relationships with an offeror are considered in the same light as other types of advisory relationship. Whilst it is accepted that the strength and nature of broking relationships, and the services provided under them, vary widely, such relation-ships generally create a potential conflict of interest.

In one or two recent cases, groups have assumed that a potential conflict of interest arising from an offeror broking relationship can be addressed satisfactorily by the broker standing down from its role for the duration of the offer. The Executive's view is that this action will not normally be sufficient to resolve concerns as to independence. Therefore, in cases where an offeree adviser's group has an offeror broking relationship, the Executive should be consulted at an early stage."

The Executive outlined its approach to determining whether an adviser is independent for these purposes in Practice Statement No.21, which also explained something of a relaxation in its approach in recognition of the fact that relationships between companies and financial advisers are less exclusive than was previously the case. In considering whether an adviser is independent, the Executive will examine the strength of the overall relationship between the offeror and the adviser's group, including:

1. the nature of all matters in relation to which the adviser has provided the offeror with advice over the preceding 12 to 24 month period and any matters in contemplation— this is not limited to corporate finance advice, but includes other services, for example leading a debt syndication;
2. the size of past transactions on which the adviser's group has advised over the relevant period and the locations in which they were undertaken;
3. the frequency with which the adviser's group has advised the offeror and the extent to which the offeror has instructed other financial advisers during the relevant period; and
4. the fee income paid to the adviser and its group during the period, both in terms of total fees and their significance to the adviser's group.

As a result, the Executive may conclude that a recent, or even a current, advisory role for the offeror may not be material and therefore should not compromise the independence of the adviser (which is a relaxation of its previous position that advising the offeror on any matter at the same time as the proposed offer would generally mean the adviser should not be considered independent). However, the Executive continues to take the view that an adviser which is in the same group as a corporate broker to an offeror is not independent for these purposes.

Appendix 3 also deals with the problem of conflicts of interest and "material confidential information", particularly where the financial adviser has previously advised one of the other parties to the bid. This arose specifically out of the difficulties which ensued on the TKM bid for Molins, which were dealt with in Panel Statement 1987/13. The conclusion is that conflicts of interest cannot necessarily be resolved by the creation of internal Chinese walls.

The Panel has also considered whether the nature of a financial adviser's fee arrangements may give rise to a conflict of interest that would prevent it from acting as a Rule 3 adviser. In Panel Statement 1999/11, the Panel stated:

> "Arrangements which reward an adviser to the offeree dependent on failure of a hostile offer, irrespective of the offer price, give rise to, or create the perception of, an actual or potential conflict of interest. In these circumstances, the adviser will normally be disqualified from acting as independent Rule 3 adviser. Similar considerations will apply to any fee payable on failure of an offer below an unrealistically high price. The Executive should be consulted in any case of doubt. The Panel may in appropriate cases require disclosure in the offer documentation to enable the arrangements to be subjected to public scrutiny."

This followed the takeover by The Great Universal Stores of Argos. A new Note 3 on Rule 3.3 was introduced into the Code in July 2000 implementing this statement and requiring consultation with the Panel where fee arrangements might be such as to create a conflict of interest. The Note does not, however, require a success fee to be disclosed, as was envisaged in the statement.

Chapter 3

Share Dealings and Holdings—Restrictions and Disclosure Requirements

Andy Ryde

Partner

Slaughter and May

Roland Turnill

Partner

Slaughter and May

3.1 Introduction

This Chapter is principally concerned with the Rules of the Code which restrict, or require the disclosure of, dealings in shares before and during a takeover bid. However, there are additional Rules that apply to dealings in shares at any time, such as the Companies Act 2006 (the 2006 Act), the Disclosure and Transparency Rules (the DTRs), the Criminal Justice Act 1993 (the CJA 1993), the Financial Services and Markets Act 2000 (the FSMA) and the Financial Services Act 2012 (the FS Act 2012). These additional Rules will also be considered in this Chapter.

It will be apparent from the above list of sources that one of the principal concerns in the takeovers field is to ensure that all the different sets of Rules which apply to the transaction in hand have been identified and, where they overlap, to ensure that each is complied with. Steps taken with one set of regulations in mind may have adverse consequences under another and a balance may have to be struck. Furthermore, not all Rules are absolute in their application; in particular, the Rules set out in the Code are not always strictly construed and, even where their meaning appears clear, may be relaxed or perhaps even extended by the Panel in particular circumstances. How such Rules should be applied is often a matter of judgment based on experience, but discussions with the Panel on points of difficulty will be a regular feature of major transactions.

Two sets of regulations not addressed in detail in this Chapter (although there are references where appropriate) are the FCA Listing Rules and the FCA Prospectus Rules (collectively, the Listing Regime) of the Financial Conduct Authority (the FCA) (formerly known as the Financial Services Authority (the FSA)). This is on the basis that the Listing Regime is not normally directly relevant to dealings in shares during a takeover bid. However, it should be borne in mind that it may be relevant in certain circumstances (particularly those Rules relating to the announcement of, or the obtaining of share-holder consent for, significant transactions and limiting the scope of indemnities which a listed company can give to third parties buying shares on its behalf).

Practitioners will be aware of the changes introduced on April 1, 2013 by the FS Act 2012 to the UK financial regulatory landscape. The FCA has taken over the FSA's former responsibility for the regulation of markets, and the prudential supervision of those not supervised by the new Prudential Regulation Authority (the PRA). Panel Statement 2013/3 details the amendments made by the Code Committee to the Code under Instrument 2013/1 to implement the changes required by the FS Act 2012. For the purposes of this Chapter, the impact of the FS Act 2012 is limited, with the majority of the amendments replacing references to "FSA" with those to "FCA". The FS Act 2012's more substantive changes to the regulation of misleading statements and practices are addressed at 3.3.4.1.

3.2 Applicability of the Rules

The first question to be addressed in this area is: in what circumstances do each of the particular sets of Rules or provisions apply, if at all?

3.2.1 The Code

Until recently, the Code broadly speaking applied to offers for all companies (and Societas Europaea) which had their registered offices in the United Kingdom, the Channel Islands or the Isle of Man and had securities which were (or, in certain cases, had been) traded on a regulated market in the United Kingdom. It also applied to public companies (such as AIM-listed companies) which did not have securities traded on a regulated market but which were considered by the Panel to be resident in the United Kingdom, the Channel Islands or the Isle of Man. However, in response to a 2012 consultation on the topic, the Code Committee removed the residency test with respect to public companies whose securities are admitted to trading on a multilateral trading facility (such as AIM) in the United Kingdom (see Response Statement RS 2012/3 published on May 15, 2013). As a result, regardless of the company's place of central management and control, all companies that have their registered offices in the United Kingdom, the Channel Islands or the Isle of Man are now subject to the Code if any of their securities are admitted to trading on: (i) a regulated market in the United Kingdom or any stock exchange in the Channel Islands or the Isle of Man; (ii) a multilateral trading facility in the United Kingdom; or (iii) a regulated market in one or more member states of the EEA but not on a regulated market in the United Kingdom. These changes have been effective since September 30, 2013 and an amended version of the Code implementing these changes was published on that date.

One of the main functions of the Code is to regulate changes of "control" in companies to which it applies: thus, the Code is not generally applicable to offers relating only to non-voting or non-equity capital (except offers under Rule 15 (Appropriate offer for convertibles etc.)), but it does cover transactions, not amounting to full takeover offers, in which control is obtained or consolidated. Control for Code purposes is deemed to be exercised by those with an "interest" (see 3.2.1.1 below) in 30 per cent or more of the "voting rights" in the target either alone or as part of a "concert party" (see 3.2.1.3 below).

The Rules of the Code of most relevance to dealings in shares which might result in control being obtained or consolidated are Rules 5 and 9. Rule 5 has the effect of prohibiting, subject to certain exceptions, the acquisition by a person and its concert parties of interests in shares carrying 30 per cent or more of the voting rights of a company or, where a person and its concert parties are already interested in shares carrying between 30 per cent and 50 per cent of the voting rights, the acquisition of an interest in any other shares carrying such voting rights (see further 3.3.1.3, 3.3.1.4 and 4.2 below).

The Code also contains detailed Rules concerning the disclosure of dealings during the "offer period" (principally Rule 8, see further 3.4.3.1 and 3.4.3.2 below). These Rules are not restricted to dealings by the "parties to the offer" but extend to other parties interested in "relevant securities" of the target or offeror.

The Panel has kept the dealing disclosure requirements under review with the most recent wholesale amendments to Rule 8 coming into force on April 19, 2010 (see Code Committee Instrument 2009/6 (Instrument 2009/6)). The Panel introduced the requirement for an "opening position disclosure" and extended the requirements to disclose dealings and positions on a composite basis. These most recent amendments continue the pattern of increased transparency in relation to the position of, and dealings by, persons involved in takeover bids and should enable the Panel and the market to develop a more comprehensive understanding of circumstances surrounding an offer. The Rules of the Code which restrict or require the disclosure of dealings make use of a number of important defined terms. Certain of these terms are explained below.

3.2.1.1 *Interests in securities*

When considering interests in shares or relevant securities under the Code, the focus has historically been on direct holdings of shares or relevant securities and restrictions and disclosure requirements have been applied to persons "purchasing securities". However, in recent years much market activity has moved from the cash to the derivatives market and developments in market practice mean that persons with long derivative or option positions may exercise significant de facto control over the underlying securities.

In the case of a long contract for difference (CFD), the counterparty with whom the CFD holder takes out the contract will typically hedge its exposure by acquiring the shares which underlie the CFD. The counterparty will also sometimes agree (usually informally) to exercise the voting rights attaching to these shares in accordance with the wishes of the CFD holder. Therefore, while the holder of a CFD will not appear on the register of shareholders of the company in question, it may be able to control the exercise of votes in respect of a significant proportion of its shares. Furthermore, the terms of the CFD or market practice may enable the CFD holder to receive the underlying shares acquired by the counterparty in settlement of the CFD.

For example, in the case of BAE Systems' offer for Alvis during 2004, BAE Systems obtained irrevocable commitments from a number of funds which had entered into CFDs referenced to shares representing approximately 16 per cent of the issued share capital of Alvis. Some of these funds entered into commitments with BAE Systems to

> "request physical settlement of the CFDs in accordance with market practice... and then to assent to the offer all shares received by them as a result of this physical settlement process."

Other CFD holders who did not give such a commitment to BAE Systems expressly consented to the counterparty with whom they had entered into a CFD giving BAE Systems a standard irrevocable commitment to accept the offer in respect of the Alvis shares held by it as a hedge against its position under the relevant CFD.

Similarly, in the same year a number of funds entered into long CFDs referenced to shares in Marks & Spencer during the period of Revival Acquisitions' interest in the company. These funds sought to put pressure on the board of Marks & Spencer to grant Revival Acquisitions access to carry out due diligence. The funds were aware that their statements of support would be made public and their intention was to influence the debate on whether due diligence access should be granted.

As a result of these developments, the Code Committee made a number of changes to the Code to ensure that it covers all relevant interests and not just traditional holdings of shares or other securities.

The resulting Code provisions are not just applicable to CFDs but also to other types of derivatives. Similarly, they are also applicable to dealings in options because, despite the differences between options and derivatives, counterparties to options may also hedge their exposure by acquiring the shares underlying the option and persons holding call options may obtain a measure of de facto control over shares in a similar way to holders of long CFDs.

It should be noted that a person with a short position in securities will not normally be treated as interested in them and will therefore not be subject to a disclosure obligation. The Panel has kept the disclosure of short positions under review and consulted on this point in 2009 (see Public Consultation Paper PCP 2009/1 (PCP 2009/1)). The Panel's view was that an arguable case could be made for the introduction of a "short trigger" provision, whereby the Code's disclosure requirements would apply to a person who has a significant gross short position in the relevant securities of a party to an offer but who does not have a long position of one per cent or more in any such securities. However, it concluded that it would not

be proportionate to introduce such a new disclosure requirement for the relatively unusual cases in which short positions
would not otherwise be subject to disclosure under the Code
(see Response Statement RS 2009/1: Extending the Code's
Disclosure Regime (RS 2009/1)). The Code Committee has
reserved its right to review the "short trigger" proposal in the
future but has stated that it has no current intention of doing
so.

Guidance from the Panel in its Practice Statement No.22 of July
10, 2008 indicates that where an offeror has received an
irrevocable commitment to accept its offer, that will not, of
itself, result in the offeror being considered to be interested in
the shares to which the irrevocable commitment relates (other
than for the purposes of Rule 5 of the Code). Where an
irrevocable undertaking includes a voting undertaking, the
question arises on whether this gives the offeror "the right... to
exercise or direct the exercise of voting rights attaching to
them" for the purposes of para.2 of the definition of interest in
securities. Practice Statement No.22 indicates the Panel would
not normally consider an offeror to be interested in the shares
to which the irrevocable commitment relates provided that the
voting undertaking is:

1.   given in the context of an irrevocable commitment to
     accept the offer;
2.   limited to the duration of the offer or, if earlier, until the
     irrevocable commitment otherwise ceases to be binding;
     and
3.   limited to matters which relate to ensuring that the offer is
     successful.

3.2.1.2   Dealings

The definition of "dealings" under the Code covers any action
which results in an increase or decrease in the number of
securities in which a person is interested or in respect of which
he has a short position. The definition was extended in 2005 to
transactions involving derivatives and options and, more
recently, new Notes 1 and 2 have been added to clarify that the

term encompasses indemnity and other dealing arrangements with concert parties, but does not include securities borrowing and lending except where Rule 4.6 applies (see Instrument 2009/6). This may change in the future as the Code Committee raised in PCP 2009/2 the question of whether the definition of dealings should be amended so as to treat borrowing and lending transactions as dealings. They decided not to put forward detailed proposals at that time, but the PCP did describe in substance the amendments that they believed might be made if detailed proposals were put forward in the future.

3.2.1.3 Concert parties

The term "concert parties", which used to describe gatherings at the end of the pier in seaside resorts, was adopted by the Panel in the early days of the Code to describe associated parties acting together. For most purposes under the Code and for disclosure purposes under the DTRs and the 2006 Act (see 3.4.1 and 3.4.2 below), the holdings or acquisitions of shares in a target by parties "acting in concert" are aggregated. The concert party concept is expressed in different ways in the Code, the DTRs and the 2006 Act and is not used as a defined term other than in the Code, but in each case concert parties are capable of being constituted even where there is no formal written concert party agreement.

The Code also previously applied to the similar category of "associates" of a party to an offer and persons falling within either or both categories were subject to disclosure requirements under the Code. Since April 19, 2010 (as a result of amendments under Instrument 2009/6) the "associate" concept has been deleted in order to simplify the application of the Code, and the provisions of the Code which previously referred to an associate of a party to an offer now refer to persons acting in concert.

For Code purposes, a concert party is a combination of persons who cooperate to achieve or consolidate control of the target or to frustrate the successful outcome of a bid (see the Definitions section of the Code). The Code definition of a concert party does not require active co-operation between the parties, is not limited to parties co-operating through the acquisition of shares by any of them and includes persons who co-operate with the target company with a view to frustrating the successful outcome of a bid. The consequences of being a member of a concert party will generally bite under Rules 5, 6, 8, 9 and 11 when any of the relevant parties acquires shares.

Furthermore, under the Code definition of acting in concert, a person and each of its affiliated persons will be deemed to be acting in concert with each other. An "affiliated person" is defined in Note 2 to the definition of acting in concert as any undertaking in respect of which any person:

1. has a majority of the shareholders' or members' voting rights;
2. is a shareholder or member and has the right to appoint or remove a majority of its board;
3. is a shareholder or member and alone controls a majority of the shareholders' or members' voting rights pursuant to an agreement with other shareholders or members; or
4. has the power to exercise, or actually exercises, dominant influence or control.

The Code also provides that certain persons, including holding companies, sister subsidiaries, 20 per cent-owned associated companies, directors, connected advisers, pension schemes and the pension schemes of associated companies are presumed to be acting in concert with a company unless the contrary is established. Likewise, investors in a bidding consortium are presumed to be acting in concert with the offeror and, if they are part of a larger organisation, the Panel should be consulted to establish which other parts of the organisation will also be regarded as acting in concert.

The notes to the Code definition of acting in concert give additional guidance as to how the term is understood by the Panel. In relation to other parts of a financial services organisation of which a consortium investor is part, for example, the Panel will consider waiving the presumption if the investment in the consortium amounts to less than 50 per cent of the share capital of the offeror. The Panel will normally waive the presumption in relation to other parts of the organisation if the investment in the consortium is 10 per cent or less (Note 6 on the Code definition of acting in concert). Similarly, the Panel will normally regard the presumption of concertedness between a company and its pension scheme as having been rebutted if an independent third party has absolute discretion regarding dealing, voting and offer acceptance decisions relating to any securities in which the pension scheme is interested (Note 7 on the Code definition of acting in concert).

The presumption that advisers will act in concert with their clients (presumption 5 of the Code definition of acting in concert) was considered in the case of Songbird Acquisition Ltd's bid for Canary Wharf Group Plc (see Panel Statement 2004/12). In its statement of April 23, 2004, the Panel made it clear that the presumption does not only apply to advisers who have been engaged to act on the offer or on a transaction related to the offer; other advisers who have a relationship with the offeror or target company (or a concert party thereof) will also be presumed to be acting in concert with that party. The presumption can, however, be rebutted (as it was in the Canary Wharf case). The question of whether or not the presumption should be rebutted is determined by the Panel, taking into account all relevant factors including whether the adviser is named in the company's annual report and accounts, and whether the adviser has stood down or offered to do so and, if so, why.

A person will not normally be treated as acting in concert with an offeror or target company by reason only of giving an irrevocable commitment, but Note 9 to the Code definition of acting in concert states that the Panel will consider the position of such a person in order to determine whether he is acting in concert if either:

1. the terms of the irrevocable commitment give the offeror or target company either the right (whether conditional or absolute) to exercise or direct the exercise of the voting rights attaching to the shares or general control of them; or
2. the person acquires an interest in more shares.

The Panel should therefore be consulted before the acquisition of any further interest in shares in such circumstances.

Further guidance from the Panel in its Practice Statement No.22 of July 10, 2008 indicates that the Panel is of the view that, although the precise wording of a voting undertaking contained in an irrevocable commitment to accept an offer may vary, it would generally comprise an undertaking to vote the relevant shares in accordance with the instructions of the offeror in the context of both resolutions required to implement the offer and resolutions which, if passed, might result in a condition of its offer not being fulfilled or might frustrate the offer in some other way.

The Panel considers that in entering into a voting undertaking of this type a shareholder is doing no more than what is logically consistent with his irrevocable commitment to accept the offer, since he is undertaking to vote the shares in a manner consistent with his acceptance decision. As such the Panel has indicated it would not consider the offeror to have acquired general control of the relevant shares for the purposes of the definition of acting in concert provided the voting undertaking is:

1. given in the context of an irrevocable commitment to accept the offer;
2. limited to the duration of the offer or, if earlier, until the irrevocable commitment otherwise ceases to be binding; and
3. limited to matters which relate to ensuring that the offer is successful.

Where the Panel agrees that the presumption is rebutted in any individual case, it may, where it considers it appropriate, require that a person who would otherwise have been treated as a person acting in concert make a private disclosure to the Panel (containing the details that would have been required under Rule 8.4) if he deals in any relevant securities during an offer period. This requirement, which was introduced by Instrument 2009/6, is set out in new Note 10 to the acting in concert definition and is designed to enable the Panel to monitor whether or not the presumption of concertedness should continue to be treated as rebutted during the offer period.

In addition to the definition and the notes which follow it, there are a number of other provisions of the Code which are relevant to understanding the concept of acting in concert. These provisions include, notably, the Notes on Rule 9.1 (see further 3.3.1.4 below).

Note 2 on Rule 9.1 provides that the Panel will normally presume that shareholders who make or threaten to make a "board control-seeking proposal" at any general meeting of a company are acting in concert with each other and with their proposed directors. Parties will be presumed to be acting in concert from the time that an agreement or understanding between them is reached, so any purchase of the company's shares by any of them thereafter could give rise to a mandatory offer obligation. However, it should be noted that the Panel takes a retrospective approach to the determination of appropriate consideration in respect of bids involving concert parties: although a concert party relationship may only arise at a certain point, the dealings of the parties prior to that point may be relevant for the purposes of determining the level and nature of consideration under a subsequent offer (see further 3.3.1.5 (Rule 6) and 3.3.1.6 (Rule 11) below).

Concerns were raised by various shareholders as part of the 2009 Walker Review of Corporate Governance of the UK Banking Industry that these provisions acted as a barrier to cooperative action by fund managers and institutional shareholders. In response, the Panel issued Practice Statement No.26 on September 9, 2009 which sought to provide clarification of when a mandatory offer would be triggered by activist shareholders cooperating with each other. In this, the Panel confirmed that, of themselves, the following factors would not lead to the conclusion that the parties were acting in concert:

1. discussions between shareholders about possible issues which might be raised with a company's board;
2. joint representation by shareholders to the board; and
3. the agreement by shareholders to vote in the same way on a particular resolution at a general meeting.

The Panel also notes in this Practice Statement that even if a "board control-seeking" resolution were to be proposed by activist shareholders, no mandatory offer would be required if, at the time that any such agreement or understanding is reached, steps are taken to prevent the acquisition of interests in securities in the relevant company by those shareholders.

Separately, Note 5 on Rule 9.1 provides that the Panel must be consulted before the acquisition of an interest in shares where:

1. the aggregate number of shares in which the directors, any other persons acting, or presumed to be acting, in concert with the directors and the trustees of an employee benefit trust (EBT) are interested will carry 30 per cent or more of the voting rights (or, if already carrying 30 per cent or more, will increase further) as a result of the acquisition; or
2. a person or group of persons acting, or presumed to be acting, in concert is interested in shares carrying 30 per cent or more (but does not hold shares carrying more than 50 per cent) of the voting rights and it is proposed that an EBT acquires an interest in any other shares.

Note 5 goes on to provide that no presumption of concerted-ness will apply in respect of any shares held in an EBT that are controlled by the beneficiaries.

The Note states that the Panel will consider "all relevant factors" in concluding whether the trustees of an EBT are acting in concert with the directors and/or a controller or group of persons acting, or presumed to be acting, in concert. The Note contains a non-exhaustive list of factors which will be taken into account.

For the purposes of Rule 9.1, the Panel has traditionally treated a group of persons acting in concert as a single person. Usually, therefore, the person responsible for making the mandatory offer (the person whose acquisition triggered the mandatory bid) will extend it to shareholders outside the concert party but not to members of the concert party itself. Following the Panel's Annual Report for 2002/3, however, the person responsible for making the offer may extend it to other concert party members if it wishes, although it is under no obligation to do so.

Similarly, the 2006 Act treats persons as acting together in a less formal manner than the normal, strict legal meaning of contractual agreement; for instance, ss.824 and 825 when read together treat two or more persons as one (such that each party to the agreement is interested in all the shares in which any other party to the agreement is interested) where there exists any "agreement or arrangement" between them for the acquisition of shares. Section 824 makes it clear that "agreement or arrangement" includes a non-legally binding agreement or arrangement, provided there exists a mutuality of undertakings, expectations or understandings.

3.2.2 The 2006 Act

The 2006 Act will be relevant in a variety of circumstances. The acquisition of any shares in a UK-incorporated public company may lead to an obligation to disclose, at the request of that company, whether the acquiror is, or has within the previous three years been, interested in its shares, along with certain other details (s.793, as to which, see further 3.4.2.3 below).

The 2006 Act contains powers compulsorily to purchase minority shareholdings once an offer for shares in the target has been accepted by holders of 90 per cent of the shares of the relevant class to which the offer relates, excluding any shares in the company held as treasury shares. Hence, any shareholder with a holding of more than 10 per cent of the shares to which an offer relates is able to thwart the operation of this mechanism and remain an unwanted minority holder.

Finally, as became apparent in the aftermath of the takeover by Guinness of the Distillers Company, restrictions on a public company giving financial assistance in connection with the purchase of its own shares (now contained in Ch.2 of Pt 18 of the 2006 Act) may apply to a takeover, not only in connection with any purchase of shares in a target, but also in relation to indemnities given by offerors in connection with various aspects of share-for-share offers.

3.2.3 DTRs

Chapter 5 (Vote Holder and Issuer Notification Rules) of the DTRs applies to: (1) United Kingdom and overseas companies whose home state is the United Kingdom and which have shares traded on a regulated market; and (2) UK companies with shares traded on a prescribed market (for example AIM). It does not apply to non-UK issuers whose home state is not the United Kingdom.

Non-EEA companies may benefit from an exemption from the requirements of DTR 5 if they are subject to equivalent requirements under their domestic legislation. At the date of writing, the FCA has determined that the laws of the United States of America, Japan, Israel and Switzerland impose equivalent requirements (see *http://www.fca.org.uk/firms/markets/ukla/information-for-issuers/non-eea-regimes* [Accessed July 14,, 2014]). The notification obligations are discussed at 3.4.1 below.

At the end of each calendar month, an issuer must (assuming an increase or decrease has occurred) announce the total number of voting rights and capital in respect of each class of share which it issues, and the total number of voting rights attaching to shares held in treasury. However, following the FSA's January 2010 Quarterly Consultation (No.23) and subsequent DTR amendments effective from November 1, 2010, an issuer must now disclose changes in total voting rights and capital, other than those which are immaterial, as soon as possible (and in any event no later than the end of the business day following the day on which the increase or decrease occurs). The issuer must make the decision as to what is immaterial but the FCA's guidance makes it clear that an increase or decrease of 1 per cent or more is likely to be material. It is the responsibility of each shareholder to monitor company announcements: the number of issued shares as announced by the company is taken as the denominator for determining whether disclosure thresholds have been reached by a shareholder (even where it has not engaged in any dealings). In addition, DTR 5 contains announcement obligations on an issuer which acquires or disposes of its own shares, in cases where the percentage held reaches, exceeds or falls below five or ten per cent of the voting rights.

The DTRs also place an obligation on "persons discharging managerial responsibility", which includes directors, to notify listed companies of share dealings, which the company must then announce. These obligations are not discussed in this Chapter.

3.2.4   CJA 1993 and FSMA

Part V of the CJA 1993 applies to dealings in shares on a regulated market, including the Main Market of the London Stock Exchange, regardless of the place of incorporation or residence of the company whose shares are being transferred. Its primary purpose is to prohibit certain dealings by, and certain activities of, persons who have inside information. In particular, when in possession of inside information, it is an offence for an individual not only to deal or to "encourage" others—such as corporate employees or clients—to deal, but also to disclose the information other than in proper performance of the functions of his employment, office or profession.

FSMA controls the manner in which securities may be offered and admitted to listing on the Official List. It also contains provisions relevant to all takeovers, such as restrictions on financial promotions (s.21). Prior to the regulatory changes introduced by the FS Act 2012 on April 1, 2013, FSMA contained a provision for an offence relating to misleading statements or courses of conduct (s.397). This provision has now been repealed and replaced by three offences relating to the making of misleading statements or courses of conduct under Pt 7 of the FS Act 2012. Two of these offences largely replicate the old s.397 offences; the third covers the making of false or misleading statements, or the creation of false or misleading impressions, in relation to "relevant benchmarks" (with the London Interbank Offered Rate (LIBOR) being the only relevant benchmark specified so far).

In addition, FSMA contains a statutory regime for the control of market abuse, which implements the Market Abuse Directive (2003/6/EC).

These provisions result in a considerable potential overlap between the jurisdiction of the FCA and the Panel. In light of this, the FCA and the Panel have agreed a set of operating guidelines which are intended, inter alia, to assist in determining how each of them should exercise its functions in cases of jurisdictional overlap. The operating guidelines provide that where, during a takeover bid, matters arise which may amount to market misconduct, the FCA will not exercise its powers during the bid save in exceptional circumstances (see 3.3.4.3 below).

3.2.5 Other Rules

Finally, it will always be necessary to consider whether law and regulation in specific industries and/or in other jurisdictions will be relevant to share dealings in a takeover situation. Particular care will need to be taken where securities are listed on more than one market to ensure that the requirements of each stock exchange (which may conflict) are complied with.

3.3   Restrictions on the freedom to deal

We will first deal with Rules prohibiting or restricting share dealings which only apply in the context of a takeover, and then turn to restrictions with general application.

3.3.1   *The Code*

3.3.1.1   *Dealings by offerors and persons acting in concert*

Before turning to the detailed Rules of the Code, it is worth recording that there was, during 1997, speculation that the Panel might change the Code to restrict the ability of a bidder and its advisers to buy shares in the market during an offer period. This was largely prompted by the takeover in December 1996 of Northern Electric by CalEnergy, the US utility. Some commentators have said that Northern Electric was acquired too cheaply because CalEnergy had an unfair advantage as it was able to buy 30 per cent of Northern Electric's shares while the price was depressed owing to the possibility of a referral to the former Monopolies and Mergers Commission. The price recovered when the bid was cleared and the offer received only 20 per cent acceptances. But with 30 per cent already in hand, CalEnergy gained control by the narrowest of margins. Some have, therefore, called on the Panel to adopt the US practice where a bidder is barred from market purchases once an offer has been made. Others, including Northern Electric's chairman, have asked for the 30 per cent threshold up to which a bidder can buy to be cut to 15 per cent, or for purchases to be prohibited at a time when there is regulatory uncertainty. However, many others take the view that there is no good public policy reason for restricting market activity during a bid. If shareholders are willing to sell out early at or below the offer price in return for certainty, then that is their prerogative (and the bidder will be barred by the insider dealing legislation from buying if it has price-sensitive information about a likely regulatory outcome that the market does not, as to which see 3.3.3.4 below). It appears that the Panel has no current plans to amend the Code in this regard, which is in keeping with its preferred approach of a generally permissive regime on dealings, focusing on consequences and disclosure.

3.3.1.2 *Rule 4—restrictions on dealings prior to and during the offer period*

Between the time when there is reason to suppose an offer or approach is contemplated and the announcement of that offer or approach (or the termination of discussions), Rule 4.1 prohibits all dealings in the securities of the target or (on a share-for-share offer) the offeror by any person who is privy to price-sensitive information concerning the offer or possible offer, apart from dealings in target securities by the offeror itself.

One difficulty which sometimes arises in this context, normally in connection with joint or consortium offers, is the identification of the offeror (i.e. the party which is permitted to deal in target securities notwithstanding its being in possession of confidential price-sensitive information). Note 2 on Rules 4.1 and 4.2 provides that the Panel must be consulted before any acquisitions of interests in target company securities are made by members or potential members of a consortium and that it will not normally be appropriate for members of a consortium to acquire interests in such securities unless, for example, there are arrangements to ensure that such acquisitions are made proportionate to members' interests in the consortium company or under arrangements which give no profit to the party making the acquisition. These restrictions will not, of course, apply to a party which can properly be characterised as an offeror (including a joint offeror).

Note 3 provides a limited exception to the Rule 4.1 prohibition allowing a party acting in concert with the offeror to deal provided that it is done on the basis that the offeror carries the economic risk and is entitled to the rewards of the transaction. Careful consideration of the insider dealing legislation and

Listing Rules provisions on indemnity arrangements (see Listing Rule 10.2.4) will, however, be required before any such transaction is implemented.

Note 4 amplifies Rule 4.1 and provides that where an announcement has been made that an offer is contemplated and discussions are then terminated or the offeror decides not to proceed with the offer, no person (including the offeror) privy to this price-sensitive information may deal until the position is publicly clarified. Note 5 further prohibits directors and financial advisers from dealing contrary to advice given by them in relation to an offer.

Once an offer has been announced, Rule 4.2 prohibits the offeror and its concert parties from selling any securities in the target except with the prior consent of the Panel and following 24 hours' public notice that such sales might be made; the Panel's consent will not be given where the offer is a mandatory offer under Rule 9, and no sales at a price below the value of the offer will, in any event, be permitted. Once notice of a possible sale has been given under this rule, neither the offeror nor its concert parties may acquire an interest in any target securities and any revision to the terms of the offer will be permitted only in exceptional circumstances. The Panel should also be consulted whenever the offeror or its concert parties proposes to enter into or close any type of transaction which may result in target securities being sold during the offer period (either by that party or by the counterparty to the transaction). The rule is designed to prevent offerors and persons acting in concert with them from misleading or manipulating the market and is also therefore a reflection of General Principle 4 of the Code which prohibits the creation of false markets.

The Panel will give dispensation in exceptional circumstances from the usual consequences of a sale under Rule 4.2 as it did in March 2003 in connection with the hostile offer by Capital Management and Investment Plc (CMI) for Six Continents Plc (Six Continents). The offer involved the issue of a very large number of CMI shares as consideration relative to the number already in issue. In order to avoid potential concerns under Rule 6 (see 3.3.1.5 below) about whether the offer could be valued at a price at or above the prices paid by CMI as part of its pre-offer stake-building, the Panel Executive agreed with CMI's proposal that it would sell those shares which had been acquired and donate the profit to charity. The Panel Executive ruled (Panel Statement 2003/7) that the disposal by CMI of its shares in Six Continents was not intended to mislead or manipulate the market but rather was a pragmatic solution to any potential concerns arising under Rule 6. The Panel Executive therefore gave its consent under Rule 4.2 to the sale by CMI of its shares in Six Continents and ruled that the usual consequences of a sale under Rule 4.2 should not apply in this case.

Panel Statement 2003/5 addressed Rule 4.2 in light of the behaviour of Indigo Capital LLC (Indigo) in relation to Regus Plc (Regus). In this case, Indigo had entered into CFDs referenced to shares in Regus. The Panel Executive considered that the closing out of such a CFD by Indigo during the offer period should be treated as equivalent to the sale of the underlying shares represented by the CFD, and as such subject to Rule 4.2. This was on the basis, discussed above, that it will most often be the case that a party with whom a CFD is entered into will hedge its exposure by acquiring an equivalent number of shares in the target company in the market. Accordingly, when such a CFD is closed out, the party with whom the CFD was entered into can reasonably be expected to sell the shares it had acquired to hedge its exposure.

In addition, as mentioned above, Rule 4.2 requires that when a sale of relevant securities is permitted by the Panel Executive, no such sale can be made at below the prevailing offer price and thereafter neither the offeror nor any person acting in concert with it may acquire an interest in any securities of the target company. The Panel Executive said that in a case such as the Indigo case where the offeror had not announced the price of its offer, it would normally treat the requirement of Rule 4.2 that sales cannot be made at below the offer price as setting a ceiling on the price at which the potential offeror would subsequently be allowed to make its formal offer, that ceiling being the price at which the relevant securities were sold.

In the Indigo case itself, however, in view of the fact that the closing out of the CFD was not disclosed to the market at the time (as it should have been) such that, in fact, there was no misleading impression that could have been created and also that to set a ceiling on the price would have the undesirable effect of possibly depriving Regus shareholders of any offer being made by Indigo at above the price at which they closed out the CFD, the Panel Executive ruled (on an ex parte basis) that the closing out of the CFD should not set a ceiling on the price of any future offer for Regus by Indigo. The Panel Executive also considered it relevant in making this ruling that further CFDs in respect of the same aggregate number of underlying shares were entered into by Indigo on the same date as the closing out of the CFD and that the number of underlying shares concerned was small.

The Panel Executive, however, ruled that the restriction on future purchases of shares set out in Rule 4.2 should apply as a consequence of the closing out of the CFD, such that during the offer period neither Indigo, nor any person acting in concert with it, would be permitted to acquire any further Regus shares or to enter into any further derivatives referenced to Regus shares. Indigo accepted the ruling.

In July 1998, the Panel introduced Rule 4.4 which prohibited financial advisers and stockbrokers (and their related entities except for "exempt principal traders" and "exempt fund managers") to a target company (or any associated companies) from dealing in interests in target company securities during an offer period. Following amendments to the Code in 2006, the prohibition now prevents financial advisers and corporate brokers during an offer period from:

1. either for their own account or on behalf of discretionary clients, acquiring interests in target company shares; or

2.   making any loan to a person to assist them in acquiring any such interests (save for lending in the ordinary course of business to established customers); or
3.   entering into any indemnity or option or other arrangements which may be an inducement for a person to retain, deal or refrain from dealing in relevant securities of the target company.

The introduction of this rule followed controversial examples of purchases by a target's advisers. A note on Rule 4.4 now makes it clear that restriction (3) above does not prevent an adviser to a target company from procuring irrevocable commitments or letters of intent not to accept an offer.

The Panel has also encountered some instances of offerors, target companies and persons associated with them borrowing or lending securities or seeking to unwind such transactions during an offer period. The Panel expressed concern that the purpose underlying the borrowing or lending may have been to secure a tactical advantage or to manipulate the price or location of securities (see PCP 2004/3) and introduced Rule 4.6 to address these concerns. Rule 4.6 prohibits the following persons from entering into or taking action to unwind a securities borrowing or lending transaction in respect of relevant securities of the target during an offer period without first obtaining the consent of the Panel:

1.   an offeror;
2.   the target; and
3.   any person acting in concert with an offeror or with the target.

Consent of the Panel was previously also required in relation to entering into or taking action to unwind securities borrowing or lending transactions in respect of relevant securities of an offeror but, as from April 19, 2010, such consent has only been required in respect of relevant securities of the target.

With effect from April 19, 2010, a new Rule 4.6(b) was introduced which requires persons who are subject to Rule

4.6(a) and who enter into or take action to unwind a securities borrowing or lending transaction in respect of relevant securities of an offeror (other than a cash offeror) or, with the consent of the Panel under Rule 4.6(a), the target to disclose details of the transaction in accordance with Rule 8 (see Note 5(l) on Rule 8).

In addition, Rule 4.6 now also applies to the entry into of certain financial collateral arrangements in relation to a target's relevant securities (see new Note 4 to Rule 4.6).

It is worth noting that persons who have borrowed or lent shares will be treated for the purposes of Rule 9 as if they are interested in such shares provided that they have not been on-lent or sold. Note 17 to Rule 9.1 states that the Panel must be consulted where such action may result in an obligation to make a mandatory offer. Note 17 was amended on April 19, 2010 to clarify that intra-day securities borrowing and lending will only be relevant to whether a mandatory offer has been triggered if these transactions would result in an increase to the person's "net borrowing position" in a company's shares at midnight on the day in question.

3.3.1.3   Rule 5—timing restrictions on acquisitions

Subject to certain exceptions, Rule 5.1 prohibits the acquisition by any person of interests in shares if the result of such acquisition would be: (i) to increase the number of shares in which that person is interested (when aggregated with the holdings of that person's concert parties) to a number of shares carrying 30 per cent or more of the target's voting rights; or (ii) to increase (by any amount) a similarly aggregated interest in 30 per cent or more of the target's voting rights. The rule ceases to apply once a person acquires interests in shares carrying more than 50 per cent of a company's voting rights.

The preamble to Rule 5 specifies that, for the purposes of Rule 5 only, "the number of shares in which a person will be treated as having an interest includes any shares in respect of which he has received an irrevocable commitment". The definition of "irrevocable commitments and letters of intent" in the Code includes both commitments to accept and commitments not to accept an offer, and both therefore count towards the relevant threshold.

As will be seen below, one of the exceptions to Rule 5.1 is that the relevant acquisition immediately precedes the announcement of a recommended offer. Accordingly, although the restrictions in Rule 5 are capable of applying to irrevocable commitments, they can be avoided if the irrevocable commitments are executed immediately before the announcement of a firm intention to make an offer, provided the offer is to be recommended. This is another reason why it is often appropriate for irrevocable commitments to be executed on the evening prior to any announcement of an offer.

It should be noted that Rule 5 differs from the mandatory offer provisions in Rule 9 (see 3.3.1.4 below) in that receipt of an irrevocable commitment only constitutes an interest in securities for the purposes of Rule 5, and not for Rule 9. This means that a bidder can obtain irrevocable commitments over 30 per cent or more of the target's voting shares where permitted by Rule 5 (most significantly where the offer is recommended) without triggering the mandatory offer provisions in Rule 9. However, Rule 5 would preclude a bidder from obtaining irrevocable commitments over 30 per cent or more of the target's voting shares in the context of a hostile bid (unless it fell within the "single shareholder" exemption in Rule 5.2(a), as to which see further below). It should further be noted that, even if the offeror does not mind incurring a Rule 9 obligation, he may be prevented from doing so by Rule 5.

The main exceptions to Rule 5.1 (set out in Rule 5.2) are acquisitions of interests in shares carrying voting rights:

1. from a single shareholder where it is the only acquisition within a period of seven days (although this exception is not available in respect of an acquisition made after the announcement of a firm intention to make an offer where posting of the offer document is not subject to a

111

pre-condition, nor where the acquisition is from a principal trader or a fund manager managing investment accounts on behalf of more than one underlying client, regardless of whether or not on a discretionary basis);

2.   which immediately precede and are conditional upon the announcement of a recommended offer (or, if the offer is not recommended, the acquisition is made with the consent of the board of the target);

3.   made after the announcement of a firm (unconditional) intention to make an offer:
     (a)   with the agreement of the target's board;
     (b)   where either that or any competing offer is or has been recommended;
     (c)   where the first closing date of that or any competing offer has passed; or
     (d)   where the offer has become unconditional in all respects;

4.   by way of acceptance of an offer; or

5.   if the acquisition is permitted by Note 11 on Rule 9.1 or Note 5 on the Notes on Dispensations from Rule 9.

There are a number of Notes to Rule 5.1 which clarify its scope. For example, Note 5 states that Rule 5.1 does not apply to acquisitions of interests in shares which do not increase the percentage of shares carrying voting rights in which that person is interested (for example if a shareholder takes up his entitlement under a fully underwritten rights issue or if a person acquires shares on exercise of a call option). Similarly, Note 2 provides that the Rule does not cover acquisitions of new shares, securities convertible into new shares, rights to subscribe for new shares (other than pursuant to a rights issue) or new or existing shares under a share option scheme (albeit that the acquisition of new shares as a result of the exercise of conversion or subscription rights or options must be treated as an acquisition from a single shareholder falling within exception (1) above).

Acquisitions of interests in shares under exception (1) above must be notified by noon the following business day to the target, a Regulatory Information Service (RIS) and the Panel under Rule 5.4. Rule 5.3 states that any such acquisition of interests in shares will preclude the possibility of making further acquisitions under that exception unless the acquiror makes an offer for all the shares in the target and that offer subsequently lapses.

It should be noted, however, that any acquisition made under one of the exceptions to Rule 5 will almost inevitably bind the acquiror to make an offer under Rule 9, as referred to below.

The Panel stated in PCP 2009/3 of December 9, 2009 that it is proposing in due course to undertake a general review of Rule 5 in order to establish whether there might be a case for amending or deleting certain (or even all) of the provisions of the rule. However, the Panel noted in RS 2009/3 of March 5, 2010 that it is not currently clear when such review might be undertaken.

3.3.1.4 Rule 9—the mandatory offer

Rule 9 was amended in May 2006 in light of the requirements of the European Directive on Takeover Bids (Directive 2004/25) (the Takeover Directive) and to reflect the broader concept of interests in securities which is now used in the Code. The rule now states that, where a person acquires an interest in target shares which (taken together with shares in which he and persons acting in concert with him are interested) carry 30 per cent or more of the voting rights in the target, the acquiror and (depending on the circumstances) its concert parties are required (except with the consent of the Panel) to make a cash offer for the outstanding shares in the target (although the offer need not extend to shares held in treasury) at a price not less than the highest price paid for target shares by the acquiror or its concert parties during the 12 months prior to the announcement of that offer. This requirement is also triggered by any acquisition of an interest in shares by a person who, together with his concert parties, is interested in shares carrying not less than 30 per cent of the voting rights in the target if such person does not hold shares carrying more than 50 per cent of such voting rights and if the effect of such acquisition is to increase the percentage of the shares carrying voting rights in which that person is interested.

The changes made to the Code in light of the Takeover Directive make it explicit in Rule 9.5(b) that if the offeror or its concert parties acquire any interest in target shares after the announcement of an offer under Rule 9 and before the offer closes for acceptance, the offer price must be increased to not less than the highest price paid for those target shares. It was also clarified in Rule 9.1 that an offer will not be required where control of the target is acquired as a result of a voluntary offer.

A mandatory offer made pursuant to Rule 9 may not be subject to any conditions other than a 50 per cent acceptance condition (which will be satisfied upon the offeror having received acceptances in respect of shares which, together with shares acquired or agreed to be acquired before or during the offer, will result in the offeror and concert parties holding shares carrying more than 50 per cent of the voting rights in the target (Rule 9.3(a))). Pursuant to Note 2 to Rule 9.3 (as amended with effect from April 19, 2010), the Panel must be consulted if an offeror, or a person acting in concert with it, has borrowed or lent target shares so that the Panel can consider how such shares should be treated for the purpose of the acceptance condition. Rule 9.3(a) is reinforced by Rule 9.3(b) which provides that no acquisition of any interest in shares which would trigger a mandatory offer obligation may be made if the making or implementation of such an offer would or might be dependent on the passing of a resolution at any meeting of shareholders of the offeror or upon any other conditions, consents or arrangements.

In addition, any offer made under Rule 9 must (if the relevant jurisdictional criteria are met) contain a term that it will lapse if, before the first closing date of the offer or the date when the offer becomes unconditional (whichever is the later), it is referred to the Competition and Markets Authority under Sch.4 to the Enterprise and Regulatory Reform Act 2013 (defined in the Code as a "Phase 2 CMA reference"), or the European Commission initiates Phase 2 proceedings under art.6(1)(c) of Council Regulation 139/2004 (Rules 9.4, 12.1(a) and 12.1(b)).

Section 2 of the Schemes Appendix to the Code (Appendix 7), which was adopted on January 14, 2008, clarifies that an obligation to make a mandatory offer under Rule 9 may not be satisfied by an offer structured as a scheme of arrangement unless the Panel consents and Note 1 sets out the factors that the Panel will take into account when considering whether to so consent. Note 2 provides that an offeror using a scheme should not trigger a mandatory offer under Rule 9 without the Panel's prior consent to either satisfy its mandatory offer obligation by way of a scheme or to switch the transaction to a contractual offer structure.

Most of the difficult issues which arise in the context of Rule 9 concern whether or not particular persons are acting in concert. Such issues are the subject of 3.2.1.3 above and Ch.4. Issues do also arise, however, in relation to whether or not particular acquisitions of interests in shares or securities should have the effect of triggering the mandatory offer obligation.

In this connection, Note 11 on Rule 9.1 previously stated that normally, where shareholdings in a company are reduced by sales or diluted as a result of an issue of new shares, the provisions of Rule 9 will apply to the reduced or diluted holding. As a result, controlling shareholders were not able to restore their holdings to original levels by the acquisition of shares without incurring an obligation to make a general offer. In July 1999, the Panel considered the position of controlling shareholders and concluded that it was appropriate to permit controlling shareholders some ability to purchase further shares, notwithstanding that they (or the concert party of which they formed part) held 30 per cent or more of the voting rights in a company. Accordingly (and after further amendment in May 2006), Note 11 now provides that if a person or group of persons acting in concert reduces its interest in shares, but without reducing its interest to less than 30 per cent, such person or persons may subsequently acquire an interest in further shares without incurring an obligation to make a Rule 9 offer, provided that: (i) the total number of shares in which interests are acquired on this basis in any period of 12 months does not exceed one per cent of the voting share capital for the time being; and (ii) the percentage of shares in which the relevant person or persons acting in concert are interested following any such acquisition does not exceed the highest percentage of shares in which such person or persons were interested in the previous 12 months. Parties with a controlling interest will not, as a result, be permitted to increase the percentage of shares in which they are interested progressively from one year to the next. A reduction of the percentage of shares in which a person or concert party is interested by dilution will be treated in the same way as a sale for these purposes.

Similarly, Rule 37.1 provides that when a company redeems or purchases its own voting shares, any resulting increase in the percentage of shares carrying voting rights in which a person is, or a group of persons acting in concert are, interested will be treated as an acquisition for the purposes of Rule 9. Note 1 on Rule 37.1, however, provides that a person so interested who comes to exceed the limits in Rule 9.1 as a result of a company's redemption or purchase of its own shares will not normally incur an obligation to make a mandatory offer unless that person is a director, or the relationship of the person with any one or more of the directors is such that the person is, or is presumed to be, acting in concert with any of the directors. For this purpose, a person who has appointed a representative to the board of the company is treated as a director. Note 1 goes on to provide that there is no presumption that any or all of the directors are acting in concert solely by reason of a proposed redemption or repurchase or by reason of a decision to seek shareholder authority for a redemption or repurchase.

It is worth noting that the exception provided for in Note 1 on Rule 37.1 will not apply if a person (or any relevant member of a group of persons acting in concert) who is interested in shares has acquired an interest at a time when he had reason to believe that a redemption or purchase by the company of its own shares would take place (Note 2). In any event, the Panel must be consulted in advance in any case where Rule 9 might be relevant (Note 4). This will include any case where a person or group of persons acting in concert is interested in shares carrying 30 per cent or more of the voting rights of a company, but does not hold shares carrying more than 50 per cent of such voting rights, or where such person(s) may become interested in shares carrying 30 per cent or more of such voting rights on full implementation of the proposed redemption or purchase of own shares. Further, the Panel must be consulted if the aggregate interests of the directors and any other persons acting in concert, or presumed to be acting in concert, with any of the directors amount to 30 per cent or more of such shares, or may be increased to 30 per cent or more on full implementation of the proposed redemption or purchase of own shares.

Notwithstanding the foregoing, there are certain circumstances in which the Panel will be prepared to waive an obligation which would otherwise arise under Rule 9 including, for example, where there is an independent vote at a shareholders' meeting (see Note 1 of the Notes on Dispensations from Rule 9). Rule 37.1 (see above) contains a similar provision regarding the waiver of a mandatory offer obligation which would otherwise arise following the redemption or purchase by a company of its own shares. Detailed Rules concerning the obtaining of a waiver are set out in Appendix 1 to the Code (the Whitewash Guidance Note).

It should be noted, however, that the Panel will not (as specified in Note 1 of the Notes on Dispensations from Rule 9) normally grant a waiver if the person to whom the new securities are to be issued or any persons acting in concert with him have purchased shares in the company in the 12 months prior to posting of the shareholder circular relating to the proposals but subsequent to negotiations, discussions or the reaching of understandings or agreements with the directors of the company in relation to the proposals. Similarly, any waiver will be invalidated if there are any such purchases between the posting of the circular and the holding of the meeting of independent shareholders.

On August 16, 2002 (in Panel Statement 2002/17), the Panel announced that it had dismissed an appeal against the decision of the Panel Executive to grant a waiver from the obligation that would otherwise have arisen under Rule 9.1 in connection with a proposed issue of shares in Alexanders Holdings Plc (Alexanders) to Orb Estates Plc (Orb Estates) as consideration for the acquisition by Alexanders of certain subsidiaries of Orb Estates. The shares proposed to be issued to Orb Estates amounted to approximately 75.1 per cent of Alexanders' enlarged share capital. On August 19, 2002 (in Panel Statement 2002/18), the Panel gave the reasons for its decision. The decision of the Panel considered, inter alia, disqualifying transactions, put options and equality of treatment. The Panel Executive confirmed that the provision regarding disqualifying transactions (referred to above) was introduced to ensure equality of treatment for all shareholders and to prevent some shareholders being allowed a cash exit from the company while the remaining body of shareholders was not afforded that option. Accordingly, this safeguard should not apply when an acquisition of shares is made at a time when a proposed transaction which will give rise to a change in control is not in contemplation. It is only where the transaction and the purchase of target company shares can be regarded in some way as part of the same overall transaction that there can be equality concerns.

Similarly, the Panel held that the relevant date for determining whether the constituent elements of a disqualifying transaction are present in relation to the entry into of a put option is the date on which the put option agreement is executed. This is when the acquiror incurs the potential obligation to acquire the shares and, therefore, when equal treatment of all holders of target securities under General Principle 1 should be considered.

Rule 9 was amended on March 30, 2009 to remove the requirement to seek the consent of the Panel to board appointments of nominees of Rule 9 offerors. Rule 9.7 was also introduced with the aim of clarifying both the requirements relating to the disposal of interests in shares by persons who have triggered a mandatory bid obligation and the application of restrictions on the exercise of voting rights attaching to shares in which such persons are interested. The principal purpose of these restrictions is to prevent a potential offeror acquiring shares that would trigger a Rule 9 offer, exercising rights attaching to the shares and then disposing of the shares as an alternative to making an offer pursuant to Rule 9.1.

3.3.1.5 *Rule 6—minimum level of consideration*

Under Rule 6.1, an offer may not be made on less favourable terms (but need not necessarily be in cash, even if the acquisitions were for cash (although see 3.3.1.6 below)) than the highest price paid by the offeror or its concert parties (as to which see 3.2.1.3 above) for interests in target shares during the three months prior to the commencement of the offer period or during the period between commencement of the offer period and formal announcement of the offer. This obligation may also arise in respect of acquisitions made prior to this three-month period if the Panel considers there are circumstances which render this necessary to give effect to the general principle that all holders of securities be treated equally. The Panel will not normally exercise this discretion unless the sellers, or other parties to the transactions giving rise to the interests, are directors of, or other persons closely connected with, the offeror or target (Note 2).

Note 4 on Rule 6 explains how to calculate the highest price paid. The price paid for purchases of shares is simply the price agreed between the purchaser and the vendor. In the case of an unexercised call option, the price paid will normally be treated as the middle market price of the relevant shares at the time the option is entered into. In the case of a call option which has been exercised, the price paid will normally be treated as the amount paid on exercise of the option together with any amount paid by the option-holder on entering into the option. In the case of a written put option (whether exercised or not), the price paid will normally be treated as the amount paid or payable on exercise of the option less any amount paid by the option-holder on entering into the option. In the case of a derivative, the price paid will normally be treated as the initial reference price of the underlying derivative together with any fee paid on entering into the derivative. However, if any of the option exercise prices or derivative reference prices are calculated by reference to the average price of a number of acquisitions by the counterparty of interests in underlying securities, the price paid will normally be determined to be the highest price at which such acquisitions are actually made. The Note also indicates that when calculating the figure any stamp duty or broker's commission payable should be excluded.

Note 1 on Rule 6 provides that the Panel will, "in exceptional circumstances", permit offers at a price which does not match one paid less than three months earlier. The factors which the Panel will take into account in determining whether to exercise this discretion include whether the relevant acquisition was made on terms then prevailing in the market, changes in the market price of the shares since the relevant acquisition and whether interests in shares have been acquired at high prices from directors or other persons closely connected with the offeror or target.

If, following the formal announcement of an offer, any interest in target shares is acquired at a price exceeding the offer price, the offer must be revised immediately to reflect the terms of such purchase (Rule 6.2).

Both Rules 6.1 and 6.2 acknowledge that acquisitions of interests in shares giving rise to obligations under those Rules may also give rise to obligations under Rule 11 (see 3.3.1.6 below). Compliance with Rule 11 will normally be regarded as satisfying Rule 6.

Note 3 on Rule 6 applies where interests in shares in a target have been acquired at a relevant time and the offer includes securities as consideration. The Note makes clear that the securities offered as consideration must, at the date of announcement of the firm intention to make the offer, have a value at least equal to the highest relevant price paid. The Note goes on to say that if there is a restricted market in the securities of the offeror, or if the amount of securities to be issued is large in relation to the amount already issued, the Panel may require justification of prices used to determine the value of the offer. Note 3 was discussed in Panel Statement 2003/7 published in March 2003 in connection with the hostile offer by CMI for Six Continents, referred to at 3.3.1.2 above.

CMI was an AIM-listed cash shell with a net asset value of about £41 million. Six Continents was a FTSE 100 company. Prior to announcement of its offer, CMI acquired shares representing about 0.3 per cent of Six Continents' issued share capital. CMI's basic offer was on a share-for-share basis with a partial cash alternative. The Panel Executive stated that, given the very great number of new CMI shares that were being offered as consideration, Note 3 was applicable in establishing whether the value of the offer was at least equal to the highest price paid by CMI in buying Six Continents shares in the market. The Panel Executive said that Note 3 recognised that, in cases where the amount of listed securities to be issued was large in relation to the amount already issued, the market price of the offeror's shares at the time of announcement of the offer might not be capable of providing an accurate yardstick against which to determine whether the offeror had satisfied its Rule 6 obligation. As discussed earlier, the Panel Executive went on to explain that it had accepted CMI's proposal that it should sell the Six Continents shares it had acquired and donate the profits to charity in order to solve any potential concerns under Rule 6. This ruling by the Panel Executive makes it clear that a listed bid vehicle which is proposing a reverse takeover containing a share-for-share element and which has recently acquired target shares in the market may find it very difficult to justify to the Panel its valuation of the offer for Rule 6 purposes. The Panel Executive also ruled that the sale by CMI of the shares it had acquired in Six Continents would not give rise to any consequences under Rule 4.2 (see 3.3.1.2 above).

3.3.1.6 Rule 11—mandatory cash offers and mandatory securities offers

Under Rule 11.1, acquisitions for cash by an offeror or its concert parties (as to which see 3.2.1.3 above):

1. during the offer period, and within 12 months prior to its commencement, of any interests in shares of any class under offer carrying 10 per cent or more of the voting rights exercisable at a class meeting of that class; or
2. during the offer period, of any interests in shares of any class under offer,

will require the offeror to make its offer for that class in cash, or to make a cash alternative available, at not less than the highest price paid for the relevant interest in shares during those 12 months or during the offer period, as appropriate. Note 1 on Rule 11.1 explains how to calculate the highest price paid for different types of interest in shares in these circumstances. The process is exactly the same as that set out in Note 4 on Rule 6 (see 3.3.1.5 above).

Interests acquired in exchange for securities will normally be deemed to be acquired for cash unless the seller, or other party to the transaction giving rise to the interest, is required to hold the securities received or receivable in exchange until either the offer has lapsed or the offer consideration has been posted to accepting shareholders (Note 5 on Rule 11.1). This Rule was amended in July 1998 to include the requirement to make a cash alternative available where any target shares of the class under offer are purchased by the offeror or its concert parties during the offer period. This amendment followed criticism of offerors using the 10 per cent threshold as a loophole to allow them to make cash purchases during the offer period favouring a minority of shareholders.

On February 21, 2002, the Code Committee inserted a new Rule (Rule 11.2) which requires the making of a securities offer in similar circumstances to those in which a cash offer is required by Rule 11.1. The effect of Rule 11.2 is to require a securities exchange offer if, during or within three months prior to the commencement of the offer period, the offeror and persons acting in concert with it have acquired, in exchange for securities, interests in shares of the class under offer carrying 10 per cent or more of the voting rights exercisable at a class meeting of that class. An obligation to make a cash offer under Rule 11.1 will also arise in these circumstances, unless there is an obligation on the vendor to hold on to the securities received or receivable until the offer has lapsed or consideration has been posted.

There are a number of important Notes on Rule 11.2:

1. Note 1 provides that the securities offered pursuant to Rule 11.2 must be offered on the basis of the number of consideration securities received or receivable by the relevant sellers, or other parties to the transactions giving rise to the interests, for each target company share rather than on the basis of securities equivalent to the value of the securities received or receivable by the sellers or other parties at the time of the relevant purchases. The Panel clarified in Response Statement RS 6 that, in considering the required level of an offer, it will take into account a corporate action (such as a rights issue or a share split) if as a result shareholders would not be treated equally and will also require any special features attached to securities offered to a seller (such as contingent value rights) to be attached to the securities to be made available under any offer.
2. Note 2 provides a discretion to the Panel to require a securities offer even where the 10 per cent threshold has not been reached, or where the relevant purchase took place more than three months prior to the commencement of the offer period. Exercise of the discretion will normally be limited to situations where the sellers of the relevant shares or other parties to the transactions giving rise to the

interests are directors of, or other persons closely connected with, the offeror or target company.

3.   Note 3 makes clear that where an offeror acquires target
shares in exchange for securities and the offeror has
arranged for these securities to be immediately placed for
cash on the seller's behalf (a vendor placing), then there
should be no obligation to provide a securities offer to all
shareholders.

Finally, the Panel clarified in July 2000, by the addition of a
new Note 12 on Rule 11.1, that where a new offer is announced
in accordance with Rule 12.2(b)(ii) (i.e. following anti-trust
clearance from the Competition and Markets Authority or the
European Commission), acquisitions of interests in target
company shares made for cash during the competition
reference period will be deemed to be acquisitions during the
new offer period for the purposes of Rule 11.1(b). Note 7 on
Rule 11.2 makes clear that acquisitions during the competition
reference period will also be deemed to be acquisitions during
the new offer period for the purposes of Rule 11.2 (and so may
trigger an obligation to make a securities exchange offer
available to all shareholders).

3.3.1.7   Rule 16—special deals and management incentivisation

When an offer is in progress or is reasonably in contemplation,
Rule 16.1 prohibits (without the consent of the Panel) the
offeror or its concert parties from dealing in target shares or
entering into arrangements which involve acceptance of the
offer, if there are favourable conditions attached which are not
available to all target shareholders. Irrevocable undertakings to
accept an offer should not, therefore, confer any valuable
benefit on the person giving the undertaking—a point also of
importance in ensuring that the shares which are the subject of
such an undertaking count for the purposes of the squeeze-out
provisions of the 2006 Act.

In addition, an arrangement made with a person who, while
not a shareholder, is interested in shares carrying voting rights
in a target (such as options or derivatives holders), is also

prohibited under Rule 16.1 if favourable conditions are attached which have not been extended to the shareholders. However, there is no requirement to extend any offer, or any "special deal" falling within Rule 16.1, to persons who are interested in shares but are not shareholders.

Note 1 on Rule 16.1 specifies that arrangements where there is a promise to make good to a seller of shares any difference between the sale price and the price of any subsequent successful offer are arrangements to which Rule 16.1 applies. Similarly, an irrevocable undertaking, combined with an option to put if the offer fails, will be prohibited by Rule 16.1.

The Panel has over time developed a flexible approach to interpreting Rule 16.1 where one or more shareholders in the target company participate in a vehicle making the offer. Otherwise, management buy-outs would effectively be prohibited, to the potential detriment of existing target shareholders, as well as offers by one or more such shareholders. The Panel has therefore usually ruled that when two or more persons form a consortium whereby each can properly be considered to be a joint offeror, Rule 16.1 is not contravened if one or more of them is already a shareholder in the target company. Subject to that, joint offerors may make arrangements between themselves concerning the future membership, control and management of the business being acquired.

In the context of what constitutes a joint offeror, the Panel issued Panel Statement 2003/25 on November 21, 2003 concerning Brascan Corporation's appeal against an earlier Panel ruling that arrangements between the members of a consortium, formed with a view to the potential acquisition of Canary Wharf Group Plc, did not contravene Rule 16. The Panel stated that the criteria for assessing whether or not a person was a joint offeror were as follows.

1. What proportion of the equity share capital of the bid vehicle will the person own after completion of the acquisition?

2. Will the person be able to exert a significant influence over the future management and direction of the bid vehicle?
3. What contribution is the person making to the consortium?
4. Will the person be able to influence significantly the conduct of the bid?
5. Are there arrangements in place to enable the person to exit from his investment in the bid vehicle within a short time or at a time when other equity investors cannot?

In dismissing the appeal, the Panel stressed that each case must be decided upon its own facts and that earlier decisions on different facts are of little precedent value.

With effect from January 25, 2010, the Code Committee has introduced a new Rule 16.2 to simplify the manner in which the Code applies to management incentive arrangements and reduce the range of circumstances in which consultation is required (see Code Committee Instrument 2009/5).

Rule 16.2 provides that (absent consent from the Panel) where an offeror has entered into or reached an advanced stage of discussions on proposals to enter into incentivisation arrangements with members of the target's management who are interested in target shares, relevant details of the arrangements or proposals must be disclosed and the independent adviser to the target must state publicly that in its opinion the arrangements are fair and reasonable. Where the value of the arrangements entered into or proposed to be entered into is significant and/or the nature of the arrangements is unusual either in the context of the relevant industry or good practice, the Panel must be consulted and its consent to the arrangements obtained (Rule 16.2(b)). The Panel may also require, as a condition to its consent, that the arrangements be approved at a general meeting of the target's independent shareholders.

Where the members of the management are shareholders in the target, and, as a result of the incentivisation arrangements, they will become shareholders in the offeror on a basis that is not being made available to all other target shareholders, Rule

16.2(c) requires that such arrangements be approved at a general meeting of the target's independent shareholders.

Note 1 on Rule 16.2 provides that where members of the target are to receive offeror securities pursuant to an appropriate offer or proposal made in accordance with Rule 15, Rule 16.2 will apply, but shareholder approval will not normally be required in respect of such offer or proposal.

If the only target shareholders who receive offeror securities are members of the target's management, Note 2 sets out that the Panel will not, so long as the requirements of Rule 16.2 are complied with, require all target shareholders to be offered offeror securities pursuant to Rule 11.2, even though such members of management propose to sell, in exchange for offeror securities, more than 10 per cent of the target shares.

3.3.1.8 *Competitive bid processes*

The Panel raised concerns in a consultation paper issued in October 2001 about the ability of the then framework of the Code to resolve competitive situations in an orderly fashion and create as little uncertainty for the shareholders of the target as possible.

With these concerns in mind the Panel adopted a number of changes to the Code which, it was hoped, would limit the times when the Code fails to resolve a competitive situation in an orderly and timely manner. In terms of the subject matter of this Chapter, the introduction of Rule 35.4 is particularly relevant. This states that, except with the consent of the Panel, where an offer has been one of two or more competing offers and has lapsed, neither that offeror, nor any concert party of that offeror, may acquire any interest in shares in the target company on more favourable terms than those made available under its lapsed offer until each of the competing offers has either been declared unconditional in all respects or has itself lapsed. This amendment has closed the loophole which previously allowed lapsed competitive bidders the possibility of frustrating another offeror's bid.

3.3.1.9 *Disenfranchisement of shares acquired during an offer period*

Following the Panel's June 2010 review of certain elements of the Takeover Code, respondents suggested that the Code be amended to remove the ability of shareholders to vote shares acquired after the commencement of an offer period. Another suggestion was the creation of "qualifying periods" which would similarly govern when votes attaching to shares could be exercised. The respondents suggesting such amendments were keen to counter perceived short-termism, exemplified by investors who may be acquiring shares following the announcement of a possible offer in the expectation that the offer price would exceed their acquisition cost. Following a consultation, the Code Committee affirmed that such changes would offend General Principle 1 of treating all shareholders equally and the generally accepted position of "one share, one vote". The Code Committee stated that it would not propose such changes without an equivalent change in company law (see Panel Statement 2010/22).

3.3.2 *The 2006 Act*

Although the 2006 Act does not expressly prohibit or restrict dealings in shares during a takeover, there are certain aspects of the compulsory acquisition procedure (set out in ss.979 to 982 of the 2006 Act) which may impact on the desirability of such dealings by an offeror or its associates.

In order to exercise the right to purchase compulsorily outstanding minority shareholdings following a bid, an offeror must have acquired or unconditionally contracted to acquire "by virtue of acceptances of the offer": (i) not less than 90 per cent in value of the shares of the class "to which the offer relates"; and (ii) 90 per cent of the voting rights attaching to those shares. The definition of "shares" for these purposes excludes treasury shares.

In considering these tests, shares in the target purchased by an offeror after the offer has been made (i.e. after the posting of the offer document) may also be treated as acquired by virtue of an acceptance of the offer (ss.979(8) and (10) of the 2006 Act) if:

1. the value of the consideration for which they are acquired or contracted to be acquired (the "acquisition consideration") does not at that time exceed the value of the consideration specified in the terms of the offer; or
2. those terms are subsequently revised so that, when the revision is announced, the value of the acquisition consideration (calculated at the time of the acquisition) no longer exceeds the value of the consideration specified in those terms.

Shares in the target purchased after the offer has been made by those who are "associates" of the offeror for the purposes of these provisions (including group companies, companies in which the offeror is substantially interested, nominees and concert parties (s.988(1)) may be "shares to which the offer relates" if their purchase fulfils either condition (1) or (2) above (s.979(9)). If the purchasing associates then assent such shares to the offer, they may thus be counted towards the 90 per cent threshold for the exercise of compulsory purchase rights. However, any shares owned by associates before the offer is made by the posting of the offer document are ignored in calculating whether the 90 per cent level has been attained (s.977(2)).

Purchases of target company shares by an offeror or its associates after the making of an offer (i.e. after the posting of the formal offer document) should, therefore, have no adverse effect on the offeror's ability to reach a position where it can exercise compulsory acquisition rights over minority shareholdings. However, where shares are purchased either by the offeror or an associate before the offer is formally made, the level of acceptances required for the exercise of compulsory purchase rights will be 90 per cent of a correspondingly smaller proportion of the target's total share capital (and, therefore, potentially more difficult to achieve).

Another point to note relates to the drafting of irrevocable commitments to accept an offer. A "takeover offer" is defined in s.974 of the 2006 Act as "an offer to acquire all the shares... other than shares that at the date of the offer are already held by the offeror" being an offer in respect of which the terms are the same "in relation to all the shares to which the offer relates".

Section 975(2) provides that

> "the reference in Section 974(2) to shares already held by the offeror does not include a reference to shares that are the subject of a contract... entered into by deed and for no consideration, for consideration of negligible value or for consideration consisting of a promise by the offeror to make the offer."

It follows from this that irrevocable commitments should:

1. be drafted so as to be for no consideration and executed as a deed;
2. contain negligible consideration; or
3. contain as their sole consideration a promise by the offeror to make the offer.

Otherwise, the shares which are the subject of irrevocable commitments are excluded for compulsory acquisition purposes (in the same way that a market purchase of shares made before the offer would be excluded) counting neither towards the numerator nor towards the denominator in determining whether the 90 per cent threshold has been reached and thus making it more difficult to apply the compulsory acquisition procedure.

3.3.3   CJA 1993

3.3.3.1   CJA 1993 offences

Part V of the CJA 1993 came into force on March 1, 1994 and was designed to bring English law into line with the EC Insider Dealing Directive (89/592). The CJA 1993 renders it an offence for an individual to:

1. deal in price-affected securities if he has inside information relating thereto which he holds as an "insider" (i.e. by virtue of his directorship, employment, shareholding, office or profession or which he has obtained from an inside source) (s.52(1));
2. encourage any other person (which would include a company) to deal in securities which he himself is prohibited from dealing in (s.52(2)(a)); or
3. disclose the inside information to another person other than in the proper performance of the functions of his employment, office or profession (s.52(2)(b)).

It should be noted that, as referred to above, these offences can only be committed by individuals (and not by companies). However, the scope of the offence provided for in s.52(1) extends to catch individuals who procure dealings by other persons, including companies (s.55).

3.3.3.2   Relationship with FSMA

There are certain aspects of the insider dealing prohibition provided for in CJA 1993 which are similar in application and scope to the FSMA market abuse regime. Market abuse is addressed further in 3.3.4.2 below.

3.3.3.3   Contravention

A contravention of Part V of the CJA 1993 results in exposure to the risk of a fine or imprisonment under s.61(1). However, s.63(2) makes it clear that no contract is void or unenforceable merely because it is made in contravention of the Act. In March

2013, Richard Joseph, formerly a futures trader, was found guilty of six counts of conspiracy to deal as an insider and sentenced to four years on each count, to be served concurrently. To date, the FCA, and previously the FSA, have secured twenty three convictions in relation to insider dealing and is currently prosecuting seven other individuals (see FCA press notice FCA/PN/110/2013).

3.3.3.4   *Consequences for takeovers*

The insider dealing legislation will normally have the effect of preventing share dealing in price-affected securities by a potential offeror who, as part of pre-bid due diligence, has been given price-sensitive information by the target. This is because the individuals in receipt of the price-sensitive information are likely to be taken to have procured or encouraged any such dealings in contravention of s.52(1) or 52(2)(a). Similarly, such individuals, the directors of the offeror and others in the know will be prohibited from dealing in price-affected securities on their own account and, even in the absence of receipt of confidential information, they will be prevented from dealing on their own account by their knowledge that a bid is in contemplation.

However, most of the prohibitions in the Act do not apply where the only relevant inside information is that the acquiring party is contemplating a takeover offer and the dealings are made to facilitate the offer—the "market information" defence (s.53(4), para.3, Sch.1, Pt V of the CJA 1993). It is, therefore, not an offence for directors or employees of a potential offeror to procure purchases of the shares of a target by the offeror or others in the knowledge that a full scale bid is in contemplation, if the dealing is to facilitate the completion or carrying out of the bid, provided they have no other relevant inside information.

It is important to consider the implications of undertaking due diligence prior to the announcement of an offer, as this may affect the availability of the market information defence. Even where pre-bid due diligence is proposed, it may be possible to avoid insider dealing concerns by setting up an information barrier arrangement within the financial adviser to the offeror. Under such an arrangement, information provided by the target would be vetted for price-sensitivity by employees of the offeror's financial adviser who were not engaged in providing advice to the offeror. Only information which was not price-sensitive would be passed to the offeror and the offeror's advisory team. It is worth noting that, for CJA 1993 purposes, there is no reason why the information barrier arrangement should not be set up within the offeror rather than within its financial adviser. However, this would give rise to market abuse concerns under FSMA (as a result of the fact that both companies and individuals can commit market abuse) (see further 3.3.4.2 below).

In general, CJA 1993 should not normally inhibit purchases of target shares following an announcement of a bid. This is because, if the bid is hostile, then the offeror is unlikely to have received confidential information and, if recommended, it is unlikely that any information will remain price-sensitive following announcement of the bid, since the target will have taken all information into account in recommending the offer. This point is not, however, beyond doubt and the offeror will need to be satisfied that there is no expectation of profit attributable to the price-sensitive information, because the information is reflected in the offer price.

3.3.3.5 *Appointment of investigating inspectors*

Section 168 FSMA confers power on the Secretary of State, FCA and the PRA to appoint inspectors to investigate whether any offence under Pt V of the CJA 1993 has been committed. Section 177 then lays down penalties for refusal to comply with these investigations. Although a refusal to answer any questions put by the inspectors will entitle the inspectors to bring the case before the court, the court may only punish a reluctant interviewee if it is satisfied that he has acted without reasonable excuse in refusing to reply.

3.3.3.6 CFDs—no longer a loophole

It is no longer possible to offset the expenses of a bid by the use of cash-settled derivatives (including CFDs) linked to the share price of the target or the share prices of companies in the same business sector as the target. Such contracts were controversially used in the bid by Trafalgar House for Northern Electric. Trafalgar House effectively bet that the share price of a number of electricity distribution companies (including Northern Electric) would rise as a result of its offer by striking a series of CFDs with its investment bank, Swiss Bank Corporation. After consultation with the Panel (which had initially concluded that Trafalgar House's strategy was legitimate), the Securities and Investment Board (later the FSA and now, the FCA) effectively prohibited the use of derivative contracts for the purpose of offsetting the expenses of a bid by issuing a guidance document in December 1996 (under s.206 Financial Services Act 1986) which stated that such contracts should not be entered into on the basis of inside information (including information that a bid may be made) where they would provide only a cash benefit and would not constitute a step towards the accomplishment of the takeover. The guidance reflected legal advice received by the Securities and Investment Board to the effect that cash-settled derivatives do not facilitate the accomplishment of takeovers and that the parties to them cannot therefore rely on the CJA 1993 "market information" defence. Although the Securities and Investment Board guidance no longer has any statutory underpinning (the Financial Services Act 1986 having been repealed in its entirety by FSMA), it is nevertheless still considered to reflect best practice and to be an accurate statement of the law. The Code of Market Conduct (made under s.119(1) FSMA) reinforces the position by stating that an example of market abuse would be

> "an offeror or potential offeror entering into a transaction in a qualifying investment, on the basis of inside information concerning the proposed bid, that provides merely an economic exposure to movements in the price of the target company's shares (for example, a spread bet on the target company's share price) (MAR 1.3.2(2)(E))."

It should be noted, however, that neither CJA 1993 nor the Securities and Investment Board's guidance (nor, indeed, the FSMA market abuse regime) has the effect of completely prohibiting the use of derivative contracts in the context of takeovers (particularly where such contracts provide for physical settlement). Indeed, there have been a number of recent examples of their use or attempted use as part of pre-bid stake-building efforts. As will be evident, however, the legal and regulatory consequences of their use are not wholly straightforward.

3.3.4 FSMA and the FS Act 2012

3.3.4.1 Sections 89 to 91 FS Act 2012—misleading statements and practices

Section 90(1) of the FS Act 2012 may be particularly significant in the context of takeovers. As part of the changes introduced by the FS Act 2012, Pt 7 of the Act repealed s.397 of FSMA, which had prohibited the making of misleading statements and market manipulation, and replaced it with ss.89 to 91 of the FS Act 2012, which makes it a criminal offence to:

(i)   make false or misleading statements (s.89);
(ii) create false or misleading impressions (s.90); and
(iii) make false or misleading statements or create a false or misleading impression in relation to the setting of relevant benchmarks (s.91).

Sections 89 and 90 largely replicate the effect of s.397 of FSMA. The only "relevant" benchmark under s.91 will be LIBOR and the provision is a reaction to recent global investigations into LIBOR's alleged manipulation by a number of banks.

Section 90 of the FS Act 2012 makes it an offence to do any act or engage in a course of conduct which creates a false or misleading impression as to the market value of any investments if this is done for the purpose of creating that impression and of thereby: (i) inducing a person to deal, or refrain from dealing, in those investments; and/or (ii) obtaining a profit or avoiding a loss. It is a defence under s.90(9) to show that a person reasonably believed his act or conduct would not create a false or misleading impression.

If associates of a target purchase shares as a defensive tactic against a dawn raid, the clear aim is to create a misleading impression as to the value of the target's shares. However, it seems (at least, it is the BIS's view) that if all relevant facts are disclosed, no such impression will be created. Hence, if the associate puts his motives on the screen at the time of his bid for the stock, it seems that no offence would be committed. Of course, this suggested course is unlikely to arouse much enthusiasm among the broking community and, if he immediately discloses his dealing under Rule 8 of the Code (see 3.4.3.1 below), probably there would be little risk of prosecution. The position would be similar in respect of agreements with the target to sell its shares.

Liability may also be incurred by the offeror and its associates. Purchases of the offeror's shares by associates in takeovers where the consideration includes shares in the offeror could amount to a breach of s.90(1). Much will depend upon the purpose of such acquisition: if it is genuinely for a long-term investment, it is hard to see how the section is contravened, but if the main purpose is merely to inflate the value of the offeror's share price, there may be a breach. A share support operation, of the type carried out on the Guinness bid for Distillers, would therefore be a criminal offence under s.90(1) (at the time of these events the relevant statutory provision was s.13(1)(a)(i) of the Prevention of Fraud (Investments) Act 1958).

Further criminal liability may be incurred if purchases of offeror shares are carried out by an associate with the benefit of an indemnity from the offeror as this may also involve unlawful financial assistance by the offeror for the purpose of the acquisition of its own shares, which is an offence under s.678 of the 2006 Act. In this area it should be noted that, if a false market in any listed securities arises, then the relevant listed company must consider whether it is required by the DTRs to release information to the public. Where a company is under such an obligation, a failure to comply with it can, arguably, amount to a course of conduct for s.90 purposes.

3.3.4.2 The market abuse regime

The general impact of the Market Abuse Directive (2003/6) (the Directive) of January 28, 2003 on insider dealing and market manipulation (and certain secondary legislation adopted under it) is outside the scope of this Chapter. However, the Financial Services and Markets Act 2000 (Market Abuse) Regulations 2005 (the Regulations), which implement certain provisions of the Directive and came into force on July 1, 2005, made considerable changes to the statutory market abuse regime put in place under FSMA.

3.3.4.2.1 Categories of abusive behaviour

The Regulations introduced s.118 FSMA. Instead of the three categories of abusive behaviour which used to exist (misuse of information, misleading conduct and market distortion) there are now seven categories, which cover similar ground but which set out more precise descriptions of the behaviour that is prohibited. These categories are:

1. an insider deals or attempts to deal in a qualifying investment or related investment on the basis of inside information relating to the investment in question;
2. an insider discloses inside information to another person otherwise than in the proper course of the exercise of his employment, profession or duties;
3. behaviour (not falling within (1) or (2) above) which:
   (a) is based on information which is not generally available to those using the market, but which, if available to a regular user of the market would be or would be likely to be regarded by him as relevant when deciding the terms on which transactions in qualifying investments should be effected; and
   (b) is likely to be regarded by a regular user of the market as a failure on the part of the person concerned to

observe the standard of behaviour reasonably expected of a person in his position in relation to the market;

4. the behaviour consists of effecting transactions or orders to trade (other than for legitimate reasons and in accordance with accepted market practices) which:
    (a) give or are likely to give a false or misleading impression as to the supply of or demand for, or as to the price of, one or more qualifying investments; or
    (b) secure the price of one or more such investments at an abnormal or artificial level;

5. the behaviour consists of effecting transactions or orders to trade which employ fictitious devices or any other form of deception or contrivance;

6. the behaviour consists of the dissemination of information by any means which gives or is likely to give a false or misleading impression as to a qualifying investment by a person who knew or could reasonably be expected to have known that the information was false or misleading; and

7. the behaviour (not falling within (4), (5) or (6) above):
    (a) is likely to give a regular user of the market a false impression as to the supply of, demand for or price or value of qualifying investments; or
    (b) would be or would be likely to be regarded by a regular user of the market as behaviour that would distort or would be likely to distort the market in such an investment,

and the behaviour is likely to be regarded by a regular user of the market as a failure on the part of the person concerned to observe the standard of behaviour reasonably expected of a person in his position in relation to the market.

The behaviour described in paras (1) to (7) above, whether by one person alone or by two or more persons acting jointly or in concert, must occur in relation to (i) qualifying investments admitted to trading on a prescribed market, (ii) qualifying investments in respect of which a request for admission to trading on such a market has been made, or (iii) in the case of behaviour under (1) or (2) above, investments which are related investments in relation to such qualifying investments.

The regular user test in the previous s.118 does not appear in the Directive and is therefore retained only for those categories of abusive behaviour which are not drawn from the Directive (namely ss.118(4) and 118(8), see (3) and (7) above). These provisions were given a limited lifespan and would have automatically fallen away on June 30, 2008 had they not been extended. HM Treasury consulted on whether to extend these provisions so that the findings of the EU review of the Directive and its implementation currently taking place could be considered before reaching a final conclusion on the retention of the provisions. In response to this consultation, the retention of these provisions has been extended on three occasions, the latest being until December 31, 2014.

The FSA previously stated that it was their ultimate aim to align the UK market abuse regime with the European model. A European public consultation process took place in June 2010 and on October 20, 2011 the European Commission published its proposals to replace the existing Directive with (i) a new regulation on insider dealing and market manipulation and (ii) a new directive on criminal sanctions for insider dealing and market manipulation (CSMAD). The European Commission amended these proposals on July 25, 2012 to prohibit the manipulation of benchmarks in the wake of the LIBOR scandal and on December 7, 2012, European justice ministers in the Council of the European Union agreed on the introduction of the new directive (see MEMO/12/963). The Council adopted CSMAD on February 5, 2014 and the new regulation on April 14, 2014. Together, the legislative package (collectively, MAD II) will replace the existing Directive. The regulation will be directly effective from 24 months after its entry into force (on which date the Directive will be repealed) and Member States will have two years to transpose CSMAD into national law, although the UK government announced in 2012 that it will not opt in for the time being.

3.3.4.2.2 Prescribed markets and qualifying investments

The Regulations extended the scope of the United Kingdom's market abuse regime. Prescribed markets include all EEA regulated markets, except in relation to the "regular user" categories of abuse, which are not drawn from the Directive. Any financial instrument admitted to trading on a regulated market is covered. This means that behaviour is now covered if it happens:

1. in the United Kingdom in relation to financial instruments traded on prescribed markets which are based in the EEA; or
2. in the United Kingdom or abroad in relation to financial instruments traded on prescribed markets which are based in the United Kingdom.

3.3.4.2.3 Insiders

An "insider" is defined in s.118B FSMA as any person who has inside information:

1. as a result of his membership of an administrative, management or supervisory body of an issuer of qualifying investments;
2. as a result of his holding in the capital of an issuer of qualifying investments;
3. as a result of his having access to the information through the exercise of his employment, profession or duties;
4. as a result of his criminal activities; or
5. which he has obtained by other means and which he knows, or could reasonably be expected to know, is inside information.

3.3.4.2.4 Inside information

Section 118C FSMA defines "inside information". The definition varies slightly, depending upon the type of investment to which the information relates and the nature of the "insider" in question. The common features are that the information:

1. must be of a precise nature;
2. must not be generally available; and
3. (except in relation to commodity derivatives) would, if generally available, be likely to have a significant effect on the price of the qualifying investments.

3.3.4.2.5   Consequences of market abuse

The FCA has wide-ranging powers of penalty under FSMA. The FCA is able to impose an unlimited fine (s.123(1) refers to "a penalty of such amount as it considers appropriate"). The FCA also has the option of electing not to impose a fine but to publish a public censure of the offender instead (s.123(3)).

The largest fine levied for market abuse by the FSA was imposed in 2004 on Shell Transport and Trading Company, Royal Dutch Petroleum Company and the Royal Dutch/Shell Group of Companies (Shell), who were fined £17 million for market abuse and breach of the Listing Rules without admitting or denying culpability. The market abuse occurred in relation to the misstatement of its proved reserves, which led to Shell being investigated for the old "misleading conduct" limb of market abuse. Individuals have also received large fines: on November 9, 2011, Mr Rameshkumar Goenka, a Dubai-based private investor, was fined US $9,621,240 for manipulating the closing share price of Reliance Industries Limited in order to avoid a loss under an over-the-counter structured product. This is the largest fine by the FSA against an individual for market abuse to date (see FSA press notice 94/2011).

As referred to above (see 3.3.3.2), much of the behaviour prohibited by FSMA bears some resemblance to the offence of insider dealing provided for in CJA 1993 and many of the cases brought by the FSA since the market abuse regime first came into force on December 1, 2001 were for the misuse of information. For example, on January 25, 2012, Mr David Einhorn, owner of the US hedge fund Greenlight Capital (Greenlight), was fined £3,368,000 for allegedly using inside information about an upcoming rights issue to order the sale of part of Greenlight's stake in Punch Taverns Plc (Punch), thereby avoiding a significant loss when Punch's share price subsequently dropped by around 30 per cent.

3.3.4.2.6 Defences

Under s.118A(5) FSMA as amended on December 31, 2009, behaviour does not amount to market abuse if:

1. it conforms with a Rule which includes a provision to the effect that behaviour conforming with the Rule does not amount to market abuse;
2. it conforms with Regulation 2273/2003 of December 22, 2003 regarding exemptions for buy-back programmes and stabilisation of financial instruments; or
3. it is done by a person acting on behalf of a public authority in pursuit of monetary policies with respect to exchange rates or the management of public debt or foreign exchange reserves.

Furthermore, the FCA is not able to impose a penalty where there are reasonable grounds for it to be satisfied that the relevant person believed, on reasonable grounds, that his behaviour did not amount to market abuse and took all reasonable precautions and exercised all due diligence to avoid engaging in market abuse (s.123(2)). This is a defence only against a penalty and not against a finding of market abuse. In order to utilise this defence, the grounds on which the person believed that he was not committing market abuse must be objectively reasonable.

The FCA has produced a Code of Market Conduct (as required under s.119(1) FSMA—the code is set out in MAR 1 of the FCA Handbook) which, inter alia, outlines behaviour that will not amount to market abuse. Most notably in the context of takeovers, the Code of Market Conduct includes provisions which are similar in effect to the market information defence provided for in CJA 1993 (see 3.3.3.4 above).

Compliance with the Code of Market Conduct and reliance on legal advice may be helpful in discharging the burden of proof for the purposes of s.123(2).

3.3.4.3 *The effect of FSMA on the Panel*

As a result of the market abuse regime, there is a significant potential overlap between the jurisdiction of the Panel and that of the FCA in relation to takeovers. Under the old FSA regime, there was some initial concern that this overlap might result in hostile participants dragging the FSA into contested bids as a tactic. In order to allay these fears, the Government introduced a provision into FSMA to enable the FSA (with Treasury approval) to establish a safe harbour for behaviour which complies with the Code (s.120). The FSA did this at MAR 1.10.3G to 1.10.6C of its Code of Market Conduct (the same provisions exist in the FCA's Code of Market Conduct which state that compliance with certain, specified, Rules of the Code will not constitute a breach of the market abuse regime).

The 2000/2001 Annual Report of the Panel stated that the FSA was keen to minimise the situations in which it may be required to interpret the Code. It was partly due to this concern that the FSA, when drafting the safe harbour provisions, avoided giving a blanket safe harbour for the entire Code.

In addition (and as mentioned in 3.2.4 above), the Panel and the FCA have agreed a set of operating guidelines (the Operating Guidelines) which are intended, inter alia, to assist in determining how each of them should exercise its functions in cases of jurisdictional overlap. The Operating Guidelines provide that where, during a takeover bid, matters arise which may amount to market misconduct, the FCA will not exercise its powers during the bid save in exceptional circumstances. The exceptional circumstances referred to in the Operating Guidelines are:

1. where the Panel asks the FCA to use its power to impose penalties or its powers to seek injunctive or restitutionary relief from the courts;

2. where the suspected misconduct falls within the misuse of information prohibition under the market abuse regime (s.118(2)—(4) FSMA) or Pt V of the CJA 1993 (insider dealing);
3. where the suspected misconduct extends to securities or a class of securities which may be outside the Panel's jurisdiction; or
4. where the suspected misconduct threatens or has threatened the stability of the financial system.

In any event, the FCA will consult with the Panel before taking any action which may affect the timetable or outcome of a takeover bid. The Operating Guidelines also contain similar principles relevant to situations where there is jurisdictional overlap between the Panel and the FCA but no takeover bid is actually in progress.

3.4 Disclosure of share dealings

Next, we will address the subject of disclosure of share dealings. Although disclosure should be no more than a mechanical exercise, it may be important in the early, planning stages of a transaction and is easy to overlook once a bid is underway, when information may be difficult to collect in the time required. Further, the disclosure requirements of the Code have been considerably extended in recent years, most recently in April 2010.

3.4.1 DTRs

The obligations under DTR 5 relate to: (i) shares of UK and non-UK issuers which are admitted to trading on a regulated market in the United Kingdom; and (ii) shares of UK issuers which are admitted to trading on a prescribed market (such as AIM). DTR 5.1.2 provides that a person (which includes a natural person, a legal person or an unincorporated body such as a partnership) must notify an issuer of shares, in accordance with prescribed procedures and including prescribed information, of certain voting rights which it holds as shareholder (including direct and indirect holdings of shares and depository receipts, and including discretionary proxies), or which it holds through a direct or indirect holding of certain financial instruments with a right under a legally binding agreement to call for issued shares carrying voting rights. The relevant financial instruments include transferable securities, options, futures, swaps, forward rate agreements and some other derivatives.

The FSA previously estimated that approximately 30 per cent of equity trades were in some way driven by CFD transactions referenced to underlying shares and, as these positions did not previously have to be disclosed under DTR 5, it used to be impossible to determine who had significant economic exposure to an issuer's shares. In June 2009 the FSA therefore amended DTR 5 to introduce a general disclosure regime of long positions in CFDs and other derivative instruments that may have a similar effect with the aim of achieving greater disclosure (see PS09/3).

Notifications required by DTR 5 must be made as soon as possible and in any case not later than two trading days (or four trading days for non-UK issuers) after the date on which the notifying person learns—or should have learnt—of the event that has given rise to the requirement to make the disclosure. Even if the disclosing person does not learn of the event, he will in general be deemed to have knowledge of the event two trading days after the event has taken place. When disclosure is made to an issuer whose shares are traded on a regulated market, a copy of the notification must also be filed electronically with the FCA. The issuer must as soon as possible make the disclosure public.

Notification must be made if the percentage of voting rights held reaches, exceeds or falls below three per cent or any subsequent one per cent. These thresholds for notification are the same as was the case under the Companies Act 1985. Higher thresholds apply to non-UK issuers (thresholds at each 5 per cent interval, up to 30 per cent, and then at 50 per cent and 75 per cent). The DTR 5 notification requirements also apply where a holding changes as a result of changes to the structure of the share capital of an issuer, and where information announced by the issuer in respect of the total number of voting rights and capital in respect of each share class would cause a holding to be re-calculated.

DTR 5.1.3 provides that a notification need never be made in respect of:

1. shares acquired for clearing and settlement purposes within a four-day settlement cycle;
2. shares held by a custodian or nominee (in its capacity as such), provided that the custodian or nominee receives its instructions in written or electronic form;
3. shares held by a market maker in its capacity as such, up to a 10 per cent holding and subject to certain conditions;
4. shares held by a credit institution or investment firm, provided they are held on the trading book, they do not exceed a five per cent holding, and the voting rights are not used "to intervene in the management of the issuer";
5. shares held under a collateral transaction, provided voting rights are not exercised; and
6. shares acquired under a stock loan, provided the borrower on-loans the shares or equivalent stock by the end of the next trading day, and does not exercise voting rights.

DTR 5.1.5 provides that a notification need only be made at five per cent, 10 per cent and higher thresholds in respect of:

1. an FCA-authorised manager's interest in voting rights attaching to shares managed for the shareholder under a written agreement;
2. voting rights exercisable by the operator of an authorised unit trust scheme, a recognised scheme or a UCITS (Undertakings for Collective Investment in Transferable Securities) scheme;
3. voting rights exercisable by an ICVC (Investment Company with Variable Capital); or
4. voting rights exercisable by certain prescribed categories of investment entity (this includes US investment advisers,

who are treated in the same way as EEA investment managers for the purposes of DTR 5).

DTR 5.3.1R details the financial instruments holdings of which may trigger the notification obligation under DTR 5.2.1R. Following FSA Quarterly Consultation (No.23) and from November 1, 2010, the FSA exempted receipts of nil-paid rights and rights to apply for open offer shares from the category of financial instruments within DTR 5.3.1R. As such, these interests will not be aggregated with other interests for the purposes of calculating the thresholds in DTR 5.2.1R.

Under DTR 5.2.1(e) and 5.2.2G(1), a parent company must generally aggregate its holdings with those of its "controlled undertakings" (this term, as defined in the FCA Handbook Glossary, includes most entities that would fall within the definition of subsidiary undertaking for the purposes of the 2006 Act). In certain circumstances, holdings of an asset manager and its parent may be required to be aggregated (see DTR 5.4). To avoid the requirement for such aggregation, a parent undertaking must ensure that it does not, and must be able to demonstrate to the FCA that it does not, interfere with the exercise of voting rights by the asset manager.

3.4.2 The 2006 Act

3.4.2.1 An "interest" for the purposes of the 2006 Act

For the purposes of disclosure of interests, when required, under the 2006 Act (see 3.4.2.2 and 3.4.2.3), an "interest" includes any interest in shares, including where a person has entered into a contract to acquire shares, or, not being the registered holder, is entitled to exercise any right conferred by holding the shares (or control the exercise of that right by another) (s.820(4)).

An option constitutes a disclosable interest. For the purposes of s.793 only (see further below), a right to subscribe for shares is also disclosable (s.821). A person is also deemed to be "interested" in shares (under s.823(1)) if a body corporate is interested in them and the directors of that body corporate are accustomed to act on the first person's instructions, or the first person is entitled to exercise or control the exercise of one-third of the voting rights of the body corporate in a general meeting. Similarly, shares of spouses, civil partners, infant children and step-children are aggregated for the purposes of these provisions under s.822.

3.4.2.2 Concert parties

Section 824 of the 2006 Act requires the disclosure of interests arising under concert party arrangements, where such disclosure is required pursuant to a s.793 notice (see 3.4.2.3 below). "Concert party arrangements" are not defined, but the arrangements covered include a non-legally binding arrangement where the parties have mutuality of undertakings, expectations or understandings, but exclude underwriting and sub-underwriting agreements (s.824(6)). The concept of an "arrangement" would probably catch circumstances where parties merely communicate in some way without necessarily any express oral or written statement, and thereby create expectations in each other of how each will behave in the future. Hence, potentially, the ambit of these provisions, like those under the Companies Act 1985 that these provisions replace, is very wide. However, the concert party agreements and arrangements concerned are only those which include provision for the acquisition by one or more of the parties of interests in the shares of a target company and which impose obligations with respect to "their use, retention or disposal" (s.824(2)).

The consequence of such an agreement or arrangement is that, under s.825, each of the parties to it is deemed to be interested in all the shares in which each of the other parties is interested. It is, therefore, not possible secretly to build a significant stake in a target company by means of splitting holdings between numerous concert parties. In discharging notification obligations under these provisions, concert parties are required to specify in which shares they have interests by virtue of them being deemed to have interests in shares in which other parties

148

are interested (s.825(4)); in addition, they must state the names and (so far as known to them) addresses of the other concert parties.

3.4.2.3 *Section 793 notices*

Section 793 notices were previously known as s.212 notices, in reference to the relevant provision of the Companies Act 1985.

Pursuant to s.793 a public company may require any person whom the company "knows or has reasonable cause to believe" to be, or to have been at any time during the three immediately preceding years, interested in any of its shares (whether or not the number of shares exceeds the three per cent level):

1. to confirm or deny that fact;
2. to give particulars of any interests he has or has had during the previous three years;
3. if any other person is or has been interested in the same shares, to give "so far as lies within his knowledge" particulars with respect to that other interest; and
4. if he is no longer interested in shares in the target, to give "so far as lies within his knowledge" particulars of the identity of the person who acquired his interest.

It is worth noting that, at least on one view, a potential offeror will have an interest in the relevant share capital of the target company if it obtains an irrevocable commitment from a shareholder to accept the offer when made. Accordingly, a target company would, on this basis, be entitled to serve a s.793 notice on a potential offeror to ascertain details of any irrevocable commitments received. There is, therefore, a clear advantage for the offeror in irrevocable commitments not normally being entered into until the evening prior to the announcement of an offer or possible offer.

A reply to any notice given by a company under s.793 must be given within any "reasonable time as may be specified in the notice" (s.793(7)). In cases of urgency (for example during the closing stages of a contested bid) a "reasonable time" would not generally be more than two days (see *Lonrho Plc v Edelman* (1989) 5 B.C.C. 68, which was decided under the equivalent provisions in the Companies Act 1985) and may be 24 hours, or even less. Here, too, a person is deemed to be interested in shares if he is a party to a concert party arrangement (s.793(5)).

For the purposes of s.793, references to "shares" are to the relevant company's issued shares with voting rights, including treasury shares. Temporary suspension of voting rights does not cause shares to be excluded from this definition.

For the purposes of s.793, a person is deemed to be interested in shares even if he is interested only as a nominee. Thus a nominee can be required to give details, so far as known to him, of the true owner of the shares; clearly this is the most sensible approach since the section aims at ensuring the fullest information possible is available to a company. Where, however, the true owner is not required by the DTRs himself to give notice of his interest (by virtue of that interest not being a notifiable interest, for example if he is a nominee), it may be possible to extend the period during which a target company is unable to ascertain the true owner of some of its shares by the device of giving instructions for the acquisition of shares through a chain of nominees each of whom is unaware of the identity of any others in the chain apart from those immediately next to him. The target company would then be obliged to send out a series of notices before identifying the person at the end of the chain.

It is worth noting that Swiss banks, for example, have regarded themselves as bound by secrecy laws which prevent them from answering s.793 notices. There are, however, doubts, both (it appears) under Swiss law and (certainly) in relation to the obligations under English law as to whether reliance on such grounds for refusing to answer a s.793 notice may be regarded as excusing the recipient from the consequences of such refusal (see *Re Geers Gross Plc* [1987] 1 W.L.R. 1649; (1987) 3 B.C.C. 528).

3.4.2.4   Consequences of contravention of the 2006 Act

The failure of a person to respond to a notice under s.793, or responding in a manner which a person knows to be false or reckless, is an offence which may be punished by imprisonment or a fine (s.795). In addition, the shares in question may be disenfranchised; disenfranchisement may be effected by the target under powers in its articles of association or by the court at the instigation of the target company under s.794 (in the case of failure to answer a s.793 notice). The basic approach of the courts in this area has been that the company has an unqualified right to know who owns its shares (see *Re Geers Gross Plc* [1987] 1 W.L.R. 1649; [1988] B.C.L.C. 140). However, problems may arise in an interlocutory application in deciding whether there has genuinely been an untruthful answer to the notice. It should be noted that a person does not commit an offence by failing to respond to a s.793 notice if he can prove that the request in the notice was frivolous or vexatious (s.795(2)).

Companies are required to maintain registers of notices given and replies received under s.793 (s.808). Obviously, these registers may contain information useful to any person contemplating a bid for the company concerned and the registers are required to be made available for inspection. But although s.793 gives a company extensive powers in relation to its shareholders, it is perhaps worth mentioning that many companies continue to be ignorant of the identity of their shareholders because they do not exercise their rights. In many instances, therefore, there is no register from which information may be gleaned. Even where companies do have such registers, attempts have been made to avoid publicising the information which a s.793 notice may reveal by sending out notices which appear to be given under that section, but which (arguably) are not; replies are then not registered. The effectiveness of such ploys must be open to doubt.

3.4.3 The Code

The provisions of the Code relating to disclosure of holdings and dealings normally only apply during an offer period (i.e. after the time when an announcement has been made of a proposed or possible offer).

3.4.3.1 Disclosure of opening positions

Prior to April 19, 2010, the disclosure regime under Rule 8 only related to dealings in relevant securities during the offer period. However, in May 2009 the Code Committee issued PCP 2009/1: Extending the Code's Disclosure Regime, which put forward proposals regarding, inter alia, a requirement for various persons to publicly disclose their holdings of relevant securities following the commencement of an offer period, regardless of whether or not a dealing had taken place. The purpose of this change was to increase transparency as to where voting control of securities lay as the Code Committee was of the view that the Code's disclosure regime did not fully achieve this objective as persons were not required to disclose their holdings of relevant securities unless and until they dealt in them.

With effect from April 19, 2010, Rule 8 therefore requires those subject to the Code's disclosure regime (as described below) to disclose their positions in relevant securities of the target and (in the case of a securities exchange offer) the offeror, regardless of whether they have dealt in relevant securities of the company concerned, by way of an "opening position disclosure".

Certain definitional changes have also been introduced.

1. A definition of "cash offeror" has been included in the Code which includes an offeror (or potential offeror) which has announced, or in respect of which the target has announced, that its offer is, or is likely to be, solely in cash.

2. "Parties to the offer" is now a defined term and covers the target, the offeror and any competing offeror whose identity has been publicly announced (including a potential target or offeror).
3. The Code Committee concluded that reference to "associates" of the offeror and target in Rule 8 (and elsewhere in the Code) should be replaced with references to persons acting in concert and the definition in the Code of associates has therefore been deleted.
4. For the purposes of Rule 8 only, the term "relevant securities" does not include securities of a cash offeror.

An opening position disclosure (as described below) is required to be made by the following persons:

1. the offeror (after its identity is first publicly announced) (Rule 8.1(a));
2. the target (Rule 8.2(a));
3. any person who is interested in one per cent or more of any class of relevant securities of any party to the offer (other than a cash offeror) at the time of the announcement that commences the offer period or the time of announcement that identifies an offeror (as the case may be) (Rule 8.3(a) and Note 7); and
4. exempt principal traders connected with an offeror or the target who do not have recognised intermediary status (who were previously subject to Rule 38.5(b)) or who do have such status but who hold any interest or short position in or right to subscribe for any relevant securities of any party to the offer (other than a cash offeror) in a proprietary capacity (Rules 8.5(a) and (b)).

As noted above, if a potential offeror has not yet been identified as such, it will not need to make an opening position disclosure under Rule 8.1(a) (which applies only to the offeror) until after the announcement that first identifies it publicly as an offeror (Note 12). However, a potential offeror will still need to make an opening position disclosure in accordance with Rule 8.3 (which applies to persons with interests in securities representing one per cent or more) if applicable, but it is not required to disclose the fact that it is a potential offeror.

The new regime does not require that persons acting in concert with a party to the offer make an opening position disclosure since the details of their holdings, if any, are required to be included in the opening position disclosure made by the party to the offer with whom he is acting in concert (Notes 2(c) and 5(a)(iv)).

If members of a consortium that has not been publicly identified as such may be required to issue an opening position disclosure under Rule 8.3(c), they will not normally be required to make a joint opening position disclosure which could identify them as such, although any member of the consortium who is interested in one per cent or more of a class of relevant securities of the target would be required to make an individual opening position disclosure under Rule 8.3(a) (Note 12(b)). In any such situation, the Panel must be consulted.

The opening position disclosure must be made no later than 12.00 (or, in the case of persons disclosing under (3) above, 15.30) on the tenth business day after the commencement of the offer period or, if later, after the announcement that first identifies a paper offeror as such (Note 2). The Code Committee gave careful consideration to the appropriate deadline for opening position disclosures and this period has been adopted to enable the offeror and the target to collect and collate accurate details of the positions not only held by themselves but also their concert parties. This is likely to be less time consuming for other market participants (who will generally be required to ascertain details of their own positions only); however, the Code Committee rejected the idea of setting different deadline dates for different classes of person.

If an offeror announces a firm intention to make an offer prior to the latter of the deadlines for releasing an opening position disclosure set out above, the offeror's opening position disclosure in relation to relevant securities of the target and the offeror itself should be made at the same time as its Rule 2.7

announcement (Note 2(a)(i)). If it is not practicable to ascertain all relevant details in respect of its concert parties by this time, this fact should be stated and a further opening position disclosure containing such details should be made as soon as possible and, in any event, before the deadlines referred to above. The Panel should be consulted in all such cases.

If a person is required to make an opening position disclosure and it deals in relevant securities of any party to the offer (other than a cash offeror) before midnight on the day before the deadline for releasing the opening position disclosure, that person (other than in the case of a party to the offer) is not required to release an opening position disclosure as it is required instead to make a dealing disclosure (as to which see 3.4.3.2 below) (Notes 2(b)(i) and 2(d)(i)). In the case of a party to the offer, such dealing disclosure would only be in respect of its own positions and holdings and, as such, a separate opening position disclosure is still required, which would include the information in respect of any persons acting in concert with it (Note 2(a)(i)).

Notes 4 and 5 set out the information that must be contained in an opening position disclosure and specimen disclosure forms are available online or may be obtained from the Panel. One point to note in this regard is that the opening position disclosure must be made on the basis of "composite disclosure", which means that the person who is required to make an opening position disclosure due to the size of his holding of relevant securities in one party to the offer, is required also to disclose all holdings of relevant securities in all parties to the offer (other than a cash offeror).

3.4.3.2 *Disclosure of dealings*

Rule 8 continues, as it did prior to April 19, 2010, to require various persons to publicly disclose their dealings in relevant securities of any party to the offer, other than a cash offeror. The persons who are required to make dealing disclosures are the same as those required to make an opening position disclosure (see 3.4.3.1 above) plus any person acting in concert with a party to the offer (Rules 8.1(b), 8.2(b), 8.3(b), 8.4 and 8.5(c)). The obligation in respect of the parties to the offer and their concert parties only applies to dealings on their own account or for discretionary clients.

The dealings disclosure must be made by 12.00 (or, in the case of a person disclosing due to having an interest in relevant securities of one per cent or more, 15.30) on the business day following the dealing.

By virtue of amendments following RS 2011/1 to Note 12, the Rule 8.1(b) obligation to disclose dealings extends to cover a potential offeror (and persons acting in concert with it) which has been referred to in an announcement but not publicly named. A potential offeror (and its concert parties) is therefore required to make a dealing disclosure in respect of any dealings in relevant securities of the target after the time of that announcement and, as a new requirement from April 19, 2010, is also required to make an announcement that it is considering making an offer under Rule 2.9. Of course, the circumstances in which this obligation will be relevant from a practical perspective are now more limited following the introduction of amended Rules in relation to the identification of potential offerors (see further Ch.2).

A party to the offer and its concert parties must also disclose the procuring of irrevocable commitments or letters of intent in accordance with Rule 2.11, which replaced Rule 8.4 with effect from April 19, 2010 (see 3.4.3.3 below).

The Panel has stated that it attaches great importance to compliance with Rule 8.3 on the basis that "disclosure underpins market transparency which, in turn, constitutes a fundamental protection for shareholders and others who deal in the United Kingdom securities markets" (Panel Statement 2003/16). Where people act pursuant to any sort of understanding to acquire or control an interest in relevant securities, they will normally be deemed to be a single person for the purposes of this rule (Rule 8.3(c)); and where relevant securities are managed on a discretionary basis by an investment management group then (unless the Panel agrees) all funds under management will be treated as the investments of a single person (Rule 8.3(d)).

Recently, the Code Committee has proposed in PCP 2010/2 that the threshold for disclosure in Rule 8.3 should be reduced from 1 per cent to 0.5 per cent. However following a consultation, on October 21, 2010 the Code Committee concluded that in light of the relatively recent overhaul of Rule 8, the appropriateness of the disclosure threshold should be monitored and the change was rejected (see Panel Statement 2010/22).

Rule 8.3 applies equally to exempt fund managers (whether or not connected with the offeror or target) as to any other one per cent holder. It does not, however, apply to a recognised intermediary acting in a client-serving capacity unless the recognised intermediary is an exempt principal trader connected with the offeror or target (Rule 8.3(e) and Note 9) (see 3.5.1 below), or is a concert party of the offeror or target (in which case disclosure under Rule 8.4 is required). See 3.5.2 below for further information about recognised intermediary status.

Rule 8.3 was considered by the Panel in connection with BC Capital Partners' proposed offer for Mitchells & Butlers Plc (M&B) (Panel Statement 2003/9). M&B was to become one of two successor companies to Six Continents following the latter's demerger. This prompted the question of how to determine a one per cent holder in relation to M&B, prior to the time of the demerger becoming effective and dealings in shares in M&B commencing. The Panel Executive ruled that a relevant person's percentage holding in the When Issued shares of M&B should be aggregated with that person's percentage holding in Six Continents' shares since a holding in Six Continents' shares would, at the time the demerger became effective, translate into an equivalent holding in M&B shares. Therefore, a person that held 0.5 per cent of Six Continents' shares and acquired 0.8 per cent of the When Issued shares of M&B was treated as being a one per cent holder in relation to M&B (although not

Six Continents, see below), notwithstanding that he did not hold one per cent in either stock individually.

Six Continents itself was already in an offer period following an announcement made by Sun Capital Partners Limited. However, as a holding of When Issued shares in M&B would not translate into an effective holding in Six Continents, there was no need to aggregate shareholdings in M&B and Six Continents when calculating percentage interests in Six Continents.

Rule 8 was substantially modified in the wake of the Guinness affair. In particular, Note 10 now states that intermediaries are expected to co-operate with the Panel in its enquiries, including by identifying clients. The requirement for co-operation with the Panel is now reinforced by provisions set out in the Market Conduct volume of the FCA Handbook. These state, in broad terms, that a firm which acts for any person in connection with a transaction to which the Code applies must cease to act for that person if it has reasonable grounds for believing that the person in question, or his principal, is not complying or is not likely to comply with the Code; and provide such information and assistance as the Panel may reasonably require to perform its functions.

In order to assist the Panel's monitoring of compliance with Rule 8.3, Rule 22 has been amended with effect from April 19, 2010 to oblige the offeror and the target to assist the Panel in identifying persons who are interested in one per cent or more of any class of relevant securities of that party and, in particular, to provide the Panel promptly after commencement of the offer period with details of all persons who are reasonably considered to be so interested. As an additional obligation, at the same time as the information is provided to the Panel, the offeror and the target are required to send all such persons an explanation of their disclosure obligations under Rule 8. However, if the target has sent those persons a copy of an announcement or circular in accordance with Rule

2.12, (and these would summarise the requirements of Rule 8), then there is no requirement to separately notify them of their Rule 8 obligations.

The Code Committee originally proposed in PCP 2009/2 that Rule 22 be amended to require that offerors and targets take all reasonable steps to identify persons who are interested in one per cent or more of any class of relevant security, including requiring the issue of s.793 notices (as to which see 3.4.2.3 above). However, following consultation, the Code Committee accepted that this would be unduly onerous and that boards should only be required to provide information that is readily available. In RS 2009/1 the Code Committee has therefore clarified that in complying with the requirements of amended Rule 22, it would expect boards to normally provide the Panel with details from the following sources:

1. the company's shareholder register;
2. notifications received pursuant to the DTRs and responses to s.793 notices (to the extent that the company has issued such notices); and
3. analysis previously received, or readily available, from the company's brokers or other advisers.

Dealing disclosures under Rule 8 must contain the information set out in Note 5 and as detailed in the Panel's specimen disclosure forms (which are available online or may be obtained from the Panel).

As is the case for opening position disclosures, with effect from April 19, 2010, dealing disclosures must be made on a composite disclosure basis. This is reflected in Note 5 and requires that:

1. any person who has a gross long interest of one per cent or more in a class of relevant securities of any party to the offer (other than a cash offeror) is required to disclose any dealings in relevant securities not only of that party but of any other party to the offer (other than a cash offeror); and

2.   any person who is required to make a dealing disclosure is required to disclose details of his interests and short positions in the relevant securities of both the party to the offer in whose relevant securities the dealing occurred and any other party to the offer (other than a cash offeror).

If a person is disclosing details in respect of more than one party to the offer at the same time, a separate disclosure form must be used for each such party.

The Panel Executive considers it best practice for incorrect details to be corrected in a separate disclosure rather than in a disclosure containing details of previously undisclosed dealings. Note 14 on Rule 8 requires that any incorrect details included in a dealing disclosure should be corrected as soon as practicable in a subsequent disclosure and that such disclosure should:

1.   state clearly that it corrects details previously disclosed;
2.   identify the disclosure or disclosures being corrected; and
3.   provide sufficient detail for the reader to understand the nature of the correction.

In the case of any doubt, the Note suggests the Panel be consulted. Private dealing disclosures are required to be made to the Panel:

1.   by a party to the offer and any person acting in concert with that party if it deals for the account of non-discretionary investment clients in any relevant securities of any party to the offer (other than a cash offeror) during an offer period (Rule 8.7); and
2.   in certain circumstances by exempt fund managers (Rule 8.6) (see 3.5.3.2).

3.4.3.3   Disclosure of irrevocable commitments and letters of intent

Rule 2.11 (which from April 19, 2010 replaced Rule 8.4) requires a party to the offer or any concert party thereof who procures an irrevocable commitment or letter of intent during the course of an offer period to disclose the details publicly by no later than 12 noon the following business day (Rule 2.11(a)). Such a disclosure must also include details of any other commitments or letters of intent which have been procured prior to the date of that disclosure and which have not been previously disclosed for example because they were obtained prior to the commencement of the offer period (Rule 2.11(c)). However, no separate announcement is required where an offeror sets out these details in its Rule 2.7 announcement which is published no later than noon on the business day following such procurement (Note 1).

As noted in 3.4.3.1 above, details of any irrevocable commitment or letter of intent procured by a party to the offer, whether procured before or during the offer period, must be included in that party's opening position disclosure (Rule 2.11(b)).

Rule 2.11(d) states that if a person who has given an irrevocable commitment or letter of intent either becomes aware that he will not be able to comply with the terms of that commitment or letter or no longer intends to do so, that person must promptly announce the updated position or so notify the relevant party to the offer and the Panel. Upon receipt of such notification, the relevant party to the offer must then promptly announce such information.

In a situation where a party to the offer has procured a letter of intent prior to the commencement of the offer period, the relevant party should ensure that the letter of intent continues to represent up-to-date intentions of the shareholder or other person concerned (Note 4 on Rule 2.11). This requirement is similar to the requirement in the Note on Rule 19.3 for a party to an offer to verify the up-to-date intentions of the shareholders or other person before making a "statement of support".

3.4.3.4 *Other disclosure obligations under the Code*

Rule 7.1 requires an immediate public announcement to be made whenever there is an acquisition of an interest in shares which triggers an obligation to increase an offer under Rule 6, to make a mandatory offer under Rule 9 or to make a mandatory cash or securities offer under Rule 11. Such an announcement should, whenever practicable, state the nature of the interest, the number of shares concerned and the price paid.

Following an acquisition of an interest in shares from a single shareholder permitted by Rule 5.2(a), a public announcement is required not later than 12.00 on the following business day (Rule 5.4); normally, however, such an announcement will be preceded by the announcement of a Rule 9 offer.

Disclosures of shareholding interests and of dealings are also required when an announcement is issued on a bid closing date, or on an offer being declared unconditional as to acceptances, or on an offer being revised (Rule 17), and must be included in offer and defence documents (Rules 24.4 and 25.4). Following the June 2010 review of certain aspects of the Takeover Code, the Code Committee explained that some respondents to the consultation had suggested that offeree company shareholders should be compelled to disclose either their acceptance of an offer or their vote in favour of a scheme. The perceived benefit to this arrangement would be greater accountability and transparency as regards institutional investors. The Code Committee rejected these proposals and in Panel Statement 2010/22 explained that it perceived little practical benefit from such disclosures.

A Rule 17 announcement and offer and defence documents are required to include the full extent of the relevant securities of the target in which the offeror (or persons acting in concert with it) is interested or in which it has a short position. In addition, a Rule 17 announcement requires details of acceptances, including the extent to which acceptances have been received from persons acting in concert with the offeror or in respect of shares which were the subject of an irrevocable commitment or letter of intent; and details of any relevant securities of the target in respect of which the offeror (or any person acting in concert with it) has an outstanding irrevocable commitment or letter of intent. In addition, a Rule 17 announcement and offer and defence documents must detail securities borrowed or lent by the offeror (or persons acting in concert with it) in order to facilitate a full understanding of the extent to which the voting rights attached to the relevant securities of the parties to the offer are currently controlled by such persons.

The Panel amended what is now, following RS 2011/1, Note 2 on Rule 24.4 on February 21, 2002. This amendment had the effect of relaxing the restrictions on disclosing dealings in shares before or during the offer period on an aggregated basis (subject to the requirement that no significant dealings are thereby concealed). The Code Committee was of the opinion that there are occasions when there is little benefit in listing a large number of transactions during or shortly before the offer period. It therefore decided that all purchases and sales during the offer period can be aggregated. Furthermore, the Code Committee decided:

1. to extend to three months the period prior to the offer period during which dealings may be aggregated on a monthly basis; and
2. to permit dealings in the nine months prior to that period to be aggregated on a quarterly basis.

The Note requires that acquisitions and disposals should not be netted off, that the highest and lowest prices should be stated and that disclosure should distinguish between different categories of interest in relevant securities and short positions. The entirety of the provisions in Note 2 on Rule 24.4 are now subject to a full list of all dealings (together with a draft of the proposed aggregate disclosure) being sent to the Panel for approval prior to the posting of the offer documentation, and being available for inspection. It is also worth noting that Note 4 on Rule 24.4 and Note 2 on Rule 25.4 now require details of securities of competing offerors to also be included in the relevant documents.

3.5   Miscellaneous

We will now deal briefly with some miscellaneous topics concerning share dealings of which advisers on a takeover will need to have some understanding.

3.5.1   *Dealings by principal traders and fund managers*

There has historically been a good deal of confusion about how the Code treats dealings by connected principal traders and fund managers. On April 25, 2005, following the consultation on market-related issues, the Code was amended, mainly to clarify and codify elements of the Panel's practice which had developed over time. It is, perhaps, simplest to address the provisions which apply to both principal traders and fund managers before looking at the Code provisions which are specific to one or the other.

The term "market maker" was previously used in the Code, but was replaced with the term "Principal trader" on April 25, 2005, as the Panel had adopted this term following the introduction of SETS (see 3.5.4 below), after which there were no recognised market makers in SETS-traded securities. It also reflects the policy which has been adopted by the Panel for some time that all principal trading activities (not just market making activities) should be eligible for exempt status (see below).

The amendments made on April 25, 2005 also introduced a new defined term, that of "connected adviser". Connected advisers normally include only:

1.   in relation to the offeror or target—an organisation which is advising that party in relation to the offer and a corporate broker to that party; and
2.   in relation to a person who is acting in concert with the offeror or the target—an organisation which is advising that person either in relation to the offer or in relation to the matter which is the reason for that person being a member of the relevant concert party.

The Code definition of acting in concert contains a presumption (presumption 5) that a connected adviser acts in concert with its client and, if its client is acting in concert with the offeror or the target, the connected adviser is also presumed to act in concert with the offeror or target, in respect of the interests in shares of that adviser and the persons controlling, controlled by or under the same control as, that adviser. Hence, when the adviser is part of a larger financial services organisation, the presumption of concertedness extends to all entities within that group.

However, principal traders and fund managers who can demonstrate to the Panel's satisfaction their independence from corporate advisory and corporate broking operations in their group are granted exempt status. Exempt status is obtained by application to the Panel. The Panel will consider all relevant factors in deciding any applications including group structure, separate physical location, the history of the organisation as a whole (including past records of cooperative or independent action), the extent of the use of common services, common directorships, financial interests of the relevant executives in the group as a whole and the existence of an effective compliance department. The effect of exempt status is to remove the principal trader or fund manager from the presumption of concertedness that would otherwise apply. However, the principal trader or fund manager will still be regarded as connected with the offeror or target company, as appropriate (see Note 3 on the definitions of exempt fund manager and exempt principal trader).

It should be noted that exempt status is not relevant unless the sole reason for the connection is that the principal trader or fund manager is controlled by, controls or is under the same control as a connected adviser to the offeror, target, or person acting in concert with the offeror or target (Note 2 on the Code definitions of exempt fund manager and exempt principal trader). If a fund manager or principal trader's exempt status is not relevant, or if they do not have exempt status, Rule 7.2 applies. Connected fund managers and principal traders will not normally be presumed to be acting in concert with an offeror or potential offeror until that party's identity as an offeror or potential offeror is publicly announced, or (if earlier) the time at which the fund manager or principal trader had actual knowledge of the possibility of an offer being made by a person with whom it is connected (Rule 7.2(a)). When this is the case, Rules 4.2, 4.6, 5, 6, 9, 11 and 36 will be relevant. Similarly, under Rule 7.2(b), connected fund managers and principal traders will not normally be presumed to be acting in concert with the target until the commencement of the offer period, or (if earlier) the time at which the fund manager or principal trader had actual knowledge of the possibility of an offer being made. Rules 4.4, 4.6, 5 and 9 may then be relevant.

The Code reflects the Panel's practice of permitting a connected non-exempt principal trader or fund manager, after it is presumed to be acting in concert, to acquire or sell interests in target shares so as to flatten its book position within a short period (usually 24–48 hours) of being presumed to be acting in concert. The Panel will then not apply the usual Code consequences to dealings undertaken with its consent in this way (see Notes 3 and 4 to Rule 7.2).

3.5.2 *Recognised intermediary status*

As part of the amendments made to the Code in relation to dealings in derivatives and options, the Code Committee reviewed the status of investment institutions under the Code. The product of this review was the creation of a new "recognised intermediary status" for trading desks which trade as principal for client-serving purposes. This status allows the interests of the recognised intermediary in shares as a result of positions in derivatives and options not to be taken into account in establishing whether the trading desk (or the organisation of which it forms part) is interested in 30 per cent or more of a company's shares carrying voting rights for the purposes of Rule 9.

The rationale behind the introduction of recognised intermediary status is that certain investment institutions, especially client-serving desks of investment banks, are likely to have substantial derivatives and options positions in the ordinary course of their business and this should not require them to make mandatory offers under Rule 9.1.

To obtain recognised intermediary status, the desk must apply to the Panel and satisfy a number of suitability conditions regarding the nature of its activities and the organisation of which it forms part.

It should be noted that recognised intermediary status is an entirely separate regime from the exempt status regime. Hence, where a recognised intermediary is (or is part of) an exempt principal trader connected with an offeror or target company, the position under the Code remains unchanged.

3.5.3   *Fund managers*

3.5.3.1   *Restrictions on dealings*

Although Rules 38.1 to 38.4 (see 3.5.4.1 below) do not specifically apply to exempt fund managers, the Panel has stated that it: "would not expect such a fund manager to take any action with the intention of assisting the group's corporate finance clients because this would undermine the basis on which exempt status was granted to it."

3.5.3.2   *Disclosure—Rule 8*

An exempt fund manager who is connected with the offeror or target, and who deals in relevant securities for the account of discretionary investment clients, is required to make private disclosure of such dealings to the Panel (Rule 8.6(a)). If, however, a connected exempt fund manager holds a greater than one per cent interest in the relevant securities, then it will have to make the usual public disclosure under Rule 8.3 (in which case, private disclosure will not normally be required in addition (Rule 8.6(b)). The latter is also true, of course, of non-connected fund managers holding a one per cent (or greater) interest, but non-connected principal traders are under no such obligation.

Connected fund managers which do not enjoy exempt status must make public disclosure of their dealings in the normal way.

3.5.4 Principal traders

3.5.4.1 Restrictions on dealings

Granting exempt status to principal traders left a risk of concerted action, which was considered by the Panel to be more acute in respect of market making, involving the use of the organisation's own capital, than in respect of discretionary fund management, where managers owe fiduciary duties to their investment clients and are therefore less likely to take action to assist the organisation's corporate finance clients. Accordingly, Rule 38.1 prohibits an exempt connected principal trader from dealing with the purpose of assisting the offeror or target; Rule 38.2 also prohibits the offeror and its concert parties from dealing as principal, during the offer period, with an exempt principal trader connected with the offeror in shares of the target; Rule 38.3 states that such a principal trader may not assent its shares to the offer or purchase such shares in assented form until after the offer is unconditional as to acceptances; and Rule 38.4 prohibits shares owned by an exempt connected principal trader from being voted in the context of an offer. In order to ensure compliance with Rules 38.1 and 38.2, the Code now states that during an offer period, an offeror and persons acting in concert with it must not acquire an interest in any securities of the target company through any anonymous order book system, or through any other means, unless it can be established that the seller (or other party to the transaction in question) is not an exempt principal trader connected with the offeror (Rule 4.2(b)).

Dealings by exempt principal traders are also relevant for the purposes of Rule 9. The Panel Executive has adopted a standard approach to aggregation which requires compliance officers of multi-service financial organisations to monitor closely the aggregate holdings of the group so as to ensure that Rule 9 is not breached. This is now reflected in Note 16 on Rule

9.1, which states that Rule 9 will be relevant if the aggregate number of shares in which all persons under the same control (including any exempt fund manager or exempt principal trader) are interested carry 30 per cent or more of the voting rights of the relevant company. However, if recognised intermediary status has not fallen away under Note 3 of the definition of recognised intermediary, a recognised intermediary acting in a client-serving capacity will not be treated as interested in any securities, unless they are held in a proprietary capacity and fall within para.3 or 4 of the definition of interests in securities. Note 16 also provides that if such a group of persons includes a principal trader and the aggregate number of shares in a company in which the group is interested approaches or exceeds 30 per cent of the voting rights, the Panel may consent to the principal trader continuing to acquire shares in the company without consequence under Rule 9.1, provided that the company is not in an offer period and the number of shares which the principal trader holds does not at any relevant time exceed three per cent of the voting rights of the company.

3.5.4.2 *Disclosure*

Before the Code Committee amended the Code to take into account dealings in derivatives and options, an unconnected principal trader who dealt in that capacity did not have to make disclosure under Rule 8.3 when his holding rose above one per cent (in contrast to the position for an unconnected fund manager and all other shareholders). As part of its review of the status of investment institutions under the Code, the Code Committee has developed further the Code's long-standing disclosure exception for recognised market makers and other intermediaries. Under the amended regime, the exception from disclosure under Rule 8.3(d) applies to all investment desks enjoying recognised intermediary status. In practice, this exception is more widely available than previously, when it was only available to unconnected principal traders. For example, a trading desk not registered as a market maker with the LSE or an LSE-registered member firm dealing as principal in order book securities could potentially apply for recognised intermediary status but would not constitute a principal trader. Some commentators assume that connected principal traders have a similar immunity from disclosure so that market-making arms of investment banks are able secretly to build up stakes in the target while another part of the organisation is advising the bidder. In fact, this is not the case. Exempt connected principal traders (i.e. within the same group as the financial adviser or broker) are already required to disclose all dealings (although in aggregated form) under Rule 8.5 (which replaced old Rule 38.5 with effect from April 19, 2010) (see Note 9 on Rule 8) via an RIS by 12.00 on the business day following the dealing, while connected principal traders which are not exempt will have disclosure obligations under Rules 8.3 and 8.4.

Chapter 4

Mandatory and Voluntary Offers and their Terms

Christopher Pearson

Partner

Norton Rose Fulbright LLP

Nick Adams

Partner

Norton Rose Fulbright LLP

4.1   Introduction

Rules 9 to 13 restrict the freedom which a party has at common law in his decision whether or not to bid for control of a company to which the Code applies and, where he does make a bid, to choose the consideration he offers and the conditions which he attaches to his bid.

They do this in a number of ways.

1. Rule 9 obliges a person (or persons acting in concert) to make a bid in certain circumstances, specifies the minimum consideration to be offered and limits the conditions which can be attached to the bid;
2. Rule 10 requires a bid to contain a minimum acceptance condition;
3. Rule 11 requires a voluntary offeror in certain situations to offer a minimum cash price, a cash alternative or to make a securities offer;

4.   Rule 12 requires a particular term to be included in an offer which could trigger an in-depth ("Phase 2") investigation by the UK or EU competition authorities; and

5.   Rule 13 prohibits certain types of condition and restricts the ability of an offeror to invoke a condition to lapse an offer.

Different principles apply to partial offers, which are governed by Rule 36 and are covered in Ch.5.

Many of the Rules referred to in this Chapter are qualified by wording "except with the consent of the Panel". It is therefore important to understand the philosophy of the Panel in these matters.

Except as mentioned, the Rules referred to in this Chapter apply equally to contractual offers and to offers implemented by way of a scheme of arrangement.

4.2   The mandatory offer and its terms

Rule 9 provides that where:

1.   a person (which can be an individual as well as a company);

2.   acquires (whether by one transaction or a series of transactions over a period of time) an interest in shares in a company;

3.   which in itself, or when aggregated with shares in which the person and persons acting in concert with it are already interested;

4.   carries 30 per cent or more of the voting rights of the company,

then such person must make an offer:

1.   to acquire all other equity shares in the company (whether voting or non-voting, but excluding any shares held in treasury); and

2.   to acquire any other class of transferable securities in the company carrying voting rights (again, excluding any shares held in treasury),

on the terms and conditions required by Rule 9, and on no other conditions.

The Rule also requires such a bid where a person who (together with any persons acting in concert with it) is already interested in shares carrying 30 per cent or more of the voting rights of a company, but does not hold shares carrying more than 50 per cent of such rights, acquires (or any person acting in concert with it acquires) an interest in any other shares carrying voting rights which increases the percentage of shares carrying voting rights in which it is interested. The provisions permitting such a person to acquire up to one per cent of the voting rights in any period of 12 months were abolished in August 1998. However, the Panel has considered the position of persons (and members of concert parties) interested in shares carrying more than 30 per cent of the voting rights of companies where such interests are reduced by sales or diluted as a result of the issue of new shares but remain in excess of 30 per cent. The Panel concluded that it was appropriate to permit such persons some ability to acquire an interest in further shares in these circumstances, notwithstanding that they (or the concert party of which they form part) already hold an interest in shares carrying 30 per cent or more of the voting rights of the company. This is dealt with in more detail in 4.2.5.6 below.

A person will be treated as having an "interest in shares" if he has a long economic exposure, whether absolute or conditional, to changes in the price of shares and in particular if:

1.   he owns the shares;
2.   he has the right (whether conditional or absolute) to exercise or direct the exercise of the voting rights attaching to them or has general control of them;
3.   by virtue of any agreement to purchase, option or derivative, he has the right or option to acquire them or

call for their delivery or is under an obligation to take delivery of them (whether such right, option or obligation is conditional or absolute and whether it is in the money or otherwise); or

4. he is party to any derivative whose value is determined by reference to their price and which results, or may result, in his having a long position in them.

Consequently, the thresholds for the triggering of a mandatory offer obligation pursuant to Rule 9.1 are not limited by reference to holdings of shares carrying voting rights but will also take into account other interests in shares acquired by virtue of long derivatives, call options and written put options. A person will not normally be treated as having acquired an interest in further shares just because the nature of his interest has changed (for example, where a person acquires shares upon the exercise of a call option over existing shares). In these cases, the aggregate number of shares in which the person would be interested will usually remain the same (Note 18 to Rule 9.1).

Rule 9 is based on General Principle 1, which provides that where a person acquires control of a company, the other holders of securities must be protected.

"Control" is defined in the Definitions section of the Code as an interest, or interests, in shares carrying in aggregate 30 per cent or more of the voting rights of a company, irrespective of whether such interest or interests give de facto control.

From time to time there have been suggestions that the 30 per cent figure should be reduced. Article 5 of the Takeover Directive requires Member States to introduce Rules relating to mandatory bids but does not specify the threshold at which a mandatory bid has to be made: this is left to individual Member States to determine. In the United Kingdom, the 30 per cent threshold is thought to strike an appropriate balance between protecting minority shareholders and not unduly restricting takeover activity.

The 1991 Annual Report of the Panel contained the following helpful explanation of the philosophy underlying Rule 9:

"The philosophy underlying this Rule is that, if effective control of a company is obtained by the acquisition of shares, the principle of equality of treatment for shareholders requires that all shareholders should have the opportunity to obtain the price per share paid for that control (it will usually be a premium price) and that they should have the opportunity to get out of the company if they do not like what has happened."

An important bolstering of this principle is contained in Rule 9.6, which requires directors (and their close relatives and related trusts) who sell shares to a person (or enter into options, derivatives or other transactions with a person) which would trigger a Rule 9 obligation to make it a condition of the sale (or other relevant transaction) that the person will make a Rule 9 bid. In addition, such directors should (except with the consent of the Panel) remain on the board until the later of the first closing date or the date on which the offer becomes wholly unconditional so as to ensure proper conduct of the bid. This important provision should not be overlooked; it imposes an obligation on the seller of the shares and its significance is indicated by the fact that an equivalent of Rule 9.6 appeared in the Code before the remainder of Rule 9.

In practice, Rule 9 mandatory offers are contractual rather than effected by way of a scheme of arrangement, although Section 2 of Appendix 7 to the Code does allow a mandatory offer under Rule 9 to be implemented by way of a scheme of arrangement with the Panel's prior consent. Note 1 on Section 2 refers to the views of the offeree board and its independent adviser and the likely timetable of the scheme as being factors that the Panel will take into account in considering whether or not to permit a mandatory offer to be made by way of a scheme. Note 1 also states that, if the Panel does consent to a mandatory offer being effected by way of a scheme of arrangement and the scheme lapses for a reason that would not have caused a contractual offer to lapse (for example, the court does not sanction the scheme), the offeror must immediately make a contractual offer in compliance with Rule 9 (and the scheme circular must include a statement to that effect).

4.2.1 The terms and conditions of mandatory bids

4.2.1.1 Price

Rule 9.5(a) requires that a mandatory offer must be in cash (or be accompanied by a cash alternative) at not less than the highest price paid by the offeror or any person acting in concert with it for any interest in shares of the relevant class during the 12 months prior to the announcement of that offer. The Panel should be consulted where there is more than one class of share capital involved. Rule 9.5(b) also states that if, after a Rule 9 offer has been made for a class of shares but before it closes for acceptance, the offeror or anyone acting in concert with it acquires a further interest in shares of that class at above the offer price, it must increase its offer price for that class of shares to not less than the highest price paid for the interest so acquired.

Note 1 to Rule 9.5 explains that sometimes, where a significant number of acquisitions which have to be taken into account for the purposes of this Rule have been securities exchange transactions, the principle of equality of treatment may make it undesirable that the offer be a cash only offer, and that the same securities, but with a cash offer or alternative, must be offered.

Rule 9.5(c) grants the Panel a discretion to adjust the highest price calculated under Rules 9.5(a) and 9.5(b). Note 3 to Rule 9.5 identifies some of the considerations which the Panel might take into account in deciding whether to make such an adjustment; one situation might be where the mandatory bid is being made as part of a rescue operation. The price payable in any of the situations set out in Note 3 will be the price that is fair and reasonable taking into account all the factors that are relevant to the circumstances. In any case where the highest price is adjusted, the Panel will publish its decision.

The other notes to Rule 9.5 give further guidance on calculation of the price to be offered, including where dealings in options and derivatives are relevant.

4.2.1.2 *Competition references*

Rule 9.4 requires any mandatory bid to which Rule 12 applies (see 4.4 below) to contain the term required by Rule 12.1 providing that the offer will lapse in the event it is referred for a Phase 2 investigation by either the UK or EU competition authorities. If a mandatory bid lapses pursuant to Rule 12.1 and competition clearance is then obtained, the offer must be re-made on the same terms as soon as practicable, although Note 1 to Rule 9.4 envisages situations where intervening action taken with the consent of the Panel may make this unnecessary. However, it cannot be a condition of a mandatory bid that clearance is received from the competition authorities.

4.2.1.3 *Acceptance condition*

Rule 9.3 requires that, except with the consent of the Panel, a mandatory bid must be conditional only upon acceptances being received which (together with shares acquired or agreed to be acquired before or during the offer) will result in the offeror and its concert parties holding shares carrying more than 50 per cent of the voting rights. Note 1 to Rule 9.3 recognises that there will be no such condition where 50 per cent of the voting rights are already held before the offer is made. Although the Code has not formally disapplied Rule 9.3 in the case of a mandatory offer implemented by way of a scheme of arrangement, in practice this provision can only apply to a contractual offer as an offer by way of a scheme requires approval by the relevant majority of shareholders in a Court convened shareholder meeting (as well as court sanction) rather than acceptance by individual shareholders.

4.2.1.4 *Other conditions*

Rule 9.3 prohibits other conditions being attached to mandatory bids. As a consequence it is not possible to include in mandatory offers the detailed protective conditions customarily included in voluntary offers (see 4.3.3 below) regarding material adverse change, or consents of shareholders, or clearances by third parties.

As far as material adverse changes are concerned, these are treated as entirely the risk of the person whose acquisition has triggered the obligation to make a mandatory bid.

As far as consents of an offeror's shareholders are concerned, again this is treated as something the offeror should have thought about before triggering the bid, although Note 3 to Rule 9.3 indicates that the Panel will consider a request for dispensation, which will be heavily qualified, in exceptional circumstances such as where the necessary cash is to be provided, wholly or in part, by an issue of new securities for which listing is a pre-condition.

As far as regulatory clearances are concerned, the difficulties to which this would give rise are such that Rule 9.3(b) prohibits the making of an acquisition which would trigger a mandatory bid if the mandatory bid's implementation would be dependent upon such a clearance (or indeed on any other conditions, consents or arrangements), although Note 3(b) to Rule 9.3 envisages situations in which a dispensation from this may be granted.

4.2.2 Who are deemed to be "persons acting in concert"?

This question is a crucial one, since the aggregation of the interests in shares of people who are deemed to be acting in concert may result in an obligation to make a bid. The opening sentence in the Notes to Rule 9.1 states: "The majority of questions which arise in the context of Rule 9 relate to persons acting in concert".

The Definitions section of the Code defines the term as follows:

"Persons acting in concert comprise persons who, pursuant to an agreement or understanding (whether formal or informal), cooperate to obtain or consolidate control... of a company or to frustrate the successful outcome of an offer for a company . . ."

There is a deeming provision in the definition which states that a person and each of its "affiliated persons" will be acting in concert all with each other. Affiliated persons include undertakings in respect of which any person has a majority of, or controls a majority of, the shareholders' voting rights, has the right to appoint or remove a majority of the board of directors or has the power to exercise, or actually exercises, dominant influence or control.

The definition of "acting in concert" then continues with a series of presumptions as to those persons who are in concert. These fall into six self-contained categories; someone in one of these categories is presumed to be in concert only with those in the same category and not with those in another category. However, the presumptions are rebuttable, and they are not meant to be exhaustive. They are followed by a series of Notes discussed in other contexts in this Guide. In addition, the presumptions are supplemented in some cases by guidance issued by the Panel Executive on how the presumptions are applied (see for instance, Practice Statement No.12 on the application of presumption (4)). This Chapter will concentrate on the guidance given in those Notes and in the Notes to Rule 9.1 which is of particular relevance to Rule 9.

4.2.2.1 *Persons coming together to act in concert or shareholders voting together*

If persons already interested in shares carrying 30 per cent or more of the voting rights in a company but not previously acting in concert merely decide to co-operate to obtain or consolidate control of a company, this will not normally trigger a bid (provided that acquisitions made prior to coming together were made without the knowledge of the other concert parties). However, once they have come together, the acquisition by one of them of any further interest in shares carrying voting rights in that company could trigger a mandatory offer (Note 1 to Rule 9.1), with purchases made over the previous 12 months then becoming relevant for the purpose of determining the price to be offered even if such purchases had been made without the concert parties' knowledge and prior to coming together (Rule 9.5).

The Panel does not normally regard the action of shareholders voting together on particular resolutions, discussing possible issues which might be raised with a company's Board or making joint representations to a company as indicative of a group acting in concert. An exception to this general principle is contained in Note 2 to Rule 9.1. Practice Statement No.26 on shareholder activism contains guidance on the application of Note 2. In summary, the Panel will normally presume shareholders who requisition or threaten to requisition the consideration of a "board control-seeking proposal" at a shareholders' meeting, together with their supporters, to be acting in concert with each other and with the proposed directors, with the result that subsequent acquisitions of interests in shares could trigger a mandatory offer. In determining if a proposal is board control-seeking, the Panel will have regard to a number of factors, including the specific factors listed in Note 2. The most important factor is whether there is a relationship (other than an insignificant relationship) between the proposed directors and the shareholders proposing them or their supporters. If such a relationship exists then the other factors set out in Note 2 will also need to be considered to determine whether the proposal is board control-seeking, including the number of directors to be appointed or replaced compared with the total size of the board and the board positions held by the directors to be replaced. In practice, board control-seeking resolutions are relatively rare and, in the majority of normal collective shareholder actions, no mandatory offer issues would therefore arise.

4.2.2.2 Break-up of concert parties

Note 1 to the definition of "acting in concert" indicates that the Panel needs clear evidence before it will accept that parties, once held to be in concert, are no longer in concert. This will be particularly relevant where, the original objective of the concert party having been achieved and co-operation having ceased, one of its members wishes to make a further acquisition without triggering a mandatory offer.

The composition of concert parties can also change. The sale of its interest in shares by an outgoing member of the concert party to a continuing member may, in certain circumstances, trigger an obligation on the part of the purchaser to make a mandatory bid. Note 4 to Rule 9.1 describes these circumstances.

4.2.2.3 *Acquisition of part only of an interest in shares*

Difficult questions arise when a shareholder who holds more than 30 per cent sells less than 30 per cent to a single purchaser or two or more purchasers who are acting in concert. One often sees a sale of 29.99 per cent in these circumstances, obviously designed to protect the purchaser from Rule 9. In such circumstances the Panel are rightly concerned as to whether seller and purchaser are effectively acting in concert in respect of all their shares, or the seller has allowed the purchaser to acquire a significant degree of control over the retained shares, so that a mandatory offer should be made.

The Panel will take account of such factors as whether the seller is an "insider", whether the price paid effectively contained a control premium, and whether there are any arrangements (however informal) between seller and purchaser regarding the seller's retained shares. Obviously fine judgments will be involved and the fact that the seller retains a substantial number of shares over which it intends to act independently will be helpful in rebutting any presumption of concerted behaviour. Similar considerations will arise where the seller remains interested in shares but without itself owning any of such shares, or where the acquisition is not of the shares themselves but of another type of interest in shares. Note 6 to Rule 9.1 provides guidance on the point, but each case is inevitably different and the Panel should always be consulted.

4.2.2.4 Employee benefit trusts

Note 5 to Rule 9.1, introduced in 2002, concerns trustees of employee benefit trusts (EBTs) as potential concert parties. The Panel must be consulted in advance when an acquisition is proposed and the aggregate number of shares in which the directors, those persons acting in concert with them and the trustees of an EBT are interested would as a result carry 30 per cent or more of the voting rights or, if already carrying 30 per cent or more, would increase further. Similarly, the Panel must be consulted where a person or a group of persons acting in concert is interested in shares carrying 30 per cent or more (but does not hold shares carrying more than 50 per cent) of the voting rights of a company, and it is proposed that an EBT acquires an interest in shares. The mere establishment and operation of an EBT will not by itself give rise to a presumption that the trustees are acting in concert with the directors and/or a controller (or group of persons acting in concert). However, the Panel will consider all relevant factors in making their determination, including the non-exhaustive list contained in Note 5.

4.2.3 Dispensations from Rule 9

The Code acknowledges that in certain circumstances it would be inequitable, and therefore unnecessary in order to satisfy the equality of treatment principle, to require a mandatory bid to be made.

There is a specific dispensation at the end of Rule 9.1 for control achieved through a voluntary bid. In addition, there are a series of notes (Dispensation Notes) at the end of Rule 9 which list six situations in which the Panel may, or will, dispense with the need to make an offer. These are as follows.

4.2.3.1 The "Whitewash" procedure

The Whitewash dispensation is available on the issue of new securities, either as consideration for an acquisition or on a cash subscription. Where such an issue is of such a size that it would otherwise trigger a Rule 9 bid, the Panel will normally waive the obligation to make the bid if the requirements of Dispensation Note 1 and of Appendix 1 to the Code are complied with. Particular features of these requirements (which are additional to those of the UK Listing Authority (the UKLA)) are:

1. the issue must be approved at a shareholders' meeting of the company issuing the securities, the vote must be conducted by poll rather than a show of hands, and only independent shareholders may vote;
2. the circular to shareholders convening the meeting must give full details of the transaction, comply with the detailed requirements of para.4 of Appendix 1 as to its contents, contain a number of warnings and include competent independent advice on the proposals. It is noteworthy that a Whitewash circular is one of the few documents that the Panel insists it must approve before it is sent to shareholders; and
3. the Whitewash dispensation is not normally available if there have been "disqualifying" acquisitions of interests in shares of the company during the preceding 12 months by the person or persons to whom the new securities are to be issued (or persons acting in concert with it or them) and those dealings occurred after discussions on the trans-action to be approved by the Whitewash had begun (see para.3 of Appendix 1).

The philosophy behind this dispensation is that the vote gives independent shareholders the opportunity to veto the change of control before it takes place. Further, if there is a premium for control involved it accrues to the company, and therefore to all shareholders, rather than to a selling shareholder.

Consistent with this philosophy, the persons to whom the new shares are to be issued (and persons acting in concert with them) may not otherwise acquire any interest in shares in the company during the period between posting of the circular and the time shareholders' approval is obtained. Once approval has been obtained, there is no restriction (apart from those restrictions applying generally by virtue of Rules 5 and 9) on such persons acquiring any interest in other shares in the company (save that where shareholders approve the issue of convertible securities, options or warrants where no immediate voting rights are obtained, any further acquisition of shares should be discussed with the Panel to establish the number of shares to which the waiver will be deemed to apply given that the number of shares to be issued on conversion or exercise (as applicable) may be uncertain).

4.2.3.2   Enforcement of security for a loan

Where shares or other securities are pledged as security for a loan and the lender enforces as a result of the borrower's default, the lender may find itself (either alone or with persons with whom it is in concert) holding an interest in shares carrying more than 30 per cent of the voting rights. Where the threshold is crossed purely as a result of such an enforcement, the Panel will not normally require the lender to make a mandatory offer provided that a sufficient number of the shares over which it has an interest are sold within a limited period to persons unconnected with the lender. In order to prevent the lender exercising control, it must consult with the Panel as to the ability to exercise its voting rights prior to such a sale.

The Panel will apply similar principles to the appointment of a receiver, an administrator or a liquidator. That person will not normally be required to make a mandatory offer, but a purchaser from him will be subject to Rule 9.

4.2.3.3   Rescue operations

Where a company is insolvent or prospectively insolvent because it is undercapitalised, the directors will obviously wish to restore it to solvency, either by issuing new shares in exchange for new cash or by arranging with certain of its loan creditors to exchange their debt for shares. Usually its financial difficulties will be such that its existing equity shares are worth little, so that meaningful new capital is likely to represent more than 30 per cent of the voting share capital after the rescue.

However, sometimes the financial crisis may be such that there is no time to go through the Whitewash procedure before the directors would have to call in the receiver. Dispensation Note 3 indicates that in such circumstances the Panel may, out of financial necessity, waive the need for a mandatory bid without the need for a Whitewash resolution provided that shareholder approval is given for the rescue operation as soon as possible after it has happened or the Panel is satisfied that some other provision is made for the protection of independent shareholders. If neither of these solutions is available, the rescuer will be required to make a mandatory offer, although the Panel may consider an adjustment to the highest price required for such offer by Rule 9.5(a).

4.2.3.4   *Inadvertent mistake*

Dispensation Note 4 acknowledges that sometimes there may be a crossing of the 30 per cent threshold as a result of an innocent mistake. In that event the Panel will not normally require a mandatory offer if the holding is within a short period reduced to below 30 per cent by sales to persons unconnected with the purchaser (or the percentage of shares carrying voting rights in which the person, together with persons acting in concert with him, is interested in is otherwise reduced to below 30 per cent in a manner satisfactory to the Panel). In order to prevent any such person exercising control in the meantime, the Panel must be consulted as to the ability to exercise voting rights prior to such sales.

It should be noted that a dispensation is not necessarily available if a purchaser knowingly acquires an interest in shares carrying more than 30 per cent of the voting rights on the basis that it will place out a sufficient percentage of this interest to reduce its holding to below 30 per cent. Note 7 to Rule 9.1 envisages situations in which dispensation may be given in such circumstances, but if the Panel regards it as a situation in which a premium has been paid for control it may require a mandatory offer to be made.

4.2.3.5 *Where 50 per cent will not accept*

Dispensation Note 5 acknowledges that there is no point in making a mandatory offer if persons holding shares carrying 50 per cent or more of the voting rights state in writing that they will not accept it. This is because it is pointless to make the offer if the acceptance condition will not be satisfied. However, the Panel must be consulted so that it can be assured of the factual background.

4.2.3.6 *Enfranchisement of non-voting shares*

If a person crosses a Rule 9 threshold as a result of non-voting shares in which it is already interested being enfranchised, Dispensation Note 6 provides that it will not be required to make a mandatory offer unless shares or interests in shares have been acquired at a time when it had reason to believe that enfranchisement would take place. This dispensation reflects the fact that the person has not crossed the threshold by a voluntary act.

4.2.4 *Redemption or purchase by a company of its own shares*

The position where a person's interest in shares is caused to cross the threshold by reason of a redemption or purchase of its own shares by the company itself is covered by Rule 37.1 rather than a Dispensation Note to Rule 9. Rule 37.1 states that subject to prior consultation with the Panel, the Panel will normally waive an obligation to make a mandatory offer arising by a person's interest in shares crossing the relevant mandatory offer threshold by reason of a redemption or purchase of own shares, provided that there is a vote of independent sharehold-ers and a procedure similar to that of the Whitewash procedure (see 4.2.3.1 above) is followed. Persons typically caught by Rule 37.1 are usually only directors and their concert parties. The removal in August 1998 of the one per cent "creeper" provisions (see 4.2 above) resulted in a number of perceived difficulties in the application of Rule 37.1, particularly as regards directors. Following a detailed review, the Panel's policy is now set out in Panel Statement 1999/17.

4.2.5 *Other points in relation to Rule 9*

4.2.5.1 *Who must make the offer*

The person whose acquisition causes the 30 per cent threshold to be crossed or who acquires an interest in further shares triggering a Rule 9 obligation has primary responsibility to make the bid (Rule 9.1). However, Rule 9.2 provides that where there is a concert party the principal members of the party may also be obliged to make the offer depending on the circumstances of the case. The Note to Rule 9.2 provides some guidance, but consultation with the Panel as to who should make the bid where there is a concert party is highly desirable. The person required to make a mandatory offer may extend the offer to other concert parties, but will not normally be required to do so.

4.2.5.2 *The chain principle*

If a person or group of persons acquires shares resulting in a holding of over 50 per cent of the voting rights of any company which is interested, either directly or through intermediate companies, in shares of a second company, the Panel may require a mandatory bid if such a bid would have been triggered if that person or group of persons had directly acquired the interest in the shares of the second company owned by the first company. Generally speaking, however, the Panel will not apply this principle (which is set out in Note 8 to Rule 9.1) unless either the interest in shares which the first company has in the second company is significant in relation to the first company (taking account of a number of factors including, as appropriate, the assets, profits and market values of the respective companies, with relative values of 50 per cent or more normally regarded as significant), or unless securing control of the second company might reasonably be considered to be a significant purpose of acquiring control of the first company. The Panel should be consulted in any relevant case.

4.2.5.3   *Triggering Rule 9 during the course of a voluntary offer*

Rule 5.2 may in certain circumstances, subject as set out in the next paragraph in the case of a scheme, permit a voluntary offeror to take its interest in shares in the offeree above the 30 per cent threshold during an offer period (although Note 4 to Rule 32.1, which only applies to contractual offers, may preclude it from doing so unless the offer can remain open for acceptance for at least 14 further days following the date on which the amended offer document is posted). The obvious situation in which an offeror might want to trigger a Rule 9 bid would be one where it felt obliged to pick up a parcel of shares overhanging the market. If it does so, it must immediately waive all conditions other than those permitted by Rule 9 and must announce the mandatory offer immediately. If a voluntary offeror (or any person acting in concert with it) wishes to make such an acquisition, Note 9 to Rule 9.1 requires the Panel to be consulted in advance.

Note 2 on Section 2 of Appendix 7 of the Code provides that, where a voluntary offer is proceeding by way of a scheme of arrangement, the offeror (and persons acting in concert with it) must not acquire an interest in shares in the offeree company which would trigger a mandatory offer under Rule 9 unless it has first obtained the Panel's consent either to satisfy its obligation under Rule 9 by way of a scheme or to switch to a contractual offer. This reflects the requirement referred to above that a mandatory offer cannot be made by way of a scheme of arrangement without the prior consent of the Panel.

4.2.5.4   *Restrictions on exercise of control by an offeror*

Rule 9.7 provides that where the Panel has required a person who has triggered a Rule 9 obligation to dispose of interests in shares as an alternative to making a mandatory offer, and in certain other specified circumstances, the Panel must be consulted as to the application, pending completion of the disposal, of restrictions on the exercise of voting rights attaching to the shares in which the offeror and its concert parties are interested. The Note to Rule 9.7 provides guidance on the number of shares to which voting restrictions will normally be applied. The Panel has confirmed that any restrictions imposed on a person under Rule 9.7 will necessarily result in a proportionate increase in the percentage of voting rights exercisable by independent shareholders that are not subject to such restrictions (Takeover Panel Statement 2013/2).

4.2.5.5 *Convertible securities, warrants and options*

Generally speaking, the acquisition of securities convertible into, warrants in respect of, or options or other rights to subscribe for, new shares does not give rise to an obligation to make a general offer under Rule 9, although the subsequent exercise of the conversion or subscription rights or options will be treated as an acquisition of an interest in the shares for the purposes of the Rule. Even then the exercise of those conversion or subscription rights will not usually be regarded as triggering a general offer if the issue of the convertible securities or subscription rights was approved by a Whitewash procedure, unless there have been intervening acquisitions of further interests in voting shares.

If a fund management organisation (or persons under the same control as it) hold convertibles, options, warrants or other rights to subscribe for shares carrying voting rights in an investment company or investment trust at the time of its IPO, which on exercise or conversion (as appropriate) would otherwise result in a mandatory offer obligation being triggered, no such obligation will normally arise provided that the terms have been disclosed in the prospectus (and such disclosure has been approved by the Panel) (see Panel Practice Statement No.12).

Any holder of conversion or subscription rights who intends to exercise such rights and will, as a result, become interested in shares carrying 30 per cent or more of the voting rights of a company must consult the Panel before doing so to determine whether a mandatory offer obligation would arise under Rule 9 and if so at what price?

4.2.5.6 *The "bounceback" principle*

A person's interest in shares can be reduced by a number of events, such as a sale by it or an issue of further shares by the company itself or a transfer by the company of shares out of treasury. If the effect of this event is to reduce its interest in shares to below 30 per cent of the voting rights, it will still have to make a mandatory offer if it subsequently makes a further acquisition and as a result the number of shares in which it is interested would, once again, carry more than 30 per cent of the voting rights (unless it qualifies for one of the dispensations). It is treated for all purposes as starting from the base of its reduced percentage and subsequently crossing the 30 per cent threshold by voluntary action. These principles, which are referred to in Note 11 to Rule 9.1, can give rise to practical difficulties and again consultation with the Panel will usually be required.

Note 11 to Rule 9.1 permits, in limited circumstances, acquisitions by persons (or groups of persons acting in concert) who are interested in shares carrying more than 30 per cent of the voting rights of a company. If such a person or group of persons reduces its interest but not to less than 30 per cent, then they may subsequently acquire an interest in further shares, subject to the following restrictions, without incurring an obligation to make a general offer:

1. the total number of shares in which interests may be acquired in any period of 12 months must not exceed one per cent of the voting share capital for the time being (and reductions cannot be netted off against acquisitions for these purposes); and
2. the percentage of shares in which the relevant person or group of persons acting in concert is interested following any acquisition must not exceed the highest percentage of

shares in which such person or group of persons was interested in the previous 12 months.

The Panel will regard a reduction of the percentage of shares in which the person or group is interested as a result of dilution following the new issue of shares as also being relevant for these purposes. However, where an existing shareholder participates in a placing then the Panel will look at the shareholder's percentage interest following completion of the placing, rather than treating it as a reduction in percentage interest followed by a subsequent increase.

4.2.5.7 *Gifts*

Note 12 to Rule 9.1 requires the Panel to be consulted if a person receives a gift of shares or an interest in shares which takes the aggregate number of shares in which he is interested to 30 per cent or more.

4.2.5.8 *Insincere Rule 9 bids*

A mandatory offer may also be triggered, for example, by an existing major shareholder who acquires a block of shares to increase their holding in the offeree company but does not necessarily want to acquire the rest of the share capital or during the course of, for example, a management buy-in by an entrepreneur who needs a listed vehicle and who has to buy more than 30 per cent of a listed company, but where acceptances are placed out in order to secure a sufficient spread of shareholdings to maintain a quotation; these bids are generally known as insincere Rule 9 bids. An insincere Rule 9 bid is treated in the same way as any other Rule 9 bid for the purposes of the Code. There has been some recent debate about the impact of insincere Rule 9 bids and whether the existing system offers enough protection to minority shareholders in these circumstances, in particular where the insincere Rule 9 bid may result in de-listing of the offeree company were sufficient shareholders to accept it and shareholders may therefore feel obliged to accept rather than risk being left holding shares in an unlisted company.

4.2.6   Practical effects of Rule 9

Rule 9 has three important effects in practice:

1. it discourages a holding of interests in shares which carry more than 29.99 per cent of the voting rights of a company;
2. it discourages a voluntary offeror from making a market purchase permitted by Rule 5.2 if it wants to maintain a full set of conditions to its offer; and
3. it encourages persons who might be in concert and who are close to (or over) the 30 per cent threshold to consult the Panel.

For the above reasons Rule 9 bids are not frequent.

4.3   The voluntary offer and its terms

In accordance with Rule 2.7(c)(iii) an offeror is required to announce all the conditions of an offer at the time that a firm intention to make a bid is announced. Generally speaking, the conditions attaching to an offer to purchase the share capital of an offeree company are a matter for the offeror. However, the Code does impose certain restrictions so as to ensure that its General Principles are honoured.

4.3.1   When a particular form of consideration is required

Rule 11.1 requires an offer to be in cash, or have a cash alternative, if:

1. the offeror and its concert parties have acquired interests in shares of any class under offer in the offeree company during the offer period or within the preceding 12 months for cash, and the interests so acquired carry 10 per cent or more of the voting rights currently exercisable at a class meeting of that class (in which case the cash price offered must be not less than the highest price paid during such period);

2. any interest in shares of any class under offer in the offeree company is acquired for cash by an offeror or any person acting in concert with it during the offer period (in which case the cash price offered must be not less than the highest price paid during such period); or
3. in the view of the Panel there are circumstances which render such a course necessary in order to give effect to General Principle 1.

This requirement is additional to the minimum value requirement contained in Rule 6 (see Ch.3).

The Notes to the Rule contain guidance on how the price paid for any acquisition of an interest in shares (either through the direct purchase of shares or through entering into an option or derivative) will be determined. There is also particular guidance in relation to the conversion or exercise of securities convertible into, warrants in respect of, or options or other rights to subscribe for, new shares.

There are a number of other important points contained in the Notes to Rule 11.1. Note 2 provides that the Panel will not normally allow sales to be netted off against acquisitions in calculating the 10 per cent limit. Note 5 indicates that acquisitions of interests in shares in exchange for securities will normally be deemed to be acquisitions for cash on the basis of the value of the securities at the time of the acquisition (unless the recipient is required to hold the securities received or receivable until either the offer has lapsed or consideration has been posted to accepting shareholders). Note 8 provides guidance as to how the percentages are calculated if there is a rights issue in progress.

It is important to note that Rule 11.1 can be triggered after the offer period commences, although the Notes to Rule 32.1 contain restrictions on this in the 14 days before the last date on which the offer can become unconditional as to acceptances (in the case of a scheme of arrangement, Section 7 of Appendix 7 contains a similar restriction, requiring Panel consent before any revision can be made in the 14 days before the date of the shareholder meetings to implement the scheme). If an acquisition of an interest in shares is made which triggers Rule 11.1 at a time when there is a cash alternative which is not lower than the acquisition price, there is no problem. If there is no cash alternative, Note 6 requires an immediate announcement of the necessary revision of the offer to include a cash alternative at not less than the transaction price. Similarly there must be a revision and an immediate announcement if the transaction price exceeds the present offer price. Difficulties can arise if it is a person deemed to be in concert with the offeror, rather than the offeror itself, which makes an acquisition which triggers the Rule; in the Guinness/Distillers bid a purchase of shares in Distillers at above the bid price was made by a party which the Panel ruled, after completion of the bid, to have been in concert with Guinness; the Panel ruled (Panel Statement 1989/13) that Guinness should top up, by payments to Distillers' former shareholders, its purchase price to the level to which it would have been required to revise its offer by Rule 11.1.

The Rule is effectively an (albeit limited) exemption from General Principle 1, in that it enables an offeror to acquire an interest in shares for cash without making a cash alternative available to other shareholders provided that the aggregate interest acquired represents less than 10 per cent and no interest in shares is acquired for cash during the offer period. It is for this reason that Rule 11.1(c) envisages that there may be circumstances in which General Principle 1 requires there to be a cash alternative even if the 10 per cent threshold is not crossed. Note 4 indicates that this discretion will not normally be exercised unless the vendors or the parties to the transactions giving rise to the interests are directors of, or otherwise closely connected with, the offeror or the offeree company.

Rule 11.2 requires that, where interests in shares of any class of the offeree company carrying 10 per cent or more of the voting rights currently exercisable at a class meeting of that class have been acquired by an offeror and any person acting in concert with it in exchange for securities in the three months prior to the commencement of and during the offer period, such securities will normally be required to be offered to all other holders of shares of that class. Note 1 to Rule 11.2 provides that any securities required to be offered must be offered on the basis of the same number of consideration securities received or receivable by the vendor or other party to the transaction for each offeree company share rather than on the basis of securities equivalent to the value of the securities received or receivable at the time of the relevant acquisition.

Rule 11.3 enables an offeror to seek dispensation from the obligation to pay the highest price given during the relevant period and the Note to that Rule sets out the factors which the Panel might take into account when considering such an application. These factors are not expressed to be exhaustive; the Panel may take into account a substantial collapse in the offeree company's share price after the acquisitions were made as a result of new information about its business becoming publicly available where the acquisition had been made before these events.

4.3.2 The acceptance condition

In any contractual offer (as opposed to an offer effected by way of a scheme of arrangement) for voting equity share capital or for other transferable securities carrying voting rights, Rule 10 requires there to be an unwaivable condition that the offer will not become or be declared unconditional as to acceptances unless the offeror has acquired or agreed to acquire (either under the offer or otherwise) shares carrying over 50 per cent of the voting rights.

The rationale for the 50 per cent threshold for contractual offers is that the offeror will control the board of the offeree company, and thus have management control. The Panel normally regards 50.01 per cent control as determinative. In PCP 2010/2, the Panel consulted, amongst other things, on raising the minimum acceptance condition threshold. In Panel Statement 2010/22, the Panel confirmed that respondents were almost unanimously opposed to raising the minimum acceptance threshold on the basis that it is inextricably linked to the threshold for passing an ordinary resolution (which itself would enable Board changes to be made). In the Minorco/ Consgold bid, the Panel required Consgold to withdraw a US anti-trust action once Minorco held over 50 per cent, even though the directors of Consgold had received Counsel's opinion that having decided that the action was in the interests of Consgold they were not free as a matter of law to change their position without there being a relevant change in the interests of the company (which did not mean the interests of the majority shareholder).

Note 1 envisages that there can be certain exceptional circumstances where Rule 10 can be waived, but it would be important to consult the Panel at the earliest stage in such a situation. If an offeror wished to acquire less than 50 per cent it might consider the alternative of making a partial offer under Rule 36 (see Ch.5).

In the 1995 Granada/Forte bid, such dispensation was granted by the Panel. The Council of Forte, although holding less than 0.1 per cent of Forte's shares, held a majority of the voting rights in Forte. Rule 10 requires that an offeror acquires over 50 per cent of voting rights before a bid can be declared unconditional. However, when Granada made the initial offer it was unclear whether the Council would be legally able to accept the offer. The Panel agreed that Granada could make its offer conditional on acceptance by a majority of ordinary shareholders.

Note 2 to the Rule requires the offeror to take account in its acceptance condition of all shares carrying voting rights which are unconditionally allotted or issued before the offer becomes or is declared unconditional as to acceptances. By implication it does not allow the condition to take into account shares which can be issued as a result of conversion rights or options being exercised after the offer closes. It is a common feature of conversion rights and share option schemes that they can be exercised in connection with a takeover and normally these rights will persist for a period after the offer closes.

The difficulties which this can cause were illustrated in the Boots offer for Ward White in 1989. Ward White had a class of convertible preference shares which, if fully converted, would have increased the ordinary share capital of Ward White by more than 40 per cent. Boots made offers, each subject to a separate acceptance condition, for both the convertible preference shares and the ordinary shares. The last date for lodging conversion notices was the day before the last day on which Boots could (by virtue of Rule 31.6) declare its offers unconditional as to acceptances (failing which declaration its bids would have to lapse). The question arose as to whether ordinary shares which would in due course be allotted on conversion, but which could not yet be allotted, should or should not be taken into account in deciding whether the acceptance condition in the offer for the ordinary shares was satisfied. A decision either way could have produced a bizarre result, depending upon patterns of exercise of the conversion rights which could not be known when the Panel had to make its decision. The difficulties inherent in deciding which approach was preferable were indicated by the fact that the Panel Executive's ruling was reversed by the full Panel on appeal, who decided that the literal interpretation of Note 2 should be followed and that only ordinary shares actually allotted could be taken into account.

This ruling (Panel Statement 1989/15) makes it important that offerors carefully consider all potential subscription and conversion rights when framing and deciding upon the timing of their offers. In order to ensure that an offeror has sufficient information for this purpose, Note 3 to Rule 10 requires the offeree company to provide all such information to an offeror on request.

Given the number of respects in which a 50 per cent level of acceptances triggers actions under the Code, and also the psychological effect of an offeror announcing that it has achieved over 50 per cent acceptances, the Panel attaches considerable importance to the verification of acceptances. In 1988, Blue Circle declared its bid for Birmid Qualcast unconditional as to acceptances when it thought it had attained that

197

level, but in fact had not done so because of a mistaken double counting. In the aftermath of that bid the Panel introduced a number of detailed provisions relating to the verification of acceptances, which are set out in Notes 4–7 to Rule 10 and in the Receiving Agents' Code of Practice set out in Appendix 4 to the Code.

One feature of these provisions is that an offeror's receiving agent can only treat an acceptance as valid if it is accompanied by the relevant share certificate, or in the absence of such a certificate, specified confirmatory documentation. This Rule reflects the basic equitable principle that a vendor's inability to produce his share certificate puts his purchaser on notice that there might be inconsistent proprietary rights. In the case of shares held through CREST, proof of ownership of shares in dematerialised form is provided electronically to the offeror's receiving agent.

Notwithstanding that Rule 10 only requires a 50 per cent acceptance condition, it is usual for offer documents to specify a 90 per cent level in the acceptance condition. This level is chosen because it is the threshold at which the compulsory purchase provisions of Ch.3, Pt 28 of the Companies Act 2006 can apply. Attainment of that level also facilitates the conversion of the offeree company to a private company, able to take advantage of the more liberal regime in UK companies legislation for private companies, following completion of the takeover. However, such conditions retain to the offeror the right to waive that condition down to a lower level, subject to the Rule 10 minimum of over 50 per cent. An offeror may choose to declare the offer unconditional as to acceptances once the 50 per cent level has been obtained so as to accelerate further acceptances, although this is very much a tactical consideration. For example, financiers of a bid (particularly where the bid is highly leveraged, such as in most MBOs) may require a guarantee and supporting charges from the offeree company; this can only be given after the offeree has become a private company and is no longer subject to the financial assistance prohibition applicable to public companies under the Companies Act 2006. Generally speaking, it is necessary to be certain that the compulsory purchase provisions can be activated to achieve this, and in such cases it may not be possible to waive the 90 per cent level (this is because the holders of five per cent or more of the offeree company could in theory apply to the court for cancellation of any special resolution passed to convert the offeree into a private company). Another possibility might be where the offeree company is in financial or other difficulty and unfettered control is considered necessary.

Where an offer includes shares held by the offeree company in treasury, the offeree company is not permitted to accept the offer until after it has become unconditional as to acceptances (Rule 4.5), so treasury shares cannot be used to meet the 50 per cent acceptance condition.

Rule 10 does not apply to an offer effected by way of a scheme of arrangement. This is because schemes of arrangement do not involve approval by individual shareholders; instead they require approval by offeree shareholders being a majority in number of those voting, representing at least 75 per cent in nominal value of shares voted, at a shareholders' meeting at which only independent shareholders may vote, with subsequent sanction by the court. Once a scheme has obtained shareholder approval and court sanction and has become effective, all offeree shareholders are bound so that the issues referred to above relating to non-accepting shareholders do not apply.

4.3.3 *Other conditions*

Offer documents in voluntary bids usually contain very detailed conditions. They need to be identified at the earliest stage, since Rule 2.7(c)(iii) requires all conditions to be identified when a firm intention to make an offer is announced.

These conditions generally fall into three categories, namely those:

1. requiring specific action in order to enable the offer to proceed;
2. concerning possible governmental action or regulatory action which might be triggered by the offer; and
3. giving the offeror the opportunity to withdraw if there is material adverse change in relation to the offeree company.

4.3.3.1 *Conditions requiring specific action*

If the takeover is a Class 1 transaction for the offeror, or if an offeror is offering shares and its directors' share issuing powers are insufficient to implement the offer, the offeror will have to make its offer conditional upon the necessary resolutions of its own shareholders.

It is standard practice for offeror shareholder resolutions to approve not only the offer but also any increased or revised offer approved by the offeror's board. This is both to give the offeror flexibility and because the Code timetable might render it impracticable to convene another general meeting to seek further shareholder approval. However, as a result of a change to the UKLA's Listing Rules made in 2007, a further shareholder authority will be required where the takeover constitutes a Class 1 transaction for the offeror and it proposes to increase the consideration payable under the offer by 10 per cent or more or make any other material change to the terms of the transaction.

Where offeror shares are to be issued by way of consideration, a listing for them will have to be a condition. Where a cash bid is being financed by the issue of offeror securities, the bid may only be conditional on matters that are necessary, as a matter of law or regulatory requirement, to issue those securities (Rule 13.4). Generally the only permissible conditions will be the passing of any necessary shareholder resolution and listing of the securities. It will not be appropriate, therefore, for the offer to be conditional upon any placing, underpinning or under-writing agreement in relation to the issue of the new securities becoming unconditional and/or not being terminated. A condition of this nature is not necessary as a matter of law or regulatory requirement in order to issue the new securities or, therefore, to implement the offer. The Panel has said that where an offer lapses or is withdrawn as a result of a failure to fulfil a condition relating to the issue of offeror securities where such issue was to finance the offer, it will want to be satisfied that on announcement, the offeror and its financial adviser had every reason to believe that it could, and would continue to be able to, implement the offer (in accordance with Rule 2.7(a)). The Panel also stated that it will need to be satisfied that the offeror used all reasonable efforts to ensure the satisfaction of the condition as required by Rule 13.5(b) (See Panel Practice Statement No.10).

When the offer is conditional on an offeror shareholder approval, as a result of a change in circumstances the offeror directors may determine that they are no longer able to recommend that shareholders approve the necessary resolution. In those circumstances the Panel will be concerned to ensure that, in making the bid, the offeror complied with the provisions of General Principle 5 and Rule 2.7(a) and had given the proposed offer careful and responsible consideration before announcement and having done so had no reason to believe it would not be able to implement it. Subject to this, the Panel may, in appropriate circumstances, agree to the bid being withdrawn (such as in WM Low's lapsed bid for Budgens in 1989) or, with the consent of the target, to a revised and lower bid (such as in the 2008 bid by Lloyds TSB for HBOS).

If the offeree company has already put proposals to its own shareholders for some transaction or other, it is permissible to make it a condition of the bid that the proposals are approved, or alternatively voted down. For example, in 2003 Capital Management & Investment, the bid vehicle of Hugh Osmond, made its bid for Six Continents conditional on Six Continents' shareholders not approving the proposed demerger of Six Continents' pub and hotel businesses (and its bid lapsed when the demerger proposals were approved). If such a transaction is proposed by the offeree company's board to its shareholders after the bid is announced, this situation will normally be covered by one of the conditions referred to in 4.3.3.3 below.

If the offeree company's Articles of Association contain restrictions on the ownership of shares, these will need to be amended before the bid can be completed.

4.3.3.2 Regulatory matters

Where some form of licence is fundamental to the offeree company's business, the confirmation of the relevant regulatory authority's approval to the change of control is usually made a specific condition.

Bids will usually contain a condition about merger clearance from the UK (or, where relevant, EU) competition authorities (a condition which supplements the Rule 12 provision referred to in 4.4 below) and those involving an important US dimension will refer to the expiry of all US anti-trust waiting periods.

Such specific provisions are usually backed up by more general provisions referring to all necessary official authorisations being obtained and no adverse regulatory action being taken. Such regulatory action, particularly when taken overseas, is in many ways analogous to the situation which can arise in relation to a UK or EU reference for an in-depth competition investigation. There is, however, an important difference between what happens to a bid if there is a reference to competition authorities of the kind envisaged in Rule 12 and what happens if there is a reference to a regulatory authority only covered by the more general condition. This is because, if a bid lapses as a result of a "Rule 12 reference", the offeror must normally clarify its intentions (by either announcing a firm intention to make an offer or making a no bid statement) within 21 days of obtaining merger clearance from the UK or EU competition authorities, whereas if an offeror lapses its offer because of another type of regulatory reference it is precluded by Rule 35.1 from re-bidding within 12 months unless the Panel gives it dispensation.

This distinction did not make any difference in the 1989 Hoylake bid for BAT. BAT had an insurance subsidiary in the United States and various US regulatory reviews were instituted, as a result of which Hoylake had to lapse its bid. The regulatory procedures having been completed, Hoylake requested Rule 35.1 dispensation in order to re-bid. This was given (Panel Statements 1989/20 and 1989/21) on the basis that the new bid would have to follow exactly the same shortened timetable as applies when a bid which has lapsed under Rule 12 is remade. The analogy with the Rule 12 situation was clear in this bid, but may not always be so; Note (b) to Rules 35.1 and 35.2 encourages reference to the Panel as soon as possible where delays in regulatory reviews become apparent.

Another important distinction is that the restrictions on invoking conditions referred to in 4.3.4 below will not apply to UK or EU competition conditions. This means that a bidder may invoke such a condition without restriction, whereas in invoking a regulatory condition a bidder will have to comply with the materiality test contained in Rule 13.5.

4.3.3.3 *Material change in circumstances conditions*

Such conditions perform a very important function, at least in theory, because (if the offeror cannot lapse its bid under the acceptance condition or Rule 12) they give the offeror its only opportunity to walk away from the bid if it finds something seriously amiss with the offeree company's business in the course of the takeover. It has no opportunity to exact warranties, and where the bid is not recommended will have had no opportunity to conduct a due diligence exercise. Further, an offeree company is likely to publish more information during the course of a takeover bid than it would normally do—indeed it is obliged by General Principle 2 and Rule 23 to give shareholders sufficient information to enable them to reach a properly informed decision on the bid and not to withhold relevant information from them. Apart from this, offeree companies tend to become subjected to heavy press scrutiny. Much about the offeree's business will therefore become public knowledge during the course of the bid, and if the information is bad news the offeror will want the opportunity to withdraw.

Material change conditions will usually cover a number of situations, including transactions outside the ordinary course of business, litigation, the discovery of provisions of loan documents or contractual obligations which would restrict completion of the bid or affect the offeree company's business and compliance with environmental laws.

The words "material" and "adverse" appear with some regularity in these conditions, as they do in certain regulatory conditions. This, and indeed the general approach to regulatory and material change conditions, is governed by two requirements of Rule 13. The first of these requirements is that an offer must not normally be subject to conditions which depend solely on subjective judgments by the directors of the offeror. It is acknowledged in the Rule that elements of subjectivity are unavoidable in certain circumstances, but it is clear that the Panel will expect to be consulted unless such conditions follow the usual form. The second requirement is covered in 4.3.4 below.

4.3.4 Invoking conditions

Rule 13.5 provides that an offeror should not invoke a condition (other than an acceptance condition or a condition included pursuant to Rule 12) so as to cause its offer to lapse or to be withdrawn unless the circumstances which give rise to a right to invoke the condition are of material significance to the offeror in the context of the offer. Practitioners were reminded that the Panel may restrict the circumstances in which a condition may be invoked in the Corporate Services Group (CSG) case (Panel Statement 1999/7) where an offeror made an offer conditional on there being no changes to the board of CSG, and later sought to invoke the condition following certain board changes. The Panel Executive ruled that the condition could not be invoked because the changes could not be regarded as sufficiently material.

The issue was looked at again by the Panel in connection with the offer by WPP for Tempus (Panel Statement 2001/15). The Panel met on October 31, 2001 to hear an appeal by WPP against the Panel Executive's refusal to allow WPP to invoke the material adverse change condition in relation to its offer for Tempus. WPP was of the view that there had been a material adverse change in the prospects of Tempus after the announcement of WPP's offer and, in particular, following the events in the United States on September 11, 2001.

It was agreed between the parties that the issue for the Panel was whether WPP had established that there had been a material adverse change in the prospects of Tempus which was of material significance to WPP in the context of its offer for Tempus. There was disagreement, however, about the definition of "material" for these purposes.

The Panel received submissions in relation to the various commercial issues, including in relation to the prospects of Tempus and its profitability. The Panel also had regard to the rationale for the acquisition as expressed in the WPP offering documentation.

As regards "materiality" the Panel took the view that meeting the test specified in the Code requires an adverse change of very considerable significance striking at the heart of the purpose of the transaction in question, analogous to something that would justify frustration of a legal contract. The Panel took the view that to accept a lower test would allow an offeror to use a material adverse change condition to defeat the object of the Code Rules and previously expressed Panel policy. The Panel, accordingly, did not accept the test proposed by WPP that it is sufficient if there has been "a change which undermines, from the offeror's perspective, the rationale for having made the offer at the price and on the terms specified".

The Panel did consider that a change in general economic circumstances may legitimately be relied upon when seeking to invoke the relevant condition, but only if and to the extent that the requirements mentioned above are met.

The Panel's conclusion is worth noting:

"For an offeror to invoke a material adverse change condition and so withdraw its offer requires, in the opinion of the Panel, the offeror to demonstrate to the Panel that exceptional circumstances have arisen affecting the offeree company which could not have reasonably been foreseen at the time of the announcement of the offer. The effect of the circumstances in point must be sufficiently adverse to meet the high test of materiality [mentioned above] and judged, at least in the present type of case, not in terms of short-term profitability but on their effect on the longer-term prospects of the offeree company. Indeed, as WPP made clear it was the longer-term prospects of Tempus which had provided the strategic rationale for the offer and this seemed to the Panel to be central to the value which WPP placed on Tempus at that time.

The Panel considered the submissions of the parties and the arguments they made at the time of the hearing, including but not limited to the basis of the attempts to predict the future profits of Tempus, the longer term effects of the events of September 11 on Tempus, the general economic decline affecting the advertising industry before and after the posting of the offer and the strategic reasons for WPP's offer for Tempus. The Panel came to the conclusion, on the evidence before it, that WPP had failed to demonstrate that... there was a material adverse change in the context of the bid such as to entitle them to invoke the material adverse change condition, and had so failed by a considerable margin. The appeal, therefore, failed."

WPP's arguments would not have been assisted by the market purchases of Tempus shares which it made on September 17. However, the Panel's ruling is not based on those purchases.

The Panel Executive issued Practice Statement No.5 in April 2004 which clarified the statement it had made that the test of "material significance" required an adverse change that was "analogous... to something that would justify frustration of a legal contract". Some practitioners had interpreted this to mean that an offeror would need to demonstrate legal frustration in order to be able to invoke a condition to an offer. The Panel Executive confirmed that although the standard required is high, it does not require the offeror to demonstrate frustration in the legal sense.

In August 2004 the Code Committee issued Panel Consultation Paper 2004/4 which contained a number of proposed changes to the Code relating to conditions. In this paper the Code Committee considered whether the strict test for invoking conditions contained in Note 2 to Rule 13 (now Rule 13.5) should apply to bespoke conditions, which may have been heavily negotiated between the offeror and the offeree. Although the Code Committee concluded that Note 2 on Rule 13 should apply in all cases, a new Note to Rule 13 was proposed which would make it clear that in determining whether a condition can be invoked the Panel should be able to take account of whether or not the condition was the subject of negotiation, whether the condition was expressly drawn to the offeree company shareholders' attention in the offer document and its consequences clearly explained and whether the condition was included to take account of the particular nature of the business of the offeree company. This proposal was, however, withdrawn by the Code Committee following consultation, largely on the basis that inclusion of a list of specific factors to be taken into account might result in undue weight being given to those factors. Nevertheless, the Committee reiterated that the factors listed above remain of general relevance.

An example of where the Panel did allow an offeror to invoke a condition under Rule 13.5(a) so as to lapse its offer was the Pension Corporation's bid for Telent which was announced in September 2007. In this case the offeror included in its offer a condition that no changes had been made to any relevant pension schemes. As well as being included with the other conditions in an appendix to the offer document, the condition (unlike any of the other conditions) was expressly referred to and brought to offeree shareholders' attention in the main body of the offer document. In the event, the Pensions Regulator replaced the trustees to the offeree's pension scheme with three of its own choice who could not be removed for six months. The replacement of the trustees could have been an obstacle to restructuring the pension scheme, which included a significant sum in an escrow account (more than the total value of the bid) and in these circumstances the Panel permitted the offeror to withdraw its offer (although in fact the offer was not ultimately withdrawn). Such examples are very rare and are likely to depend on the extent to which the factors referred to above are met in the particular circumstances.

An amendment to the Code made in April 2005 imposes an obligation on an offeror to use all reasonable efforts to ensure the timely satisfaction of the conditions to its offer (Rule 13.5(b)). This is to prevent an offeror seeking to cause a condition which is not subject to a materiality threshold (such as a condition included pursuant to Rule 12) not to be satisfied in order to lapse a bid where the offeror would be unable to rely on a material adverse change condition or other protective condition to do so.

The Panel Executive issued a further practice statement in April 2005 (Practice Statement No.11) regarding the acceptability of offer conditions relating to working capital requirements of the enlarged offer group after the completion of an offer. The Executive clarified that an offeror will not, other than in exceptional circumstances (such as those described in Rule 13.4(c) of the Code in relation to financing pre-conditions), be permitted to include such a condition to its offer and, if working capital concerns arise after announcement of the offer, the offeror will only be able to allow its offer to lapse if it is able to invoke one of the conditions to the offer in accordance with the application of Rule 13.5.

In some circumstances an offer will include conditions relating to the offeror which benefit the offeree company (known as "offeree protection conditions"), as well as standard conditions which benefit the offeror. Offeree protection conditions are generally only found in securities exchange offers, particularly where the offeror and offeree company are of a similar size. Rule 13.6, introduced in April 2005, provides that an offeree company should not invoke (or cause or permit the offeror to invoke) such a condition unless the circumstances which give rise to the right to invoke the condition are of material significance to the shareholders of the offeree company in the context of the offer. Note 1 to that Rule makes it clear, however, that the circumstances in which the Panel may permit an offeree company to invoke (or cause or permit the offeror to invoke) a condition are not necessarily the same as those in which an offeror would be permitted to invoke a condition. The Panel retains flexibility to consider each case on its merits, taking into account the circumstances giving rise to the right to invoke the condition, for example, the size of the offeree company relative to the offeror and the recommendation of the board of the offeree company may be a relevant consideration. Rather than simply having to decide whether an offer should lapse or not, Note 2 (which does not apply to an offer implemented by way of a scheme of arrangement) provides that the Panel should also have the flexibility to require, as an alternative, the introduction of withdrawal rights, so that shareholders who had accepted the relevant offer would be given a period of time to withdraw their acceptance.

Rule 35.1 reinforces Rule 13, in that an offeror which lapses its offer will, subject to certain exceptions set out in the notes to Rule 35, have to wait a year before bidding again.

An interesting insight into the Panel's attitude to such situations arose in the Severn Trent bid for Caird in 1990. Early in 1990 Caird had issued a profit forecast for the year. When Severn Trent announced its offer for Caird later in the year it made it a condition that the board of Caird would re-confirm the profit forecast. It did not, reducing the forecast downwards by some 15 per cent. Severn Trent decided to lapse its bid and applied to the Panel for dispensation under Rule 35.1 to re-bid at a lower price. In the meantime it had acquired more than 10 per cent of Caird's ordinary share capital in the market at its original offer price, so that the Panel would also have had to give dispensation under Rule 11.1. The Panel declined dispensation purely by reference to Rule 35.1. In its ruling (Panel Statement 1990/20) it noted that Severn Trent must have been somewhat sceptical as to the likelihood of the profit forecast being reaffirmed when it made that reaffirmation a condition of the bid; it did so aware of the provisions of Rule 35.1 and therefore must live with the consequences.

The question was looked at again in 1995 when the Panel was asked to permit Trafalgar House to make a new bid for Northern Electric following its decision to lapse its offer following a substantial fall in the market value of the Regional Electricity Companies as a result of a statement by Professor Littlechild, the Director General of the Office of Electricity Regulation. At the time it decided to lapse Trafalgar House held 76 per cent acceptances.

Trafalgar House submitted that the circumstances were so exceptional as to justify the Panel permitting a new offer. It contended that shareholder interests would best be served by a new offer. There was substantial shareholder support for a new offer. The Northern Electric Board stated it would not agree to a new offer until the regulatory uncertainty was removed. The Panel refused to consent to Trafalgar launching a new bid. Although unusual, the circumstances did not justify the granting of a dispensation under Rule 35.

4.4 Competition law issues

Offerors also have to consider the possible application of competition laws—in particular, UK merger control under the Enterprise Act 2002 and EU merger control under the EU Merger Regulation. The application of any merger control rules will at the very least have an impact on the timetable, especially if a Phase 2 investigation is opened by the UK or EU competition authorities.

There are specific jurisdictional tests for determining whether these merger control rules apply. The UK test is based on the UK turnover of the offeree company or the parties' shares of the supply of a particular good or service in (a substantial part of) the UK. The EU test is based on the parties' turnovers derived worldwide, within the European Union and within the individual EU Member States. A transaction may fall under either set of rules (and in limited circumstances under both). Generally, if the transaction falls within the scope of the EU merger control rules, the European Commission is granted exclusive jurisdiction over the transaction thereby precluding examination by the national competition authorities in the individual EU Member States. However, there are two exceptions, one of which allows the merger to be referred back to the national competition authorities and the other of which enables them to take parallel jurisdiction over certain aspects of the transaction. Also, in limited circumstances, the European Commission may be requested to review a transaction over which it does not otherwise have jurisdiction, instead of the national competition authorities.

Rule 12 requires every offer to which either of these competition regimes might be relevant to contain a term whereby it will lapse if, before the first closing date or the date when the offer becomes or is declared unconditional as to acceptances, whichever is the later (or, in the case of an offer implemented by way of a scheme of arrangement, before the shareholder meeting or meetings which will need to be held to approve the scheme):

1. the merger is referred to a Phase 2 investigation by the Competition and Markets Authority (CMA) in the UK; or
2. the European Commission initiates Phase 2 proceedings under the EU Merger Regulation, or refers the merger back to the United Kingdom and it is then referred to a Phase 2 investigation by the CMA.

Both the UK and the EU competition authorities are subject to timetables within which decisions on whether an in-depth competition investigation is to be opened must be taken, which

211

timetables do not necessarily tie in with the first closing date. Both authorities are well aware of the timetabling constraints of the Code, but cannot always meet them. If there is a delay the Panel will usually "freeze" the bid timetable at the request of either the offeror or the offeree company. If the competition authority concerned subsequently decides not to refer the transaction for a Phase 2 investigation, Note 3 to Rule 31.6 provides that the bid timetable will normally start again on the second day following the announcement of such decision.

If there is a Phase 2 investigation by either the UK or EU competition authorities, the offer must lapse, and there will usually be a lengthy period whilst the competition determination is being made. The underlying aims of the Code in such circumstances are to acknowledge that an offeror subject to such an investigation is in a similar position to a "potential offeror", to prevent a continuation of an offer campaign during this period and to ensure equality of information amongst competing offerors. During this period Rule 21 continues to apply, with limited exceptions. The requirements of the Code relating to the release of information by either the offeror or the offeree do not normally continue to apply, but Rule 19.7 provides that any statements made during such a period must be substantiated or withdrawn if the merger is subsequently cleared by the competition authorities and a further offer is made. Note 2 to Rule 12.2 sets out the other provisions of the Code which remain relevant, in most cases with some specific modifications. Where an offer was announced subject to a pre-condition relating to merger control clearance, the offer period will generally continue if there is a Phase 2 competition investigation, with the Code applying in the usual way, although Note 3 to Rule 12.2 provides that the Panel may grant dispensations from the applicable Rules if it would be proportionate in the circumstances to do so.

If the merger is cleared at the end of the in-depth competition investigation, Rule 12.2(b)(ii) provides that the offeror may make a new offer provided that it does so within 21 days after the announcement of the clearance decision. If the merger is prohibited, Rule 12.2(b)(iii) will prevent the offeror, together with any person acting in concert with it, from making a new offer for six months from the date of the decision.

Chapter 5

Provisions Applicable to all Offers, Partial Offers and Redemption or Purchase by a Company of its own Securities

Mark Gearing

Partner

Allen & Overy LLP

5.1   Introduction

This Chapter deals with three sections of the Takeover Code:

1. provisions applicable to all offers (Section H);
2. partial offers (Section P); and
3. redemption or purchase by a company of its own securities (Section Q).

The Rules of the Code, like the General Principles, are applied by the Panel in accordance with their spirit to achieve their underlying purpose. In order to understand the practical application of the Rules, it is therefore important to appreciate the spirit or philosophy underlying the particular Rules, and not just the precise wording used. A common purpose of the three sections covered by this Chapter is to ensure that offeree company (i.e. target) shareholders are treated fairly and that shareholders of the same class are afforded equivalent treatment. This reflects General Principle 1 and is one of the principal purposes of the Code as stated in its introduction.

5.2 Provisions applicable to all offers

Section H of the Code falls into two parts:

1. a substantive part, comprising Rules to ensure equivalent treatment (Rules 14 to 16); and
2. an administrative part, comprising Rules on the timing and content of announcements of acceptance levels and provisions relating to proxy forms (Rules 17 and 18).

5.2.1 Equivalent treatment

Rule 14 contains requirements for comparable offers where there is more than one class of equity share capital and Rule 15 contains requirements for appropriate offers for convertible securities (including warrants and options). Rule 16 prohibits special deals being made with certain shareholders (or other persons interested in shares carrying voting rights) which offer them favourable conditions. Rule 16 also contains special Rules for dealing, in particular, with management incentive arrangements.

5.2.1.1 Rule 14—comparable offers for different classes of equity

Rule 14.1 provides that, where an offeree company has more than one class of equity share capital, the offeror must make a comparable offer for each class, whether such class carries voting rights or not. If, however, an offer is made for non-voting shares only, it is not necessary to make an offer also for the voting class. This reflects the fact that the Code is principally concerned with the acquisition of voting control. The Panel requires prior consultation in all Rule 14 cases.

5.2.1.1.1 The meaning of "equity share capital"

If shares have uncapped rights to either dividends or capital, they will be equity share capital for the purposes of s.548 of the Companies Act 2006. The Code acknowledges, however, that the requirement to make a comparable offer need not apply to shares which are equity only on technical grounds. For instance, some shares which are designed to be equity share capital under the Companies Act may have extremely limited or remote equity rights. Unless a company is in financial difficulties, and there is a real possibility of a winding up, the existence or otherwise of uncapped rights to dividends (as opposed to capital) is likely to be the most relevant factor. If, for example, these rights are subject to the company first having to make an unrealistic level of profits (making the shares so-called "technical equity" only), the Panel will not usually regard the shares as equity for the purposes of Rule 14.1.

5.2.1.1.2 Conditionality

In order to save holders of non-voting (or limited voting) equity shares from being "stranded" because of low acceptances for that class, Rule 14.1 states that an offer for such shares should not be conditional upon any particular level of acceptances in respect of the class in question, or on the approval of that class, unless the offer for the voting equity is also conditional on the success of the offer for the non-voting (or limited voting) equity. In practice, therefore, such a condition in the offer for the voting equity cannot be waived unless the acceptance condition in the other offer is waived or deemed to be satisfied. An alternative is to include the acceptance condition for the non-voting equity in the conditions of the offer for the voting equity. The Code does not expressly prevent the offer for the non-voting equity share capital from being made subject to other conditions which are different and independent from those in the voting equity offer. Rule 14.2 provides that separate offers must be made for each class of shares.

5.2.1.1.3 Different classes of equity

In what circumstances can a company have more than one class of equity shares? In the case of certain companies, there may be one class of voting equity shares and another class of non-voting equity shares, or only limited voting, or perhaps weighted voting, equity shares. Other companies (principally investment trusts) divide their equity capital into income shares and capital shares with rights deferred to another class of equity.

There are a number of companies whose shares are admitted to trading on a UK regulated market (such as the Main Market of the London Stock Exchange) or multilateral trading facility (such as the London Stock Exchange's Alternative Investment Market, AIM) and which have two or more classes of publicly quoted equity shares. However, the Code applies more broadly to all public companies (including those without securities admitted to trading on a relevant public market), as well as to certain private companies where there has been some public involvement in the previous ten years, if they are registered in the United Kingdom, the Channel Islands or the Isle of Man and have their place of central management and control in one of those jurisdictions—see Section 3(a) of the Introduction to the Code, and also Response Statement 2012/3 for a synopsis of the types of company which are subject to the Code. There is, therefore, considerable scope for the potential application of Rule 14.

Over the years, there have been a number of offers for companies with two or more classes of equity shares. Examples include the offers by Fuller, Smith & Turner for George Gale and Company (ordinary shares and "A" ordinary shares) and the offers by James Reed & Partners for Reed Health Group (ordinary shares and "B" ordinary shares), both dated November 2005.

The question of whether separate classes of share existed arose in connection with the Eurotunnel restructuring in 2007. In that case, the same offer was made to those Eurotunnel shareholders who were entitled to travel privileges on the Eurotunnel shuttle as was made to shareholders who did not have any travel privileges. The shareholders who had travel privileges argued that this amounted to a breach of General Principle 1 (on the basis that they would lose their privileges if they accepted the offer, whereas other shareholders would not be so affected) and also Rule 14 (on the basis that their shares were a separate class for this purpose and should therefore have received a separate offer). Both the Panel Executive and the Hearings Committee rejected these arguments, and certain of the shareholders affected appealed to the Takeover Appeal Board. The Board rejected the appeal on the basis that the travel privileges were personal rights and were not attached to or an integral part of the share rights. Accordingly, there was found to be no separate class and therefore no requirement for separate offers (see Takeover Appeal Board Statement 2007/2).

5.2.1.1.4 What is a "comparable" offer?

Where an offeree company does have more than one class of equity shares, it will be necessary to determine what is a "comparable" offer for the purposes of Rule 14.1. A number of questions will arise. For instance, where there are differing voting rights, should the offeror give a premium for voting control and, if so, how much? Can it offer a different type of consideration, such as shares or other paper for one class and cash for the other?

The Code sets down a method of assessing the comparability of offers involving two or more classes of equity share capital where the prices for all the classes involved are published in the Daily Official List. It states that the ratio of the offer values for the different classes should normally be equal to the average of the ratios of the middle market quotations taken from the Daily Official List over the course of the six months preceding the offer period. The Panel will not normally allow any other ratio to be used unless the advisers to the offeror and the offeree company are jointly able to justify it. Thus, in practice, an alternative ratio can usually only be used in the case of an agreed, recommended bid.

The six month average ratio was used, for example, in the two offers by Clayform Properties for Stead and Simpson in 1988 and 1989. But the use of that ratio can produce some odd results. What happens if the difference between the prices of the two classes of share has been affected by rumours of a takeover bid or by the offeror's purchases of offeree company shares? The offeror, if it is seeking to gain control, is almost inevitably going to be purchasing voting shares in preference to limited voting or non-voting shares. Even if it does not make purchases, the possibility of a bid is likely to drive up the price of the voting shares compared with the other shares.

For instance, the first offer by Clayform for Stead and Simpson put values on the two classes of share, one voting and one non-voting, of £14.50 and £1.51 (a ratio of 9.6:1). By the time of the second bid a year later, however, the market price of the voting shares had increased significantly and the ratio of the prices under the second bid was 14.2:1.

As noted above, the Code only stipulates a method of valuation where the prices for all the relevant share classes are published in the Daily Official List. If prices for one or more of the classes are not published in the Daily Official List, no specific guidance is given—the Code merely requires that the ratio of the offer values must be justified to the Panel in advance. This is what happened, for example, in the recommended offers by American Express for Sharepeople Group (an unlisted company), made in December 2000, where the offeror was able to justify to the Panel the proposed ratio of the offer values as between the offeree company's ordinary shares and two classes of preference shares, which were both treated as equity. It is no doubt easier to justify a ratio to the Panel where the offers are recommended by the offeree company's directors, and supported by its independent financial adviser, than where they are hostile.

The Code also does not provide any guidance on the question of comparability in the type of consideration under offer, save to say that a comparable offer need not necessarily be an identical offer. In practice, an offeror may find it difficult to persuade the Panel that one type of consideration (for example cash) can be offered to one class of equity and another type of consideration (for example securities) be offered to another class. It is possible, however, to offer different types of securities to different classes.

5.2.1.1.5   Interaction with other Rules

Finally, it should be noted that, although Rule 14 does not require comparable offers to be made for non-voting, non-equity share capital, offers for non-equity securities may be required under Rule 15 (see 5.2.1.2 below) if, for example, they are convertible into equity shares.

5.2.1.2   Rule 15—appropriate offers for convertibles, options etc.

If an offer is made for voting equity share capital or for other transferable securities carrying voting rights (the "voting equity offer") and the offeree company also has in issue securities which are convertible into, or which comprise options or other rights to subscribe for, securities to which the voting equity offer relates ("Rule 15 securities"), Rule 15 requires an appropriate offer (or proposal) to be made for those Rule 15 securities. The purpose of Rule 15 is to safeguard the interests of the holders of Rule 15 securities in their capacity as potential holders of the shares to which the voting equity offer relates. The Executive's interpretation and application of certain of the provisions of Rule 15 is the subject of a practice statement (see Practice Statement No.24 in relation to appropriate offers and proposals under Rule 15).

5.2.1.2.1   What is an "appropriate" offer or proposal?

The Code does not elaborate on what is meant by "appropriate" but informal guidance is contained in Practice Statement No.24. In order to be "appropriate", the Executive considers that a Rule 15 offer or proposal should be for no less than the "see through" price—i.e. the price which would be payable under the main voting equity offer for any shares which would arise from the exercise of the conversion, option or subscription rights, less a deduction for any price payable on the exercise of such rights.

As convertible securities do not have an exercise price, their see through value will always be positive. Therefore, an offer or proposal at no less than see through will always be required for convertible securities, even if it would be below their market price. Where the market price (if any) of any Rule 15 securities is higher than their see through value (for example, where a convertible security may be trading as a fixed income security), the Executive does not require the Rule 15 offer or proposal to be at market price or above.

As with Rule 15 offers and proposals generally, the terms offered or proposed in relation to convertible securities may nonetheless be more generous than simple see through. In the case of Agip Investments' recommended cash offer for Lasmo in December 2000, the Panel agreed that the redemption of Lasmo's convertible bonds in accordance with their terms was sufficient for Rule 15 purposes and that no separate offer or proposal was necessary. This was on the basis that the conversion terms were significantly less attractive to holders than redeeming the bonds at par. Agip also stated in the offer document that it would procure redemption of the bonds within a certain timeframe.

In the case of Vista Funds' recommended acquisition of Misys in April 2012, on the other hand, the conversion terms in relation to Misys' convertible bonds were more attractive to holders than a redemption of their bonds at par (plus accrued interest) and the offeror therefore made a separate cash offer for the bonds in accordance with Rule 15. Under the convertible bond offer, bondholders were entitled to receive a cash payment equivalent to the amount a converting bond-holder would have received if he had converted his bonds at the enhanced conversion price applicable on a change of control (under the terms of the bonds) and been entitled to the same cash consideration for his resulting shares under the terms of the main voting equity offer. Similar see-through cash offers, reflecting an enhanced conversion rate applicable on a change of control, were made by joint offerors William Hill and GVC in relation to Sportingbet's convertible bonds in January 2013 and by Dentsu in relation to Aegis' convertible bonds in March 2013.

In the case of Vodafone's recommended acquisition of Cable & Wireless Worldwide in May 2012, Vodafone also made a separate cash offer for C&W's convertible bonds in accordance with Rule 15. Under Vodafone's convertible bond offer, C&W bondholders were entitled to receive an amount equal to the value of all remaining payments of principal and interest on their bonds up to and including the scheduled maturity date of the bonds, discounted to the settlement date. Bondholders could also exercise their conversion rights and accept the Vodafone offer for their resulting shares, but they were advised that the consideration payable to them under the main voting equity offer was expected to be lower than the consideration which would be payable under the separate convertible bond offer.

So far as other types of Rule 15 security are concerned, if the see through value is zero or would leave a negative figure (for example options that are "out of the money"), no Rule 15 offer or proposal will normally be required so far as the Panel is concerned. See, for example, ESWC's offer for Prologic in March 2012, where no Rule 15 offer or proposal was made in respect of employee share options or warrants to subscribe for Prologic shares as they were all "out of the money", and the main equity offer expressly did not extend to any shares which might be allotted or issued pursuant to the exercise of such options or warrants whilst the offer was open for acceptance. In other cases, however, even if the rights are "out of the money", an offeror may nonetheless want to make an offer in order to encourage holders of the securities to sell out, particularly if their conversion or subscription rights do not lapse at some stage following the voting equity offer. Furthermore, if a takeover offer is made for convertibles or warrants, as a separate class, non-assented securities may be subject to the statutory squeeze-out provisions if sufficient acceptances are received (see 5.2.1.2.3 below).

The Executive does not require any particular form of consideration to be offered to holders of Rule 15 securities, and there is no requirement for them to be offered the same form of consideration as offered under the voting equity offer. One way of making an appropriate offer for Rule 15 securities could, for example, be to offer an equivalent convertible or option in the offeror company. The offer by Hiscox for Hiscox Select Insurance Fund in December 1997, for example, included an offer of a substantially equivalent convertible loan stock in Hiscox for the convertible loan stock in Hiscox Select Insurance Fund.

The offer to exchange an option for an equivalent option over shares of the offeror can be of particular value to employees with share options in the offeree company provided the option scheme under which the options were granted is appropriately worded. The offer of an equivalent option would enable them to take advantage of the roll-over provisions in Sch.3 (for all employee "Save As You Earn" share option schemes) or Sch.4 (for discretionary "Executive" share option schemes) to the Income Tax (Earnings and Pensions) Act 2003, where the share option scheme is tax approved, and so preserve their tax approved status. If an exchange of options is offered, the offeror should take care to ensure that, by granting options over its shares to the offeree company's employees, it does not breach any limit on the total number of its shares that may be made available under employee share plans and that the subscription price payable under the new options (which should reflect the price payable under the original options granted by the offeree) is not less than the par value of its shares unless there are arrangements enabling the shortfall to be paid up out of reserves.

Equality of treatment is required as between holders of the same class of Rule 15 security (for example option holders in the same scheme), but it is acceptable for there to be different treatment as between holders of different classes and as between such holders and the offeree company shareholders (unless the different treatment is being done as a way of giving particular shareholders a special deal which would contravene Rule 16—see 5.2.1.3 below).

Where the voting equity offer is a securities exchange offer but offeror securities are not being offered to the holders of the

Rule 15 securities, the see through value of the Rule 15 securities should normally be calculated by reference to the value of the voting equity offer on the latest practicable date prior to the despatch of the Rule 15 offer or proposal. If offeror securities are also being offered to the holders of Rule 15 securities, the exchange ratio offered to such holders should be no less favourable than that offered under the voting equity offer.

An "appropriate" offer or proposal is not required to reflect "time value" considerations—i.e. the timing of when the holders of the Rule 15 securities may be entitled to exercise a conversion, option or subscription right. If, however, the rights attaching to the Rule 15 securities include an adjustment mechanism which affects the exercise terms of the securities in the event of an offer for the offeree company, an "appropriate" offer or proposal should normally take the adjusted terms into account. The Executive should be consulted if the adjusted exercise terms are not capable of immediate determination.

5.2.1.2.2 "Exercise and accept" proposals

If the holders of Rule 15 securities are able to exercise their rights prior to (or on) the voting equity offer becoming wholly unconditional, a proposal that such holders exercise their rights so as to be able to accept the voting equity offer (an "exercise and accept" proposal) is normally regarded as sufficient for Rule 15 purposes.

In the case of Electrabel's recommended acquisition of International Power (IPR) in May 2012, for example, conversion rights in respect of IPR's three outstanding series of convertible bonds were all currently exerciseable and bondholders also benefited from enhanced conversion terms for a limited period after the main voting equity offer (which was implemented by a scheme of arrangement) became effective. Accordingly, Electrabel's basic proposal for Rule 15 purposes was "exercise and accept", and bondholders were also recommended to convert by no later than the end of the special conversion period in order to receive the enhanced conversion terms. As is

225

usual with schemes of arrangement, if conversion rights were exercised after the record time for the scheme, changes to the offeree company's articles of association, which were approved by offeree shareholders at the same time as the scheme, ensured that the resulting shares were automatically transferred to the offeror in exchange for the offer consideration. The terms of the IPR bonds also gave the bondholders a right of redemption (although this was less favourable than "exercise and accept" in the circumstances) and the issuer a squeeze-out right once 85 per cent of the bonds had been converted or purchased and cancelled.

Where, however, there are alternative offers for the voting equity an "exercise and accept" proposal may not be sufficient if the alternative offer with the highest value ceases to be open for acceptance earlier than the end of the minimum 21 day period during which the Rule 15 offer or proposal should be kept open (see 5.2.1.2.3 below). The reason for this is that holders should not be required to exercise their conversion, option or subscription rights before knowing whether or not the voting equity offer will be successful. In the share for share offer by Goshawk Insurance Holdings for Matheson Lloyd's Investment Trust in June 1997, for example, warrant holders could not exercise their warrants in time to benefit from a partial cash alternative and they therefore received a separate cash offer.

Consideration should be given to the tax consequences, especially for option holders, of exercising their rights and accepting the offer as compared with other forms of proposal, for example cash payments for releasing their rights or the grant of equivalent rights in the offeror. If the rights do not lapse (but will continue to be exercisable in the future), it may be in the interests of the offeror, just as much as the holders of the rights, for proposals to be made to get rid of those rights.

5.2.1.2.3 Timing of a Rule 15 offer or proposal and conditionality

All relevant documents, announcements and other information sent to offeree company shareholders and other persons with information rights in connection with an offer must also, where practicable, be sent at the same time (for information) to the holders of Rule 15 securities. If the terms of the Rule 15 securities enable the holders to exercise their conversion, option or subscription rights during the course of the voting equity offer and to accept the offer following any such exercise, that fact must also be made clear in the relevant documents, announcements and other information.

Rule 15 requires that, wherever practicable, the offer or proposal for the Rule 15 securities should also be despatched at the same time as the main voting equity offer. If this is not practicable (and often it is not in the case of employee share options, particularly in hostile offers where the offeror is unlikely to have full details of the options outstanding), the Panel must be consulted. The Executive will normally expect the Rule 15 offer or proposal to be despatched, at the latest, as soon as possible after the voting equity offer is declared wholly unconditional. In practice, at least so far as employee share options are concerned, the offer document will usually state that proposals will be made to option holders in due course. This will typically be done shortly after the offer is declared wholly unconditional, unless the voting equity offer is recommended and any competing bid looks unlikely, in which case the proposals may be made earlier to enable option holders to choose between any alternatives which may be made available and so as to receive any consideration due to them sooner rather than later.

Where the voting equity offer is being implemented by scheme of arrangement, however, option holder proposals will typically be made at or around the same time that the scheme document is posted to shareholders. This enables the effect of the proposals on the interests of the offeree company directors to be addressed in the explanatory statement sent to shareholders in the scheme document, which is a statutory requirement (see s.897(2) of the Companies Act 2006). It also makes it possible to satisfy the court that option holders' interests have been dealt with, when the court is asked to sanction the scheme, and allows the option holders themselves to exercise their options promptly on the scheme becoming effective.

Rule 15 provides that the offeree company's board must obtain independent advice on the offer or proposal (including if it is simply "exercise and accept"). The substance of this advice must be made known to the holders of the securities in question, together with the board's view. It is particularly important to note this requirement in the case of a hostile offer as it will usually be desirable for at least some of the offeree company's directors to remain in office for a short period after the main voting equity offer is declared wholly unconditional, assuming the offer is successful, so as to give an independent board view on any subsequent Rule 15 offer or proposal. In any event, care should be taken to ensure that the mandate of the independent adviser for Rule 3 purposes extends to advising on any Rule 15 offer or proposal.

To protect individual holders of Rule 15 securities from being "stranded" against their will, the Code provides that the offer or proposal to them should not normally be made conditional on any particular level of acceptances. It is permissible, however, to include a condition in the main voting equity offer requiring a particular level of acceptances under the Rule 15 offer (for example a 90 per cent acceptance condition may be included in relation to a separate offer for convertibles or warrants, where relevant, given that they are capable of being subject to the statutory squeeze-out provisions in Ch.3 of Pt 28 of the Companies Act 2006, unlike employee share options).

Depending on the terms of the Rule 15 securities in question, it may also be possible to put the Rule 15 proposal forward by way of a scheme of arrangement to be considered at a meeting of the relevant holders—where the resolution to approve the scheme will require approval by a majority in number of holders present (in person or by proxy) representing 75 per cent or more in value of the relevant securities voted. Normally such a proposal, once approved by the relevant holders and sanctioned by the court, is binding on all the holders of the rights in question. If, however, a Rule 15 proposal put by way of a scheme is not so approved, or not sanctioned by the court, the offeror will be required to make a further Rule 15 offer which is not conditional on any level of acceptances or approval.

A Rule 15 offer or proposal is normally required to be kept open for at least 21 days following the date on which the relevant documentation is sent to the holders of the Rule 15 securities concerned. However, if the only Rule 15 offer or proposal is "exercise and accept", the Executive's normal practice is to require the voting equity offer to remain open for not less than 21 days after the later of the date on which the documentation containing the "exercise and accept" proposal is despatched and the date on which the voting equity offer is declared wholly unconditional.

5.2.1.2.4   Interaction with other Rules

If an offer for convertible securities is required by Rule 9 or Rule 14, compliance with the relevant Rule will be regarded as satisfying the obligation to make an appropriate offer or proposal under Rule 15.

It is possible for a particular type of share to be both equity, at least in the technical sense, and also convertible (for example a convertible preference share will be treated as equity share capital, for the purposes of s.548 of the Companies Act 2006, if it includes a right to participate in any dividends paid to ordinary shareholders in addition to any preferential dividend right it may also enjoy). In these circumstances, the question arises whether there should be a "comparable" offer under Rule 14 or an "appropriate" offer under Rule 15. As noted above, this can lead to a significant difference in the required offer value. In a hostile situation, where any Panel Executive ruling prior to the offer announcement is likely to be ex parte only, and therefore subject to the Executive being able to hear the views of other parties involved after the announcement is made, an offeror may wish to make its offer conditional on Panel confirmation that the shares in question will be treated under, say, Rule 15 and not Rule 14. An example of this approach occurred in TI's offer for Dowty in April 1992.

A Rule 15 offer or proposal can, as noted above, be made on more favourable terms than see through. However, where certain holders of Rule 15 securities are also offeree company shareholders (for example directors or a significant shareholder perhaps), and the proposed Rule 15 offer or proposal is to be made on more generous terms than see through, the Executive will be concerned to ensure that the Rule 15 offer or proposal does not have the effect of indirectly giving such holders more favourable treatment than other shareholders in a manner prohibited by Rule 16 (see below).

5.2.1.3 *Rule 16—special deals and management incentivisation*

Rule 16.1 is a more detailed expression of General Principle 1 of the Code which provides that all holders of securities of the same class in an offeree company must be afforded equivalent treatment.

Rule 16.1 prohibits an offeror (or persons acting in concert with it) from making arrangements with shareholders or dealing in shares in the offeree company if there are favourable conditions attached which are not extended to all offeree company shareholders. The prohibition applies both during an offer and when one is reasonably in contemplation, and it also extends to entering into arrangements to deal in shares or arrangements which involve acceptance of an offer. It also applies in the six months following a successful offer, during which period Rule 35.3 prohibits a successful offeror from acquiring further shares in the offeree company at a price higher than that available under the offer.

Rule 16.1 also prohibits any arrangement with a person who is interested in shares carrying voting rights in the offeree company (for example a person with a long derivative or option position, who is not necessarily a shareholder) if favourable conditions are attached which are not being extended to all shareholders. There is, however, no requirement for an offeror to extend any offer, or any "special deal" falling within Rule 16.1, to persons who are not shareholders of the offeree company but who have another interest in offeree company shares.

The prohibition on special deals imposed by Rule 16.1 frequently raises difficult issues for both practitioners and the Panel. The Code gives specific guidance regarding four circumstances which have commonly or historically required consideration under this Rule: top-ups, disposals of offeree company assets and finders' fees (which are expressly dealt with in Notes 1, 2 and 3 respectively of Rule 16.1); and management incentive arrangements (which are dealt with in some detail in Rule 16.2).

The Panel Executive has also published a Practice Statement in relation to debt syndication during offer periods which describes, amongst other things, how the provisions of Rule 16 may be applicable in this context and the steps that may be taken to avoid breaching the rule in relevant cases (see Practice Statement No.25).

5.2.1.3.1 Top-ups

One sort of special deal which is expressly prohibited is where the offeror buys shares outright but the seller says that he wants a top-up if the offeror subsequently pays more under a general offer for the target. Top-ups of this nature were quite common at one time, but now they are prohibited (see Panel Statement 1988/11 for an example of a case where the question whether such a top-up arrangement existed was under consideration). To enable certain shareholders to be able to hedge their bets (i.e. to get their money whether or not the offer succeeds but also to get the maximum paid under the offer) would not be treating all shareholders equally. Similarly, the Rule also prohibits shareholders entering into an irrevocable commitment to accept an offer if it is combined with a put option exercisable if the offer fails. But what about an irrevocable commitment combined with a put option exercisable if the offer is not made? Also, what about a top-up in the event of a third party offer at a higher price? Arguably, such arrangements may not fall foul of Rule 16.1 but the Panel would need to be consulted. An offeror may obtain an irrevocable commitment combined with a call option over the shares in question, as the shareholder is not then given a definite exit.

Arrangements made by an offeror with a person acting in concert with it, whereby that person acquires an interest in offeree company shares, are not prohibited provided that the offeror bears all the risks and receives all the benefits and the concert party receives no other benefit (or potential benefit), for example a fee for undertaking the acquisition, beyond normal expenses and carrying costs. In cases of doubt, the Panel should be consulted. Rule 4, which contains certain restrictions on dealings, will also be relevant in these circumstances (see Note 3 to Rules 4.1 and 4.2).

5.2.1.3.2   Disposal of assets

Another way of giving a special deal to a person interested in shares in the offeree company would be to enter into a transaction to dispose of some of the offeree company's assets to him at a favourable price. To guard against this, the Panel has said that, if the disposal is agreed before the offer is unconditional, then it will normally require that:

1. the independent adviser to the offeree publicly states that the terms of the transaction are fair and reasonable; and
2. the offeree company's shareholders give their approval at a general meeting (at this meeting the vote must be a separate vote of independent shareholders and the votes must be given on a poll).

Accordingly, a disposal of assets in these circumstances is normally only possible in a recommended offer situation. If the assets in question are not material in the context of the offer (for example they represent, say, less than one per cent of the value of the offer), the Panel may be satisfied with a "fair and reasonable" statement from the offeree company's independent adviser without also requiring independent shareholder approval; the Panel would need to be consulted where this might be a possibility.

The arrangements between Guinness and LVMH, in the context of the Guinness/GrandMet merger in November 1997, potentially fell within this category. LVMH was a substantial holder of GrandMet shares and its arrangements with Guinness included an extension of the brands distributed through their joint distribution network, to include certain GrandMet brands, as well as payment of a significant sum to LVMH. The GrandMet directors were required to state in the merger document that, having been so advised by their independent financial adviser, the arrangements were fair and reasonable so far as the other GrandMet shareholders were concerned. In addition, LVMH did not vote at the meeting of independent GrandMet shareholders required to approve the merger, which was effected by means of a scheme of arrangement of GrandMet.

Another example is provided by the offer by NTL for Virgin Mobile in April 2006. Virgin Enterprises, a member of the Virgin Group which held approximately 71 per cent of the existing issued share capital of Virgin Mobile, entered into a brand licence which allowed the NTL Group to make use of the Virgin brand. Since members of the Virgin Group were both a party to the brand licence and shareholders in Virgin Mobile, the Panel required the licence to be approved by a simple majority of independent Virgin Mobile shareholders voting at a general meeting of Virgin Mobile. In addition, the independent Virgin Mobile directors stated in the offer document that the terms of the brand licence represented "an arm's length, commercially negotiated agreement and, therefore, [were] fair and reasonable". A similar statement was made by Virgin Mobile's independent financial adviser.

233

If a disposal is agreed after an offer has become unconditional, the Panel will look into it and will want to be satisfied that there was in fact no pre-arrangement. The Panel will be similarly concerned if, for example, more favourable trading arrangements are entered into with shareholders after an offer has become unconditional.

A disposal of certain of the offeror's assets to an offeree shareholder would also need to be considered in terms of Rule 16.

5.2.1.3.3   Finders' fees

If a person interested in shares in the offeree company is paid a finder's fee for the part he has played in promoting an offer, this may be a special deal. The Panel will, however, normally permit a finder's fee if the finder's interest in the offeree shares is not substantial (less than one per cent, say) and the amount of the fee is not abnormal–that is, it is not more than would have been paid to the finder if he was not interested in the offeree company's shares. Finders' fees are now rarely encountered in practice.

5.2.1.3.4   Management incentive arrangements

An offeror will often wish to incentivise the management of the offeree company so that they remain with the enlarged group. This is likely to arise, in particular, in connection with so-called "public to private" transactions involving private equity and other financial investors, as well as management buy-outs (MBOs) and similar types of transaction, as the Panel's Annual Report for 1997–1998 highlighted. It can, however, arise in any type of transaction wherever the offeror wishes to retain and incentivise particular members of the offeree company's existing management.

Management incentive arrangements can take a number of different forms. In "public to private", MBOs and similar types of transaction, it will often be desirable to allow certain members of management to exchange (i.e. "roll over") their shares in the offeree company for securities in the offeror bid vehicle, whereas non-management shareholders will not be given the same opportunity. In other cases, management may be financially incentivised by reference to underlying profitability and/or share price performance without acquiring an interest in any offeror securities. An offeror may also wish to offer particular members of the offeree company's management enhanced remuneration packages, which may take the form of new or improved service contracts or bonus arrangements or the opportunity to participate in the offeror's own employee share plans (which would confer a right to receive shares in the offeror at some future point in time).

Where the management concerned also holds shares in the offeree company, incentive arrangements can give rise to concerns relating to General Principle 1 (which requires offeree company shareholders to be afforded equivalent treatment). They can also give rise to concerns as to their effect on the offeree board's assessment of a proposed offer and/or the amount of consideration that might be left for non-management shareholders. Accordingly, Rule 16.2 of the Code provides various procedural safeguards to ensure that the philosophy underlying General Principle 1 and Rule 16.1 is respected whilst enabling management to participate in the ongoing business through different types of incentive arrangement which are not necessarily extended to all other offeree company shareholders.

Rule 16.2 came into effect on January 25, 2010, replacing what was previously Note 4 on Rule 16. The aim of Rule 16.2 is to clarify and simplify the manner in which, and increase the consistency with which, the Code applies to management incentive arrangements; it also aims to reduce the range of circumstances in which consultation with the Panel is required in this context (see Section 3 of Panel Consultation Paper 2009/2 and also Section 3 of Response Statement 2009/2).

The basic requirement is that, where an offeror enters into (or reaches an advanced stage of discussions or proposals to enter into) any form of incentivisation arrangements with members of the offeree company's management who are interested in shares of the offeree, the relevant details of the arrangements (or proposals) must be disclosed and the independent adviser to the offeree company must state publicly that in its opinion the arrangements are fair and reasonable. When forming its opinion, the independent adviser is expected to consider whether the incentives being offered to management are fair and reasonable in the context of the managers acting in their capacity as such (which is acceptable) or whether, implicitly, the arrangements also include additional benefits and incentives which are being made available to them because they are interested in shares (which is not acceptable). The independent adviser will be expected to have regard to the whole of the incentive arrangements being offered (including any enhanced remuneration package). The independent adviser will also be expected to take into account all relevant circumstances, including for example the particular skills of the individual concerned, the circumstances of the company in question and/or comparable remuneration packages provided to management of peer group companies.

The question also arises whether independent shareholder approval will be required, in addition to the "fair and reasonable" opinion required of the independent adviser to the offeree company. Where managers who are also shareholders in the offeree company are being offered shares in the offeror on a basis that is not being made available to all other offeree company shareholders then, in order to comply with the requirement of the Takeover Directive that any derogation from the Rules must "respect" the General Principles (see arts 3(1)(a) and 4(5) of the Takeover Directive), independent shareholder approval must always now be obtained (Rule 16.2(c)). See, for example, the offer by Goliath for Goals Soccer Centres in July 2012, which involved the management team (and their connected persons) exchanging a substantial portion of their existing shareholdings in the offeree company, as well as shares resulting from the exercise of their "in the money" options, for loan notes in the bid vehicle which were in turn exchangeable for securities in the offeror's ultimate holding company, an arrangement which was not extended to other shareholders in the offeree company who were only entitled to the basic cash offer. See also the offer by Tracsis for Sky High in March 2013, in which three executive directors and three senior managers of Sky High agreed to apply the proceeds of the cash consideration received for their Sky High shares under the terms of the Tracsis offer in acquiring Tracsis shares, an arrangement which was also not made available to other shareholders in the offeree.

Rule 16.2 is focussed on members of management who are also interested in shares of the offeree company. The Panel believes, however, that management incentive arrangements can still be relevant to offeree company shareholders even where members of management are not interested in shares (and thus independent shareholder approval is not required in order to comply with the Takeover Directive). This may be the case, for example, by virtue of the influence which such arrangements might have on the board's recommendation or on the amount of consideration left over for non-management shareholders. The Panel therefore requires to be consulted in cases where significant and/or unusual incentive arrangements are proposed in relation to members of the management of the offeree who are not interested in shares of the offeree.

It will be a question of judgment whether the value of incentive arrangements for members of management who are not interested in shares is significant and/or the nature of the arrangements is unusual, and this needs to be assessed both in the context of the relevant industry in which the companies operate and by reference to good practice. This places the burden on the offeree company's independent adviser to decide whether arrangements are sufficiently significant or unusual to require consultation with the Panel and, if they are in any doubt, they will be expected to consult the Executive. In certain circumstances, in addition to requiring a "fair and reasonable" opinion from the independent adviser to the offeree company, the Panel may make its consent to such arrangements conditional on independent shareholder approval (Rule 16.2(b)). This is what happened, for example, in the case of the offer by Tracsis for Sky High, where the proposed cash bonus incentivisation arrangement between Tracsis and two executive directors of Sky High (one of whom was not an offeree company shareholder) was also made subject to independent shareholder approval.

Some limited guidance is provided in Response Statement 2009/2 on the question of whether independent shareholder approval is likely to be required in relation to new remuneration packages. It is said that, where these simply reflect the existing remuneration policy of the offeror, they would not normally be viewed as significant and/or unusual in which case they would not need to be approved by shareholders. The independent adviser to the offeree company will, however, still be required to publicly state that any such enhanced remuneration packages are, in its opinion, fair and reasonable.

Where shareholder approval is required, it must be provided by way of a separate vote of independent shareholders, taken on a poll. It is not therefore possible to include such an approval as part of a composite resolution to approve other matters in relation to an offer, for example a resolution of offeree company shareholders to approve a scheme of arrangement to implement the acquisition by the offeror. Panel practice does, however, allow the passing of any resolution(s) that may be required in connection with an offer to be made inter-conditional with any resolution required to approve management incentive arrangements, with the result that the offer may lapse if the resolution to approve the management incentive arrangements is not approved.

The term "management" is not defined for the purposes of Rule 16.2 and the Executive adopts a flexible approach. In practice, the Executive usually interprets "management" to comprise those directors and senior executives of the offeree who have the power to make managerial decisions affecting the future development and business prospects of the company concerned. The Executive may also be prepared to allow the holdings of those directors' immediate families to be included in the management's arrangements, if otherwise permitted. In addition, the Executive may be prepared to allow management below offeree company board level to participate in the arrangements, provided they are sufficiently key personnel (for example they are directors of a principal operating subsidiary): see, for example, the recommended proposals for the acquisition of the Peacock Group by Henson No.1 Ltd in November 2005, where the holdings of the spouse of one of the executive directors and of two members of management below board level were included in the share exchange proposals. The holdings of self invested personal pensions (SIPPs) and fund managers linked to members of management may also be included: see, for example, the management incentive arrangements associated with Sanlam's offer for Merchant Securities in November 2011. The Executive expects to be consulted on all situations where it is unclear which individuals may be viewed as part of the "management" camp for these purposes.

Rule 16.2 also includes a requirement to consult the Panel if any changes to the status of management incentive arrangements are made after the offer document has been published. If the changes are material, disclosure of the relevant details and a statement by the offeree company's independent adviser that the arrangements are fair and reasonable will be required and, if merited on the facts, independent shareholder approval may also need to be obtained.

In some cases, an offeror may choose to refrain from holding any incentivisation discussions with the offeree company management until after the offer has completed. However, it should be noted that, if it is intended to put incentivisation arrangements in place after completion of an offer, but either no discussions or only limited discussions have taken place, this fact must be publicly stated and relevant details of any discussions which have taken place must be disclosed. Where no incentivisation arrangements are proposed, this must also be publicly stated.

Rule 16.2 is also capable of applying in whitewash transactions, where some form of incentivisation arrangement is being provided to the management of the company which is treated as the "offeree company" in these circumstances (i.e. the company issuing the new securities and seeking the white-wash) by any member of the "offeror" camp (i.e. any potential controlling shareholder receiving new shares in the offeree)—see Section 4(f) in Appendix 1 to the Code. A recent example of this occurred in connection with the potential acquisition by Bidtimes of PowerHouse Energy in April 2011. The acquisition constituted a reverse takeover for Bidtimes, given that it needed to increase its share capital by well over 100 per cent to satisfy the share consideration being offered to PowerHouse shareholders, and a whitewash vote of independent Bidtimes shareholders was required in order to exempt certain of the selling PowerHouse shareholders (who were treated as acting in concert) from having to make a general offer for Bidtimes under Rule 9 by virtue of receiving in excess of 30 per cent of Bidtimes as a result of the acquisition. The approval of independent Bidtimes shareholders was also required under Rule 16.2 in relation to a success fee which was payable by one of the principal members of the concert party to a company advising it on the transaction, given that a director and controlling shareholder of the corporate adviser was also a director and shareholder in Bidtimes.

5.2.1.3.5 Joint offerors

In the same way that Rule 16 does not apply to a genuine offeror who already holds shares in the offeree company, in respect of any arrangements it may make regarding its own shares in the offeree company or otherwise, the Panel acknowledges that Rule 16 is not relevant where two or more persons come together to form a consortium on such terms and in such circumstances that each of them can properly be considered to be a joint offeror.

Rule 16 will not, therefore, apply where the offeree company's management can properly be characterised as acting as joint offeror. In these circumstances, the management of the offeree company that is acting as joint offeror will be free to enter into its own arrangements without the need for those arrangements to require a fair and reasonable opinion from an independent adviser or independent shareholder approval. By way of example, when BL Davidson (a 50/50 joint venture company owned by the Davidson family and the British Land Company) made a cash offer for Asda Property Holdings in August 2001, the Davidson family and British Land were treated as joint offerors with the result that Rule 16 did not apply to the arrangements whereby the Davidson family exchanged its 29 per cent stake in Asda for shares in the bidding vehicle. This may be contrasted with the offer by Dundonald Holdings for Grantchester Holdings in August 2002, where it could not be said that the management team, who agreed to subscribe for a proportion of the shares in the bidding vehicle (and to "roll over" certain of their options in the offeree company for options over preference shares in the bidding vehicle), were acting as joint offerors and therefore the arrangements needed independent shareholder approval.

The distinction between receiving a special deal as offeree company shareholder (which is subject to the prohibitions and restrictions in General Principle 1 and Rule 16) and acting as joint offeror (where it is not) can be a fine one. A genuine offeror is seen as a person who, alone or with others, seeks to obtain control of an offeree company and who, following the acquisition of control, can expect to exert a significant influence over the offeree company, to participate in distributions of profits and surplus capital and to benefit from any increase in the value of the offeree company, while at the same time bearing the risk of a fall in its value resulting from the poor performance of the company's business or adverse market conditions.

In determining whether a person can properly be considered to be an offeror (or joint offeror), rather than simply acting in concert with the offeror, the Panel Executive will consider the following factors.

1. What proportion of the equity share capital of the bid vehicle will the person own after completion of the acquisition?
2. Will the person be able to exert a significant influence over the future management and direction of the bid vehicle?

3. What contribution is the person making to the consortium?
4. Will the person be able to influence significantly the conduct of the bid?
5. Are there arrangements in place to enable the person to exit from his investment in the bid vehicle within a short time or at a time when other equity investors cannot?

The appropriateness of these factors was endorsed by the Panel in the case concerning Canary Wharf Group (see Panel Statement 2003/25). The Panel did, however, stress that the above factors should not be regarded as exhaustive, and that it is also necessary to ensure that, even if the criteria seem to be satisfied to a degree sufficient to justify treating the person in question as an offeror, the arrangements looked at as a whole are consistent with General Principle 1 and Rule 16. The Panel also said that no single factor should be regarded as determinative, nor is it necessary that a person satisfies each factor.

In the Canary Wharf case, the Panel was satisfied that a particular offeree company shareholder should be treated as a joint offeror and that, accordingly, the terms of the consortium arrangements in which he was involved did not infringe General Principle 1 or Rule 16. It was found, in that case, that the shareholder concerned would have in excess of 30 per cent of the equity in the bid vehicle, making him the largest single shareholder, and that the consortium arrangements gave him significant influence over the direction of the bid vehicle and the future management of the business. It was also found that the shareholder was making a substantial contribution to the consortium, both in financial and managerial terms, and that he was exposed to substantial risks and had no arrangements for a short-term exit. The Panel did, however, also stress that each case must be decided upon its own facts and that therefore previous decisions arrived at on different facts are likely to be of little help in determining the acceptability of consortium arrangements in other cases.

A more recent example of a bid by joint offerors was the offer for eircom Group in May 2006 by BCM Ireland Holdings, a bid vehicle formed for the purpose of making the offer by Babcock & Brown Capital and the eircom Employee Share Ownership Trust. These two shareholders held approximately 28.8 per cent and 21.4 per cent respectively of eircom's issued ordinary share capital and, following completion of the offer, they would hold 65 per cent and 35 per cent respectively of the issued ordinary share capital of the bid vehicle. Both shareholders provided equity financing for the offer and both had the ability to exert significant influence over the business of eircom following completion of the transaction.

It follows that, where an offeree company shareholder cannot be characterised as a joint offeror, and is not involved in the management of the offeree company as referred to in 5.2.1.3.4 above, a special deal involving a "roll over" into shares in the bidding vehicle (when all other shareholders would not be given the same opportunity) is not generally permissible, even with the benefit of a fair and reasonable statement from the offeree company's independent financial adviser and an independent shareholder vote, and will be prohibited by the overriding requirement for shareholders of the same class to be afforded equivalent treatment as set out in General Principle 1.

5.2.1.3.6 Debt syndication

Practice Statement 25 describes the way in which the Executive normally interprets and applies certain provisions of the Code, including Rule 16, in the context of the primary syndication of debt financing for an offer during offer periods. Rule 16 may be in point where a debt finance provider who is allocated a debt participation following the completion of the syndication process, or a potential debt finance provider who is approached to take part in a proposed debt syndication, (in either case, a "syndicate") also holds shares in the offeree company, or acquires such shares during the offer period. The Executive's concern in this context is primarily based on the possibility that favourable debt terms might be used as a means of providing additional value to a syndicatee in its capacity as an offeree company shareholder. This would be the case if, for example, a syndicatee's equity department agreed that it would accept a lower offer for its shares in the offeree company than would otherwise have been the case because the syndicatee's debt department was allocated a participation in the syndicate, perhaps on attractive terms. In addition, the Executive is concerned to ensure that the decision of a syndicatee's equity department as to whether or not it should accept the offer should not otherwise be influenced by the participation of the syndicatee's debt department in the syndicate.

The Executive believes that the knowledge that a syndicatee's equity department has about the participation of its debt department in a debt syndication, and the terms of that participation, is critical in determining the application of Rule 16. This is because the Executive considers that, without this knowledge, it would be unlikely that value would be transferred between the equity and debt components of the transaction or that the decision of the equity department as to whether or not it should accept an offer would be influenced.

In view of this, the Executive normally takes the view that, in relation to a syndicatee which holds shares in the offeree company or which acquires shares during the offer period, no problems would arise under Rule 16 provided effective information barriers are in place between its equity and debt departments. Paragraph 6 of Practice Statement 25 sets out the minimum standards which the Executive has identified for an information barrier to be effective in preventing issues arising under Rule 16 in this context.

If, however, an effective information barrier has not been established then the Executive will want to establish whether or not the debt being syndicated is on "market terms":

1. if the offeror is able to demonstrate to the Executive's satisfaction that the debt being syndicated is on "market terms", the Executive would not normally consider there to be an issue under Rule 16. This is on the basis that, if an offeror is able to prove that a syndicatee has been allocated "plain vanilla" debt with no special features which is on

similar terms to debt issued in comparable transactions, the Executive would consider the scope for a transfer of value to occur as between the equity and debt components of the transaction, or for the decision of the syndicatee's equity department to be influenced, would be minimised;

2. if, on the other hand, the debt being syndicated is not on "market terms", the Executive will normally require further information in order to determine whether there is an issue under Rule 16. For example, the Executive would seek to gain an understanding of the identity of the syndicatees, the reasons why the syndicatees were invited to participate in the syndicate, the basis and terms on which the debt was allocated to syndicatees, and the extent to which syndicatees hold shares in the offeree company.

5.2.1.3.7 Other cases

Rule 16 is concerned with special deals for particular shareholders which are (or may be) on favourable terms. It follows, therefore, that Rule 16 (and General Principle 1) will not be relevant where a particular shareholder voluntarily accepts a less favourable deal than other shareholders (as happened, for example, in the offer by Britannia Living for The Range Cooker Company in November 2002, where one of the offeree company directors agreed to waive his entitlement to part of the cash consideration payable under the terms of the offer).

Rule 16 will also not be relevant where all offeree shareholders are being offered the same opportunity to exchange their shares in the offeree company for securities in the offeror, such as a bidding vehicle, even if it is clear that the opportunity provided will not be attractive to all of them. This is what happened, for example, in the offer for Delancey Estates in April 2001: all shareholders were offered cash for their Delancey shares and two types of loan note, one guaranteed and the other unguaranteed but convertible into the unlisted equity of the ultimate parent company of the bidding vehicle. A mechanism was thereby found to enable those offeree shareholders who wished to have a continuing equity partici-pation post completion (which included both management and non-management shareholders) to do so, whilst affording all other shareholders the same opportunity in compliance with General Principle 1.

A similar situation arose, for example, in the buyout offer by RAB Capital Holdings for RAB Capital in July 2011, where the offeree company directors leading the buyout elected to receive an unlisted share alternative which was also made available to all other shareholders but which was not recommended to them by the offeree company's independent directors or adviser. See also the offer for Theo Fennell in August 2013 which included an unlisted share alternative comprising shares in the bid vehicle which was made available to all offeree shareholders but which was not recommended. In that case, various other arrangements involving one or more offeree company director shareholders also required a "fair and reasonable" statement from the offeree company's independ-ent adviser as well as independent shareholder approval: these comprised a "sweet equity" arrangement by way of manage-ment incentivisation, new director service agreements, a so-called "brand repatriation" agreement and a separate purchase agreement relating to shares in an associated com-pany.

5.2.1.3.8   Interaction with other Rules

Where members of the management of the offeree company are to receive offeror securities pursuant to an appropriate offer or proposal made in accordance with Rule 15, relevant details of the arrangement must be disclosed and the independent adviser of the offeree must give a fair and reasonable opinion in accordance with Rule 16.2(a), but the Panel will not need to be consulted (and shareholder approval will not normally be required) unless the value of the arrangement is significant and/or its nature is unusual.

If the only shareholders in the offeree company who receive offeror securities are members of the management of the offeree company, the Panel will not, so long as the requirements of Rule 16.2 are complied with, require all offeree shareholders to be offered offeror securities pursuant to Rule 11.2, even though such management members propose to sell more than 10 per cent of the offeree company's shares in exchange for offeror securities.

In addition to the requirement to disclose relevant details of any management incentive arrangements or proposals under Rule 16.2(b), it is also worth noting that full particulars of any special arrangements between the offeror or any person acting in concert with it and any of the directors, shareholders or recent shareholders of the offeree company, having any connection with or dependence upon the offer, also need to be disclosed in the offer document under Rule 24.5.

5.2.1.4 Compensation rulings

Section 10(c) of the Introduction to the Code provides that, where a person has breached the requirements of (amongst others) Rules 14, 15 or 16.1 of the Code, the Panel may rule that the person concerned must make a payment to the shareholders, or former shareholders, in the offeree which ensures that such holders receive what they would have been entitled to receive if the relevant Rule had been complied with. The ruling may also require interest to be paid up to the date of payment.

5.2.2 Administrative provisions

Rules 17 and 18 contain certain administrative provisions relating to all offers. Rule 17 deals with announcements of acceptance levels and Rule 18 with certain provisions in forms of acceptance.

5.2.2.1 Rule 17—announcements of acceptance levels

5.2.2.1.1 Timing and contents

Rule 17.1 requires an announcement of the level of acceptances to be made after the occurrence of certain events, namely:

1. any expiry date—that is, any date on which the offeror could allow the bid to lapse if insufficient acceptances have been received. This will obviously include the first closing date of an offer, usually the minimum period of 21 days after the despatch of the offer document; it will also include any subsequent closing date if the offer is extended; the Code also states that a date on which any alternative form of consideration available under the offer expires is also to be treated as an expiry date, even if the offer itself is not due to expire at that time;

2. when the offer becomes or is declared unconditional as to acceptances—which may of course also be an expiry date, though not necessarily, and it could be before or after the first closing date;

3. whenever the offer is revised—including where a revision is required as a result of a purchase of offeree company shares above the then current offer value, if otherwise permitted, in which case the announcement required by Rule 7.1 should also include the information required under Rule 17.1; and

4. whenever the offer is extended—that may also be an expiry date, though not necessarily.

The deadline for announcements required by Rule 17.1 is 08.00 on the first business day following the relevant event. However, on the final day of the offer (i.e. the day beyond which the offer cannot be extended if not unconditional as to acceptances, which is normally the 60th day after posting unless the offeror has made a "no extension" statement for an earlier date or the Panel has consented to a later date which it may do in certain circumstances), the announcement must normally be made by 17.00 on that day—not 08.00 on the following business day. If an offer is likely to reach the final day, the offeror and its advisers should consider Rule 31.6 closely in advance as it has a number of detailed requirements about timing.

Rule 17.1 also specifies that the following must be included in the announcement:

1. the number of shares for which acceptances of the offer have been received, specifying the extent to which acceptances have been received from persons acting in concert with the offeror or in respect of shares which were subject to an irrevocable commitment or a letter of intent procured by the offeror or any person acting in concert with the offeror;

2. details of any relevant securities of the offeree company in which the offeror or any person acting in concert with it has an interest or in respect of which he has a right to subscribe, in each case specifying the nature of the interests or rights concerned (similar details of any short positions, whether conditional or absolute and whether in the money or otherwise, including any short position under a derivative, any agreement to sell or any delivery obligation or right to require another person to purchase or take delivery, must also be stated);

3. details of any relevant securities of the offeree company in respect of which the offeror or any person acting in concert with it has an outstanding irrevocable commitment or letter of intent; and

4. details of any relevant securities of the offeree company which the offeror or any person acting in concert with it has borrowed or lent, save for any borrowed shares which have been either on-lent or sold,

and the announcement must specify the percentages of each class of relevant securities represented by these figures.

A Rule 17 announcement must also include a prominent statement of the total number of shares which can be counted towards satisfaction of the acceptance condition and must specify the percentages of each class of relevant securities represented by these figures. The Code has strict Rules for determining what acceptances and share purchases may be counted towards fulfilling an acceptance condition (see Rule 10 including, in particular, Notes 4 and 5). Accordingly, an acceptance of the offer may only be counted for this purpose if (in cases where the acceptance is effected by means of CREST without an acceptance form) the transfer to the relevant

249

member's escrow account has settled in respect of the relevant number of shares on or before the last time for acceptance or (where the acceptance is effected by means of an acceptance form) the acceptance is received by the offeror's receiving agent on or before such time, the form is completed to a suitable standard and:

1. the form is accompanied by the relevant share certificates and, where necessary, any other documents required to show title; or
2. in the case of a holding in CREST, it is covered by a transfer to the relevant member's escrow account, details of which are provided in the form; or
3. the acceptor is registered in the register of members as the holder of the shares in question as at the final time for acceptance and those shares are not included as acceptances in any other respect; or
4. the acceptance form is certified by the target's registrar.

Similarly, share purchases may only be counted if:

1. the offeror (or its nominee or, in a Rule 9 offer, a person acting in concert with it) is the registered holder of the shares; or
2. a duly executed transfer in favour of the offeror (or its nominee or, in a Rule 9 offer, concert party) has been received and is accompanied by the relevant share certificates or is certified by the target's registrar.

The Panel should be consulted if the offeror wishes to make any other statement about acceptance levels in a Rule 17 announcement. In practice, if it is wished to refer to other acceptances and share purchases which do not meet the above standards, this is usually permissible, subject to prior Panel approval, provided they are referred to separately and their status is made clear.

If an offer is to become or be declared unconditional as to acceptances before the final closing date, the criteria for determining which acceptances and purchases can be counted towards fulfilling the acceptance condition (although not necessarily for the purposes of a Rule 17 announcement) are more strict in one particular respect (see Rule 10, Note 6). In these circumstances, it is not possible to take account of acceptances solely on the grounds that they are from a registered holder, unless they are also accompanied by share certificates or (in the case of a holding in CREST) covered by a transfer to the relevant member's escrow account or (in any case) certified by the target's registrar.

In addition, before the offer becomes or is declared unconditional as to acceptances, the offeror's receiving agent must have issued a certificate which states the number of acceptances and purchases which comply with the above requirements. A copy of that certificate must be sent to the Panel and the offeree company's financial adviser as soon as possible.

The above requirements were introduced in to the Code following the situation which arose in the Blue Circle offer for Birmid in 1988. In that case there was an announcement that there were sufficient acceptances and purchases for the bid to become unconditional. It was, however, subsequently found that some incomplete purchases had been included and a further announcement had to be made that the bid had in fact lapsed (see Panel Statements 1988/4 and 1988/22).

Rule 24.7 of the Code requires an offer document to state that the offeror will make announcements on the required occasions and what will be included within those announcements.

An announcement under Rule 17 must be published in accordance with the requirements of Rule 2.9. However, in the case of companies whose securities are not admitted to listing or trading, it would normally be permissible to send a notification to all shareholders and persons with information rights instead of making an announcement.

5.2.2.1.2 Failure to announce

If the offeror, having announced the offer to be unconditional as to acceptances, fails to announce the details required by Rule 17.1 by 15.30 on the following business day, then automatically every acceptor has the right to withdraw his acceptance. Subject to Rule 31.6, that right to withdraw cannot be terminated for at least eight days and then it can only be terminated by the offeror reconfirming that the bid is unconditional, assuming of course that by the end of that eight days it is still unconditional. If too many people have withdrawn, the bid may no longer be capable of being reconfirmed as unconditional as to acceptances.

On the final day, however, when Rule 31.6 applies, an offer must either become or be declared unconditional as to acceptances or lapse. If it becomes or is declared unconditional as to acceptances, it is generally not then capable of becoming conditional as to acceptances again. The words "Subject to Rule 31.6" in Rule 17.2(a) seem to infer that the right of withdrawal cannot be terminated beyond the 60 day limit. What is less clear, but is presumably the case, is that the withdrawal rights themselves cease to be exercisable beyond the final time for lodging acceptances which can be taken into account for the purposes of Rule 31.6. This would be consistent with when the general right of withdrawal ceases to be exercisable under Rule 34.1.

Rule 17.2 also used to provide, as an alternative sanction for failure to announce within the requisite time limits, for the temporary suspension of listing of the offeree company's shares (if admitted to the Official List) and, if appropriate, the offeror's shares. This alternative sanction has, however, been removed on the basis that it was unlikely to be imposed in practice in any event.

5.2.2.1.3 General statements about acceptances and withdrawals

During an offer, particularly in a competitive situation, an offeror or its advisers may be tempted to make general statements about the level of acceptances received, or the number or percentage of shareholders who have accepted the offer. In these circumstances, the Panel will require an immediate announcement to be made in conformity with Rule 17. As noted above, a formal Rule 17 announcement will need to make clear which acceptances can be counted towards fulfilling the acceptance condition.

Conversely, in the case of a hostile offer, an offeree company may wish to draw attention to withdrawals of acceptances. In this case, the Panel requires prior consultation before any announcement is made. The Panel is usually concerned to ensure, in particular, that the market is not misled by conflicting announcements of withdrawals and acceptances. Rule 19.3 will also be relevant: an offeree company should not make statements about levels of support from its shareholders unless their up-to-date intentions have been clearly stated to the company or its advisers and satisfactory verification (which usually means written) can be provided to the Panel.

5.2.2.1.4 Schemes of arrangement

Rule 17 is not applicable in the case of schemes of arrangement. In its place, the provisions of Section 5 of Appendix 7 of the Code provide that an announcement should be made as soon as practicable after the results of the shareholder meetings are known, stating whether or not the resolutions were passed by the requisite majorities and giving details of the voting results in relation to the meetings including (where applicable) the number of votes cast for and against the resolutions and the number of shareholders who voted for and against them. Announcements are also required as soon as practicable following the court sanction hearing and, assuming the scheme proceeds to that stage, the scheme effective date.

5.2.2.2 *Rule 18—the use of proxies in relation to acceptances*

Rule 18 relates to the appointment of proxies to exercise voting rights and other sorts of rights. The offeror will usually include, as part of the terms of acceptance, a provision by which an accepting shareholder appoints the offeror, or someone nominated by him, as the acceptor's proxy and authorises that person to exercise rights on his behalf. The purpose of this is normally to enable the offeror to exercise the rights attached to the acceptor's shares in the offeree company between the time when the offer goes wholly unconditional and the time when the offeror gets itself registered on the register of members. In the absence of any other arrangement, until the offeror becomes the registered holder of the shares, the rights attached to them would continue to be exercisable by the accepting shareholder.

Rule 18 states that the appointment as proxy should be expressed in terms that it will become effective only if the offer has become wholly unconditional or (in the case of voting by the proxy) if the resolution in question concerns the last remaining condition of the offer (other than any admission to listing or admission to trading condition) and the offer would either become wholly unconditional (save for satisfaction of any such condition) or lapse depending upon the outcome of the resolution in question. This exception is to enable votes to be cast at a general meeting of the offeree company if one is needed for the purposes of the offer. In order for an offeror to benefit from the appointment, it may be necessary for it to waive any outstanding, waivable conditions save for the admission to listing or admission to trading condition which, if applicable, will always be the last condition to be satisfied.

One other circumstance in which the Panel is likely, in practice, to permit the offeror to use proxies acquired as a result of the acceptance process, before the offer has become wholly unconditional, is where the offeree company proposes to dispose of certain assets for which shareholder approval is required and the offer is conditional on the proposed sale not being approved at the offeree company's general meeting.

The Code goes on to say that the offeror can only use the votes to satisfy the conditions of the offer. In other words, it would not be possible for the offeror (for example if it had cold feet about the offer) to exercise voting rights over shares in the offeree company to defeat the conditions of its offer. In these circumstances, however, an offeror may be able to lapse its offer on an expiry date if it has failed to satisfy the 90 per cent acceptance condition which is usually inserted for compulsory acquisition purposes (although this "get out" would not be available where the offeror has chosen to implement its offer by means of a scheme of arrangement).

The proxy form must also make it clear that the appointment ceases to be valid if the acceptor withdraws his acceptance.

Finally, it has to be made clear that the appointment relates only to the shares which are the subject of the acceptance. In other words, if (say) Barclays Bank has several million shares in the offeree company registered in its name, all as nominee, and it is instructed by one person to accept the offer, an appointment of the offeror as a proxy in relation to those shares may not be taken as an appointment in relation to all the other shares in the offeree company held by Barclays.

Rule 18 does not restrict the terms on which a proxy may be obtained, or other shareholder rights acquired, otherwise than as a term of acceptance (for example, as part of a separate proxy solicitation exercise).

Rule 18 is not applicable in the case of schemes of arrangement and is disapplied by virtue of Section 16 of Appendix 7 to the Code.

5.3 Partial offers

The provisions of the Code on partial offers (Section P, Rule 36) are also concerned with the application of General Principle 1 regarding equivalent treatment.

A partial offer is an offer for less than 100 per cent. of the voting share capital of a company, taking into account any shares already owned by the offeror and persons acting in concert with it. In other words, a partial offer is one which is not capable of resulting in the offeror and its concert parties being interested in 100 per cent of the voting rights of a company.

Partial offers are relatively uncommon for the simple reason that offerors usually wish to acquire 100 per cent control, which avoids the need to take account of the interests of minority shareholders longer term, whilst offeree company shareholders are usually reluctant to cede control without the ability to get out for 100 per cent of their holdings. Nonetheless, partial offers may prove attractive in certain circumstances.

Some notable examples of partial offers in recent years include the offer by Zoo Hotels to acquire up to 29 per cent of the Groucho Club London in April 2001, the offer by Carnival Corporation to acquire up to 20 per cent of P&O Princess Cruises in March 2003 (in connection with the proposed combination of Carnival and P&O Princess under a dual listed company structure), the hostile offer by GPG Group to acquire an additional 25 per cent of De Vere in March 2004, the offer by Leander Group to acquire 74.9 per cent of Real Office Group in October 2008 and the hostile offer by Thalassa to acquire an additional 25.89 per cent of Rock Solid Images in April 2012.

Panel consent is always required for a partial offer. This consent is normally granted if it would not result in the offeror and its concert parties being interested in shares carrying 30 per cent or more of the votes. A person can, of course, buy shares to give himself up to 29.9 per cent without incurring a mandatory bid obligation under Rule 9 of the Takeover Code and, following the abolition in May 2006 of the Rules Governing Substantial Acquisitions of Shares (the "SARs" as they used to be known), there is no longer any restriction on the speed with which a person may acquire shares (or interests in shares) below the 30 per cent level.

There are three ways in which a person is able to acquire shares (or interests in shares) of up to 29.9 per cent of a company to which the Code applies:

1. by stakebuilding through the purchase of individual holdings;
2. by means of a tender offer (the Rules for which are contained in Appendix 5 of the Code); or
3. by means of a partial offer.

Share purchases may, for example, be made from particular shareholders or as part of a market operation conducted by the purchaser's broker. However, if the purchaser wishes to make an offer to all shareholders, he will need to do a tender or partial offer. A tender offer is made by means of a simple advertisement which must be published in two national newspapers (although a circular in the same form as the advertisement may also be posted to shareholders) and it need only be open for a minimum period of seven days. A tender offer provides a more straightforward procedure than a partial offer, which is subject to the other provisions of the Code in the normal way and is therefore a lengthier and more costly process. A tender offer may also be particularly relevant in the context of companies whose shares are not admitted to trading (where it is not therefore possible to acquire shares in the market).

A tender offer must, however, be for cash only and cannot be made subject to any conditions, other than receipt of acceptances amounting to at least one per cent. Thus, where the offer consideration is to include securities or conditions need to be attached to the acquisition of shares (for example the approval of the purchaser's own shareholders or, possibly, regulatory conditions), a purchaser will have to resort to a partial offer regulated under the Code.

The amount of information which can be imparted during a tender offer is also strictly limited; in particular, no form of argument or persuasion is allowed, whereas a partial offer under the Code is not so restricted. Zoo Hotels, for example, had to proceed by way of partial offer rather than tender offer, in its attempt to acquire up to 29 per cent of the Groucho Club, both because its offer consideration comprised Zoo shares and because its offer was unsolicited and competitive with another, general offer which meant it needed to be able to argue the relative merits of its partial offer. Zoo Hotels' partial offer was not, however, subject to any conditions: partial offers which cannot result in the offeror holding 30 per cent or more need not be subject to any acceptance condition although an offeror may choose to include one. Thalassa's hostile partial offer for Rock Solid Images, for example, which included a share alternative and, if accepted in full, would have given the offeror 29.99 per cent of the offeree company, also included a minimum acceptance condition.

A tender offer would also not be an option for an offeror who wants to acquire shares carrying 30 per cent or more of the votes, unless the offeror already controls the majority of the votes (i.e. over 50 per cent) and the Panel believes the circumstances justify the use of a tender offer.

Where a partial offer is made which could result in the offeror and its concert parties being interested in shares carrying 30 per cent or more of the voting rights, the Panel will normally grant its consent, but only on the following conditions:

1. the holders of over 50 per cent of the voting rights in the offeree company (excluding those held by the offeror and its concert parties) must approve the offer, even though they do not necessarily accept the offer; the way in which such approval would normally be sought is that, in the acceptance form sent out with the partial offer document, or possibly in a separate form, there will be a box for shareholders to tick to indicate their approval to the partial offer (this is what was required, for example, in the partial offer by GPG Group to acquire an additional 25 per cent of De Vere, given that GPG Group already held a 10 per cent stake; similarly, for example, in the partial offer by Jardine Matheson Holdings for an additional 10 per cent of Jardine Lloyd Thompson Group in September 2011, which

resulted in an increased aggregate holding for Jardine Matheson Holdings of 40.35 per cent); and

2.   where the offer could not result in the offeror holding more than 50 per cent of the voting rights of the offeree company, the offer must not be declared unconditional as to acceptances unless acceptances are received for not less than the number of shares offered for—that number must be stated precisely in the offer document (see, again, the partial offers by GPG Group for De Vere and Jardine Matheson Holdings for Jardine Lloyd Thompson Group).

The purpose of the first condition is to ensure that "over 50 per cent" approve the making of a partial offer which, if successful, will result in the offeror and its concert parties acquiring "control" of the offeree company without all shareholders being given the opportunity to exit for 100 per cent of their shareholdings. Rule 36.5 makes clear that the "over 50 per cent" approval requirement applies to over 50 per cent of the voting rights held by shareholders who are "independent" of the offeror and persons acting in concert with it, rather than over 50 per cent of the voting rights not held by the offeror concert party.

The purpose of the second condition above is to prevent an offeror acquiring what is effective control without paying the full price—that is the offer must be fully successful. Normally, an offeror under a partial offer will permit shareholders to accept an offer for as many shares as they like, guaranteeing that their acceptances will be accepted only to the extent of their proportionate holdings. Thus, if a significant number of shareholders accept for amounts substantially in excess of their proportionate holdings, the offeror may well receive acceptances for more than the total number of shares it has offered for. In view of this, it is not normally difficult to satisfy the second condition if the price is attractive enough.

Partial offers which could result in the offeror and its concert parties being interested in shares carrying 30 per cent or more (but less than 100 per cent) of the voting rights of a company will not normally be permitted if there have been selective or

259

significant acquisitions by the offeror or its concert parties in the previous 12 months or if interests in shares were acquired by any of them after the offer was reasonably in contemplation. The reason for this is, again, so as not to favour certain shareholders (i.e. those who were able to sell out in full as a result of one of the offeror's earlier acquisitions) over other shareholders who would only receive the possibility of a partial exit under the partial offer.

For the same reason, the Code (Rule 36.3) prohibits the acquisition of any interest in offeree shares being made either:

1. during the partial offer (and this applies even for offers for less than 30 per cent); or
2. in the 12 months after the end of the offer period if the offer was successful, unless the Panel consents.

The 12 month moratorium on acquisitions also applies following an unsuccessful partial offer for 30 per cent. or more of the voting rights of the offeree company (see Rule 35.2).

These Rules apply to concert parties (including any connected but non-exempt discretionary fund managers or principal traders who will be presumed to be acting in concert with the offeror or potential offeror once its identity has been publicly announced or is otherwise known to them) just as much as they do to the offeror.

The Panel is likely to grant its consent only if:

1. the successful offer results in less than 30 per cent being owned by the offeror and its concert parties (subject, of course, to Rules 5 and 9); or
2. there are circumstances in which, under Rule 35, an offeror would be allowed to renew a full offer within 12 months of its lapsing (for example, if the offeree company's board recommends it or if a rival offer is made by a third party).

The Code does not expressly deal with the situation where a partial offer is made which could only result in the offeror and persons acting in concert with it being interested in shares carrying less than 30 per cent. of the voting rights of the offeree company, and that offer is unsuccessful. It seems clear, however, that in these circumstances the failed offeror should be free to acquire shares immediately following the lapse of its offer without the 12 month moratorium applying. This is what happened, for example, following Thalassa's partial offer for less than 30 per cent. of Rock Solid Images. Thalassa had chosen to include a minimum acceptance condition in its offer and, following the lapse of its offer for non-satisfaction of this condition, Thalassa was nonetheless allowed to acquire shares by private treaty from certain of the shareholders who had previously accepted its offer.

In the case of a partial offer which could result in the offeror holding shares carrying over 50 per cent of the voting rights of the offeree company, Rule 36.6 requires the offer document to contain specific and prominent reference to this and to the fact that, if the offer succeeds, the offeror and its concert parties will be free (subject to Rule 36.3 and, where relevant, Note 4 on Rule 9.1) to acquire further shares without incurring any obligation under Rule 9 to make a general offer (i.e. it will have what is known as "buying freedom"; Note 4 on Rule 9.1 will be relevant where, as a result of the partial offer, the offeror does not itself hold shares carrying over 50 per cent of the voting rights). Such a disclosure was required, for example, in the partial offer by Amor Holdings to acquire approximately 51 per cent of Partridge Fine Arts. It is also noteworthy in that case that the offeror undertook to offer to purchase the remaining shares not acquired by it pursuant to the partial offer, but not any earlier than 12 months after the partial offer became unconditional.

Rule 36.7 specifies how scaling down of acceptances is to be effected. All shareholders' acceptances up to the relevant percentage of their holdings offered for must be accepted in full. Where shares in excess of that percentage have been tendered by shareholders, the same proportion of such excess shares to the number tendered must be accepted from each shareholder.

261

Rule 36.8 states that, if a partial offer is made for a company with more than one class of equity share capital which could result in the offeror and its concert parties being interested in shares carrying 30 per cent or more of the voting rights, comparable offers must be made for each class (see Rule 14). Although the Code is silent on the point, the question also arises whether an appropriate offer or proposal needs to be made for any convertible securities (see Rule 15) and, if so, whether for all such securities or only on a partial basis.

In July 1992 Jack Chia MPH made an offer for all the shares in Boustead. The offer was structured so that the first three out of every five Boustead shares were offered one cash sum, with a lesser cash sum being offered for all or any part of the balance of shares held. Following this offer, the Panel inserted a new Note to Rule 36 stating that its consent must be sought if any such dual consideration offer is contemplated, where a lower consideration is offered for the balance of shareholders' holdings, and that it may treat such an offer as a form of partial offer. The later two-tier offer by Panther Securities for Elys (Wimbledon) in March 1996, in which Panther offered a higher price for the first one out of every three Elys shares held, was accordingly treated as a partial offer.

In July 2003 a shareholder in Monsoon made an offer to sell put options over shares representing 20 per cent of Monsoon's issued share capital. The shareholder and its concert parties already owned 72.5 per cent and therefore the offer meant that this combined shareholding would increase to 92.5 per cent on the offer becoming unconditional and the put options being exercised. The offer was not, however, treated as a partial offer (or tender offer) regulated by the Code. It appears that the principal reason for the Panel taking this view was that it was an offer to sell put options, as opposed to an offer to buy shares directly. As a general principle, however, the Panel was concerned to see that all shareholders were treated equally.

Generally speaking, the other provisions of the Code (for example as to disclosure) apply to a partial offer regulated by the Code, in the same way as they do to a general offer, except to the extent the context otherwise requires. Where it is proposed to implement a partial offer by way of a scheme of arrangement, the Panel requires prior consultation.

5.4 Redemption or purchase of own securities

Section Q (Rule 37) of the Code deals with the redemption or purchase by a company of its own securities. Such purchases can, of course, effectively be a backdoor method of obtaining control. If a director or a person acting in concert with him was to hold a substantial block of voting shares, any purchase of other voting shares by the company concerned would reduce the number of shares in issue (outside of treasury, where relevant) and increase the percentage which the existing block represents. It would, therefore, give that person greater control.

To protect the minority and to preserve the principle that a person may not obtain or consolidate effective control of a Code company without making an offer to all shareholders, Rule 37.1 provides that a mandatory offer obligation (under Rule 9) will arise in certain circumstances if the percentage of shares carrying voting rights in which a person or group of persons acting in concert is interested increases beyond the limits provided for in Rule 9 as a result of the redemption or purchase by a company of its own shares.

A company which is subject to the Companies Act and which purchases its own shares can choose whether to cancel them immediately or to hold them in treasury. Treasury shares can be used to satisfy awards under a company's employee share plans, resold for cash or cancelled at some future date, or they can simply continue to be held in treasury. Shares held in treasury continue to form part of the company's issued share capital but, for so long as they are held in treasury, the voting rights in respect of them are suspended. Accordingly, for the purposes of the Code (including, for example, the calculation of percentages for Rule 9 and Rule 37 purposes), it is only shares which are in issue outside of treasury which are relevant (see Panel Statement 2003/26 and the definition of "treasury shares" in the Definitions section of the Code).

There have been a number of changes to Rule 37.1 over recent years. Prior to Panel Statement 1999/17, there was a presumption that all the directors of a company, including any shareholders represented on the board, were acting in concert simply by reason of the company seeking shareholders' authority (and being authorised) to redeem or purchase any of its own securities. Where a company annually renewed its authority to buy-in its own shares, which is often the case in practice, this had the effect of all the directors being perpetually presumed to be acting in concert with each other for this purpose. This meant, in turn, that the ability of any director to buy further shares was severely inhibited where all the directors had a combined holding of between 30 per cent and 50 per cent, particularly following the abolition in August 1998 of the "creeper" provision (which had allowed a person holding between 30 per cent and 50 per cent to buy further shares carrying up to one per cent of the voting rights of a company in any 12 month period without triggering a mandatory offer). After a brief experiment at allowing directors some limited purchasing freedom to mitigate the effect of abolishing the "creeper" provision, the Panel then abolished the presumption that the directors as a whole are acting in concert solely by reason of a proposed redemption or purchase by a company of its own shares or the decision to seek shareholders' authority for any such redemption or purchase (see Panel Statement 1999/17).

Accordingly, Rule 37.1 is now applied on the following basis:

1. a director or a person acting in concert with him will normally incur an obligation to make a mandatory offer under Rule 9 (unless a whitewash is obtained as referred to in paragraph 4 below) if, as a result of a redemption or purchase by a company of its own shares, that director and any concert party comes to be interested in 30 per cent or more of the voting rights of the company in question or, if already interested between 30 per cent and 50 per cent, his

percentage interest is increased (but, as noted above, the directors as a whole are no longer presumed to be acting in concert with each other solely by reason of the proposed redemption or purchase);

2. a person who has appointed a representative to the board of the company, and managers of investment trusts, will be treated on the same basis as directors and may incur a mandatory offer obligation under Rule 9 in the circumstances described in 1 above;

3. any other person (i.e. one who is not a director, nor acting in concert with any director, nor represented on the board, nor a manager of an investment trust) will not normally incur an obligation to make a mandatory offer under Rule 9 provided that he has not purchased any shares in the company at a time when he had reason to believe that a redemption or purchase for which requisite shareholder authority existed was being, or was likely to be, implemented in whole or in part (see, for example, the buy-back authority sought by Stobart Group in March 2014 which made clear that a 35.9% shareholder, who was neither represented on the board nor acting in concert with any director, would not be subject to any obligation to make a mandatory offer in the event that its interest increased as a result of the buy-back authority being utilised); and

4. the Panel will usually waive any mandatory offer obligation resulting from a redemption or purchase by a company of its own shares provided there have been no disqualifying transactions (see Section 3 of Appendix 1 to the Code) and there is a vote of independent shareholders and the other procedures set out in Appendix 1 to the Code are followed before the implementation of any redemption or purchase (any such waiver, or "whitewash", must be renewed at the same time as the relevant shareholders' authority for the purchase of shares is renewed under Ch.4, Pt 18 of the Companies Act 2006. There are numerous examples of such waivers being sought in any given year).

Each individual director is required to draw the attention of the board to any interest in relevant securities of that director and any person acting in concert with him at the time any redemption or purchase of the company's own shares is proposed, and whenever shareholders' authority for any such redemption or purchase is to be sought. The Panel requires prior consultation in any case where Rule 9 might be relevant. In appropriate cases, the Panel may require inclusion in the circular to shareholders of confirmation by the directors that they are not aware of any agreements or understandings between directors or persons acting in concert with them.

When is Rule 37 likely to be relevant? It is likely that the maximum number of shares which a company admitted to the Official List will propose to buyback will normally be less than 15 per cent of its equity, in view of the additional requirements imposed by the Listing Rules where 15 per cent or more is to be bought back (see para.12.4 of the Listing Rules). If, for example, there is a buyback of 15 per cent, an interest in 25.5 per cent before the buyback will become an interest in 30 per cent afterwards. In other words, in these circumstances, any director (and persons acting in concert with him) would have to be interested in at least 25.5 per cent of the voting rights before a whitewash is needed. Thus, if a director and his concert parties are interested in 25.5 per cent or more of the voting rights, they should stop all purchases of voting shares as soon as the board starts contemplating proposals for the company to buy back its own shares. Even if they are interested in less than 25.5 per cent of the voting rights, they may be prohibited from purchasing shares for other reasons (for example because of the Model Code (see Annex 1 to Ch.9 of the Listing Rules), Rule 4 of the Code or the insider dealing or market abuse legislation). If they are already interested in between 30 per cent and 50 per cent, they should of course not make any further purchases in any event if, absent some other dispensation, they wish to avoid a mandatory offer obligation.

The share buyback authority sought by Mallett in April 2002 provided an example of where a director was deemed by the Panel to be acting in concert with a family trust, in which the director was also a beneficiary, as a result of which a whitewash was needed to waive the obligation that would otherwise have arisen to make a general offer to all shareholders following implementation of the proposed share buyback.

There are certain cases when a buyback may not be permitted at all, even if a whitewash had previously been obtained, without a further, specific shareholders' approval. Normally a buyback will not be allowed (without such further approval) during an offer or if the target company's board has reason to believe that an offer might be "imminent" (Rule 37.3(a)). The notice of the shareholders' meeting called to approve a buyback in such circumstances must contain information about the offer or anticipated offer. The Panel may, however, consent to the buyback without a further shareholders' approval if it is in pursuance of a contract entered into earlier or another pre-existing obligation (see also art.9 of the Takeover Directive). If it is felt that these circumstances exist, the Panel must be consulted and its consent to proceed without a shareholders' meeting obtained.

An interesting question arises where a company already has a buyback programme in place which is managed by an independent third party (for example its broker) and the board subsequently has reason to believe that an offer for the company might be imminent: would the company need to obtain a further, specific shareholders' approval to continue with the buyback programme in these circumstances? Listing Rule 12.2.1(2) allows purchases by or on behalf of a listed company of its own shares to continue to take place in a prohibited period, provided that the company's broker makes its trading decisions in relation to the company's shares independently of, and uninfluenced by, the company concerned. It is suggested that, in these circumstances, it should be possible for such a buyback programme to continue provided that the original instruction to the company's broker was given before Rule 37.3 came into play, it is irrevocable and the broker does not know of any approach to the company concerned. The Panel should be consulted in cases where this might be an issue.

In practice, a company seeking to defend itself against an unwelcome bidder is unlikely to want to buy back its own shares during the course of the offer as that would increase the percentage of shares in issue (outside of treasury, where relevant) which any unwelcome bidder (or stake builder) may be interested in. Where a buyback forms part of an offeree company's defence strategy, it will therefore usually propose the buyback subject to the hostile offer lapsing (i.e. being defeated). This is what Blue Circle did, for example, as part of its successful defence against an offer from Lafarge in the first half of 2000. This case also provides an example of the Rule, referred to above, that a mandatory offer obligation will not be imposed on an unwelcome shareholder in such circumstances. During the course of its offer, Lafarge had purchased 19.99 per cent, and its financial adviser had purchased 9.61 per cent, of Blue Circle. As part of its defence, Blue Circle promised to return capital to its shareholders, in part through a purchase of its own shares, if Lafarge's offer did not succeed. Blue Circle duly followed up with a share buyback in May 2000, after the lapse of Lafarge's offer. On the basis that Lafarge was not represented on the board of Blue Circle and that both Lafarge and its financial adviser agreed not to vote on the shareholder resolution to authorise the share buyback, the Panel agreed that any increase in their combined holding to 30 per cent or more, as a result of the buyback, would not give rise to a mandatory bid obligation under Rule 9.

If, unusually, a buyback is effected by the offeree company during an offer, there will be an obligation to disclose it as a dealing under Rule 8 and in the offeree company's circular to its shareholders under Rule 37.3(c). The circular will in any event have to contain details of all shares bought back during the 12 months before the offer. Similarly, if the offeror purchases its own shares during the course of a share exchange offer, that counts as a dealing in relevant securities which will have to be disclosed under Rule 8 and in the offer document under Rule 37.4(b). Rules 37.3(c) and 37.4(b) also require the offeree company and the offeror, respectively, to disclose in the documents which they publish in connection with an offer the extent to which shares repurchased in the offer period (and, in the case of the offeree company only, during the 12 months prior to its commencement) were cancelled or held in treasury.

In practice, where an offeree company or an offeror redeems or purchases its own securities, the Panel Executive would normally grant it a dispensation from having to make a dealing disclosure under Rule 8 provided that it includes the necessary details in the announcement it is required to make under Rule 2.10 (regarding any change in the number of relevant securities in issue outside of treasury). In its latest Consultation Paper issued on July 16, 2014, the Code Committee is proposing to codify this practice (see s.8 of Panel Consultation Paper 2014/1). As the reason for requiring shareholder approval for the purchase or redemption by an offeree company of its own shares is because this might constitute "frustrating action", the Code Committee is also proposing to introduce additional wording into Rule 21.1 to deal with this point in lieu of Rule 37.3(a). If the proposed changes are adopted, these will also involve the removal of the remainder of Rule 37.3 and Rule 37.4.

The redemption or purchase of non-voting shares (for example, most preference shares) will not be relevant for the purposes of Rule 37 which (like Rule 9) is concerned with voting rights.

Before a company starts a buyback programme, it is always worth considering if there are any Code implications, in addition to the usual tax, financial and corporate law considerations.

Chapter 6

Documents from the Offeror and the Offeree

Carlton Evans

Partner

Linklaters LLP

6.1   Introduction

Takeover documentation, particularly in contested offers, may often appear at first sight to be subject to few guiding principles. However, the content of takeover documentation is closely controlled in respect of both general approach and detailed contents, principally by the Code and, to a lesser extent, by a number of other sources of regulation, such as the Listing Rules, the Prospectus Rules and the Disclosure and Transparency Rules (the Disclosure Rules) of the UK Financial Conduct Authority (the FCA) and the Financial Services and Markets Act 2000 (the FSMA 2000).

Over the years there has been an increase in the detailed information required by the Code in offer documentation and in the precision with which the more technical elements are drafted. This is partly due to the fact that the Code has become a document drafted in increasingly legal terms which require close study in order that all of its provisions can be properly reflected in offer documents. In addition, the offer document is a legal document constituting an offer which, on acceptance, establishes a contractual relationship between the offeror and the offeree's shareholders. The offer document and related documents may also have other legal consequences (for example, if they contain misrepresentations or defamatory statements) and their drafting therefore needs to reflect this.

On September 19, 2011, significant reforms to the Code were adopted (the 2011 Amendments). These resulted in a number of important changes to UK takeover practice, especially in relation to the announcement process during the early stages of a potential offer, as well as to the contents requirements for takeover documentation. The 2011 Amendments arose primarily from issues which occurred in the bid by Kraft for Cadbury, notably concerns over:

1. the length of time between a possible offer announcement and a firm offer being announced; and
2. the fact that, having announced during the offer that it thought it would be able to continue to operate a UK Cadbury facility (which Cadbury had announced would be subject to a phased closure), Kraft changed its mind after the offer had become wholly unconditional. Kraft was publically criticised for doing so—for breaching Rule 19.1 in not satisfying Code standards as to the accuracy of statements made during offers.

Subsequently, the Panel published additional consultation papers proposing further changes to the Code which have impacted on offer document contents (the July 2012 Consultations). These proposals related primarily to the rights of an offeree's pension scheme trustees, publication on an ongoing basis of material changes to information previously disclosed by parties to an offer and publication of profit forecasts and quantified financial benefits statements. Response Statements have subsequently been issued by the Takeover Panel, and new Rules introduced into the Code, in respect of these issues.

Most recently, on July 16, 2014 the Panel issued Consultation Paper PCP 2014/1 (the "2014 Consultation"), inviting comments on it by September 12, 2014.

6.2 General obligations in respect of documents

6.2.1 *The spirit of the Code*

The Introduction to the Code identifies the difference between its General Principles and its Rules. The General Principles are expressed in broad terms and are "essentially statements of standards of commercial behaviour". The Rules fall into two categories: some of them expand on the General Principles and others are provisions governing specific aspects of takeover procedure. Neither the General Principles nor the Rules are framed in technical language and both are to be interpreted so as to achieve their underlying purpose. Thus, the Code is to be interpreted in accordance with its spirit rather than its letter—although its letter, in giving detailed guidance as to procedure, must not be ignored.

This approach applies as much to documentation as to any other aspect of a takeover. The documents issued by a company to its shareholders, or to the shareholders of another company, have to be drafted in a way which both complies with the detailed requirements of the Code and also enables shareholders and other persons interested in the offer to consider and evaluate fairly the arguments put forward in the course of a takeover.

6.2.2 *General responsibilities in respect of offer documentation*

In the context of documentation, the General Principle of the Code that is particularly relevant is General Principle 2, which requires that:

> "The holders of the securities of an offeree company must have sufficient time and information to enable them to reach a properly informed decision on the bid; where it advises the holders of securities, the board of the offeree company must give its view on the effects of implementation of the bid on employment, conditions of employment and the locations of the company's places of business."

This Principle is, to a large extent, repeated in Rule 19.1 and is supplemented by Rule 23.1. These Rules state:

"19.1 Standards of care

Each document or advertisement issued, or statement made, during the course of an offer must be prepared with the highest standards of care and accuracy and the information given must be adequately and fairly presented. This applies whether it is issued by the company direct or by an adviser on its behalf."

"23.1 Sufficient information

Shareholders must be given sufficient information and advice to enable them to reach a properly informed decision as to the merits or demerits of an offer. Such information must be available to shareholders early enough to enable them to make a decision in good time. No relevant information should be withheld from them. The obligation of the offeror in these respects towards the shareholders of the offeree company is no less than an offeror's obligation towards its own shareholders."

As mentioned above, Kraft was publically criticised for breaching Rule 19.1 in its offer for Cadbury.

As Note 1 on Rule 19.1 makes clear, it is important to note that the Panel regards financial advisers as being responsible for guiding their clients and any relevant public relations advisers with regard to information released during the course of an offer.

Whatever the detailed information, comment or advice contained in offer documentation, the correct approach is that of common sense and commerciality—namely, do the documents say what they are intended to say, do they give fair and adequate information and are they likely to be understood by the persons who are to receive them, not all of whom will have the same level of commercial knowledge and sophistication?

6.2.3 Specific standards of care—the Notes on Rule 19.1

Rule 19.1 contains a number of notes intended to emphasise and enlarge upon the obligations of that Rule. Accordingly, the language used in documents, announcements, information, releases or advertisements should be unambiguous so as to reflect "clearly and concisely" the position being described. The source for any fact that is material to an argument must be clearly stated, together with sufficient detail to enable the significance of the fact to be assessed. Quotations must not be taken out of context, details of their origin must be given, and the board of the company using the quotation must be prepared to substantiate or corroborate comments quoted.

Pictorial representations and diagrams must be presented without distortion, and charts, graphs and other similar diagrams must be to scale. The parties to a takeover will often want to use performance figures in a way which bolsters their respective arguments—this is not forbidden, but graphs and charts used must give a fair view and the basis for them should be justifiable. The Panel must be consulted in advance if television, videos, audio tapes, etc. are to be used.

In addition, Note 3 on Rule 19.1 (adopted under the 2011 Amendments) emphasises that any public statement of intention made by a party in the context of the offer and relating to any action that it intends to take, or not take, after the end of the offer period (whether in a document, announcement or otherwise) must be adhered to during the 12 months after the end of the offer period (or for whatever time period is referred to in the public statement). It is, however, permissible for the offeror or offeree to be released from adhering to such a statement if there has been a "material change in circumstances", although no further gloss is provided on what this could mean in practice. (This arose primarily out of the Kraft bid for Cadbury where, as mentioned above, Kraft changed its mind after the offer about closing a facility.)

Finally, Note 8 on Rule 19.1 refers to potential liabilities for market abuse imposed by FSMA and for financial services offences under the Financial Services Act 2012 (see 6.12.5 below).

6.2.4 Directors' responsibility statements—Rule 19.2

The above provisions are buttressed by the requirement in Rule 19.2 that the directors of the relevant company should expressly accept responsibility as individuals for the information contained in each document or advertisement published in connection with an offer and should confirm that, to the best of their knowledge and belief (having taken all reasonable care to ensure that such is the case), the information contained in the document or advertisement is in accordance with the facts and, where appropriate, that it does not omit anything likely to affect the import of such information.

This Rule is applied slightly differently depending on the nature of the offer.

In a hostile offer the directors of the company issuing the document generally have to accept responsibility for everything in it. However, a modified form of responsibility statement is permitted when information about another company contained in a document has been compiled from published sources (such as its report and accounts). In that case, responsibility need only be taken for "the correctness and fairness of its reproduction or presentation" (see Note 3 on Rule 19.2). Accordingly, on a hostile bid, the factual information set out in the offer document relating to the offeree will be covered by such a qualified form of responsibility statement.

In a recommended offer, responsibility for information will generally be split between the offeror and offeree directors. The board of the offeree will be required to take full responsibility for information relating to the offeree and the board of the offeror will accept responsibility for the rest of the document.

In a securities exchange offer, where an offer document constitutes, or is accompanied by, a prospectus (or a document containing information which is regarded by the FCA as being equivalent to that of a prospectus), under the Prospectus Rules the offeror directors may be required to take responsibility for the whole of the prospectus or equivalent document, notwithstanding the ability under the Code to split responsibility between offeror and offeree directors.

In "public to private" takeovers (or P2Ps), the persons within a private equity house required by the Panel to take personal responsibility will often be extended to include the investment committee and/or senior employees working on the transaction, as well as directors of the actual bidco.

In exceptional circumstances, the Panel may be willing to consent to the exclusion of a director from the responsibility statement, and sometimes agrees to this in the case of overseas offerors with large numbers of non-executive directors or with a two-tier board structure. In such cases, the omission and the reasons for it may occasionally be required to be stated in the document or advertisement.

Furthermore, certain types of advertising (such as product or corporate advertising not bearing on an offer) (see 6.9.4 below), and separate opinions of the offeree's employee representatives and its pensions scheme trustees on the effects of the offer, do not need to carry a responsibility statement.

Finally, where investment analysts' forecasts are published by the offeree or a securities exchange offeror on its website, it must be prominently stated that the forecasts are not endorsed by the company and that they have not been reviewed or reported on in accordance with the Code.

6.2.5 *Appointment of board committees and verification*

Since many boards of directors are too large to be a viable body for preparing documentation (and most executive directors will continue to spend the majority of their time running the business), it is common practice for a board of directors to delegate day-to-day conduct of the offer to a committee, including the detailed consideration of documentation. The directors must believe that the members of the committee are competent to do the work and must disclose all relevant facts relating to themselves or otherwise relating to the documentation. Notwithstanding any delegation, however, all the directors retain ultimate responsibility, as is made clear by Section 1 of Appendix 3 to the Code. This requires the circulation of papers and information to the board (including all non-routine agreements and other obligations entered into by a company in the context of the offer) and the holding of board meetings, as necessary, throughout the offer period. By this means, no director is likely to be able to claim that he has been relieved from his responsibility for ensuring the accuracy of the contents of documentation.

6.3   Early stage documents

6.3.1   Initial offer announcements

In the early stages of a bid, a number of documents may be issued by or on behalf of the parties.

The first of these documents will be either an announcement of a possible offer under Rule 2.4 or an announcement of a firm intention to make an offer under Rule 2.7. Practice Statement No.20 sets out the ways in which the Panel will normally interpret certain provisions of Rule 2, including when a possible offer announcement may be required and the contents of such an announcement.

The first of these announcements to be issued in any bid will start an offer period in respect of the offeree. This is important since various Rules in the Code then begin to apply.

As soon as possible thereafter, and at latest by 09.00 on the following business day, the offeree (and the offeror, or publically identified potential offeror, in the case of a securities exchange offer) must announce details of its issued share capital (under Rule 2.10). In practice, this information is often included in the main first announcement. The 2014 Consultation proposes to replace this time of 09.00 with 07.15.

Thereafter, the offeree (and, in the case of a securities exchange offer, the offeror or publically identified potential offeror) must then provide the Panel with details of persons reasonably considered to be interested in 1 per cent or more of their share capital (Rule 22). These provisions are supported by Rule 8 which requires offerors, offerees and persons with 1 per cent interests to announce their interests publicly—generally within 10 business days of the commencement of the offer period or the announcement first identifying the offeror. The Rule also requires disclosure of dealings during the offer period.

The 2014 Consultation proposes various changes to these disclosure requirements, including in relation to the disclosure of irrevocable commitments and letters of intent under Rule 2.11.

6.3.2 *The new "put up or shut up" (or PUSU) regime*

As discussed above, the 2011 Amendments implemented significant new requirements in relation to possible offer announcements under Rule 2.4. These changes were driven by the overall approach of the 2011 Amendments to strengthen the position of offerees. In particular, the Rules were revised so as to reduce the period of time during which an offeree might be under siege from a potential offeror, following a possible offer announcement, without such potential offeror being required to launch a formal offer or announce that it has no intention of doing so.

Under Rule 2.4(a), a possible offer announcement by an offeree must identify any potential offeror with which it is in talks or from which an approach has been received (and not unequivocally rejected), irrespective of which potential offeror was the subject of the rumour and speculation which gave rise to an announcement obligation under Rule 2.2. As mentioned above, this announcement will also commence an offer period.

The Panel may grant a dispensation from the requirement for such an announcement if it is satisfied that the potential offeror has ceased active consideration of an offer (see Note 4 on Rule 2.2). In the event of such a dispensation, various restrictions then apply to the potential offeror. The 2014 Consultation proposes to make certain amendments to these restrictions.

Under Rule 2.6(a), any announcement which commences an offer period under Rule 2.4(a), and any subsequent announcement which first identifies a potential offeror under Rule 2.4(b) (see below), will trigger an automatic, compulsory 28-day "put up or shut up" or "PUSU" deadline within which any named potential offeror will be required either to announce a firm intention to make an offer or to state that it has no intention to do so. The announcement must specify the date on which the 28-day deadline will expire and include a summary of the provisions of Rule 8 in relation to disclosure of dealings and positions.

In the case of multiple competing offerors, each potential offeror is subject to its own 28-day deadline from the date on which it is publicly identified—there is no common deadline for all, allowing any new potential offeror at least the same amount of time to consider its bid as any initial potential offeror.

6.3.2.1 PUSU Extensions

Under Rule 2.6(c), extensions can be granted to the 28-day period. Extensions have occurred in a number of possible offers and are typically only granted towards the end of the 28-day, or previously extended, deadline to avoid the prospect that, otherwise, extension requests at the start of the 28-day period would become standard practice.

Extensions will normally be permitted with the consent of the Panel—but only at the request of the offeree, and after taking into account "all relevant factors", including the status and anticipated timetable for completion of negotiations. The offeree therefore, in theory at least, has the ability to request: (i) different extensions to a put up or shut up deadline and/or (ii) an extension for a preferred potential offeror and not, if it so chooses, an unwelcome potential offeror. However, this is probably unlikely to occur in practice.

Put up or shut up periods can be subsequently re-extended multiple times. Any extension, together with the status and timing of negotiations, must be promptly announced by the offeree.

6.3.2.2 White Knights

After an offer period has begun, the offeree is not required to announce the existence of a new potential offeror with which it has thereafter begun talks or from which it receives an approach. This is an important exception since it provides an offeree with the freedom to approach a potential white knight without triggering an announcement obligation and, therefore, the automatic put up or shut up deadline. An announcement may, however, be required if "rumour and speculation accurately and specifically identifies a potential offeror which has not previously been identified in any announcement" (Note 3 on Rule 2.2). If required, any such announcement must identify that potential offeror (Rule 2.4(b)). The Rules do not expand on the "accurately and specifically identified" test but, in practice, this is likely to require more than speculation in the form of an educated guess as to who else might be interested in making an offer.

6.3.2.3 Public Auctions

Note 2 on Rule 2.6 provides a further exception to the naming and compulsory put up or shut up deadline for potential offerors—it applies in the case of a public auction sale process that is initiated by the offeree. For these purposes, the Panel has stated that an announcement by an offeree of a strategic review of its business will not be sufficient to trigger this formal sale process exemption (although such a public auction can be instigated by an offeree following, and separate from, a strategic review).

6.3.2.4 End of PUSU Periods

If all identified potential offerors announce that they have no intention to make a firm offer, the offer period will end, notwithstanding that, at that time, the board of the offeree company may still be in discussions with a white knight or other potential offeror whose existence is not known to the market. In such a situation, the offeree would, however, at least need to consider whether it should issue an announcement to avoid more general false market concerns.

Once a potential offeror has announced a firm intention to make an offer, the relevant put up or shut up period will no longer apply to any other potential competing offerors (Rule 2.6(b)). In addition, any party that previously announced that they had no intention to make a firm offer will no longer be bound by such a statement and may also make a competing offer (Note 2(b) on Rule 2.8). In that case the offeror need not make the offer if any subsequent competing offeror announces an intention to make a higher offer (Rule 2.7(b)).

Conversely, where a potential offeror states that it has no intention to make an offer after a competing offeror has already made a firm offer, the Panel will not usually consent to the potential offeror setting aside such statement unless that original offer has been withdrawn or lapsed (Note 2(a) on Rule 2.8). (Note 2 on Rule 2.8 also sets out other circumstances where a statement of no intention to make an offer may be set aside—see further details in Ch.2.)

6.3.3 Misleading statements of intention

Rule 19.3 requires that parties to an offer (and their advisers) must take care not to issue statements which, whilst not factually inaccurate, may be misleading or may create uncertainty. This may arise in the early stages of an offer (for example when more than one potential offeror is named by the offeree) or, after an offer is launched, when a possible competing bidder may wish to alert the market to the fact it is considering a bid—for example, with a view to reducing the chances of the initial bidder being able to purchase shares in the market in the meantime. Equally, however, it may be relevant later on in an offer.

This general provision is supplemented by one specific example of an unacceptable statement, namely a statement by an offeror "to the effect that it may improve its offer, or that it may make a change to the structure, conditionality or the non-financial terms of an offer, without committing itself to doing so and specifying the improvement or change". This therefore includes statements about switching from an offer to a scheme of arrangement or vice versa (see Panel Statement 2007/35 concerning the breach of this Rule by Standard Life in its bid for Resolution).

This Rule is a reflection of General Principle 4 (which requires parties to endeavour to avoid the creation of a false market) and is designed to prevent an offeror indicating that it might increase, or otherwise alter the terms of, its offer before it is able to commit itself to doing so.

Practice Statement No.19 issued by the Panel Executive illustrates the Panel's approach in this area. It advises that, during the course of an offer, any suggestion of an improvement or change to an offer will be of particular sensitivity since it could lead to a false market being created in the securities of the offeree. It adds that, if an offeror wishes to make a holding statement in order to publicise its initial reaction to a particular development (such as an increase in a competing offeror's offer), it may state, for example, that it is "considering its position" or that it is "considering its options". It should not, however, use language which implies that it might improve or change the terms of its offer.

6.3.4 Clarification of possible offer announcements

These general obligations in Rule 19.3 are supplemented by a specific requirement to clarify possible offer announcements which are still outstanding in the later stages of an offer. This was previously dealt with in Note 1 on Rule 19.3 but, pursuant to the 2011 Amendments, this requirement is now in Rule 2.6(d) and (e) so that it is included alongside all the other provisions of the Code dealing with announcements of possible offers.

As mentioned in 6.3.2 above, in the case of multiple competing offerors, once one potential offeror has announced a firm intention to make an offer, any existing or new potential competing offeror is no longer subject to any put up or shut up deadline. However, in light of the potential uncertainty which could otherwise be caused by the continued presence of a potential competing offeror at the end of an offer, Rule 2.6(d) and (e) impose a deadline by when any announced potential offerors must clarify its intentions.

Under Rule 2.6(d), where it has been announced that a publically identified potential offeror might make a competing offer, whether or not such statement was made before or after the announcement of a firm intention to make an offer, it must clarify such statement in the later stages of the offer period, by a date to be decided and announced by the Panel, by announcing either a firm intention to make an offer or that it has no intention of doing so.

Similarly, under Rule 2.6(e), once an offeror has announced a firm intention to make an offer and the offeree then refers to the existence of another potential offeror without publically identifying it, such potential competing offeror must, by a date in the later stages of the offer period to be decided and announced by the Panel, either announce a firm intention to make an offer or confirm to the offeree that it has no intention to do so, which must then be promptly announced by the offeree.

These Rules are supported by a requirement for the Panel to announce the date by when the relevant possible offer announcement needs to be clarified. Where the first offeror is proceeding by way of a contractual offer (rather than a scheme of arrangement), this date will normally be a date which is on or around 10 days prior to the end of the offer period (i.e. the final day on which the first offeror's offer is capable of becoming or being declared wholly unconditional as to acceptances—Note 3 to Rule 2.6). In relation to schemes of arrangement, the date will normally be a date which is on or around 10 days prior to the date of the shareholder meetings (see the Note on Section 4 of Appendix 7 to the Code).

Finally, Practice Statement No.8 states that, if the Panel grants an offeror an extension to Day 60 (i.e. the last day generally allowed to satisfy the acceptance condition), it will normally grant a corresponding extension to any date by which a statement by a potential competing offeror must be clarified in accordance with Rule 2.6(d).

The 2014 Consultation proposes inter alia the following changes to these provisions:

(i) that the final deadline for a potential offeror to clarify its position should be by no later than 5pm on the 53rd day after publication of the initial offer document;

(ii) that, alternatively, in the case of a scheme, the potential offeror should normally be required to clarify its position by 5pm on the seventh day prior to the date of the shareholder meetings to approve the scheme (although, in appropriate cases, the Panel should continue to be able to permit the potential offeror to do so by no later than 5pm on the seventh day prior to the date of Court sanction);

(iii) that, where the Panel consents to an extension to Day 60, it will normally also grant an extension to, or re-set, Day 46; and

(iv) that, if a potential offeror acquires interests in offeree shares after making a "no intention to bid" statement when clarifying its position, it should cease to have the right to set the "no intention to bid" statement aside with the agreement of the offeree board in the event that the first offeror's offer lapses.

6.3.5 Distribution of early stage announcements

A possible offer announcement must be sent promptly by the offeree to its shareholders, persons with information rights and to the Panel (Rule 2.12(a)). Following recent Code amendments, any such announcement must also be made promptly and "readily available" by the offeree to its employee representatives or, where there are no such representatives, its employees and to the trustees of the offeree's pension scheme(s) (Rule 2.12(a)(ii)). For these purposes, and for the purposes generally of the Code, "pension schemes" must include a defined benefit element for the relevant Rules to apply.

Similarly, a "firm intention" announcement, or a circular summarising the terms and conditions of the offer, must also be sent promptly by the offeree to its shareholders, persons with information rights and to the Panel and the offeree must make that announcement or circular "readily available" to the trustees of its pension scheme(s) (Rule 2.12(b)(i)). In addition, under Rule 2.12(b), both the offeror and the offeree must also make such an announcement, or a circular summarising its terms, "readily available" to their respective employee representatives or, where there are no such representatives, to the employees themselves.

This document will often be accompanied by the offeree board's preliminary views, for example advising shareholders to take no action pending further consideration by the board, or outright rejection.

When an offeree makes an announcement or circular available to its employee representatives (or employees) and to the trustees of its pension scheme(s) pursuant to Rule 2.12(a) or 2.12(b), it must at the same time inform them of the right of employee representatives and pension scheme trustees to have separate opinions appended to the offeree board's circular pursuant to Rule 25.9. In addition, the offeree must inform its employee representative (or employees) of the offeree's responsibility to pay the costs reasonably incurred in obtaining advice required for the verification of the information contained in their opinion (Rule 2.12(d)).

Both the offeror and the offeree must explain the implications of the relevant announcement and the offeree must make clear that certain information provided by offeree shareholders, persons with information rights and other relevant persons for the receipt of communications from the offeree may be provided to an offeror during the offer period (Rule 2.12(c)).

Note 1 on Rule 2.12 makes clear that, where a circular summarising the terms of the offer is sent to shareholders, persons with information rights, employee representatives (or employees) or pension scheme trustees, the full text of the announcement must be made "readily and promptly available" to them, for example by posting it on the offeror or offeree's respective websites. Any circular summarising the Rule 2.7 announcement must also include details of the website on which a copy of the announcement is published in accordance with Rule 30.4(a) (see 6.7.6).

6.4 Offer document contents—Rule 24

6.4.1 *General requirements*

The offer document is the main document in any offer. It must normally be sent to shareholders of the offeree and others entitled to receive it within 28 days of the announcement of a firm intention to make the offer.

The following analysis of the documentation to be issued by the respective parties to a takeover assumes that an offer is not recommended. In general, however, the Rules apply equally to a recommended offer, in which case the contents requirements in respect of offeree circulars will also apply to the recommended offer document and whatever else the offeror and offeree publish jointly (see 6.5 below).

It should also be noted as a general matter that certain information can be incorporated into offer documentation by reference and that there are alternative methods of communicating Code information to shareholders (see 6.7 below).

6.4.2 Commercial issues, terms and conditions

First and foremost, the offer document will deal with the main commercial terms and arguments for the offer—the price, the commercial logic and general "puff" for the offeror, its management and its expertise. It will also set out in full all the terms and conditions attached to the offer. These terms will include:

1. information about the consideration (for example the type of consideration, any alternative consideration, whether consideration shares carry the right to the next dividend, and the rights attached to consideration preference shares or loan stock);
2. detailed information on the circumstances in which an offer can be revised;
3. the timetable for announcements and when rights of withdrawal arise;
4. detailed information about acceptances; and
5. the warranties, undertakings and authorities given by an accepting shareholder by virtue of his execution of a form of acceptance.

All terms and conditions of an offer must be set out in full, without merely cross-referencing to Rules of the Code (although this requirement has been mitigated in one respect (see 6.4.6 below)). The requirement that all the conditions be comprehensive is illustrated by Rules 31.5 and 32.2 which prohibit extensions to, or increases in, the offer in cases where the offeror has indicated that the offer will not be extended or, as the case may be, increased (unless the right to do so has been specifically reserved, with precise details being required of the circumstances which would trigger a right to extend or increase).

The specific Code requirements for an offeror to satisfy concerning the contents of an offer document are to be found in Rules 24.2–24.16. These requirements may also extend to documents that are not technically offer documents, such as circulars sent to shareholders by a potential offeror which has announced an offer but subject to a pre-condition.

6.4.3 Intentions regarding the offeree, offeror and their employees—Rule 24.2

Under Rule 24.2(a), an offeror must cover the following points in the offer document:

1. its intentions with regard to the future business of the offeree and the long-term commercial justification for the offer;
2. its intentions with regard to the continued employment of the employees and management of the offeree and its subsidiaries, including any material change in the conditions of employment;
3. its strategic plans for the offeree and their likely repercussions on employment and the locations of the offeree's places of business;
4. its intentions with regard to employer contributions into the offeree company's pension scheme(s) (including with regard to current arrangements for the funding of any scheme deficit), the accrual of benefits for existing members and the admission of new members (a new requirement implemented in 2013);
5. its intentions with regard to any redeployment of the fixed assets of the offeree; and
6. its intentions with regard to the maintenance of any existing trading facilities for the offeree's relevant securities (a requirement introduced by the 2011 Amendments).

Where the offeror is a company, and insofar as it is affected by the offer, the offeror must also state its intentions with regard to its future business and disclose information for subparas (2) and (3) above with regard to itself (Rule 24.2(c)).

In relation to subpara.(2), prior to May 20, 2006 the offeror was merely required to describe its intentions with regard to the continued employment of the employees and the practice evolved that this requirement would be met with the rather anodyne statement that the employment and other rights of employees would be "safeguarded".

Such a statement is still typically included in offer documents. However, following the events in the Kraft bid for Cadbury concerning Kraft's change of intention over closure of a facility, the 2011 Amendments deliberately aim to improve the quality of disclosure by offerors and offerees in relation to the offeror's intentions regarding the offeree's business and its employees, in order to provide meaningful information to the offeree's shareholders and employees. To that end, Rule 24.2(b) requires the offeror to make a negative statement in the offer document if it has no plans to make any changes in relation to the matters referred to in subparas (2)–(5) above. In addition, if it considers that its strategic plans for the offeree will have no repercussions on employment or the location of the offeree's place of business, the offeror must make a statement to that effect. As mentioned in para.6.2.3 above, under Note 3 on Rule 19.1, the offeror will be bound by any such statement during the 12 months following the end of the offer period, or such other time period referred to in that statement.

6.4.4   Financial and other information—Rule 24.3

Prior to the 2011 Amendments, the Code contained different disclosure requirements in respect of such information depending on: (i) the nature of the offeror, with less information being required in the case of UK listed offerors (on the basis that more extensive public information was easily available on such companies if persons wished to review it); and (ii) the nature of the offer, with more information being required if the offer included offeror securities, rather than a pure cash offer (on the basis that, in a cash offer, with the exception of any minority shareholders, offeree shareholders would not need to assess the future financial performance of the offeror).

However, the 2011 Amendments introduced a radical change of approach to the disclosure of financial information on the offeror. The rationale for this was that persons other than offeree shareholders (for example employees) have an interest in understanding the financial strength of the offeror. Accordingly, under the amended Rules, subject to certain exceptions, detailed financial information must be provided in relation to an offeror and the financing of an offer irrespective of the nature of the offer (i.e. even in the case of a pure cash offer by a UK listed company). However, the impact of this was considerably mitigated by the introduction of new Rules designed to allow financial information in particular to simply be incorporated by reference (see below).

6.4.4.1 *UK listed offerors*

Under Rule 24.3(a), where the offeror is a company incorporated under the Companies Act 2006 (or its predecessors) and its shares are admitted to trading on a UK regulated market or the Alternative Investment Market (AIM) or the ISDX Growth Market, the offeror must include in the offer document:

1. the names of its directors;
2. the nature of its business and its financial and trading prospects;
3. details of website addresses where its audited consolidated accounts for the last two financial years and any preliminary statement of annual results, half-yearly financial report or interim financial information published since the date of its last published accounts can be found, together with a statement that such statement, report or information has been incorporated into the offer document by reference to the relevant website in accordance with Rule 24.15;

4. in the case of a securities exchange offer, any known significant changes in its financial or trading position since the end of the last financial period for which audited accounts, a preliminary statement of annual results, a half-yearly financial report or interim financial information has been published (or a negative statement);
5. a statement of the effect of full acceptance of the offer upon its earnings and assets and liabilities; and
6. a summary of the principal contents of each material contract (not being a contract entered into in the ordinary course of business) entered into by the offeror or any subsidiary in the two years before the commencement of the offer period.

Under Rule 24.3(e), the information summarised under subparas (1)–(4) above must also be given in respect of the offeree (save in respect of (4) above in a recommended offer document (see 6.5.2 below)).

6.4.4.2 *Non–UK listed offerors and their participants*

Where the offeror is not a Companies Act company or its shares are not admitted to trading on a UK regulated market, AIM or the ISDX Growth Market, it must disclose as much of the information set out in Rule 24.3(a) as is appropriate and such further information as the Panel may require (Rule 24.3(b)(i)).

The Code also requires additional information about persons who are participating in an offeror whose shares are not admitted to trading on a UK regulated market, AIM or the ISDX Growth Market (for example a private equity house in a P2P or shareholders in a consortium company formed for the purposes of the offer). The identity of such persons and details of their interests must be disclosed as well as such other information as the Panel may require (Rule 24.3(b)(ii) and (iii)). The ability of the Panel to require additional information means that in appropriate cases the Panel should be consulted in advance, so that the offer document can be properly prepared.

Where an offeror whose shares are not admitted to trading on a UK regulated market, AIM or the ISDX Growth Market is the subsidiary of another company, the Panel will normally look through the offeror and require information on the ultimate holding company in the form of group accounts (Note 1 on Rule 24.3).

6.4.4.3 *Other information*

Rule 24.3(d) sets out further contents requirements for the offer document. These include:

1. a heading stating "If you are in any doubt about this offer you should consult an independent financial adviser authorised under the FSMA";
2. the date when the document is published, the name and address of the offeror (including, where the offeror is a company, the type of company and the address of its registered office);
3. the identity of any person acting in concert with the offeror and, to the extent that it is known, the offeree, including, in the case of a company, its type, registered office and relationship with the offeror and, where possible, the offeree;
4. details of each class of security for which the offer is made (including whether those securities will be transferred "cum" or "ex" any dividend and the maximum and minimum percentages of those securities which the offeror undertakes to acquire);
5. the terms of the offer, including the consideration offered for each class of security, the total consideration offered and particulars of the way in which the consideration is to be paid in accordance with Rule 31.8;
6. all conditions to which the offer is subject;
7. particulars of all documents required, and procedures to be followed, for acceptance of the offer;
8. market prices for the securities to be acquired and, in the case of a securities exchange offer, securities to be offered;
9. details of any agreements or arrangements to which the offeror is a party which relate to the circumstances in

which it may or may not invoke or seek to invoke a condition to its offer and the consequences of doing so including, to the extent permitted by the Code require-ments, details of any break fees payable as a result (see 6.8.2 below);

10. details of any irrevocable commitment or letter of intent which the offeror or any of its associates has procured in relation to relevant securities of the offeree (or, if appropri-ate, the offeror);

11. in a securities exchange offer, full particulars of the terms of the securities being offered including the rights attach-ing to them;

12. a summary of the provisions of Rule 8 (which governs the disclosure of dealings during the course of an offer);

13. the national law that will govern contracts concluded between the offeror and the holders of the offeree's securities as a result of the offer and the competent courts;

14. the compensation (if any) offered for the removal of "breakthrough" rights pursuant to art.11 of the European Directive on Takeover Bids (2004/25) (the Directive) together with particulars of the way in which the compensation is to be paid and the method employed in determining it;

15. details of any offer-related arrangement permitted under Rule 21.2 (see further 6.8.2 below);

16. a list of the documents which the offeror has published on a website in accordance with Rule 26.1 and Rule 26.2 (which set out the requirements for documents to be published on a website following the announcement of an offer or the making of an offer, respectively) and the address of the website on which the documents are published (see 6.7.9 below); and

17. any profit forecast or quantified financial benefits state-ment, and any related reports and confirmations, required by Rule 28 (as introduced following the July 2012 Consultations).

Under Rule 24.3(g), if any document published by the offeror contains a comparison of the value of the offer with previous prices of the offeree's shares, a comparison of the current value of the offer and the price of the offeree's shares on the last business day prior to the beginning of the offer period must be prominently included, no matter what other comparisons are made.

Following the 2011 Amendments, Rule 24.3(c) also requires the offer document to contain a summary of the ratings and outlooks provided by rating agencies in respect of the offeror and offeree prior to the beginning of the offer period, together with any changes made to those ratings or outlooks during the offer period and a summary of any reasons given for any such changes.

6.4.4.4 *Sources of finance to an offeror*

Following the 2011 Amendments, under Rule 24.3(f), the offer document must contain: (i) a description of how the offer is to be financed (both debt and equity) and the source(s) of the finance; and (ii) in relation to debt finance, details of the debt facilities or other instruments entered into in order to finance the offer and to refinance the existing debt or working capital facilities of the offeree, other than hedging arrangements, and in particular:

1. the amount of each facility or instrument;
2. the repayment terms;
3. interest rates;
4. any security provided;
5. a summary of the key covenants;
6. the names of the principal financing banks; and
7. if applicable, details of the time by which the offeror will be required to refinance the acquisition facilities and of the consequences if that is not done by the relevant time.

In addition, all documents relating to the financing of an offer must be put on display, along with any refinancing documents when they are entered into (see also 6.7.9 below). On occasion, however, the Panel has allowed display of market flex provisions to be delayed, for example until posting of the offer document.

6.4.5 *Shareholdings and dealings—Rule 24.4*

Rule 24.4 contains a list of information required concerning shareholdings and dealings of the offeror (and its directors) in the shares of the offeree (which can vary depending on whether the offer is a securities exchange offer or not).

Under Rule 24.4, the offer document must contain details of any shares of the offeree in which, inter alia, the offeror, its concert parties and certain other connected persons have an interest or right to subscribe or which they have borrowed or lent. "Interest" is defined as "a long economic exposure whether absolute or conditional to changes in the price of securities" and a person is treated as having an interest in shares if, inter alia, he owns them, has the right to direct voting rights, has the right or obligation to take delivery of the shares or if he is a party to any derivative whose value is determined by reference to the price of the underlying shares. Rule 24.4 also requires short positions in relation to shares and derivatives referenced to those shares to be disclosed.

Under Rule 24.4(c), dealings by any person whose interests have to be disclosed under Rule 24.4(a) are required to be disclosed for the period beginning 12 months prior to the commencement of the offer period and ending with the latest practicable date before printing of the offer document. "Dealings" is construed widely and again extends to financial products referenced to offeree shares.

In the case of a securities exchange offer, equivalent information generally has to be given by the persons required to disclose their interests and dealings in offeree shares in relation to any interests and dealings they might have in offeror shares. In the case of competing offers, certain of these disclosures also extend to the competing bidder's securities.

Note 2 on Rule 24.4 states that, provided that inter alia no significant dealings are thereby concealed, disclosure of:

1.   dealings during the offer period can be aggregated;

2.   dealings in the three months prior to that period can be aggregated on a monthly basis; and

3.   dealings in the nine months prior to that period can be aggregated on a quarterly basis.

6.4.6   Disclosure of fees and expenses—Rule 24.16

A completely new Rule was introduced as part of the 2011 Amendments to require the detailed disclosure of the fees of any advisers to the offeror (see Rule 24.16).

The offer document must contain an estimate of the aggregate fees and expenses expected to be incurred by the offeror in connection with the offer, with separate estimates in respect of: financial and corporate broking advice; financing arrangements (including full details of any commitment or drawdown fees, which may be cross-referred to the information required under Rule 24.3(f)); legal, accounting or public relations advice; and any other professional services (such as management consultants, actuaries or specialist valuers).

If a fee is variable, the offer document must disclose the minimum and maximum amounts payable. Where a fee is not subject to a maximum amount, that must be made clear and the arrangement explained (for instance, whether the fee is discretionary or relates to the final value of the offer or is calculated on a "time cost" basis). If a category of fees and expenses includes a variable or uncapped element, the figure or range given must reflect a reasonable estimate of the fees likely to be paid on the basis of the current offer. If the fee arrangement provides for circumstances where the fee may increase, for example where the offer is revised or a competitive situation arises, the higher amount is not required to be disclosed until such circumstances arise.

If any fee or expense within a particular category is likely at any time to exceed the estimated maximum previously disclosed by 10 per cent or more, or if the final fees and expenses actually paid within a particular category exceed the disclosed estimated maximum by 10 per cent or more, the offeror must promptly disclose the revised estimates, or final amounts paid, privately to the Panel, which may then require the public disclosure of such revised estimates or final amounts paid.

Rule 25.8 also requires any such fees and expenses, if applicable, to be detailed in the offeree circular (see 6.5 below).

6.4.7   Other information required by Rule 24

Other information required by Rules 24.5 to 24.14 includes:

1.   in the case of a securities exchange offer, whether and in what manner the emoluments of the directors of the offeror will be affected by the acquisition of the offeree or any associated transaction, or an appropriate negative statement (Rule 24.5);
2.   details of any agreement, arrangement or understanding (including any compensation arrangement) between the offeror or any concert party and any of the directors, recent directors, shareholders or recent shareholders of the offeree having any connection with or dependence upon the offer (Rule 24.6). This Rule also cross-refers to Rule 16.2 which requires any management or incentivisation arrangements or proposals (or discussions) to be publically disclosed and, depending on the facts, this may need to be supported by an opinion from the offeree's financial advisor and an independent shareholder vote;
3.   a repetition of the confirmation required to be included in the announcement of a firm intention to make an offer from the offeror's bank or financial adviser of the existence of financial resources to satisfy any cash payable under an offer (although this confirmation does not operate as a guarantee that funds will be available) (Rule 24.8). A conditional confirmation is not permitted. Where an offeror proposes to finance a cash offer (or a cash alternative to a securities exchange offer) by an issue of new securities, the Panel will not regard this as "exceptional circumstances" and, accordingly, will not allow the cash confirmation given to be conditional upon the success

of the issue of the new offeror securities (Practice Statement No.10), although certain necessary conditionality will be permitted—for example any required shareholder approval and/or admission of any new securities to listing. The 2011 Amendments also introduced a new Rule requiring the offeror to promptly notify the Panel if it becomes aware or considers it likely that it will not be able to satisfy a financing condition (Rule 13.4(d));

4. a statement as to the ultimate ownership of any securities acquired in pursuance of the offer (Rule 24.9);

5. a statement that, where securities offered as consideration are to be listed on the Official List or admitted to trading on AIM, the relevant listing or admitting to trading condition will only be satisfied when the announcement of admission has been made. Where securities are offered as consideration and it is intended that they should be admitted to listing or to trading on any other investment exchange, the Panel should be consulted (Rule 24.10);

6. an estimate by an appropriate adviser of the value of any class of securities proposed to be issued as consideration which is not admitted to trading (Rule 24.11). In such an offer, however, it will not normally be possible for the offeror to satisfy the Panel that the value of its offer exceeds the price of any purchases of offeree shares that might have been made to which Rule 6 applies;

7. a statement to the effect that, except with the consent of the Panel, settlement of the consideration to which any shareholder is entitled under the offer will be satisfied in accordance with the terms of the offer without regard to any other counterclaim to which the offeror may otherwise be entitled (Rule 24.12);

8. details of any arrangements in relation to certain dealings which exist between the offeror, or any person acting in concert with the offeror, and any other person, or a negative statement (Rule 24.13); and

9. a clear statement as to the procedure for shutting off any cash-underwritten alternative (Rule 24.14).

The complete and detailed list should be read from the Code itself, but there is one further and very important requirement which must be noted. According to Rule 24.7, the offer document must state the time allowed for acceptance of the offer and any alternative offer and must reflect appropriately the full terms relating to acceptance levels, time of announcements, rights of withdrawal, etc., which are contained in those parts of Rules 13.5(a), 13.6 (if applicable), 17 and 31 to 34 of the Code (see Ch.7). It must also reflect the terms of Notes 4 to 8 on Rule 10 relating to acceptances and purchases and confirmation of good title to shares. However, the amount of small print which would be required if all details were to be set out in full has been substantially reduced by the Code permitting a cross-reference to Notes 4 to 6 and Note 8 on Rule 10, since they deal with what are regarded as largely technical matters.

6.4.8 *Incorporation of information by reference—Rule 24.15*

In addition to the financial information required to be included or incorporated by reference in the offer document, Code documents may incorporate other information by reference to another source with the Panel's consent. If information is permitted to be incorporated by reference, then certain additional requirements need to be complied with under Rule 24.15 (including details of where the information is located) and recipients are entitled to request a hard copy of the relevant information.

6.5 Offeree circular contents—Rule 25

6.5.1 *Offeree recommendation*

The offeree circular (which must be issued within 14 days after issue of the offer document, if not combined with it) is subject to various general requirements set out in Rule 25.

It must first contain the opinion of the board of the offeree on the offer and any alternative offers (together with the board's reasons for forming its opinion) and the substance of the advice given to it by its independent financial advisers (Rule 25.2). In a recommended offer, the opinion of the offeree board will be contained in the offer document itself. In a hostile offer, it will be contained in the "defence document" which will seek to refute the arguments and the commercial logic put forward by the offeror. The opinion of the offeree board must include its views on:

1. the effects of implementation of the offer on all the company's interests, including, specifically, employment; and
2. the offeror's strategic plans for the offeree and their likely repercussions on employment and the locations of the offeree's place of business as set out in the offer document pursuant to Rule 24.2.

If there is no clear opinion or there is a "divergence of views" among the offeree board, or between the board and its independent financial adviser, this must be made clear in the offeree circular and an explanation given, including the arguments for or against the acceptance or rejection of the offer (Note 2 on Rule 25.2). The views of any directors who are in a minority should also be included in the circular. The Panel will also require prior consultation on such opinions and related explanations.

The 2011 Amendments implemented a new Note 1 on Rule 25.2 to make clear that the Code does not limit the factors that the board of the offeree company is able to take into account in giving its opinion on the offer—in particular, that the offeree board is not bound to consider the offer price as the determining factor.

6.5.2 Other specific content requirements

Rule 25 also sets out specific content requirements for the first major circular from the offeree board. To a large extent, Rule 25 corresponds to the information requirements imposed on the offeror by Rule 24.

Under Rule 25.3, subject as set out below, the first major circular from the offeree board advising shareholders on an offer must contain a description of any known "significant change" in the financial or trading position of the offeree since the end of the last financial period for which audited accounts, a preliminary statement of annual results, a half-yearly report or interim financial information has been published, or an appropriate negative statement.

Under Rule 24.3(e) of the Code, the offeror is generally required to include this information in its offer document in relation to an offeree. However, in a combined offer document (i.e. if the offer is recommended), this information will now be the responsibility of the offeree board and Rule 2.4.3(e) will not apply to such a statement. This gives the shareholders the benefit of knowing that such statements have been considered by those best placed to understand the offeree's affairs (i.e. the offeree's directors). In contrast, if the offeree circular follows the offer document, the information in the offeror document on any such changes need not be repeated as long as it is specifically referred to in the statement made by the offeree.

Other information that needs to be contained in the first major circular from the offeree includes:

1. interests and dealings in the offeror's and the offeree's shares and whether the offeree directors intend to accept or reject the offer in respect of their own beneficial holdings (and, if required by the Panel, which of any alternative offers they intend to elect for) (Rule 25.4);
2. information about directors' service contracts (including particulars of former contracts, if such contracts have been replaced or amended within six months of the date of the document) (Rule 25.5). This Rule is designed to ensure that any compensation payments to outgoing directors ("golden parachutes"), which are arranged at or shortly before the making of the offer, are fully disclosed to the public. Aggregation of the remuneration payable under service contracts is no longer permitted and full details of each director's remuneration package must be given;

3. any arrangement in relation to securities of the offeree, such as indemnities or options, must also be disclosed, or there should be an appropriate negative statement if there are none (Rule 25.6);

4. a summary of the principal contents of any material contract (not being a contract entered into in the ordinary course of business) entered into by the offeree or any subsidiary in the two years before the commencement of the offer period (Rule 25.7(a));

5. details of any irrevocable commitment or letter of intent which the offeree or any person acting in concert with it has procured in relation to securities of the offeree (Rule 25.7(b));

6. a list of the documents which the offeree has published on its website in accordance with Rule 26 (Rule 25.7(c));

7. any profit forecast, or quantified financial benefits statement, and any related reports or confirmations, required by Rule 28 (Rule 25.7(c)); and

8. as mentioned in 6.4.6 above, details of any fees and expenses expected to be incurred by the offeree in connection with the offer (Rule 25.8).

6.5.3 Opinions from employees and pension scheme trustees

The offeree must also append to its document any opinion from its employee representatives and/or the trustees of its pension scheme(s) on the effect of the offer on employment and/or the offeree's pension scheme(s) respectively, provided that any such opinion is received "in good time before publication". It must also publish any employee opinion or pension scheme trustee opinion on a website (and announce via an RIS that it has been so published) if it is not received prior to publication of the circular and provided that it is received within 14 days of the offer becoming or being declared wholly unconditional. Note 1 on Rule 25.9 also requires the offeree to pay for (i) the costs of the publication of the employee opinion and of any pension scheme trustee opinion and (ii) any costs reasonably incurred in obtaining advice on verification of the employee opinion.

Respondents to a previous Panel consultation on the 2006 changes to the Code in respect of employee representative opinions (which were required by the Directive) expressed concern that the effect of these Rules was to require the offeree to consult with its employees prior to the offer being announced. They claimed that this issue could be of particular concern in a recommended offer where both the announcement of a firm intention to make an offer and the combined offer document (containing information on the offeror and the offeree) could be published on the same day—this would not be possible if the offeree was required to obtain the opinion of employee representatives.

As a result, the Panel clarified that, in its opinion, both the Directive and the Code required information to be provided to employees but that consultation was not required and that there was no intention to change the practice of publishing a combined document in the case of a recommended offer. However, as mentioned in 6.3.5, above, when the offeree makes a copy of an announcement or circular available to its employees or employee representatives at the beginning of an offer period, it must at the same time inform them of the right of employee representatives to have a separate opinion appended to the circular and of the offeree's obligation to pay for advice in connection with the verification of information in that opinion.

As mentioned above, in 2013 the above provisions relating to employee representatives were extended to any opinion of the trustees of an offeree's pension schemes, save in respect of the cost of verifying such an opinion (given that any such costs might be significant).

6.6 Schemes of arrangement

Takeovers are increasingly being implemented by way of schemes of arrangement. This is often done in order to avoid the half per cent stamp duty which arises on transfers of shares in a contractual takeover offer, and also since it removes any risk of the offer succeeding but with the offeror ending up owning less than 100 per cent of the offeree securities.

In the case of a scheme, the circular which has to be sent to offeree shareholders is required to contain essentially the same Code information as an offer document in a recommended takeover. It also contains various sections necessary in order to implement the scheme itself—for example, the expected scheme timetable, an explanatory statement, notices of a general meeting and of a meeting of shareholders convened by the court, and the scheme of arrangement itself.

Takeovers implemented by way of a scheme of arrangement fall within the general scope of the Code and many of its Rules apply in exactly the same way in a scheme of arrangement as they do in a contractual takeover offer. However, some Rules are inevitably inapplicable to schemes given, for example, that there is no contractual "offer" or "acceptance" in a scheme of arrangement which is, in contrast, effected by way of a shareholder vote and court approval.

In light of this, the Panel has, over the years, applied the Code in relation to schemes of arrangement in a pragmatic way. However, due in large part to the increasing number of schemes in recent years, a new Appendix 7 was included in the Code to deal with the differences between schemes of arrangement and contractual offers, to clarify which Rules should be disapplied when a scheme is used and to set out specific Code amendments. These include the following:

1. that a mandatory bid under Rule 9 should not be able to be undertaken by way of a scheme of arrangement without the Panel's prior consent. In deciding whether to give its consent, relevant factors will be the views of the offeree and its financial adviser and the likely timetable impact. In addition, if the scheme lapses but an offer would not have done, the offeror will have to make a normal takeover offer immediately on such lapse and this must be stated in the scheme circular (Section 2 of Appendix 7);

2. a requirement for holding statements to normally be clarified on or around 10 days prior to the shareholder meetings but with Panel discretion to allow later clarifications (Section 4 of Appendix 7 and related Notes) (see 6.3.4 above, including the proposals to amend this requirement in the 2014 Consultation);

3. a requirement that announcements should be made as soon as practicable (and in some cases by no later than 08.00 on the following business day) following key events in a scheme (for example the shareholder and court meetings and the effective date (Section 5 of Appendix 7));

4. disapplying the provisions of Rule 31 ("timing of the offer") but including new provisions relating to the timing of, and revisions to, a scheme (Sections 6 and 7 of Appendix 7);

5. a requirement to consult the Panel if an offeror is considering announcing a scheme without beforehand obtaining the support of the offeree board (Section 13 of Appendix 7); and

6. a requirement that, where securities are offered as consideration, the relevant admission to listing condition must be capable of being satisfied only when all steps required for the admission to listing have been completed other than the relevant regulatory announcement of admission to listing (Section 15 of Appendix 7, implemented by the 2011 Amendments).

The 2011 Amendments prohibited implementation agreements which were generally used in schemes of arrangement and used to contain various obligations on the offeree as to the timetable for it to seek to implement a scheme (see 6.8.2 below). Instead, the 2011 Amendments include specific requirements in Appendix 7 to deal with timing obligations, conditions and other rights or restrictions which would previously have been included in an implementation agreement.

For instance, under Section 3 of Appendix 7, the offeree must: (i) ensure that the scheme circular is sent to shareholders (and persons with information rights) within 28 days of the announcement of the firm intention to launch the scheme (provided that the scheme is recommended); (ii) include in the scheme circular the expected timetable for the scheme (including certain key dates); and (iii) implement the scheme in accordance with the published timetable (for so long as the scheme remains recommended and subject to any proposed or actual adjournment of the shareholder meetings or court sanction hearing or the invocation of any condition to the scheme as permitted by the Code (see below)). On publication of the scheme circular, the offeree must also announce such publication and include the expected timetable in that announcement.

In addition, the parties to the offer are now permitted to include in the conditions to the scheme specific deadlines by when the shareholder meetings and court sanction hearing must be held (provided that the deadlines are more than 21 days after the relevant dates in the published timetable) and a long-stop date by which the scheme must become effective. Amongst other requirements, any such conditions must be given prominent reference in the offeror's firm intention announcement. While the offeror can agree an extended deadline or long-stop date with the offeree, if the relevant deadline is not met the offeror can walk away. In addition, if any condition is not capable of being satisfied by the relevant date, the offeror must make an announcement by no later than 08.00 on the business day following such date, stating whether the offeror has invoked or waived the condition or agreed a new deadline or long-stop date with the offeree.

Finally, following the 2011 Amendments, the Panel has also made clear that it will permit an offeror to switch from a scheme of arrangement to a contractual offer (with an acceptance condition of up to 90 per cent) if: (i) the board of the offeree withdraws its recommendation of the scheme or proposes an adjournment of a shareholder meeting or the court sanction hearing or if any such meeting or hearing is adjourned; or (ii) if the Panel considers that the offeree has not implemented the scheme in accordance with the published timetable (see Note 2 on Section 8 of Appendix 7).

6.7   General publication requirements

6.7.1   *Amendments to the Code*

As a result of the increasing use of websites and electronic forms of communication between companies and their shareholders, the Code was amended on March 30, 2009 in order to relax the provisions dealing with the publication and circulation of takeover documents. A summary of these provisions is set out below.

6.7.2   *Publication of documents—Rule 30.1*

Under Rule 30.1, Code documents must be published in one of the following three ways:

1.   in traditional hard copy form;
2.   by communication in electronic form (for example e-mail); or
3.   by publication on a website, provided that shareholders are notified of such website publication in accordance with (1) or (2) above (see 6.7.3 below).

These publication requirements cover all documents that are required to be issued under the Code, except that forms of acceptance, withdrawal forms and proxy forms still need to be sent out in hard copy form.

6.7.3   *Website notifications*

If a party publishes Code documents on its website, rather than publishing them electronically or in hard copy, it is also required to send a website notification to alert recipients to the website publication of such Code documents. The notification must be sent electronically or by hard copy no later than the date on which the relevant document is published on the website.

Website notifications are subject to strict content requirements (see the Note on the definition of a "website notification" in the Code). In summary, they are required inter alia to:

1. give notice of the publication of a document on a website and identify the website;
2. be prepared to the highest standards of accuracy and contain a directors' responsibility statement;
3. contain a summary of the provisions of Rule 8;
4. only include non-controversial information about an offer (and not for example include a recommendation);
5. only include certain other limited information in the same envelope as the notification;
6. include a statement about the recipient's entitlement to receive information in hard copy and details of how to do so; and
7. include a statement that the notification is not a substitute for, or a summary of, the relevant information.

6.7.4   *Ability to choose method of publishing—Rule 30.2*

Save for forms of acceptance, withdrawal forms and proxy forms, parties to an offer are generally able to choose which method of publishing a document they use. If an offeree shareholder (or person with information rights) has elected to receive documents generally from the offeree in electronic form, then Code documents can be sent to him electronically without the need for further consent. To bolster this require-ment, the offeree is required to provide the offeror with offeree shareholders' email addresses upon request following the announcement of a firm intention to make an offer.

Conversely, however, a fresh consent is required if the person has limited its e-communications election to specific docu-ments, such as notices of meetings. Similarly, previous general elections by offeree shareholders to receive documents in hard copy form prior to any offer are binding on parties to an offer during an offer.

Any person to whom a Code document is sent either electronically or by website publication is also entitled to request to receive a hard copy of that document or any future Code documents sent to him in connection with that offer (Rule 30.2). This right must be made clear in any electronic communication or website publication, together with details of how a hard copy may be obtained. A person who requests a hard copy should receive it by at the latest two business days of receipt of that request.

If a person sends a request for a hard copy to an offeror, the offeror must notify the offeree of such request, and if sent to the offeree (including by an offeror) the offeree must notify the other parties, without that person having to make separate requests of those other parties.

6.7.5 *Distribution of documents*

Under Rule 24.1(a), the offeror must normally send the offer document to shareholders of the offeree and persons with information rights in accordance with Rule 30.1 within 28 days of the announcement of a firm intention to make the offer and must make the document "readily available" to the trustees of the offeree's pension scheme(s). At the same time, both the offeror and the offeree must make the offer document "readily available" to their employee representatives or, where there are no employee representatives, to the employees themselves. It is likely that website publication will be sufficient to discharge this obligation. Under Rule 24.1(b), on the same day that the offer document is sent to shareholders, the offeror must also publish it on a website in accordance with Rule 30.4 (see 6.7.6 below) and announce via an RIS that the offer document has been so published.

Under Rule 30.3(a), an offeror is also required to lodge a copy of the offer document with the Panel, before it is made public, in hard copy and electronic form. Rule 30.3(b) also provides for copies of all other documents, announcements and information connected with an offer (including the offeree circular, if applicable) to be sent to the Panel and advisers to other parties at the time of their publication. Rule 30.3(c) also provides protection to other parties to avoid them being disadvantaged if it is proposed to publish a document, announcement or other information outside normal business hours.

If it is not combined with the offer document, the board of the offeree must normally send a circular to its shareholders (and persons with information rights) in accordance with Rule 30.1 within 14 days of the despatch of the offer document (Rule 25.1(a)). Similarly to the case of offer documents, at the same time, the offeree must make the offeree circular "readily available" to its employee representatives or, where there are no employee representatives, to the employees themselves and also to the trustees of its pension scheme(s). Again, website publication is likely to be sufficient. Finally, the offeree must also publish the offeree circular on a website in accordance with Rule 30.4, and announce via an RIS that the offeree circular has been so published, on the same day that it is sent to shareholders (Rule 25.1(b)).

6.7.6 *Information to be available on websites in any event—Rule 30.4*

A copy of most information published in relation to an offer by a party to an offer or a possible offer is required to be made available on a website (and any such document must provide details of the relevant website) by no later than noon on the following business day, even if that party does not intend to publish documents in electronic form or by means of website publication. These documents include:

1. Code documents and other information sent to shareholders, persons with information rights and other relevant persons (as mentioned above, Rules 24.1 and 25.1 now expressly require publication of the offer document and any offeree board circular, respectively, on a website in accordance with Rule 30.4);
2. any RIS announcements made by that party during the offer (whether related to the offer or not). However, this does not apply to: (i) transaction disclosures made by

311

directors and persons discharging managerial responsibilities; (ii) sales/acquisitions of major shareholdings; (iii) disclosures of increases or decreases in total voting rights and share capital; and (iv) announcements by offerees at the start of an offer period of the offeree's issued share capital, (as required by Rule 2.10); and

3. documents published on a website under Rule 26.

Conversely, however, companies are not required to publish the documents produced by another party to an offer, though they may well choose to do so in practice in the context of a recommended offer.

If a party does not have its own website (for example a bid vehicle in a P2P), the Panel may allow it to use a website belonging to a third party. The website must be maintained for the duration of the offer period as well as during any competition reference period related to the offer and all Code documents must include details of the website on which a copy is published.

6.7.7 Publishing documents to persons with "information rights"

Under ss.145 and 146 of the Companies Act 2006, shareholders may notify companies or other persons that they wish to receive information from the relevant company (for example a nominee shareholder might notify the details of the beneficial owner of the relevant shares). Persons granted such information rights will be entitled to receive Code documents at the same time and in the same manner as they are sent to offeree shareholders.

Forms of acceptance relating to an offer, however, do not need to be sent to persons with information rights on the basis that such persons are not able to transfer or dispose of the whole or any part of a shareholder's interest in shares.

6.7.8 Circulation of documents to overseas shareholders—Rules 23.2 and 30.4

Rule 23.2 provides that the requirement to make information and documents available to shareholders, persons with information rights and employees or their representatives applies wherever those shareholders or employees are located, unless there is "sufficient objective justification" for the requirement not applying.

The Note on Rule 23.2 provides a derogation setting out the circumstances in which there would be "sufficient objective justification" for not applying the Rule. Dispensations will not normally be granted in relation to recipients who are located within the EEA. However, outside the EEA, those circumstances include where the laws of a non-EEA state may result in a significant risk of civil, regulatory or criminal exposure for the offeror or offeree if the information or document is sent into that jurisdiction without amendment and either:

1. less than three per cent of the shares of the offeree are held by registered shareholders located there; or
2. circumstances are such that it would be proportionate for the Panel to grant a dispensation (having regard to factors such as the cost involved, number of shares involved and any delay to the timetable).

The introduction of this Rule in 2006 led to an updating of past advice about the risks of posting documents into certain jurisdictions and the result, in practice, has been that offer documentation is now often posted to some jurisdictions where it had not been in the past.

Overseas shareholders are also entitled to enjoy the same rights of electronic access to offer-related documents unless there is a sufficient objective justification for not doing so on the current bases set out in Rule 23.2 (see Note 3 on Rule 30.4).

6.7.9 Documents to be published on a website

Rule 26 sets out certain documents which must be and remain published by the offeror and/or offeree, as applicable, until the end of the offer (including any related competition reference period). This Rule has been amended in three important respects in the last few years.

First, all such documents must now be published on a website and the address of this website must be published in the offer document and any offeree circular and announced via an RIS. The previous requirement for hard copies of such documents to be made physically available for inspection has consequently been dispensed with.

Secondly, the Rule had previously only required publication from the date of the offer or defence document. However, the 2011 Amendments brought forward the time from when certain specific documents are required to be published on a website to no later than 12.00 on the business day following the announcement of a firm intention to make an offer (or, if later, following the date of the relevant document) (Rule 26.1).

This earlier publication requirement applies to any irrevocable commitment or letter of intent, any documents relating to the financing of the offer (save potentially for market flex arrangements), any indemnities and any offer-related arrangement permitted under the new Rule 21.2 on inducement fees, save for any such arrangements with pension scheme trustees which are not material (Note 6 on Rule 26), (see 6.8.2 below). In 2013, this list was further extended to include any agreements or arrangements (or, if not reduced to writing, a memorandum of all the terms of such agreements or arrangements) which relate to the circumstances in which the offeror may or may not invoke or seek to invoke a pre-condition or condition to its offer.

Rule 26.2 then lists a wider number of documents that must be published on a website following the publication of the offer document and any offeree board circular (or, if later, the date of the relevant document).

Thirdly, the Rule now applies on an ongoing real-time basis to new documents entered into and/or amended during the offer (including any related competition reference period). For example, as mentioned above, the requirement to publish also extends to any new documents entered into which would have had to be published on a website had they been entered into at the time of the announcement of a firm intention to make an offer or the offer document (as the case may be), as well as requiring an announcement to be released concerning the addition to the website of any such new, amended, varied or updated documents.

Similarly, Note 5 on Rule 26 makes clear that, if any relevant document is amended, varied or replaced during the period in which it is required to be published, the amended, varied or replaced document must be put on the relevant website and an announcement made explaining that this has been done.

The Rule is now further supported by the new requirement to announce, on an ongoing basis, material changes in information previously disclosed (see 6.9.2. below).

6.7.10 Revised documentation

Under Rule 32.1, if an offer is revised, a revised offer document must be drawn up in accordance with Rules 24 and 27 (see 6.9.1). The same publication requirements apply to a revised offer document as for the original, including making the revised offer document readily available to employee representatives (or employees) and the trustees of the offeree's pension scheme(s), and informing them of the right to have a separate opinion on the revised offer appended to any offeree circular.

Similarly, under Rule 32.6, the board of the offeree must draw up a circular in accordance with Rules 25 and 27 containing its opinion on the revised offer. The same publication requirements apply to such a revised circular as for the original, including with regard to the opinion of employee representatives and the pension scheme trustees on the revised offer.

6.8 Specific issues

6.8.1 Profit forecasts, quantified financial benefits statements and asset valuations (Rules 28 and 29)

It is not uncommon, particularly in contested offers, for the offeror or offeree to make a profit forecast in support of their respective positions, although this may not always be made in the first document from either side. Indeed, this may be unavoidable if, whether deliberately or not, a profit forecast has been made in some previous public statement (although this is now required in fewer situations following recent Rule changes). Similarly, statements quantifying financial benefits expected to accrue if the offer is successful, or expected cost savings if it is unsuccessful, (now known as "quantified financial benefits statements" following the July 2012 Consultations) are also fairly common. Asset valuations, which occur less frequently, tend to be made in the case of offerees with a large and potentially undervalued asset base (for example property or mining companies).

The Code lays considerable emphasis on the standards of care which are required for these types of statement and imposes material additional safeguards in relation to them.

The Rules introduced by the July 2012 Consultations have made significant amendments to the requirements relating to profit forecasts and quantified financial benefits statements. These amendments, and a summary of the more detailed Rules concerning profit forecasts, quantified financial benefits statements and asset valuations, are considered in more detail in Ch.8.

6.8.2   Offer-related arrangements— Rule 21.2

6.8.2.1   General prohibition on these arrangements

It had become common in recent years, in recommended offers, for offerors to seek the benefit of a number of deal protection measures from the offeree, such as inducement fees. In its consultation on the 2011 Amendments, the Panel expressed the view that market practice had treated deal protection measures as standard packages, which would rarely provide much scope for negotiation or resistance by the offeree and which potentially made it more difficult for a competing offeror to enter the fray. Accordingly, in a drive to strengthen the position of the offeree, the 2011 Amendments deleted the old provisions relating to inducement fees and introduced a general prohibition of inducement fees and other deal protection measures other than in certain limited cases.

Under Rule 21.2(a), except with the consent of the Panel, no offeree or any person acting in concert with it may enter into an "offer-related arrangement" with the offeror or any person acting in concert with it during an offer period or when an offer is reasonably in contemplation.

This prohibition of "offer-related arrangements" is widely drafted and includes any "agreement, arrangement or commitment in connection with an offer", which includes any inducement fee (or comparable arrangement) and extends to any other offer-related arrangement such as any exclusivity arrangements, matching rights, restrictive due diligence undertakings or where the offeree provides any ancillary benefits or undertakings to the offeror in support of the offer.

The restrictions are one-way in that, whilst they restrict the arrangements that can be entered into by the offeree company, they do not prevent the provision of undertakings by the offeror (which can still, therefore, provide reverse break fees or agree to a standstill). Note, however, that the prohibition extends to the offeror (as well as the offeree) in the context of a reverse takeover, where it may be arguable as to which party should be treated as the offeree (see Rule 21.2(b)(v)).

6.8.2.2 Permitted offer-related arrangements

Under Rule 21.2(b), the following offer-related arrangements are specifically permitted to be entered into: confidentiality undertakings; commitments to provide information or assistance for regulatory purposes or not to solicit employees, customers or suppliers; irrevocable commitments and letters of intent (as to which see below); and agreements relating to any existing employee incentive arrangement (for instance, an undertaking in relation to the number of shares to be issued or the amount payable under a bonus arrangement). While not expressly permitted under Rule 21.2, the Panel has also said that the entry into management incentivisation arrangements between offeree management and an offeror continues to be permitted.

In 2013 this list of permitted offer-related arrangements was extended to include any agreement between the offeror and the trustees of any of the offeree's pension schemes—but only in relation to the future funding of the pension scheme. Any such agreement consequently needs to be summarised in the announcement of a firm intention to make an offer and in the offer document. However unlike other offer-related arrangements (which all need to be published on a website), it will only need to be "published" on a website if it is material (Note 6 on Rule 26).

Practice Note No.27 deals with the extent to which irrevocable commitments and letters of intent are permitted offer-related arrangements in the case of persons who are both shareholders and directors of the offeree. It states that shareholder directors are permitted to enter into irrevocable commitments or letters of intent in relation to the shares held or controlled by such individuals. However, the Practice Note highlights that shareholder directors are not permitted to enter into other types of offer-related arrangements and the content of any irrevocable commitment or letter of intent is not permitted to extend beyond the scope of the decision to accept an offer or voting in favour of a scheme of arrangement.

In addition to these specific exceptions, Notes 1 and 2 on Rule 21.2 set out the following two situations when offer-related arrangements will still be permitted, in order to cater for offerees seeking a white knight and for public auctions:

1.   under Note 1, if a hostile offer has already been made and not subsequently withdrawn or recommended, the Panel will normally consent to the offeree entering into an inducement fee arrangement with any competing offeror—but only when any such white knight announces its firm intention to make a competing offer, and provided that: (i) the aggregate value of the inducement fee, or fees, that may be payable is capped at 1 per cent of the value of the offeree (calculated by reference to the price of the competing offer or, if there are two or more competing offerors, the first competing offer); and (ii) any fee is payable only after an offer becomes or is declared wholly unconditional; and

2.   under Note 2, if the offeree initiates a public auction process, the Panel will normally consent to the offeree entering into an inducement fee at the conclusion of the public auction with one offeror who had participated in that process when such an offeror announces its firm intention to make an offer. (Note 2 also states that, in exceptional circumstances, the Panel may also consent to the offeree entering into other offer-related arrangements with that offeror.)

While no express provisions are made in Rule 21.2 or the relevant Notes, the Panel has also acknowledged that offer-related arrangements might be permitted in the following circumstances:

1.   the Panel would normally expect an offeree to provide an offeror with: (i) information or notification as to the satisfaction of, or its ability to waive, the conditions to an offer; including a confirmation that no material adverse

change has occurred in relation to the offeree; and (ii) notification of any material changes in the conduct of the offeree's business since the announcement of the offer. However, the Code Committee of the Panel has stated that it does not believe that the list of permitted offer-related arrangements should be expanded to cover an agreement by the offeree to provide any such information or notification. The impact of this has in practice probably been reduced, however, as a result of the Panel's proposals in the July 2012 Consultations being adopted requiring parties to an offer to announce details of material changes to previously published information on an ongoing basis (see para.6.9.2 below); and

2. there may be circumstances in which a company is in such serious financial distress that it is actively seeking an offer to be made for it and a potential offeror will only consider making an offer if an inducement fee or other offer-related arrangement is offered to it. In such circumstances, the Panel may, following consultation, permit such an inducement fee or other offer-related arrangement to be entered into if Rule 21.2 would otherwise operate unduly harshly or in an unnecessarily restrictive, burdensome or otherwise inappropriate manner.

Practice Statement No.23 sets out inter alia various parameters for determining the maximum amount permitted for an inducement fee, in the few cases where an inducement fee might now be possible.

It states that the one per cent limit may be calculated on the basis of the fully diluted equity share capital of the offeree and, where necessary, should take into account irrecoverable VAT payable on the fee. For the purposes of determining the offeree's fully diluted equity share capital, only options and warrants that are "in the money" may be included in the calculation and such instruments must be valued on a "see through" basis (being their value by reference to the value of the offer for the shares to which they relate, net of any exercise price). In a securities exchange offer, the value of the offeree will be fixed by reference to the value of the offer as stated in the Rule 2.7 firm offer announcement.

Inducement fees have from time to time in the past been entered into between offerees and third parties as part of a defence strategy (in relation to, for example, the acquisition of an asset or business). Though not technically covered by Rule 21.2, such agreements are caught by Rule 21.1(b)(v) (whereby an offeree is prevented from entering into a contract otherwise than in the ordinary course of business during the course of an offer unless it has obtained prior shareholder approval). Accordingly, the Panel ought to be consulted if any such arrangement is ever contemplated.

6.8.2.3 *General provisions concerning offer-related arrangements*

The Panel should be consulted at the earliest opportunity if there is any doubt as to whether an agreement, arrangement or commitment is caught by the general prohibition or if the Panel's consent to an inducement fee, or dispensation from Rule 21.2, is sought.

As mentioned above, details of any permitted offer-related arrangement must be fully disclosed in the Rule 2.7 announcement of a firm intention to make an offer and in the offer document and (save for non-material agreements with pension scheme trustees) any relevant documentation or information must be put on display in accordance with Rule 26.1 (i.e. published on a website as soon as possible and in any event by no later than 12.00 on the business day following the firm intention announcement until the end of the offer period) (see 6.7.9 above).

6.9   Other documents and announcements

6.9.1   Subsequent announcements and documents

After the initial offer and defence documents have been issued, there is likely to be a succession of documents issued by the offeror and offeree containing further arguments and information. These documents must comply with the provisions of Rule 27.2 and contain details of any changes in information previously published by it in connection with the offer which are material in connection with that document and, if there have been no material changes, this fact must be stated. There must also be updated information on such matters as interests in shares and dealings, changes in the financial or trading position, offeror directors' emoluments, changes to offeree directors' service contracts, etc.

In addition, in relation to schemes of arrangement, the Panel has amended the Code so as to provide that certain key events must be announced and, in certain cases, then potentially posted to offeree shareholders (Section 5 of Appendix 7).

Where a profit forecast, quantified financial benefits statement or asset valuation has been made, any subsequent document must also contain a statement by the directors that the forecast, quantified financial benefits statement or asset valuation remains valid for the purpose of the offer and, where applicable, that the financial advisers and accountants who reported on the forecast, or the independent valuer who performed the asset valuation, have indicated that they have no objection to their reports or opinion respectively continuing to apply (see Rule 27.2(d)).

6.9.2   Continuous obligation to update material information

The requirements to update previously published information were significantly amended in the July 2012 Consultations.

In particular, a new Rule 27.1 has been introduced which requires a party to an offer to disclose, after the date of the offer document or initial defence circular (as the case may be), (i) any material changes to information disclosed in any document or announcement previously published by it in connection with the offer and (ii) any material new information which would have been required to be disclosed in any previous document or announcement published during the offer period had it been known at such time, in each case promptly by way of announcement—i.e. not merely when a subsequent document is published.

In addition, if any such announcement were required, the Panel has reserved the right to require a document setting out the relevant information to be sent to offeree shareholders and persons with information rights and made readily available to the offeree's employee representatives (or employees) and pension scheme trustees.

6.9.3 Time limits on updating material information

There is a limit to the time in which information connected with offers can be released to shareholders. Rule 31.6 basically requires that, subject to various exceptions, the acceptance condition must be satisfied by acceptances and purchases made by 13.00 on the 60th day after posting the offer document (commonly known as "Day 60"). Consequently the last document from the offeror which can contain a revision of the offer must be issued on Day 46 (in the absence of any competing offer, where an auction process will generally apply, or other exceptional circumstance). This is because Rule 32, dealing with revised offers, requires any revised offer to be kept open for at least 14 days after posting. In order to give the offeror seven days to consider the final arguments of the offeree, the offeree is, therefore, consequently restricted by Rule 31.9 from issuing new material information after Day 39 (except with the consent of the Panel).

During the bid by The Great Universal Stores Plc (GUS) for Argos Plc in 1999, the Panel allowed Argos to release certain trading information after Day 39. GUS was allowed, as a consequence, to decide whether or not it wished, in the light of this information, to increase or extend its offer. GUS chose to do neither and its offer later succeeded. The Code has since been amended to deal with this issue expressly (see Rule 31.9 and Note 5 on Rule 32.2).

In addition, the Panel has amended the Code so as to make clear, in schemes of arrangement, that the latest day for revision should normally be 14 days prior to the shareholder meetings, absent Panel consent (which will normally only be given if the Panel receives certain confirmations from the offeree and its financial adviser to the effect, broadly speaking, that the revisions will not be detrimental to the likely success of the scheme) (Section 7 of Appendix 7).

6.9.4 *Advertisements—Rule 19.4*

The provisions of the Code which apply to advertisements should also be noted. Rule 19.4 prohibits advertisements unless they fall within certain prescribed categories. This Rule was introduced after a series of high-profile advertising campaigns which were generally not considered appropriate to the proper conduct of takeovers. Accordingly, advertisements relating to an offer are, in effect, limited to statements of fact (for example reminders as to closing times, announcements which have to be made or advertisements of preliminary or interim results) and, in most cases, will have to include a directors' responsibility statement and be cleared by the Panel in advance.

6.10 Offers to holders of convertible securities and options—Rule 15

Rule 15 requires that, when an offer is made for voting equity share capital or for other transferable securities carrying voting rights and the offeree has convertible securities outstanding, the offeror must make an appropriate offer or proposal to the holders of those securities to ensure that their interests are safeguarded. "Appropriate" is often fixed by reference to the see through price of the underlying securities but, in appropriate circumstances, may be more.

Whenever practicable, the offer or proposal should be sent out at the same time as the main offer but, if this cannot be done, the Panel should be consulted and it should be sent out as soon as practicable thereafter. It should contain the advice of a competent independent financial adviser and the board's views on the offer or proposal.

Many offerees will have share option schemes outstanding and the provisions of Rule 15 apply to those schemes. In most cases it will not be practicable to send out proposals to optionholders until after the offer document has been published; indeed, in many cases, proposals will only be put to optionholders after the offer has gone unconditional. Proposals on option schemes may take a number of forms, such as providing for cash payments or rollover into an option scheme of the offeror or simply allowing optionholders to exercise their options and accept the offer as shareholders. Practice Statement No.24 issued by the Panel in 2008 (and updated to include appropriate references following the 2011 Amendments) contains various examples of how the Panel Executive applies Rule 15 in practice.

Regardless of when an appropriate offer or proposal is made, all relevant documents issued to shareholders of the offeree should, if practicable, be issued simultaneously to holders of convertible securities and options (Note 1 on Rule 15).

6.11   Offeror documents required by the Listing Rules

In some cases, information will have to be given to the shareholders of a listed offeror. An announcement will have to be made if the takeover offer is a Class 2 transaction, which will generally be the case in a transaction in which the value of any factors such as the gross assets being acquired or the profits before tax of the offeree or the aggregate value of the consideration being given exceeds five per cent (but is less than 25 per cent) of the gross assets, profits before tax, or market value of the ordinary shares (as the case may be) of the offeror (as determined by the tests set out in Ch.10 of the Listing Rules).

If the tests in Ch.10 show that the value or amount of any of the factors applicable to the offeree is 25 per cent or more of the appropriate measure for the offeror, the proposed takeover will qualify as a Class 1 transaction and the shareholders of the offeror will usually have to approve the takeover at a general meeting. In this case, a circular will be sent to them containing information about the proposed transaction (the detailed requirements are set out in Ch.13 of the Listing Rules) as well as any necessary resolutions to approve the acquisition, especially in share exchange offers. These may include, for example, resolutions to increase the directors' authority to allot shares.

A listed offeror may also have to prepare and publish a prospectus (or a document containing information which is regarded by the FCA as being equivalent to that of a prospectus—see further below) if it is offering its own securities, either as consideration or to its own shareholders to provide funds for a cash offer.

The information to be contained in the prospectus (or equivalent document) is set out in the Prospectus Rules. The prospectus should be incorporated in or sent out with the offer document. If a prospectus becomes necessary as a result of a revision to an offer, it should be sent out with the revised offer document, but it may be permitted to be sent out later. It should in any event be sent out before an offer goes unconditional in order to avoid having to adjust the information to take account of the offeree having become a member of the offeror's group.

The Prospectus Rules provide that there is no requirement for a prospectus to be published in relation to takeovers and mergers involving a securities exchange offer if an "equivalent document" is produced. However, the FCA applies a full vetting process to these documents to determine "equivalence" so the scope for circumventing the disclosure requirements of the Prospectus Rules is limited. One of the advantages of preparing an equivalent document is that there is no requirement to produce a supplementary prospectus with the effect that withdrawal rights under s.87Q(4) of FSMA do not apply. On the other hand, the main advantage of preparing a prospectus is that "passport rights" are available enabling the document to be sent to the offeree's shareholders throughout the European Union (subject to any translation requirements).

6.12 Liability for inaccurate or misleading statements in offer documentation

The inclusion of an inaccurate or misleading statement in offer documentation may give rise to liability in various ways, including in particular those set out below.

6.12.1 *Complaints to the Takeover Panel*

The most immediate remedy, used particularly in hostile or competing bids, is for parties to bids (or occasionally shareholders) to complain to the Panel about the accuracy of statements made by others involved in a particular bid with a view to seeking a public retraction or clarification. In hostile or competing bids, such complaints can occur on an almost daily basis.

6.12.2 *Liability in tort*

The public assumption of responsibility in the directors' responsibility statement under Rule 19.2 may result in such directors taking on a potential personal liability in tort to persons who act in reliance on statements contained in a document under the principle established in *Hedley Byrne & Co Ltd v Heller & Partners Ltd* (1964) A.C. 465; [1963] 3 W.L.R. 101. In effect, this states that, if a mis-statement has been made negligently to a person who is sufficiently proximate in circumstances where it is foreseeable that such person may suffer economic loss, the person making the statement will be liable in damages to a person who suffered loss by relying on the statement.

In many cases, it would be reasonable to assume that a shareholder to whom a document or advertisement is addressed may be able to show reliance on the information presented to him in considering what action he should take with regard to a takeover. The offeror or offeree making the statement may also share similar liability.

In addition, liability may arise for defamation if untrue or misleading statements are made.

6.12.3 Duty to exercise reasonable care, skill and diligence under the Companies Act 2006

Similarly to liability in tort, directors may now incur liability under s.174 of the Companies Act 2006 for inaccurate or misleading statements if they fail to exercise reasonable care, skill and diligence.

6.12.4 Criminal liability for non-compliant documents under the Companies Act 2006

Since the introduction of s.953 of the Companies Act 2006, all parties involved in a takeover offer need to take into account the criminal offence for non-compliance with the contents requirements for offeror and offeree documents set out in Rules 24 to 27 of the Code. The offence is punishable by a fine. It catches not only wilful non-compliance, but also non-compliance due to recklessness and failure to take "all reasonable steps" to ensure compliance.

With regard to the offer document, the offence is committed by "the person making the bid" and also by any of such person's directors, officers or members who caused the document to be published. It seems logical that directors, as persons responsible for the offer document under Rule 19, should be caught by this new offence but the term "officer" extends to both the company secretary and a "manager" (a term of somewhat imprecise scope in an English context).

Directors and officers of the offeree are also at risk of prosecution for the new offence, so far as offeree documents are concerned. "Members" (i.e. shareholders) of the offeror are also at risk where they cause the offer document to be published—and the scope of the offence is such that directors and officers of that member, if it is a body corporate, may also be criminally liable. This is of particular concern in the case of "take private" bids where a new bid vehicle is traditionally used, and in the case of takeover offers by wholly-owned subsidiaries.

Historically, it had been common practice for the offeror's financial adviser to make the offer to offeree shareholders on the offeror's behalf. Whilst it is arguable that it is the offeror, and not the financial adviser (as the offeror's agent), who should be regarded as "the person making the bid" in these circumstances, the legislation's lack of clarity in this regard encouraged a cautious approach from financial advisers, with the result that offers are now usually made directly by the offeror itself.

6.12.5 *Liability under FSMA 2000 and Financial Services Act 2012*

Parties must also bear in mind the provisions of s.397(1) of FSMA 2000 which makes it an offence knowingly or recklessly to make a statement, promise or forecast which is misleading, false or deceptive or dishonestly to conceal any material facts, if the statement, promise, forecast or concealment is made for the purpose of inducing another person to enter or offer to enter into, or to refrain from entering or offering to enter into, an investment agreement or to exercise, or refrain from exercising, any rights conferred by an investment. Thus, if misleading statements are made or material facts are concealed by either side in a takeover bid which induce a shareholder to accept or reject an offer or to vote a particular way on a resolution and if the statement is made deliberately or recklessly or if the concealment is made dishonestly, criminal sanctions may follow.

Similarly, liability may arise for market abuse under ss.118 to 131 of FSMA 2000 and Pt 9 (offences relating to financial services) of the Financial Services Act 2012 in appropriate cases (see Ch.9).

6.12.6 Avoiding liability in practice

The potential liabilities described above mean that great lengths are taken in order to seek to ensure the accuracy of offer documentation. In particular, the directors and their advisers usually undertake a full and detailed verification exercise to check all of the facts, and the bases and assumptions for any statements of opinion or belief, contained in such documentation.

6.13   FSMA 2000—financial promotion

Offer documents will be, but defence documents will often not be, financial promotions pursuant to s.21 of FSMA 2000—that is, communications of "an invitation or inducement to engage in investment activity". These documents can only be communicated by, or with the approval of, an authorised person unless they fall within the exemptions contained in the FSMA (Financial Promotion) Order 2005 (the Order).

Article 62 of the Order exempts from s.21 of FSMA 2000 any communication in connection with the sale of a body corporate. Offer documents appear, on their face, to fall within this exemption and this interpretation seems to have been approved by the FCA. Although the exemption was envisaged to deal with more limited transactions and HM Treasury has indicated that it may restrict the scope of the exemption, it has not done so. However, care needs to be taken before proceeding in reliance on this exemption. If this exemption is not available, offer documents do not fall within any of the exemptions contained in the Order and would, therefore, need to be communicated and/or approved by an authorised person.

The making and/or approval by authorised persons of financial promotions is governed by the FCA's Conduct of Business Rules. It contains various provisions limiting its application in respect of takeovers.

Defence documents will not, in many circumstances, fall within the definition of financial promotion (by virtue of their encouraging the offeree shareholders not to accept the offer) but, even if they do, if sent only to shareholders of the offeree, they will often be exempt by virtue of art.43 of the Order.

6.14   Companies Act 2006

6.14.1   *Payments to directors for loss of office*

Section 314 of the Companies Act 1985, which previously required disclosure in relation to compensation for loss of office in the offer document, was repealed by the Companies Act 2006 with effect from October 1, 2007. Sections 215 and 219 of the Companies Act 2006, which deal with payments for loss of office, do not require such disclosure. However, details of agreements between the offeree and directors or employees in relation to compensation for loss of office/employment that occur because of a takeover bid are now required to be disclosed in the directors' report in the relevant financial year (see Ch.4 Pt 28 of the Companies Act 2006).

6.14.2   *Squeeze out and sell out*

Sections 974 to 982 of the Companies Act 2006 provide a procedure whereby a person who has made a takeover offer can compulsorily acquire the shares held by non-accepting shareholders. However, it can only do so if inter alia it has received acceptances in respect of: (i) 90 per cent in value of the relevant shares; and (ii) 90 per cent of the voting rights of those shares (if they are voting shares). Assuming the relevant conditions are met, the documents sent to offeree shareholders to effect this will generally be prescribed forms of notice under s.979 of the Companies Act 2006.

Similarly, ss.983 to 985 of the Companies Act 2006 also provide a procedure whereby offeree shareholders who have not accepted an offer can "sell out"—i.e. force the offeror to buy them out if the offeror comes to hold more than 90 per cent in value of the shares in the target (or any class of such shares) as well as 90 per cent of the voting rights in the target.

Chapter 7

Conduct During the Offer; Timing and Revision; and Restrictions Following Offers

David Pudge

Partner

Clifford Chance LLP

Lee Coney

Partner

Clifford Chance LLP

7.1 Introduction

The Code is designed principally to ensure that shareholders are treated fairly and are not denied the opportunity to decide on the merits of a takeover, and that shareholders of the same class in the offeree company are afforded equivalent treatment. The Code is also designed to ensure that takeovers are conducted within an orderly framework, which helps to promote the integrity of the financial markets. The three areas of the Code which are the subject of this Chapter play an important role in achieving these goals and involve the balancing of the often conflicting interests of the offeror, offeree company shareholders, the offeree company itself and potential competing offerors.

The Panel has a statutory footing and a range of sanctions and powers to regulate the conduct of offers including the power to require disclosure to it of documents and information, the ability to require compensation to be paid to target shareholders and the power to seek enforcement orders from the courts. The Panel has, however, continued to operate largely on a consensual basis relying, principally, on its time-honoured sanctions of private and public censure.

The High Court decision in June 2008 in relation to the competitive bids for Expro International Group Plc reaffirmed the continuing reluctance on the part of the courts to take a more active role in determining the outcome of offers which are subject to the Code. The Court, in particular, emphasised that there should be a common approach to the conduct and regulation of bids, whether structured as a contractual offer or a court-approved scheme of arrangement.

Whilst the courts continue to be reluctant to intervene in determining issues which are subject to the jurisdiction of the Panel, the FCA does, however, remain responsible for taking enforcement action in all cases of market abuse. Although compliance with the Code will not always ensure immunity from allegations of market abuse, behaviour conforming to certain specific Rules of the Code will fall within a safe harbour from being considered to be market abuse.

A detailed review of the conduct of schemes of arrangement and the related court process in takeover situations is beyond the scope of this Chapter but it should be noted that a separate Schemes Appendix (Appendix 7 to the Code) addresses the application of the Code to schemes. The most significant area of divergence between schemes and contractual offers in relation to conduct during an offer, however, concerns the timetable for implementing the transaction. The scheme timetable is more flexible and is, to a very large extent, determined by the court process. Many of the general themes of this Chapter will, however, apply equally to contractual offers and to schemes.

In July 2014, the Code Committee of the Panel published PCP 2014/1 consulting on various miscellaneous amendments to the Code including a number of proposed changes which affect the rules covered in this chapter. The proposals include:

1. a modified default procedure for the resolution of competitive bid situations so as to give greater certainty as to the conduct and timing of the procedure—it is proposed that this will be set out in a new Appendix 8 to the Code—note that the parties will still be free to agree their own alternative auction procedure;
2. codification of Panel practice that where the Panel consents to an extension of Day 60, it will normally also grant an extension to, or re-set, Day 46 (as stated in Practice Statement No.8 (Timetable extensions in potentially competitive situations));
3. amendments to the rules on no increase statements and no extension statements including that the Panel must be consulted if a bidder wishes to include a reservation in such a statement.

7.2   Conduct during the offer

The first area covered in this Chapter, "Conduct during the offer" (Rules 19 to 22, Rule 27 and Rule 30), is principally concerned with the Rules governing the release of information during the course of a takeover and the Rules which control the taking of frustrating action by the board of an offeree company faced with a hostile takeover bid.

The cornerstone is Rule 19 (which is also addressed in Ch.6). This Rule deals with both responsibility for information released during the course of an offer and the manner of its release.

The Panel has made it clear that a breach of the Rules relating to the release of information during a bid will be treated as "a grave matter". There was in the past a perception that if the bid parties or financial advisers wanted to leak something then the public relations advisers could be left to talk freely to the press. As is made clear in the Introduction to the Code, however, the

Panel regards the Code as applying not only to financial advisers and their clients but also to any other advisers to or representatives of any entity to which the Code applies. In 1997, the Panel was heavily critical of Triplex Lloyd and its PR advisers, Citigate, over the leak by Citigate of confidential information obtained by Triplex Lloyd under Rule 20.2 (equality of information to competing offerors) in the course of the competing bids for William Cook.

A combination of the Panel seeking to crack down on leaks to the press and the steps taken to reinforce the rules regulating the dissemination of price sensitive information has resulted in the virtual disappearance of the so-called "Friday night drop", whereby a story is deliberately placed in the Sunday press ahead of a Monday announcement of a takeover bid.

7.2.1 Rule 19.1

Rule 19.1 sets out the standard of care which must be adopted not only in the preparation of formal offer documents or advertisements, but also in the making of statements to the media. Each document, advertisement or statement must be produced to the highest standards of accuracy and the information given must be adequately and fairly presented.

The Notes on Rule 19.1 deal with the following areas which are of particular concern to the Panel based on its past experience of dealing with over-imaginative offer participants:

1. language should be "unambiguous". For example, the word "agreement" must be used with care. The document or announcement should not convey the impression that there is a legally binding agreement on a particular matter when this is not the case;
2. parties to a bid must be committed to, and will be expected to adhere to, any statement of intention set out in a document published in connection with an offer; where no time period has been stated for the implementation or non-implementation of the specified course of action then the relevant party will normally be required to adhere to

its statement of intention for a period of 12 months from the date on which the offer becomes wholly unconditional unless there has been a material change in circumstances;

3. comments on future profits and prospects, asset values and the likelihood of the revision of an offer should be avoided. These may give rise to obligations to report formally on future profits or the benefits of the proposed transaction;

4. quotations should not be used out of context and must be capable of being substantiated. Copyright issues can also arise, especially if a whole article or a page from a newspaper is being reproduced;

5. diagrams should not be distorted and, when relevant, should be to scale; and

6. sources for material facts and origins for quotations must be included.

A high profile example of the high standards required in this regard was the Panel's public criticism of Kraft Foods in May 2010 in relation to its statement of belief concerning its plans for Cadbury's Somerdale facility. The Panel reiterated that where a party makes a statement of belief, that party must both honestly and genuinely hold that belief (a subjective test) and have a reasonable basis for holding that belief (an objective test). Whilst the Panel accepted that Kraft honestly and genuinely believed that it would be able to keep open Cadbury's Somerdale facility, such belief was not one which Kraft had a reasonable basis for holding. As a result, when making a statement as to its intentions about an offeree company or its employees or which is otherwise potentially controversial, an offeror will need to pay particular attention to whether it has sufficient objective information on which to base its belief and should consider whether to consult with the Panel prior to making such a statement. The effect of this ruling is potentially to set the bar at a very high level for a hostile bidder who will not have the benefit of cooperation from the offeree company and/or due diligence access to information concerning the offeree group's business.

Merger benefits statements used to be covered by this chapter as the rules were historically incorporated into Note 9 on Rule 19.1. Quantified financial benefits statements, which now include statements made by the offeree company as to cost savings etc. that it plans to implement if the offer is not successful as well as those statements made by a securities exchange offeror as to synergies if the offer is successful, are now dealt with in Rule 28 of the Code which is outside the scope of this chapter.

7.2.2 *Responsibility for information*

Rule 19.2 provides that, subject to certain limited exceptions, each document issued to shareholders or each advertisement published in connection with an offer must state that the directors of the offeror and/or, where appropriate, the offeree company, accept responsibility for the information contained in it. This involves the inclusion of a statement that, to the best of the relevant directors' knowledge and belief (having taken all reasonable care to ensure that such is the case), the information contained in the document or advertisement is in accordance with the facts and, where appropriate, that it does not omit anything likely to affect the import of such information. The implications of such an express acceptance of responsibility have been discussed in Ch.6.

As a result of changes made to the Code in September 2013, the bid parties need to keep under review whether there is any material new information which should be disclosed. Rule 27 now requires the parties to an offer to announce any material changes to information published during the offer period promptly and on a continuing basis and to announce any material new information that they would have been required to have previously disclosed, had such information been known at the relevant time. Prior to this change, information only needed to be updated as and when any new document was sent to shareholders.

Rule 19.3 prohibits the issue of statements which, while not factually inaccurate, may mislead shareholders and the market or may create uncertainty. In particular, an offeror should not make a statement to the effect that it may improve the terms or change the structure of its offer without committing itself to doing so and specifying the improvements or changes to its terms.

In October 2007, Standard Life was required by the Panel to confirm publicly that there was no certainty it would ultimately restructure its offer for Resolution Plc following an earlier announcement in which it indicated that it was exploring a number of options for restructuring the offer, including the possibility of switching from a scheme to a conventional takeover offer.

The Panel Executive has since issued Practice Statement No.19 which emphasises that, particularly in the context of a competitive or hostile bid, any suggestion of the possibility of an improvement or change to an offer will be particularly sensitive as it may lead to a false market being created in the shares of the offeree company. Therefore, while an offeror may publicise its initial reaction to a particular development and therefore may state, for example, that it is "considering its options", an offeror should not use any language which implies that it might improve or change the terms or structure of its offer and any such statements made must be unambiguous.

An example of this Rule being applied was in relation to URS Corporation's offer for Scott Wilson Group in June 2010, when URS was publicly rebuked by the Panel for stating that it was considering increasing its offer without committing itself to doing so following a competing offer being announced by CH2M HILL.

Equally, where an offeror has announced a firm intention to make an offer, and either it has been announced that another publicly identified potential offeror might make a competing offer or the offeree company refers to the existence of a potential competing offeror who has not been named, that potential competing offeror must in due course (normally at least 10 days prior to Day 60 on any relevant Code timetable or 10 days before the date of the shareholder meetings on a scheme), either announce a firm intention to make an offer or make a Rule 2.8 (no intention to bid) announcement (Rule 2.6(d) and (e), Note 3 on Rule 2.6 and Note 4 on s.4 of the Schemes Appendix).

The Notes on Rule 19.3 also highlight that neither the offeror nor the board of an offeree company may make statements about the level of support it has from shareholders or other persons (for example, holders of derivatives such as contracts for differences or persons with de facto control over the shares in question) unless the Panel is satisfied that the statement reflects the up-to-date intentions of the relevant persons and has been verified to the Panel's satisfaction. This means that a relatively simple statement about the level of shareholder support for (or opposition to) a bid can involve considerable discussion with the Panel concerning precisely what evidence is required. The evidence will normally take the form of a written confirmation from the person concerned. Letters confirming the relevant shareholder's support for, or opposition to, an offer or scheme must be publicly disclosed in accordance with Rule 2.11, details must be included in any relevant offer or defence document and a copy of the letters put on a website for public inspection by no later than noon on the business day following the date of the Rule 2.7 firm intention announcement (see Rule 26.1(a)).

An example of this Rule being enforced by the Panel occurred in relation to AbbVie's possible offer for Shire in July 2014. AbbVie was required to retract comments by its CEO that he believed major Shire investors were "generally supportive of" AbbVie's £30.14bn possible offer. In the retraction announcement AbbVie stated that it had "not received any written commitments of support and accordingly retracts the statements". The swift action taken by the Panel in forcing a retraction highlights how closely the Panel monitors statements made by the parties to a bid.

The inclusion of an express responsibility statement by the directors, the requirement for documentation to be prepared to the highest standards of accuracy and the provisions of Rule 19.3 plus the risk of civil or criminal liability for knowingly or recklessly making misleading statements have combined to make it essential to conduct a proper verification exercise. This normally involves the preparation of detailed verification notes. It is generally regarded as insufficient simply to refer to the directors' responsibilities in the board minutes which approve the relevant document. Non-compliance with certain of the contents requirements for offer and defence documentation is a criminal offence, referred to as the "bid documentation offence". Whilst scheme documents must include equivalent information to that found in offer documents and must be prepared to the same standard of accuracy, the bid documentation offence does not apply to bids implemented by way of a scheme of arrangement. The Rules covering content requirements for the purposes of the bid documentation offence are set out in Appendix 6 to the Code and principally relate to Rules 24 and 25 of the Code. The offence can be committed by the person making the bid and any director or member of the bidder who caused the offer document to be published, and in the case of the defence document, any director or officer of the company for which the bid is made. The offence occurs whether non-compliance is wilful or reckless.

From the perspective of the offeror and its directors and the offeree and its directors, comfort can be taken from the fact that criminal liability will only arise where the person knew that the offer or defence document did not comply, or was reckless as to its compliance, with the relevant disclosure obligations and failed to take reasonable steps to ensure compliance. In addition, a criminal standard of proof would apply. A properly conducted verification exercise should be effective to mitigate this risk. At the time of writing, no prosecutions have been brought in respect of the bid documentation offence.

7.2.3 *Release of information*

The following are some of the different ways in which information can be released during an offer.

7.2.3.1 *Advertisements*

Takeover advertisements are relatively rare, largely as a result of the Panel introducing Rules controlling their use following some of the more heated battles in the mid-1980s.

Rule 19.4 provides that the publication of advertisements connected with an offer or potential offer is prohibited unless the advertisement falls within one of the specific exempt categories listed in the Code. Advertisements include not only press advertisements but also advertisements in other media such as television, radio, video, audio tape and poster.

Three of the key exemptions are:

1. product advertisements not bearing on an offer or potential offer (these do not have to receive prior clearance from the Panel although if in doubt the Panel must be consulted);
2. corporate image advertisements with no bearing on the offer or potential offer, but these must be cleared by the Panel in advance. This is presumably because there is a fine line between genuine corporate image advertisements and those which, although they do not refer to the existence of an offer, are nevertheless geared to affect the market's perception of an offer; and
3. advertisements confined to non-controversial information about an offer (for example reminders as to closing time or the value of an offer). During Banco Santander's offer for Abbey in 2004, advertisements were placed in national newspapers to remind Abbey's 1.8 million retail shareholders of approaching deadlines and of the existence of a shareholder telephone helpline.

The Panel normally requires 24 hours' prior notice of a request to clear an advertisement and the proofs submitted to them must have been approved by the financial adviser. The Panel will not verify the accuracy of statements submitted for clearance but may comment on proposed wording.

Each advertisement connected with an offer or potential offer must clearly and prominently identify the party on whose behalf it is being published. Given the limited circumstances in which advertisements are permitted, it is difficult to envisage that this would not be clear in any event.

7.2.3.2 *Telephone campaigns*

Telephone campaigns designed to sway wavering shareholders or other persons interested in shares are not all that common and the Rules relating to them are complex. The key requirement is contained in Rule 19.5 which provides that, except with the consent of the Panel, telephone campaigns may only be conducted by staff of the financial adviser who are fully conversant with the requirements of, and their responsibilities under, the Code. Where this is impractical (for example because of the large number of shareholders concerned), other persons can be employed with the consent of the Panel but only in accordance with the strict procedures laid down in the Code, including supervision by the financial advisers. The Panel will also want to vet the written script for any such campaign and its principal concern will be to ensure that the information being given is fair and not misleading.

The Panel also undertakes the regulation of cold-calling on takeovers. Note 3 on Rule 19.5 provides that the Panel must be consulted before a telephone campaign is conducted with a view to gathering irrevocable commitments in connection with an offer.

7.2.3.3 *Interviews and debates*

As regards television and radio interviews, the Rules which apply here probably explain why most interviews of parties involved in takeover bids are particularly dull (except where the chairman or finance director has not been properly briefed!). Parties should in general avoid the release of any new material and any public confrontation between representatives of the offeror and offeree company, or between competing offerors. In the Panel's own words the parties should also avoid "anything... which leads to any kind of gladiatorial combat". Rule 19.6 which applies here does not say much for the level of confidence in the integrity of our media:

> "Parties involved in offers should, if interviewed on radio or television, seek to ensure that the sequence of the interview is not broken by the insertion of comments or observations by others not made in the course of the interview."

In other words, it is important for the parties to lay down the ground rules before agreeing to be interviewed so as to avoid a misleading message being broadcast.

7.2.4 Distribution and availability of documents and announcements

Rule 30.3 imposes certain practical obligations in relation to the distribution of offer documents and announcements. Before the offer document is made public, a copy must be lodged with the Panel in hard copy and electronic form. Copies of all other documents and announcements relating to a takeover and of advertisements and any material released to the press must at the time of release be lodged with both the Panel and also with the advisers to all other parties to the offer in both hard copy and electronic form. Where information has been incorporated into a document by reference, a copy of the relevant information should also be provided. Accordingly, it would not only be unprofessional but also contrary to the Code for the financial advisers to fail to organise for copies of offer documents, press announcements, etc., to be delivered to the offeree company's financial advisers at the time of issue.

Where the release of documents occurs outside normal business hours, the advisers to the other parties must be informed of the release immediately, if necessary by telephone. Special arrangements may also need to be made to ensure that the material is delivered directly to them and to the Panel.

Rules 30.1 to 30.4 deal in some detail with the Code requirements for the distribution of documents both in hard copy and electronic form. The principle behind these Rules is that no party to an offer should be put at a disadvantage owing to a delay in receiving new information. A Code document will be treated as having been "sent" to a person if it is: (i) sent to the relevant person in hard copy form; (ii) sent to the relevant person in electronic form; or (iii) published on a website, provided that the relevant person is sent a notification in respect of its publication by no later than the date on which the Code document is published. It remains market practice, however, for offer and scheme documents to be sent to offeree shareholders in hard copy form. Acceptance forms, withdrawal forms, proxy forms or other forms relating to an offer must be published in hard copy form only.

In addition, any document required to be sent, published or made available under, inter alia, Rules 30.2 and 30.4 must be sent, published or made available (as the case may be) to all persons including those located outside the EEA unless there is a sufficient objective justification for the party which publishes it not doing so on the basis described in Rule 23.2 and the Note on Rule 23.2 (see below). Certain information can be incorporated into the relevant documents by reference to another source of information (for example Annual Report and Accounts etc.), provided that such information is sent to shareholders and other relevant persons if so requested.

The Code requires that each party to an offer must make available on its website by 12.00 on the next business day all information published by it in relation to an offer (other than acceptance forms, proxy cards etc. and certain DTR announcements). The relevant website will form a single point of reference for all information published by a party in relation to an offer thereby affording easier access to such information by shareholders, potential investors and other interested persons. Access to the website can, however, be restricted via firewalls and disclaimers to address any potential securities laws issues (such as restricting access for shareholders in certain overseas jurisdictions).

7.2.5 Equality of information to shareholders

Rule 20.1 seeks to ensure that all shareholders are kept properly informed by requiring that information about companies involved in a takeover bid should be made available to all offeree shareholders as nearly as possible at the same time and in the same manner. Not only does this preserve equal treatment for shareholders but it helps to avoid the creation of a false market and reduces the potential for insider dealing.

The Panel stressed the importance which it attaches to this principle in 1995 with regard to the Kvaerner/Amec bid, where the Panel Executive investigated the source of speculation about the level of Amec's profits for 1996. In that case the Panel concluded that the PR advisers had failed to take sufficient care in their discussions with analysts when making comments about Amec's likely profits in 1996.

The requirements in the Code to encourage greater use of electronic communications, such as the obligation on a party to an offer to make all information published by it in relation to that offer available on a website, thereby forming a single point of reference for all such information published by it (Rule 30.4), seek to further strengthen this principle.

The fact that Code documents may be sent in differing forms (hard copy, electronic form or publication on a website with notification of the same) is regarded as being consistent with General Principle 1 (equivalent treatment). Shareholders, persons with information rights and other relevant persons are also able to request a hard copy version of a document which has been sent in electronic form or by website publication, and can notify a party to an offer that it would like hard copies of documents to be sent to it in future.

Consistent with the Takeovers Directive, information and offer documentation must be made readily and promptly available to shareholders at least in those Member States on whose regulated markets the offeree company's securities are admitted to trading and to representatives of the employees of the offeree company and the offeror, or, where there are no such representatives, to the employees themselves. Certain limited dispensations are available in respect of shareholders and employees in non-EEA jurisdictions. Unless significant criminal, regulatory or civil exposure can be avoided by making minor amendments to the documents, a general derogation will be available if less than three per cent of the offeree company's shares are held by registered shareholders in a particular jurisdiction or less than three per cent of employees are located there. In other instances, the Panel may grant a specific dispensation where it would be appropriate to do so.

The same dispensations are generally available in relation to the electronic communications regime, including the use of disclaimers on the gateway to a website or restrictions on access to websites from certain jurisdictions to restrict access to information where necessary, although no express reference to such mechanisms is made in the Code.

As a practical matter, the relevant overseas securities law implications need to be considered early in the bid process in order to determine whether there is a significant risk of criminal, regulatory or civil exposure in sending documentation into a particular jurisdiction.

As regards employees and employee representatives (as opposed to shareholders), the Code does not require that a copy of the relevant information or document is sent to all employees/employee representatives; it must simply be made available to them. Accordingly, this obligation can be satisfied by placing the information on an appropriate part of the company's website.

In limited circumstances, the Panel may also grant a dispensation to the equality of information principle, such as that granted in relation to Permira's bid for Just Retirement in June 2009. Just Retirement's majority shareholder, Langholm, had a representative on the Just Retirement board and therefore would be privy to information regarding the possible offer. The Panel agreed that Langholm could receive information through its nominee director.

The Notes on Rule 20.1 contain two important exceptions to the equality of information principle. The most important of these relates to the provision of information in confidence by an offeree company to a bona fide potential offeror or vice versa. The reason for this exemption is to allow an offeree company to provide a prospective offeror with certain confidential information to enable it to decide whether to proceed with an offer; without this the offeree company's shareholders might well be deprived of the benefit of an offer which would otherwise have been made for their shares (this is a theme that runs through the Code).

7.2.6 Meetings

Meetings are dealt with in Note 3 on Rule 20.1. Although meetings with selected shareholders, analysts or brokers are not prohibited, the Rules reflect the fact that the overriding objective is to prevent material new information being disclosed selectively.

The offeror or offeree company may, for example, hold meetings with selected shareholders or other persons interested in the securities of the offeror or offeree company, or with analysts or brokers, provided that:

1. no material new information is released;
2. no significant new opinions are expressed; and
3. except with the consent of the Panel, an appropriate representative of the financial adviser or corporate broker to the party convening the meeting is present. That representative must then confirm in writing to the Panel,

not later than 12.00 on the business day following the date of the meeting, that no material new information was released and that no significant new opinions were expressed at the meeting. The Panel polices this requirement strictly.

If material new information or a significant new opinion does emerge during a meeting (other than a meeting by chance), an announcement giving all relevant details must be made as soon as possible and, where appropriate, the Panel may require a document to be sent to shareholders . If, however, the meeting is held shortly before an announcement proposed to be made under Rule 2.7, the Panel may accept a confirmation from the relevant financial adviser that the information and/or opinions will be included in the Rule 2.7 announcement rather than requiring a separate document to be sent to shareholders. If the new information or opinion cannot be properly substantiated, this must be made clear and it must be formally withdrawn.

The question of what constitutes "material" new information has to be judged on a case-by-case basis. However, the Panel adopts a strict approach and the fact that information given during meetings is based upon information which has previously been made publicly available does not preclude it from being regarded as "new". Guidance on what can amount to "new" information for these purposes is provided by the Panel Executive in Practice Statement 1. For example, the provision of financial data or statistics which have been calculated from publicly available information may constitute new information, even where the data or statistics have been arrived at following a simple arithmetic process. It is therefore important to consider both the nature of the information which is given and the manner in which it is presented.

If, during the period between the start of an offer period and the release of a formal Rule 2.7 firm intention announcement, a party to the offer intends to initiate discussions with shareholders in relation to a proposed offer, particular care should be

taken to avoid triggering the obligation to make an announcement or send out a document and a dispensation should be
sought from the Panel Executive.

The requirements of the Code relating to meetings can also
extend to meetings which take place before a formal offer
period has, technically, commenced for Code purposes. In
those circumstances, the requirement is that no material
information should be released, nor any significant opinions
expressed, which will not be included in the formal announcement of the offer, if and when made.

7.2.7 Equality of information to competing offerors

As noted above, one exception to the rule on equality of
information to all shareholders is the provision of information
in confidence by an offeree company to a bona fide potential
offeror or vice versa. Rule 20.2 provides that any such
information must, however, be given on request equally and
promptly to another offeror or bona fide potential offeror even
if that other offeror is less welcome. This requirement will
usually only apply when there has been a public announcement of the existence of the offeror or potential offeror to which
information has been given. However, this obligation can also
be triggered where one potential offeror is informed authorita-
tively (normally by the offeree company or its advisers) of the
existence of another potential offeror even if there has been no
public statement made to this effect. Equally it will be triggered
if there is a public announcement of an approach or talks
concerning a possible offer even if an exemption from naming
is available such that the potential offeror involved is not
identified in that announcement.

There is a practical limitation to this Rule as the Code provides
that the less-welcome offeror must specify the questions to
which it requires answers. It cannot simply make a general
request to receive all information provided to its competitor.
This tends to lead to extremely lengthy and detailed question-
naires being sent to the offeree company's advisers by the

offeror's advisers in an attempt to catch any and all informa-tion which might conceivably be of interest.

It is important, therefore, that the flow of information from an offeree company to its preferred offeror is carefully controlled not only to avoid the prospect of having to give valuable commercial information to an unwelcome offeror but also to ensure that there is an accurate record of what information has been provided to any particular potential offeror.

It has always been clear that Rule 20.2 applies not just to information which is provided in written form but also to information which is provided orally. However, Practice Statement No.2 clarified that Rule 20.2 also extends to site visits and meetings with the management of the offeree company. As a result, if one offeror (or potential offeror) has been granted access to conduct a site visit or to talk to management then equal access must be granted to any other offeror (or potential offeror) that requests it. Offeree companies will therefore need to give particular thought to whether to allow an offeror, such as a potential white knight, to talk to management in light of the prospect of having to allow a hostile bidder similar access.

Rule 20.2 was in issue in the battle for Midland Bank in 1992. HSBC Holdings (a Hong Kong & Shanghai Bank subsidiary) announced a recommended offer for Midland and some weeks later Lloyds Bank announced that it was considering making an offer for Midland. One pre-condition of Lloyds making an offer was that it received all the information which HSBC had received from Midland and such information being satisfactory to it. Midland was concerned that passing confidential commercially-sensitive information to a competitor could ultimately cause damage to its shareholders. The Panel had to decide whether it should modify or relax Rule 20.2 since it was not disputed that Lloyds was other than a "bona fide potential offeror" for the purposes of the Rule. In the circumstances the Panel decided not to modify or relax the Rule and Midland was obliged to hand over to Lloyds the information which had previously been passed to HSBC. In the Panel's view the likelihood of damage being done to Midland shareholders was greater if the relevant information was withheld than if it were given to Lloyds.

It should also be noted that where the information was originally released by the offeree company under a confidentiality agreement then the "unfriendly" competing offeror can also be required to enter into a confidentiality agreement with the offeree company.

The only restrictions which may be placed on information which is provided under Rule 20.2 relate to:

1. maintaining the confidentiality of the information;
2. preventing the use of the information to solicit customers or employees; and/or
3. restricting the use of the information solely in connection with an offer or potential offer.

Any conditions imposed in this way should be no more onerous than those imposed on any other offeror or potential offeror to whom information is provided. The offeree company cannot insist on being provided with any equivalent "standstill" protections by the less welcome competing offeror.

If an offeree company wishes, with the consent of the relevant third party, to release to a preferred offeror information that is otherwise subject to a confidentiality agreement, the offeree company must ensure that it also has authority to pass that information to any other offeror or bona fide potential offeror in compliance with Rule 20.2.

There are specific provisions of the Code (see the Notes on Rule 20.2 and 20.3) which deal with the equality of information where the offer is from a management buyout (MBO) team. An MBO offeror must, on request, promptly furnish the independent directors of the offeree company or its advisers with all the information which it has furnished to its equity or debt financiers (Rule 20.3). This then forms the basis of the information which has to be furnished to any competing offerors but only insofar as it is information generated by the offeree company. The Panel expects the directors of the offeree company who are involved in making the MBO offer to cooperate with the independent directors of the offeree company and its advisers in assembling such information.

7.2.8 *Restrictions on frustrating action (Rule 21)*

In the year to March 31, 2014, nine out of 43 takeovers in the United Kingdom were not recommended at the time of launch. As a consequence, the provisions of the Code which restrict the ability of the offeree company to take action which might frustrate an offer must be considered carefully in practice.

7.2.8.1 *Shareholder approval*

The restrictions on frustrating action are contained in Rule 21 of the Code and are reinforced by the General Principle 3. Rule 21 prohibits the offeree board from taking any action which may result in any offer or bona fide offer being frustrated unless the board has obtained shareholder approval. This applies whether during the course of an offer or even before the date of the offer, if they have reason to believe that a bona fide offer might be imminent. If the proposed action is in pursuance of a contract entered into earlier or another pre-existing obligation or decision of the offeree company's board, the Panel must be consulted and its consent to proceed without a shareholders' meeting obtained. It should, however, be noted that the board of a company is, subject to directors' fiduciary duties, free to put in place defence planning initiatives (for example poison pills) at any time when an offer is not in contemplation (although these are very rarely employed in the United Kingdom).

Rule 21 specifically prevents any decision by the offeree company directors to:

1. issue any further shares in the offeree company;
2. grant any options over any unissued shares in the offeree company;

3. create or issue any convertible securities (for example convertible loan stock) or securities carrying the right to subscribe for company shares (for example warrants);
4. make any disposal or acquisition of assets of a "material amount" (the Panel will normally consider relative values of 10 per cent or more as being of material amount and 10 per cent becomes 15 per cent in the event that the disposal or acquisition takes place during a Phase 2 reference to the Competition and Markets Authority or where the European Commission has initiated Phase 2 proceedings); or
5. enter into any contracts other than in the ordinary course of business, unless shareholder approval is obtained.

Generally, it should be appreciated that this is a non-exhaustive list of prohibited acts. As a result, it is important that the Panel is consulted in advance if there is any doubt as to whether any proposed actions would fall foul of General Principle 3 or Rule 21.

General Principle 3 and Rule 21 are based on the premise that it is for the shareholders of the offeree company (not its directors or management) to determine the outcome of the offer. It is open to the offeree company directors to publish profit forecasts and other indications of the expected future performance of the offeree company's business and to lobby competition authorities to investigate the bid. Equally, the offeree board can put proposals to shareholders which would have the effect of defeating the bid, so long as those proposals can only be implemented with the consent of shareholders. As part of its defence against the unwelcome bid from NASDAQ in January 2007, The London Stock Exchange announced that it would return an additional £250 million to investors via a share buy-back programme. The vote on a proposal which might potentially frustrate an offer is, of course, open to all shareholders and therefore if the potential offeror has managed to establish a significant shareholding in the offeree company, it would be free to vote against the proposed course of action.

In deciding how best to defend the company against an unwelcome bid, the directors of the offeree company must, of course, have regard to their general duties as directors and in the exercise of their powers be satisfied, after taking advice, that such powers are being exercised for a proper purpose and that they are acting in accordance with their duties.

It may be tempting for the board of directors of an offeree company to consider extending service contracts or amending them to increase directors' remuneration as a protective reaction to a bid. The Panel will regard this as entering into a contract other than in the ordinary course of business and therefore as outlawed if the new or amended contract or terms contribute "an abnormal increase" in the directors' entitlements or a "significant improvement" in the directors' terms of service.

The offeree company may well have an existing executive share option scheme and the question may arise of granting further options to executives over shares in the offeree company. As already mentioned, the grant of options over unissued shares in the offeree company is prohibited unless approved by shareholders in general meeting. However, the Panel will normally permit the grant of options under an existing established share option scheme where the timing and level of the grants are in accordance with the company's normal practice (for example as regards timing, during a "window" period after the announcement of year-end or interim results). The Panel will also normally permit the issue of shares on the exercise of employee share options in accordance with their normal terms. However, a company will also need to ensure that it complies with any other obligations to which it is subject, such as the Model Code under the Listing Rules.

Other things to watch for include the payment of interim dividends otherwise than in the normal course or the making of changes to the pension scheme arrangements; in such circumstances the Panel should always be consulted in advance.

Further, it is important for an offeree board to bear in mind the aggregation principle. Separate matters may be aggregated and treated as covered by Rule 21 notwithstanding that individually they might not be regarded as sufficiently material.

In the case of a scheme, the offeree board should consult the Panel prior to taking any action which could lead to a scheme lapsing (where the offeror has not been given an opportunity to switch the structure of the transaction to a contractual takeover offer), in order to determine whether such action might constitute frustrating action.

7.2.8.2 Deal protection measures

Except in very limited circumstances, Rule 21.2 prohibits an offeree company and its concert parties from entering into any offer-related arrangement in favour of an offeror. The prohibition covers an inducement fee (often called a "break fee") arrangement, or any other deal protection measures, such as an undertaking from the offeree board to take certain actions to implement an offer (or refrain from taking action which might facilitate a competing bid) or "matching rights" provisions in the event of a competing offer. The prohibition applies both during an offer period and when an offer is reasonably in contemplation.

Derogation from this prohibition is only permitted in very limited circumstances. The prohibition does not apply where an offeree board has initiated a formal sale process to identify a buyer (at any time up to a Rule 2.7 firm intention announcement), although any break fee entered into must not exceed one per cent of the offer value/market capitalisation of the offeree company, may only be agreed with a single preferred participant in the formal sale process, and may only be payable after a third party offer becomes or is declared wholly unconditional. In exceptional circumstances, the Panel may be prepared to consent to the offeree company entering into other offer-related arrangements with the preferred offeror.

An additional white knight exception is also available in circumstances where a non-recommended offer has been announced and the offeree company wishes to obtain a competing offer from a more welcome bidder. This exception applies solely to break fees (not other offer-related arrangements); however, a white knight break fee can be agreed with more than one party provided that the maximum aggregate payment under any such break fee arrangements is one per cent of the value of the offeree company. Any such break fee agreements can only be entered into following the announcement of a firm intention to make a non-recommended offer by an initial offeror, and the fee must only be payable once a third party's offer becomes or is declared wholly unconditional.

The Panel Executive has the discretion to grant a dispensation from the prohibition on inducement fees and deal protection measures (including work fees) to a company in serious financial distress. This discretion arises under the Panel's general rights of derogation set out in the Introduction to the Code.

The prohibition on deal protection measures does not apply to arrangements between an offeror and an offeree company entered into in the ordinary course of business (although the Panel should be consulted in such circumstances), nor does it apply to any offer-related agreement which relates to an existing employee incentive arrangement. An offeror is not prevented from seeking irrevocable undertakings, confidentiality undertakings, commitments not to solicit the offeror's employees, customers and supplies, or undertakings from the offeree company to provide information required to satisfy bid conditions or obtain regulatory approvals. It should also be noted that the prohibition is intended only to apply to obligations on the offeree company and therefore an offeror may still enter into reverse break fee or other arrangements which impose obligations on the offeror itself (other than in the context of a reverse takeover). The offer by Chengdu Geeya Technology for Harvard International included a reverse break fee payable if Chengdu failed to post its offer document by a prescribed date. In addition, the merger between Glencore and

Xstrata contained a reverse break fee which was payable by Glencore in certain circumstances where its directors changed or withdrew their recommendation of the transaction. In April 2013, Kier Group agreed to reimburse May Gurney for its costs of investigating Kier's business and operations in connection with Kier's competing cash and shares bid for May Gurney and, in July 2014, AbbVie agreed a reverse break fee and cost reimbursement arrangement in connection with its cash and shares bid for Shire.

Since the introduction of the prohibition on deal protection measures, break fees in favour of an offeror have been agreed on three Code deals: Shell/Cove Energy; Ithaca Energy/ Valiant Petroleum; and The Parkmead Group/Lochard Energy Group, in each case, following the launch of a formal sale process. There have also been instances where offeree share-holders have agreed break fees in favour of the offeror, for example, Dentsu's offer for Aegis Group and the offer by Regus for MWB Business Exchange.

The prohibition on deal protection measures has addressed the Panel's concerns over what had become a growing practice of offeree companies being put under pressure to accept a "standard package" of deal protection measures. There has, however, been a notable increase in the use of matching rights and exclusivity provisions in irrevocable undertakings. Care must be taken when drafting such provisions in irrevocables given by offeree company concert parties. For example, directors and 20 per cent plus shareholders (unless the presumption of concertedness is capable of being rebutted) are presumed to be concert parties of the offeree company and will also be caught by the prohibition in Rule 21.2. In Practice Statement No.27, the Panel Executive makes clear that offeree director shareholders are permitted to enter into irrevocable commitments in relation to their shares, however, they are not allowed to enter into other types of offer-related arrangement, for example, a deal protection undertaking in favour of the offeror (or its concert parties). Undertakings aimed solely at giving effect to the irrevocable are, however, permitted, for example, an undertaking not to dispose of the shares or withdraw acceptance of the offer; an undertaking to elect for a particular form of bid consideration; and representations as to title to the relevant shares.

Aside from the Code restrictions on the amount of, and circumstances in which, a break fee (or similar) may be paid, the boards of UK companies also need to have regard to the Listing Rules, the prohibitions on providing financial assistance and their own directors' duties when considering whether to agree to enter into a break fee (or similar) agreement and, if so, the terms of that agreement and the amount of any such fee.

7.2.9 *Prohibition on share dealings by offeree company advisers*

Members of the offeree group and its financial adviser and corporate broker are not permitted to deal (or procure, facilitate, or encourage a person to refrain from, dealing) in offeree company shares during the offer period without the consent of the Panel (see Rule 4.4). This reflects the view of the Panel that it is for the offeree shareholders and not its financial advisers or other connected persons to determine the outcome of a bid. There is, however, a carve-out for the activities of exempt principal traders and exempt fund managers connected with the relevant financial adviser or broker.

The Code also contains restrictions on securities borrowing and lending transactions without the Panel's consent by offerors, the offeree company and certain other persons connected with them (Rule 4.6).

7.3 Timing and revision

The second main area covered in this Chapter, "Timing and Revision" (Rules 24.1 and 25.1 and Rules 31 to 35), is very much the "nuts and bolts" of takeover practice in that it covers the detailed and somewhat technical Rules governing the timing of the various steps in a takeover bid, the Rules relating to the introduction of different forms of bid consideration and those relating to increased offers.

The two most important basic principles underlying the Rules relating to the timing and revision of offers are as follows:

1. the duration of a bid should be limited. This is in recognition of the disruption caused by a hostile bid to the offeree company and its board in taking their attention away from the day-to-day management of the offeree group's business; and

2. the shareholders of the offeree company should, however, have sufficient time to be able to consider any offer for their shares and any competing offer for their shares on their merits.

As a result, certain events have to happen by certain times, whilst other events cannot happen before certain periods of time have elapsed.

7.3.1 *Offer timetable*

This section focuses on the Code timetable for a contractual offer (although commentary is provided on how the timetable differs on a takeover structured as a scheme of arrangement). Schemes are conducted by reference to a largely court-driven timetable and, in the absence of a competitive bid, there are no maximum time periods set out in the Code for the holding of shareholder meetings and/or the fulfilment of other conditions to a recommended scheme. As a result, a scheme can provide a greater degree of flexibility in the timetable than is the case with a contractual offer. The rules on the application of the Code to schemes are largely contained in the Schemes Appendix.

In the case of a scheme, the timetable will need to be published in the scheme circular and then adhered to by the offeree company. If the offeree company withdraws its recommendation, adjourns the shareholder meeting(s) or does not comply with the published timetable, the offeror will be permitted to switch to a contractual offer with up to a 90 per cent acceptance condition. An offeror may protect itself by including timetable-related conditions in its offer (for example, a condition that the shareholder meetings and/or the court sanction hearing must be held on or by a specific date). The inclusion of such a condition allows an offeror to lapse the scheme in the event of it being breached, without reference to the materiality thresholds set out in Rule 13.5. However, the Panel expects that any such dates stipulated in a formal condition should be more than 21 days after the date set for the relevant event in the expected scheme timetable in order to allow the offeree board flexibility to adjourn the shareholder meeting or court hearing for a short period without the offeror being immediately able to invoke a condition.

The key times or dates in a contractual offer timetable are as follows.

7.3.1.1   Posting date (Day 0)

The offer document should normally be sent to offeree company shareholders within 28 days of the announcement of a firm intention to make an offer (Rule 24.1). References to days are generally to calendar days—weekends and public holidays are treated like any other day.

In practice, the offer document is often published as quickly as possible to increase the pressure on the offeree company in the case of a hostile bid or to seek to reduce the risk of there being a competing bid in the case of a recommended offer. The Panel will not usually grant an extension of time for publishing it unless the offeree company consents.

Rule 24 is similarly applied to the publication of a scheme circular, requiring the circular to be sent to target shareholders within 28 days of the announcement of a firm intention to make a bid. In practice, however, the Panel will normally grant an extension to the publication date if that is supported by the target board as it may not always be possible to publish a scheme circular within 28 days of announcement.

Rule 24.1(a) requires the offeror to make the offer document readily available to the trustees of the offeree company's defined benefits pension scheme(s). At the same time both the offeror and the offeree company are required to make the document available to their employee representatives or, where there are no such representatives, to the employees themselves. These requirements apply equally on a scheme.

The Code provides for the opinion of employee representatives on the effects of the offer on employment and/or the opinion of the trustees of the offeree company's pension scheme(s) on the effects of the offer on the pension scheme(s) to be appended to the recommended offer document (or the offeree defence document in the case of a hostile offer—see section 7.3.1.2 below), if it is received in good time (Rule 25.9). If any such opinion is not provided to the offeree company in time, then the offeree company is required to publish the opinion on its website and to announce that this has been done via a Regulatory Information Service (for example an RNS announcement), provided that the opinion is received no later than 14 days after the date on which the offer becomes or is declared wholly unconditional. It should be noted that the offeree company is required to pay for the reasonable costs incurred by the employee representatives in obtaining advice in preparing their opinion on the effects of the offer on employment (Note 1(a) on Rule 25.9).

7.3.1.2   Day 14 *(counting forwards from the posting date and excluding the posting date)*

This is the last day for the offeree board to advise shareholders of its views on the offer. In any event, it must publish a circular containing its opinion of the offer as soon as practicable after publication of the offer document (Rule 25.1). The board of the offeree company must publish the circular to its shareholders and make it readily and promptly available to the trustees of the offeree company's pension scheme(s) and its employee representatives (or, where there are no such representatives, the employees themselves). As with the publication of an offer document, the circular must be made available on a website in accordance with Rule 26 and its publication announced in accordance with Rule 2.9. As mentioned above, the offeree board is required to append to the circular any opinion from the trustees of the offeree company's pension scheme(s) on the effects of the offer on the pension scheme(s) and/or the representatives of its employees on the effects of the offer on employment, provided any such opinion is received in good time before publication of the circular (Rule 25.9). If any such opinion is not received in good time, then the offeree company is required to publish the opinion on a website and to announce that this has been done via a Regulatory Information Service—see 7.3.1.1 above.

On a recommended offer, the offeree company's defence document would normally be incorporated within the offer document. Similarly, under a scheme of arrangement, the information required to be contained in an offer document and the information required to be contained in the offeree board circular is included in a single document, the scheme circular. Therefore, the reference to the offeree board's circular being published and made readily and promptly available after publication of the bid document is not applicable to a recommended contractual offer or a scheme.

7.3.1.3 *Day 21*

An offer must initially be open for at least 21 days after its posting (Rule 31.1). Therefore, the first closing date of an offer will normally be 21 days from the date of publication of the offer document, although it can be later than Day 21. This does not, however, prevent the offer from becoming unconditional at an earlier date or, alternatively, the first closing date being set for a date which is more than 21 days after posting (for example, to avoid public holidays etc.).

Since a scheme of arrangement does not remain "open for acceptance" in the way that a contractual offer does, Rule 31.1 is disapplied in relation to schemes. However, in order to be consistent with the position under a contractual offer, Section 3 of the Schemes Appendix provides that shareholder meetings must normally be convened for a date which is at least 21 days after the date of the scheme circular, except with the consent of the Panel.

7.3.1.4 Day 35

This is the first day on which an offer may close (i.e. no longer be open for acceptance), assuming it has been declared unconditional as to acceptances on the first closing date (assuming that is Day 21). This is because Rule 31.4 provides that after an offer has become or is declared unconditional as to acceptances, the offer must remain open for acceptance for not less than 14 days after the date on which it would otherwise have expired.

This Rule allows a shareholder who has been unable to make up his mind, or who perhaps wanted to see whether control would pass without his support, a period of 14 days beyond the date when the offer would otherwise have expired to accept the offer. When, however, an offer is unconditional as to acceptances from the outset, it is not necessary to keep the offer open for a further 14 days provided the position has been made clear in the offer document.

Since a scheme of arrangement is immediately binding on all shareholders once it has become effective, the concept of an offer remaining "open" after control has passed is not relevant and Rule 31.4 is therefore not applicable.

If the offer became wholly unconditional on Day 21, then Day 35 will also be the last date for payment of the consideration under the offer to shareholders who accepted the offer. The reason for this is that Rule 31.8 requires the consideration to be posted within 14 days of the later of:

1. the first closing date of the offer (normally "Day 21");
2. the date on which the offer became or was declared wholly unconditional; and
3. the date of receipt of a valid acceptance complete in all respects.

As a result, where an offer becomes or is declared uncondi-tional as to acceptances on Day 60 but does not become unconditional in all respects (i.e. all other conditions satisfied or waived) until Day 81, the consideration will not have to be posted until Day 95.

A scheme of arrangement has no "first closing date", is not "accepted" by target shareholders and becomes effective once the relevant court order has been duly filed, or if required by the court registered, at Companies House rather than on becoming or being declared "wholly unconditional". As a result, Section 10 of the Schemes Appendix provides that the consideration under a scheme must be posted within 14 days of the scheme becoming effective, except with the consent of the Panel.

7.3.1.5 Day 39

Except where the Panel has otherwise consented (having been consulted "in good time"), this is the last day of the offer period for the offeree board to announce "any material new information" (Rule 31.9). This Rule covers announcements relating to trading results, profit or dividend forecasts, asset valuations, quantified financial benefits statements, proposals for dividend payments and material acquisitions or disposals. This is a non-exhaustive list and these matters are referred to in the Rule as illustrative examples of the types of new information which could be considered material.

Rule 31.9 provides that, where a matter which might result in a Rule 31.9 announcement being made after Day 39 is known to the offeree company, every effort should be made to bring forward the date of the announcement. If it is not practicable to make the announcement before Day 39 or the matter arises after Day 39, then the Panel will normally extend the offer period and, in particular, move Day 46 (the last day for posting a revision of the offer) and/or Day 60 (the final date for declaring the offer unconditional as to acceptances: see 7.3.1.8 below), as appropriate, to a later date. This is precisely what happened in April 2003, in the context of the competing bids

365

for Oxford Glycosciences Plc by Celltech Group Plc and Cambridge Antibody Technology Plc. The Panel Executive extended Day 39 for up to 20 days to allow Oxford Glycosciences to announce its trading results. The offer timetable was subsequently reset, with Day 46 deemed to fall 7 days after the announcement of the trading results.

The Panel granted an extension under this Rule in relation to Kraft Foods' bid for Cadbury in December 2009 so as to enable Cadbury to release its annual trading results up to three days after the original Day 39 deadline, although the offer timetable was not reset in any other respect.

In cases where an offer is subject to a competition condition and the Competition and Markets Authority or the European Commission (as the case may be) has not yet announced whether or not a Phase 2 investigation will be initiated, the Panel will normally extend Day 39 to the second day following the announcement of the relevant decision with consequent changes to Day 46 and Day 60 (see Note 3 on Rule 31.6). Such an extension was granted in relation to Reckitt Benckiser's bid for SSL International in September 2010, Greencore's offer for Uniq in September 2011 and Motorola Solutions bid for Psion in August 2012 and the offer timetables were reset accordingly.

During the hostile bid by Saint-Gobain for BPB in 2005, Saint-Gobain sought an extension of Day 39 in circumstances where it had been delayed in making the requisite competition filing with the European Commission with the inevitable consequence that the relevant decision would be delayed beyond Day 39. Although the Panel was prepared to grant the timetable extension in these unprecedented circumstances, Saint-Gobain was required to undertake that neither it nor any of its concert parties would acquire any interest in or rights over any BPB shares (other than in very limited circumstances) until such time as the European Commission published its decision as to whether or not to initiate a second stage investigation.

The Day 39 Rule (Rule 31.9) is disapplied in relation to schemes of arrangement. Generally, schemes are implemented by agreement between the target and the bidder, therefore no specific deadline for the announcement of material new information by the target is imposed by the Code.

7.3.1.6 Day 42

This is the last date for fulfilment of all other conditions of the bid, assuming the offer became or was declared unconditional as to acceptances on the first closing date and the first closing date was Day 21.

Rule 31.7 provides that, except with the consent of the Panel, all conditions must be fulfilled or the offer must lapse within 21 days of the first closing date or the date the offer becomes or is declared unconditional as to acceptances, whichever is the later. The Panel will normally only grant consent for an extension if the outstanding conditions involve a material official authorisation or regulatory clearance in relation to the offer and it has not been possible to obtain an extension under Rule 31.6 (see 7.3.1.5 above). Thus if an offer is not declared unconditional as to acceptances until Day 60 (which is common where there are competing offers), all other conditions must normally be satisfied by Day 81 (i.e. Day 60 plus 21). (Timetable extensions are discussed in 7.3.2 below.)

The rationale behind Rule 31.6 and 31.7 is that the offeree company should not be hindered in its affairs for longer than is reasonable. On a scheme of arrangement, it is generally the target company that controls the timetable and therefore the Schemes Appendix disapplies both these Rules in relation to schemes.

Day 42 is perhaps best known because of Rule 34 which provides that the offer must confer upon an accepting shareholder a right of withdrawal of his acceptance after the expiry of 21 days from the first closing date of the initial offer (which, as indicated above, is normally Day 21) unless the offer has become unconditional as to acceptances. This is of considerable importance in a competitive bid situation since this enables an accepting shareholder to change his mind at the last minute; it is not possible for an offeror to provide in the offer document that acceptances of the offer should be irrevocable (i.e. not capable of being withdrawn) after Day 42. Equally, it is important that an offeror clearly sets out this withdrawal right in its offer document. Confusion over the timing of withdrawal rights in the Thistle/BIL bid in 2003 resulted in BIL having to allow Thistle shareholders withdrawal rights from an earlier date than the Code would otherwise have strictly required.

Competing offerors and offeree companies in hostile bids commonly try to take advantage of the existence of withdrawal rights by sending withdrawal forms to offeree shareholders pointing out that they have the right to withdraw any acceptance of the relevant offer. (This does not, however, prevent the offer from being declared unconditional at an earlier date.)

The right of withdrawal conferred by Rule 34 may, however, be varied by individual agreement and an offeror will normally attempt to extract a waiver of this right from those offeree shareholders, who agree to give irrevocable undertakings to accept the offer.

A right of withdrawal can also be imposed by the Panel as an alternative to allowing an offeree company to invoke, or cause an offeror to invoke, a so-called "offeree protection condition" (see Rule 34.2 and Note 2 on Rule 13.6).

See also 7.4 below, for a discussion of the unusual circumstances in which a right of withdrawal was made available in the context of Guoco's mandatory bid for Rank in the summer of 2011.

The Schemes Appendix disapplies Rule 34 in the case of a scheme of arrangement because shareholders generally retain the right to control and/or dispose of their shares in the target company until the scheme becomes effective and there is therefore no need for a right of withdrawal. However, Section 9(b) of the Schemes Appendix provides that a shareholder who has elected to receive a particular form of consideration in respect of any of his shares should be entitled to withdraw his election up to one week prior to the court sanction hearing.

7.3.1.7 Day 46

This is the last day for publishing a revision of the offer since an offer must be kept open for at least 14 days from the date of publishing the revised offer document to shareholders (Rule 32.1(c)) (thus giving them time to consider the revised offer on its merits) and the last day on which the offer is able to become unconditional as to acceptances is Day 60.

Rule 32.1(c) is disapplied in the case of a scheme and Section 7 of the Schemes Appendix states that any revision to a scheme should normally be made no later than 14 days prior to the date of the shareholder meetings, with revisions after that date requiring the Panel's consent. In practice, this means that there is a much shorter period in which to revise the terms of a bid which is being implemented by way of a scheme.

At the same time as publishing the revised offer, the offeror must make the revised offer document readily available to the trustees of the offeree company's pension scheme(s) and both the offeror and the offeree company must make the revised document available to employee representatives, or where there are no such representatives, employees of the offeree company themselves. The offeree company must inform the trustees of the offeree company's pension scheme(s) and the employee representatives of their right under Rule 32.6 to have a separate opinion on the revised offer appended to any response published by the offeree company in relation to the revised offer.

Day 46 will also normally be the last day for the offeror to make an announcement as to trading results, profits, dividends etc. where the offer involves an element of share exchange (i.e. the offeror is offering its shares). This is because such an announcement may have the effect of increasing the value of the offeror's shares and thus amount to a revision of its bid.

The Code contains specific Rules which address what happens if there are still two (or more) competing bidders at Day 46 (see 7.3.1.12 below).

7.3.1.8   Day 60

As indicated above, this is the final day for an offer to become or be declared unconditional as to acceptances (Rule 31.6). In other words, if the offeror has not achieved the minimum level of acceptances on which its bid is conditional by Day 60, its offer will lapse.

Day 60 can be extended with the consent of the Panel but Rule 31.6 makes it clear that the Panel will normally only consent to such an extension if:

1.   a competing offer has been announced;
2.   the offeree board agrees;
3.   there is an announcement of the offeree company's results after Day 39 (as already mentioned above);
4.   the offeror's receiving agent requests an extension for the purpose of issuing to the offeror or its financial advisers a certificate stating the number of acceptances and shares otherwise acquired, such certificate being required before an offer may be declared unconditional as to acceptances (Note 7 on Rule 10); or
5.   withdrawal rights are introduced by the Panel under Rule 13.6 as a result of an "offeree protection condition" being triggered.

The Panel has also confirmed that it would grant an extension to Day 60 (with a corresponding extension to Day 46) of the existing offeror's timetable, provided that the offeree board consented to such an extension, in a situation where a potential competing offeror, which may or may not have previously announced its interest, is still considering a possible rival offer after Day 46 of the existing offeror's offer.

The date of the shareholder meetings in a scheme of arrangement is considered to be analogous to Day 60 of a contractual offer (on the basis of this being the time by which investment decisions need to be made by offeree shareholders). Accordingly, as mentioned previously, Rule 31.6 is disapplied in relation to schemes.

An example of an extension of Day 60 occurred during the Ferrovial Consortium bid for BAA. With the support of the BAA board, the Panel granted a seven day "stay of execution" to the usual requirement under Rule 32.1 that no revised offer may be posted to offeree shareholders after Day 46 of the offer timetable, with a consequent extension of Day 60. The Panel agreed that the deadlines could be extended on the basis that a rival potential bidder in the form of a consortium led by Goldman Sachs had yet to declare its hand formally, and shareholders in BAA should be afforded the possibility of receiving a higher offer from the Ferrovial Consortium in the event of a rival bid emerging which was, indeed, what happened.

In July 2007, with the consent of the board of EMI, the Panel granted Terra Firma an extension of Day 60 to allow it more time to satisfy the 90 per cent acceptance threshold required for its offer for EMI to become unconditional. There was speculation that, at the time of the "original" Day 60 deadline, Terra Firma had not received all of the necessary supporting documentation to be able to count all of the acceptances it had received towards the 90 per cent threshold and that, due to the upheaval at the time in the debt markets, its lending banks were unwilling to allow it to waive down the 90 per cent threshold.

In circumstances where a competing offer has been announced, both offerors will normally be bound by the timetable established by the posting of the competing offer document. As a result, the normal bid timetable can be extended considerably in the event of competing bids (especially where complex competition issues are involved) and become somewhat of a marathon. This explains why bid battles can go on for some months in spite of the normal 60-day rule.

An exception to the "usual" approach to the timetable for competing bids applies in relation to so-called "pacman" bids. Pacman bids arise where, rather than simply seeking to fight off the advances of an unwelcome bidder, the offeree company accepts the commercial logic of the proposed combination and itself launches a bid for the offeror. This is a relatively rare occurrence but examples include the Friends Provident/Resolution transaction; Marstons/Wolverhampton & Dudley and EMI/Time Warner. In 2007, Resolution and Friends Provident also proposed a pacman-style restructuring of their proposed merger to reduce the potential for the deal to be blocked by an opposing minority shareholder.

Where a "pacman" situation arises, simply having both bids running on the same timetable would not work in relation to a "pacman offer" as there would be the potential for both offers to become unconditional on the same day and for general confusion among the shareholders in both companies. As a result, it is usual to freeze the first timetable when the pacman bid is launched and then restart it when the pacman offer document is posted rather than completely resetting the first timetable. A condition that the pacman offer can only succeed where the other has not succeeded is also required, as you clearly cannot have a situation where each company actually takes over the other!

It is worth noting that the Panel will not normally grant consent to an offer being declared unconditional as to acceptances after Day 60 of the relevant timetable in the case of competing bids unless the Panel's consent is sought before Day 46.

In Practice Statement No.8, the Panel Executive considered the application of Rule 31.6 and 32.1 (see 7.3.1.7 above) to a situation where a potential competing offeror, which may or may not have previously announced its interest, is considering announcing a rival offer after Day 46 of the existing offeror's offer. This Practice Statement confirms that, in such a case, the Executive would usually grant an extension to Day 60 (with a corresponding extension to Day 46) of the existing offeror's timetable, provided that the offeree board consented to such an extension. The BAA/Ferrovial example mentioned above reflects this approach.

7.3.1.9 Day 81

As referred to above, this will be the last day for fulfilment of all other conditions if the offer is declared unconditional as to acceptances on Day 60. This is another example (Day 42 was the first) of the application of Rule 31.7.

As mentioned previously, Rule 31.7 is disapplied in relation to schemes of arrangement.

7.3.1.10 Day 95

As already indicated above, the consideration must be settled no later than 14 days after the offer becomes or is declared wholly unconditional (Rule 31.8). Therefore, this is the latest theoretical date for such settlement (assuming that the offer is declared unconditional as to acceptances on Day 60 and that Day 60 is not extended).

As mentioned above, Rule 31.8 is disapplied in the case of a scheme of arrangement; in its place, Section 10 of the Schemes Appendix imposes a 14 day time limit for the settlement of consideration after the scheme has become effective.

7.3.1.11 Trigger date for compulsory acquisition of the minority

In order for an offeror to implement the compulsory acquisition of minority shareholders pursuant to the Companies Act 2006 (squeeze out), an offeror must satisfy a dual test: it needs to have acquired or unconditionally contracted to acquire both 90 per cent of the shares to which the offer relates and 90 per cent of the voting rights in the company to which the offer relates.

The squeeze-out rights must then be exercised within the period of (i) three months from the end of the time allowed for acceptance of the offer where the offeree company is a listed issuer; and (ii) six months from posting the offer document in relation to all other offeree companies (for example AIM companies and non-traded companies). This potentially provides an offeror bidding for a listed offeree company with an indefinite period of time in which to implement the squeeze-out as offers are often left open for acceptance once control has passed. In practice, however, an offeror will normally want to acquire any remaining minority as quickly as possible and the terms of any bank financing for the offer are likely to impose obligations on the offeror to implement the squeeze-out as soon as practicable.

Similarly, a minority holder has the right to require a bidder to buy his shares at the offer price if the bidder has obtained 90 per cent of the issued shares and the voting rights in the company.

Squeeze-out and sell-out provisions are not relevant in the context of a scheme of arrangement. Once a scheme has become effective, all of the target shareholders are bound by it regardless of whether or not they voted in favour of the scheme.

7.3.1.12   *Competing bids on Day 46*

The rules dealing with the relatively rare situation where there are two outstanding offers, neither of which is a "final" offer, for an offeree company on Day 46 (the last day for posting a revised offer) have undergone a number of modifications since they were first introduced.

Initially the Panel opted for a "sealed bid" approach, whereby the Panel set a deadline requiring the competing bidders to submit a sealed bid stating the maximum price which they were prepared to pay. However, this approach proved unwieldy when applied in the cases of the competing bids for

Energy Group and Hyder, which led the Panel to implement a revised "open" auction process under Rule 32.5 of the Code in 2003.

In the "open" auction process, each bidder is granted a set period within which to respond to any revised offers announced by the competing offeror, with the Panel having the power to impose a final "guillotine" on the time period over which the auction is taking place (normally a period of some days). This approach has been either utilised or proposed during takeover bids for Debenhams, QXL Ricardo, Canary Wharf and Cove Energy.

By way of an alternative, the Panel adopted an "accelerated" auction procedure involving set rules as to the number of rounds of bids that can be made, the time when bids must be submitted (usually after the markets have closed in order to minimise the risk of market speculation) and whether the competing bidder must make fixed bids or can make formula bids. A formula bid allows the bidder to state a specific amount in cash that it is willing to pay over and above the bid of the other offeror subject to a specified maximum. This "accelerated" auction procedure was first utilised during the takeover battles for Corus Plc and for Imprint Plc.

On October 20, 2006 Tata Steel Limited and Corus announced a recommended bid to be implemented by a scheme of arrangement. On November 17, Companhia Siderugica Nacional (CSN) approached Corus with a higher competing bid which culminated in a pre-conditional Rule 2.7 (formerly 2.5) announcement on December 11. The CSN offer was also to be implemented by way of a scheme of arrangement but due to concerns over whether a target company could legitimately run parallel, competing schemes, the CSN scheme was conditional upon the Tata scheme lapsing or being withdrawn. Corus shareholders were to vote on the Tata scheme on December 20, 2006. To ensure equality of information, the Panel required CSN to post an information document (containing most of the information which would have been included in a scheme document) to Corus shareholders.

In accordance with the "accelerated" auction procedure the Panel set an end date of January 30, 2007 (which would have equated to approximately Day 46 of a reset timetable if CSN had posted its scheme document shortly after announcing its bid) for the parties to announce their final offers. Although the usual position when a second bidder intervenes is for the first bidder's timetable to be reset according to when the second bidder posts its offer or scheme document (Note 4 on Rule 31.6), this could not happen in relation to CSN's bid as it was a pre-condition of CSN's bid that it would only post its scheme document if the Tata scheme failed.

On January 30, 2007 neither Tata nor CSN declared its offer final and therefore the Panel proceeded with the "accelerated" auction process. This differed from previous "open" auction procedures where the parties had to announce their bids over a number of days as it was agreed that there would be a maximum of nine rounds of bidding to take place between 16.30 on January 30, and 02.30 on January 31, 2007. This timing ensured that most of the auction would take place when the three stock markets on which the parties' shares were traded (London, New York and Mumbai) were closed in order to minimise market speculation during the bidding process. Bids were made in private to the Panel and communicated by the Panel to the bidders.

For the first eight rounds, the parties had to make fixed price bids, but for the ninth and final round they could make a formula bid stating a specified amount in cash that they would pay more than the other bidder's highest offer, subject to a specified maximum amount.

The auction was completed after Tata submitted a winning bid of 608 pence per share (significantly above the 500 pence per share that Tata was offering prior to the start of the auction process) which valued Corus at £6.7 billion. Corus posted a revised scheme document to its shareholders on February 12, 2007 and reconvened the adjourned court and shareholder meetings which then duly approved the Tata scheme.

This procedure was also adopted in February 2008 in relation to the competing bids from Hydrogen Group Plc (by way of scheme) and OPD Group Plc (by way of offer) for Imprint Plc. On November 7, 2007, OPD announced a recommended bid for Imprint to be implemented by way of a traditional cash offer; on December 20, Hydrogen announced a recommended offer for Imprint to be implemented by way of a scheme, and the shareholder meetings to approve the scheme were scheduled for February 27, 2007. In accordance with the "accelerated" auction procedure the Panel set an end date of February 4, 2008 for the parties to announce their final offers. On February 8, neither party had declared its offer final and therefore the Panel proceeded with the "accelerated" auction process whereby the three rounds of the auction took place on February 11, 12, and 13, with each party announcing its revised bid for each round by means of an announcement released via a Regulatory Information Service after the close of trading on the London Stock Exchange on the relevant day.

Following the auction procedure, both Hydrogen and OPD Group reissued scheme and offer documentation respectively, leaving it to the Imprint shareholders to resolve the impasse.

However, on February 26, 2008, a further new offeror, Premier, emerged and the Panel again determined that a competitive situation had arisen for the purposes of Rule 32.5 and held a further auction process in which all three offerors were entitled to participate. However, as none of the offerors submitted an increased offer, the Imprint board continued to recommend Premier's offer, which was ultimately successfully implemented by way of a scheme.

In June 2008, the Panel's approach in relation to the competing bids from ITW and Manitowoc for Enodis Plc signalled a return to the earlier sealed bids approach. The procedure established by the Panel for this auction consisted of a single round, which took place after markets closed. Any increased bid by either bidder was required to be at a fixed price in cash being not less than five pence higher than the price of the highest cash offer announced by either bidder prior to the commencement of the auction procedure. Any increased bid made by ITW could only be at an odd-numbered price, and any increased bid by Manitowoc could only be at an even-numbered price. As with the Imprint auction, formula bids were not allowed. Each offeror was, however, permitted to stipulate to the Panel that its bid was conditional on the other offeror also lodging an increased bid. Following the conclusion of the auction procedure, Enodis agreed to recommend Manitowoc's offer and, once the offer documentation was posted, ITW was required to withdraw its offer.

During the competitive bid for Cove Energy in 2012 which followed a formal sale process, Shell and PTTEP were unable to agree a resolution process to determine the "winning" bid, so the Panel ruled that an open auction should be conducted. The rules of the auction permitted each bidder to announce to the market one revised bid per day, such bid being revised by a fixed amount in whole pence (i.e. no minimum increment bids or by reference to a formula). The Panel had discretion to impose a final "guillotine" on the time period for announcing revised offers; in this event, the cash consideration payable under any revised offer announced by Shell needed to be at an odd-numbered price and that announced by PTTEP needed to be at an even-numbered price. A few hours before the auction was due to start, Shell announced that it would not be increasing its offer nor would it be participating in the process.

It should be noted that whilst the Panel will consider any alternative procedure which is agreed between the competing offerors and the board of the offeree company, it has previously stated in response statement RS 7 that, in the absence of agreement between the parties, its default position will be to impose an open auction procedure (as happened in connection with the competing bids for Cove).

The Code does not prescribe what timetable should apply where a scheme is proposed in competition with an existing contractual offer, or with an existing scheme, and instead this is left to the Panel to determine in the light of all the prevailing circumstances. Note 3 on Rule 32.5 requires the parties to consult with the Panel as to the applicable timetable following which the Panel will determine the date or dates on which final revisions to competing offers must be announced and on which any auction procedures will commence. It is likely that the Panel will take a stance in relation to so-called "parallel" schemes (i.e. two competing schemes) similar to its approach in relation to the situation where a scheme is proposed in competition with an existing contractual offer. In such a case, the Panel will determine the precise dates on which final revisions to the competing offers should be announced and on which the auction procedure should commence. The Corus situation provides a useful precedent in this regard.

7.3.2 Timetable extensions

As already mentioned, regulatory issues can impact on the offer timetable. Whilst the Panel attaches considerable importance to the strict offer timetable, it is prepared to be flexible in accommodating delays or extensions which arise from regulatory issues (particularly, in the case of recommended offers).

So what are the available options if the required regulatory clearances are unlikely to be obtained within the normal offer timetable?

There are, principally, three options:

1. make the offer subject to a pre-condition that regulatory approval is obtained—this approach was adopted in relation to the BHP Billiton offer for Rio Tinto; the Boots/Alliance Unichem merger; GE's offer for Amersham Plc; the Carnival/P&O Princess merger; and E.ON AG's bid for Powergen. The Panel must be consulted in advance if such a pre-conditional bid is to be announced;
2. seek an extension of Rule 31.6 (the requirement that the acceptance condition must be satisfied by midnight on Day 60). This has the effect of also extending what would otherwise be the last date for satisfying or waiving all other offer conditions; or

3.   seek an extension of Rule 31.7 (the requirement that all other conditions must be satisfied within 21 days of the offer becoming or being declared unconditional as to acceptances) in order to be able to close off withdrawal rights by declaring the offer unconditional as to acceptances whilst allowing more time to satisfy the other conditions.

Following the announcement of a firm intention to make an offer, the offeror must use reasonable endeavours to ensure the satisfaction of any conditions or pre-conditions to which the offer is subject. The Panel should be consulted in relation to any pre-conditions to which the offer is to be subject and if the relevant pre-condition has not been satisfied or waived within the period agreed with the Panel, the offeror will be required to withdraw its proposed offer.

An example of an extension of Rule 31.7 (Day 81) arose on the Federal Mogul/T&N bid. The bid was announced on November 13, 1997 and was declared unconditional as to acceptances in December 1997 before withdrawal rights arose. The Panel granted an extension of Rule 31.7 in order to allow more time in which to obtain the necessary regulatory clearances. However, the timetable became greatly extended as delays in obtaining these regulatory clearances were encountered and the offer only became unconditional in all respects in the middle of March 1998. During this period the T&N shareholders who had accepted the offer could not receive their consideration and were not free to withdraw acceptances and sell their shares in the market. There was press criticism of the Panel and the parties to the bid and questions were raised as to whether Federal Mogul should have been required to pay interest to those accepting shareholders or, alternatively, the Panel should have reintroduced withdrawal rights.

The Panel is now reluctant to accede to requests to extend Rule 31.7 and instead prefers to grant extensions to Rule 31.6 to avoid shareholders being locked in—this means that the offeror has an extended timetable in which to complete the offer but cannot declare its offer unconditional as to acceptances (thereby ending withdrawal rights) until it is satisfied that all other conditions to the offer can be fulfilled (or waived) within the next 21 days. Where it is considered more likely than not that competition issues will arise, the Panel prefers the parties to use the full 28 days following the Rule 2.7 announcement to post the offer document (or potentially a longer period, with an extension), rather than announcing and posting in quick succession and then requesting an extension in the latter stages of the bid timetable. Where it only becomes apparent later in the timetable that there will be a delay in obtaining competition clearances, the Panel is more likely to be receptive to a request to grant an extension to Day 60 (albeit still somewhat reluctant unless the target is supportive of this course of action).

Since a scheme of arrangement is not "extended" in the same way as a contractual offer, provisions of the Code regarding extensions are not generally applicable to schemes. However, in order to ensure that shareholders and other market participants are kept properly informed of the progress of a scheme, Section 6 of the Schemes Appendix provides that certain changes to the expected scheme timetable (for example, any adjournment of a shareholder meeting or court sanction hearing, or any decision by the target board to propose such an adjournment) should be announced promptly by the target in accordance with the requirements of Rule 2.9. In addition, it is worth noting that the Code Committee's response statement RS 2007/1 indicates that the Panel may hold a bidder or the target to any statements which they may make in relation to not extending the scheme timetable, including any "no adjournment statements" if it believes that shareholders or others may have relied on such statements.

7.4 Extensions of the offer

In what circumstances will an extension of the offer be important?

1. If an offeror has failed to achieve a sufficient level of control by a specified closing date, it may well wish to extend its offer to give itself more time to persuade shareholders by its arguments to accept it. As mentioned above, an offer may not be extended beyond Day 60 unless the offer has become or been declared unconditional as to acceptances by that date. Subject to this, if an offeror wishes to extend its offer, it has two options: it can either announce an extension specifying the next closing date or, if the offer is unconditional as to acceptances, it may state that the offer will remain open until further notice.

2. Once an offeror has gained control it will normally leave its offer open in order to allow dissentients to accept and to allow it to gather in further acceptances to the extent necessary to be able to utilise the compulsory acquisition provisions under the Companies Act 2006 to "squeeze out" the outstanding minority (see 7.3.1.11 above).

An offeror is not, however, obliged to extend its offer (Rule 31.3). If, for example, its acceptance condition has not been satisfied by a specified closing date then, as was the case in Vinci's bid for TBI following the 9/11 attacks in 2001, Macquarie Bank's bid for the London Stock Exchange in 2007 and KiFin's offer for Minerva in 2009, the offeror is free to lapse its offer and walk away without consequence under the Code.

Whilst an offeror is free to decide whether or not to extend its offer beyond a specified closing date where the acceptance condition has not been satisfied as at that date, it can contract out of that right. In July 2008, Barings Private Equity Asia agreed with the offeree company, Nord Anglia, that it would only be able to invoke the acceptance condition to lapse the offer if, at the relevant closing date, the level of acceptances was below 75 per cent, and that it would give Nord Anglia seven days advance notice of its intention to invoke such condition. This meant that if Barings were to have given notice of its intention to lapse the offer, the offeree company would have had an opportunity to seek to obtain sufficient acceptances during this notice period to prevent the offer from actually lapsing. In October 2010, on the Apollo/CVC consortium bid for Brit Insurance, Achilles (the consortium bidco) agreed not to cause the offer to lapse before Day 60 by reference to any non-fulfilment of the acceptance condition except in certain specified circumstances (the announcement of a competing offer, certain breaches by Brit Insurance of its covenants in the implementation agreement or a change in the independent directors' recommendation). In December 2010, in the takeover of Wellstream by GE, GE agreed to keep its offer open beyond the initial closing date regardless of the level of acceptances it received. These sorts of provision are relatively unusual but do provide considerable benefits for the offeree company and its shareholders, as they reduce the flexibility of the offeror to lapse its offer.

Rule 31.5 (and the Notes on that Rule) deal in some detail with what are known as "no extension statements". The basic idea is that shareholders should not be misled into thinking that they must accept an offer by a certain date only to find later that the offeror has granted a further extension. If an offeror wants to extend its offer it must specifically reserve the right to do so and this must be prominently displayed in the offer document and not lost in the small print of the appendices.

If, however, a competitive situation arises after an offeror has made a no extension statement, the whole picture changes and the offeror can choose not to be bound by its statement provided shareholders are informed promptly and certain other requirements are satisfied.

In addition, an offeror can choose not to be bound by a previous no extension statement in the light of material new information announced by the offeree company after Day 39 of the offer timetable (Note 5 on Rule 31.5). With the Panel's permission the offer may be extended, provided that notice to that effect is given as soon as possible, and in any event within four business days after the offeree company's announcement, with shareholders being informed in writing of this extension at the earliest opportunity.

A somewhat unusual situation arose in June 2011 when, after Guoco's hostile mandatory bid for Rank had become wholly unconditional. Guoco was permitted, with the consent of the Panel, to extend its offer until July 15, 2011 notwithstanding a previous statement that its offer would close on July 1. Guoco agreed that if, by July 15, 2011, it had received acceptances which, when combined with the Rank shares already owned by the Guoco group, represented more than 75 per cent of Rank's share capital, then the offer would remain open for acceptance for a further 7 days until July 22, 2011. This arrangement was designed to allow Rank shareholders the opportunity to wait and see whether Guoco achieved the 75 per cent threshold before deciding whether to accept the offer. In addition, Rank shareholders who had already accepted the offer were permitted to withdraw their acceptances. Guoco agreed that if it failed to reach the 75 per cent threshold by July 15, 2011, then the offer would close at that time and would not be extended further.

The driver behind these arrangements was to minimise the risk of minority shareholders being "left behind" in Rank given the possibility of the company being delisted in the event that Guoco acquired 75 per cent or more of Rank's shares. Guoco had consistently stated that it intended to retain Rank's London Stock Exchange listing regardless of the level of support for its offer but if it had ended up acquiring over 75 per cent of Rank's shares then either the London Stock Exchange could have terminated the listing (as the free float would have fallen below 25 per cent) or Guoco would have been in a position at any point in the future to proceed to delist Rank. De-listing would have had a significant adverse impact on the value of any shares held by minority shareholders. These arrangements were therefore intended to ensure Guoco remained below the 75 per cent threshold and, failing that, to give Rank shareholders an opportunity to accept the offer if the 75 per cent threshold was reached. As it turned out, Guoco ended up with 74.5 per cent and Rank has remained as a listed company.

7.5   Revisions and increases

The timing requirements relating to revisions are referred to above, for example no revision after Day 46 (see 7.3.1.7 above). Revisions will be obligatory in certain circumstances such as an acquisition of any interest in shares above the offer price (Rule 6.2) or in the event of an obligation to introduce a cash offer under Rule 11.1. Rule 32.3 provides that if an offer is revised, all shareholders who accepted the original offer must be entitled to the revised consideration.

As regards increased offers (as distinct simply from offers which are revised, although it is rare for a revision not to represent an increase), Rule 32.2 contains substantially equivalent restrictions on no increase statements as those outlined in relation to no extension statements and dealt with in Rule 31.5.

The reasons for these restrictions were explained in the 1999 Panel ruling in the context of the competing bids for CALA Plc. An MBO vehicle, Dotterel Limited, and Miller 1999 Plc had each announced bids for CALA Plc. Miller announced the revised offer of 200 pence per CALA share and stated that this increased offer was final and would not be increased further except that Miller reserved the right to increase its offer up to a maximum of 210 pence per share in the event of a bid being made for CALA at a higher value than its increased offer of 200 pence in cash.

Dotterel indicated its intention to announce a matching offer of 200 pence per share—basically relying on the shares held by management and the support of institutional shareholders for existing management to win the day. Miller sought consent from the Panel to increase its offer if a matching offer was made. The Panel ruled that as Miller had not reserved the specific right to increase its offer in the event of a matching (as opposed to higher) bid, then Miller was prohibited from doing so.

The Panel ruling went on to explain that:

"This Rule seeks to set a balance between the potential disadvantages to shareholders from this consequence and the undesirable consequences for shareholders and the markets if they cannot rely on the accuracy of statements made by an offeror. As a matter of policy, and in the absence of 'wholly exceptional circumstances', it is more important that the principle of certainty and orderly conduct should be upheld rather than to risk compromising this principle to accommodate the apparent disadvantages which may result from the application of the Rule in a particular case."

This ruling was, however, the subject of a certain amount of press criticism on the basis that this apparently inflexible application of Rule 32.2 potentially deprived the CALA shareholders of a further higher bid from Miller.

Care should also be taken to ensure that statements made by the offeror company, or its controlling shareholder, cannot be construed under Rule 32.2 as a no increase statement. It is relatively easy to be inadvertently tripped up by this Rule. In November 2002 Hugh Osmond, a controlling shareholder in Twigway which had made an indicative offer of 320–350 pence per share for the Pizza Express restaurant group, was quoted in the press as saying that the offeror company would "not reconsider the price under any circumstances unless there's some bloody good reason, and right now I can't think of one". The Panel immediately required a statement from Twigway clarifying that Mr Osmond's comments did not represent a no increase statement under Rule 32.2.

Whilst on the subject of increased offers, it is worth noting that Rule 32.4 recognises that the offeror may need to introduce new conditions into its bid in the event of a revision or an increase. For example, if it introduces a securities element to the consideration it will need a condition that the new securities be admitted to listing and/or trading. Panel consent is, however, required for inclusion of any such condition. This will only be permitted to the extent necessary to implement the revised offer.

If an offer includes both a cash and a securities element to the consideration, Panel consent will be required on a subsequent revision of the offer if the offeror wishes to remove, or reduce the amount of, one element of the consideration in substitution for an increase in a different element. The Panel is unlikely to give its consent unless the offeree company agrees to such revision.

As mentioned above, the Schemes Appendix addresses various issues in relation to the revision of a scheme and provides, among other things, that a revision to the scheme should normally be made no later than the date which is 14 days prior to the date of the shareholder meetings, with revisions after that date requiring the Panel's consent. Section 7 of the Schemes Appendix also provides that the Panel's consent must be sought to any revision of a scheme following the shareholder meetings but before the court sanction hearing. Details of the confirmations that are likely to be required from the target board and its Rule 3 adviser in such circumstances are set out in the Code Committee's response statement RS 2007/1 (but have not been reflected in the Code in order to preserve the Panel's flexibility in such circumstances).

Section 8 of the Schemes Appendix provides that the offeror may only switch from contractual takeover offer to a scheme (or vice versa) with the consent of the Panel, although it is not required to reserve the right to do so. The circumstances in which the Panel would withhold its consent are likely to be limited.

7.6 Alternative offers

Generally the Rules outlined above apply equally to alternative offers. Rule 33.1 specifies that these will include cash alternative offers. Difficult questions arise, however, with regard to alternative offers, in particular in relation to closing or shutting them off.

First, with regard to "mix and match" offers—that is, where shareholders may elect to vary the proportion in which they are to receive different forms of consideration subject to other shareholders making contrary elections (because there are limits on the different forms of consideration available)—these are not regarded as alternative offers and the availability to "mix and match" may be closed without notice on any closing date provided this has been clearly stated in the offer document.

Secondly, with regard to the shutting off of alternative offers, the general rule, as indicated, is that once an offer has become or is declared unconditional as to acceptances, all alternative offers (in the same way as the principal offer itself) must remain open for a minimum of 14 days.

Thus, waverers must also be given the benefit of jumping on the bandwagon with regard to alternative offers.

Also, as with the principal offer under Rule 31.3, if on a closing day an offer is not unconditional as to acceptances, an alternative offer may be closed without prior notice—that is, there is no obligation to extend it.

Rule 33.2 deals with shutting off cash underwritten alternatives. Cash underwritten alternatives involve large underwriting fees and offerors are naturally keen to stop commitment commissions running as soon as control of the offeree company has been won. The effect of this Rule is to allow an offeror to shut off a cash alternative earlier than other forms of consideration provided:

1. the value of the cash underwritten alternative (which must be provided by third parties) is, at the time of announcement, more than half the maximum value of the offer; and
2. it has specifically given notice that it reserves the right to close the cash alternative on a stated date, being not less than 14 days later than the date of the notice.

Rule 33.2 will not apply to a cash alternative which is provided to satisfy the requirements of Rule 9. In other words, an offeror required to make a cash bid under Rule 9 will not be able to shut it off on the date its offer becomes or is declared unconditional as to acceptances but must keep it open for a further minimum period of 14 days.

Rule 33.3 deals with the reintroduction of alternative forms of consideration. Generally, unless a statement has been made that a form of consideration will not be reintroduced, it may be reintroduced at a later date, even if it has lapsed or closed for acceptance in the interim. Reintroduction is treated as a revision and therefore must be open for 14 days and cannot be effected later than Day 46.

In the context of schemes, an election for alternative consideration under a scheme should be capable of being made at least until the date of the shareholder meetings and target shareholders who elect for alternative consideration in a scheme should have a right to withdraw such an election. The right of withdrawal must be exercisable at least until one week prior to the court sanction hearing.

7.7 Restrictions following offers and possible offers

The final area covered by this Chapter deals principally with Rule 35.1 of the Code which contains the Rule restricting a new offer from being launched within 12 months of the lapsing or withdrawal of a previous offer.

7.7.1 Circumstances when an offer must lapse

An offer must lapse if:

1. an offeror does not obtain sufficient acceptances to be able to declare its offer unconditional as to acceptances by Day

       60 (examples of this have included the NASDAQ/LSE bid; OPD's bid for Hydrogen; and TPG Capital/GlobeOp Financial Services);

2.   any detailed investigation by the relevant competition authority takes place (examples of this are the lapse of the original bid announced by William Morrison Supermarkets Plc for Safeway Plc in January 2003; the HMV bid for Ottakers; and AG Barr's all-share merger with Britvic); or

3.   having declared the offer unconditional as to acceptances, the other conditions to the offer are not satisfied within 21 days then the offer must lapse.

In November 2008, BHP Billiton's offer for Rio Tinto lapsed when it became clear that competition clearance, which was a pre-condition for the offer, would not be given without requiring significant divestments, which BHP was not prepared to make.

When an offer lapses any tendered acceptances also lapse. The offeror is therefore left with only the shares it has acquired through purchases. Its stake will usually be less than 30 per cent of the offeree company. However, if as a result of acquisitions, it was forced to make a Rule 9 offer which failed, an offeror could be left with a stake of 30 per cent or more.

Since the Schemes Appendix disapplies timing restrictions in relation to schemes, there is no pre-determined time limit by which a scheme must become effective or lapse. However, Rule 12.1 of the Code provides that the scheme will lapse and not become effective if it is the subject of a Phase 2 reference to the Competition and Markets Authority or the European Commission before the shareholder meetings have taken place. However, if the competition reference occurs after the date of the shareholder meetings, the Code will not require the scheme to lapse as a result (although it may give rise to the right for a bidder to invoke a condition to seek to lapse the offer).

7.7.2   Dealing in offeree company shares

Once the offer has lapsed, the offeror is no longer subject to the Code restriction on disposing of offeree company shares (Rule 4.2) and can therefore sell down any shareholding it has acquired in the offeree company. If it decides to retain all or some of its holding then the degree of influence it can exert over the offeree company will depend on the size of its stake.

There is generally no restriction on an offeror making market purchases after its offer has lapsed. However, where there have been competing offers, a lapsed offeror cannot acquire an interest in shares in the offeree company on more favourable terms than those made available under its lapsed offer until such time as the competing offer has either lapsed or become wholly unconditional. This is intended to prevent an offeror which has lapsed its offer from making market purchases with a view to frustrating a competing offer which is still continuing. It does not, however, prevent an unsuccessful offeror from acquiring an interest in offeree company shares once the "successful" offer has become wholly unconditional, which could potentially still frustrate the ability of the successful offeror to obtain 100 per cent control of the offeree company.

7.7.3   Rule 35—delay of 12 months

Whatever the size of the offeror's stake in the offeree company, its continued presence on the shareholder register is likely to be a source of both concern and possible irritation to the offeree company. The offeree company will not know what the offeror's intentions are.

The Code provides some protection against the "siege" being renewed immediately; the offeror cannot launch a new offer (or partial offer) within 12 months of its original offer lapsing unless the new offer is recommended (provided that three months have passed since the earlier offer lapsed), a competing offer has been made, the offeree company has announced a "whitewash" proposal or a reverse takeover, there has been a material change of circumstances, or the new offer follows the giving of clearance by the relevant competition authority (Rule 35.1 and Note on Rules 35.1 and 35.2). Accordingly, Morrison's was able to announce a renewed recommended offer for Safeway in December 2003 following the completion of the detailed review of the supermarket industry undertaken by the UK's competition authority as a result of Morrison's initial offer for Safeway in January 2003.

The Panel may also grant consent for a new offer to be made in circumstances where it is likely to prove, or has proved, impossible to obtain material regulatory clearances relating to the offer within the Code timetable.

The Panel's general approach to Rule 35.1 was explained in its statement of March 17, 1995 relating to the appeal by Trafalgar House against a Panel Executive decision that Trafalgar House should not be permitted to make an immediate new offer for Northern Electric:

> "Rule 35.1 is designed to create a reasonable balance between giving shareholders an opportunity to consider offers for their shares and enabling the business of the company in which they have invested to be carried on without continuous uncertainty and dislocation. Inevitably the effect of this Rule may be to prevent for a period of time a new offer by a failed offeror, at whatever price, being made to shareholders in the offeree company."

On that occasion the Panel made it clear that Rule 35 is regarded as one of the more important Rules of the Code and that only on rare occasions would it be prepared to grant a dispensation. Trafalgar House allowed its offer to lapse on Day 60 (with acceptances of 76.5 per cent) three days after a pricing review of all electricity companies which led to a substantial fall in the market value of shares in electricity companies generally. The Panel ruled that those circumstances did not warrant the granting of a dispensation to enable Trafalgar House immediately to make a new offer at a lower price to take account of the pricing review without having first obtained the consent of the board of Northern Electric.

Rule 35.2 makes it clear that Rule 35.1 also applies following partial offers which could result in the offeror (and its concert parties) controlling between 30 per cent and 50 per cent of the offeree company whether or not that offer has become or been declared wholly unconditional. This is to cover the possibility of successive partial offers. When such an offer has become or been declared wholly unconditional, the 12-month period runs from that date. In addition, Rule 35.1 applies following a partial offer for more than 50 per cent of the voting rights of the offeree company which has not become or been declared wholly unconditional (see Rule 35.2(b)).

In the 12 months following an offer lapsing, neither the offeror nor its concert parties can: (i) announce an offer or possible offer; (ii) acquire any interest in shares if this would give rise to an obligation to make a mandatory bid under Rule 9; (iii) acquire any interest in, or procure an irrevocable commitment in respect of, shares in the offeree if the shares in which such person, together with persons acting in concert with him, would be interested and the shares in respect of which he, or they, had acquired irrevocable commitments would in aggregate carry 30 per cent or more of the voting rights of the offeree; (iv) make any statement which raises or confirms the possibility that an offer might be made for the offeree; or (v) take any steps in connection with a possible offer for the offeree where knowledge of the possible offer might be extended outside those people within the offeror and its immediate advisers who need to know about it. However, (iv) and (v) above will not normally apply where the offer lapsed as a result of a detailed competition review being initiated or as a result of some other material regulatory approval not being obtained within the normal offer timetable and the offeror is continuing to seek the relevant approval with a view subsequently to making a new offer with the consent of the Panel.

The restrictions do not, however, prevent a lapsed offeror from acquiring further shares in the offeree company (save in the circumstances described in 7.7.2 above). However, an important restriction is that if the offeror has less than 30 per cent, it cannot acquire shares or rights over shares taking it to 30 per cent or more. Equally, if the unsuccessful offeror has between 30 per cent and 50 per cent, it cannot acquire any more shares during that 12-month period.

Once the 12 months have elapsed, an offeror is free to acquire further shares or make another offer. Rule 9 does, however, continue to apply and the offeror will be forced to make an offer if it (together with its concert parties) takes its stake from below 30 per cent to 30 per cent or more, or if it acquires any interest in further shares in the company where it already has between 30 per cent and 50 per cent.

7.7.4   Rule 35.3—6 month delay before offering better terms to any remaining minority

If an offer is declared unconditional in all respects but a minority remains outstanding then a six-month delay is likely to be required by the Panel before the offeror or any person acting in concert with him can make a second offer, or acquire any interest in shares, on more favourable terms than those which were available under the previous offer (Rule 35.3). Again this is to ensure fair treatment for offeree shareholders and to seek to establish a level playing field as between competing offerors or potential offerors.

Chapter 8

Profit Forecasts, Quantified Financial Benefits Statements and Asset Valuations

Ursula Newton

Partner

PricewaterhouseCoopers LLP

Introduction

On September 30, 2013 the Panel issued new Code Rules concerning profit forecasts and quantified financial benefits statements (formerly known as "merger benefits statements"). The aim of these rule changes, as set out in the Panel's response statement to the original consultation (PCP 2012/1), was to:

a) apply more proportionate requirements to profit forecasts than under the existing rules;

b) adopt a more logical framework for the regulation of profit forecasts;

c) achieve a greater consistency in the treatment of profit forecasts compared with other legislation, standards and guidance;

d) extend the application of the current disclosure and reporting requirements with regard to merger benefits statements to cover company cost savings statements and to all offers, not just hostile offers; and

e) adopting more detailed requirements in relation to quanti-fied financial benefits statements than under the existing rules.

As the revised Rules only came into effect from September 30, 2013 there will inevitably be a period of time before it can be seen how these will be applied in practice.

The new Rules extended the previous reporting exceptions that existed in relation to unaudited preliminary statements of annual results and interim results published during the offer period such that these are now outside the scope of Rule 28. Preliminary results, as long as they are prepared to the standard required by the UKLA Rules, will never have to be repeated and reported on because it is assumed that they will subsequently be audited. Half-yearly financial reports, or "interims", which comply with the relevant provisions of the UKLA Rules, the AIM Rules for Companies or the ISDX Growth Market Rules for Issuers will also no longer need to be repeated or reported on. Previously, a reporting exemption in respect of half-yearly financial reports was typically only available where an offer had been recommended. The new Rule 28 also excluded any other interim information which has been published by virtue of a regulatory requirement and has been prepared in accordance with International Accounting Standard 34 (or equivalent accounting standard).

It should also be noted that the Rules concerning profit forecasts and quantified financial benefits statements do not apply to forecasts or statements made by an offeror offering solely cash.

8.1 Profit forecasts

8.1.1 Introduction

Profit forecasts have historically been an extremely important feature of public takeovers in the United Kingdom, and particularly those that are contested. A forecast of the current year's profits underpins the value of any target company's shares and, where a bidder is offering paper, a forecast by the bidder can be crucial in supporting its own share price and thus supporting the value of its offer.

All the Code Rules exist for a reason and Rule 28, on profit forecasts, is no exception. Prior to the Code's introduction in the late 1960s, there were a number of scandals where takeovers were effected in circumstances where profit forecasts had been made which subsequently proved to have been exceedingly optimistic. Rule 28 is designed to ensure that shareholders are protected from being misled by inaccurate forecasts, whether too high or too low.

8.1.2   *What is a profit forecast?*

In the new Code Rules, the Panel conformed its definition of a profit forecast to be consistent with the definition in the FCA's Prospectus Rules. The principle however remains the same as previously in that a profit forecast arises from the issue of any published expectation of financial results for the last financial period (if it has not yet been audited), the current period or for a future period. Where the period has already finished, the term employed is a profit estimate, but essentially all the same rules apply whether it is a profit estimate or a forecast. It is worth noting at the outset that a profit forecast should be a best assessment made by the directors of the likely outturn for the period—it should not be a hoped for target.

This principle may appear straightforward but a company and its advisers have to take great care to ensure that the company does not inadvertently make a profit forecast. This was demonstrated in the bid by Kvaerner for AMEC several years ago, when a director of Financial Dynamics, the public relations adviser to AMEC, gave

> "an impression of a level of AMEC's future profits that was not being made public, and had not been prepared and reported on in accordance with the Code."

AMEC had subsequently to disassociate itself from the information, and Financial Dynamics was criticised by the Panel for failing to take sufficient care in its discussions with analysts which resulted in what were described as "serious breaches of the Code". Similarly, during the TI Group bid for Dowty Group, Dowty's public relations adviser was criticised by the Takeover panel for making a profit forecast which failed to meet the standards required by the Code and for giving out material new information in conversations with certain journalists and investment analysts which was not correct.

Any public statement that can be construed as putting a floor or ceiling on anticipated results would be regarded as a profit forecast, as would a statement of any data from which a calculation of future profits may be made. The Code makes it clear that it is not necessary for the statement to mention a particular figure or even the word profit. For example, a chairman might respond to questions at an AGM regarding the current year performance by commenting that the current year's results will be better than the previous year's. Such a statement would be regarded as a forecast. Another example might be where an investment trust forecasts its next year's dividend which, given that at least 85 per cent of such a trust's profits must be paid out in dividends, sets both a floor and a ceiling on the annual profits. In the 2010 takeover by Kraft for Cadbury, Kraft had included a statement in its guidance to the market, with regard to its expectation of discretionary cash flow for the year. The Panel deemed that this statement gave a measure of earnings and required the statement to be reported on as a profit forecast in the offer documents issued by Kraft.

The new Rules extended the requirements to cover references to a forecast published by third parties. Thus, if a company refers to or quotes a profit forecast relating to it that has been published by a third party, for example an investment analyst, it will be treated as having endorsed and published that profit forecast itself for the purpose of the Rules. The requirements concerning profit forecasts will then apply to this statement. The Code does provide an exemption where a company merely continues to provide details on its website of all published analyst forecasts, but as with many of the amendments to the Rules, companies and their advisors are recommended to consult with the Panel in advance of making any statements in order to ensure that they have an agreed understanding of the requirements.

The Rules were revised to clarify that they apply to a forecast which relates to any part of a company's business in the same way as to a forecast which relates to the whole of a company's business. However, in circumstances where a forecast is published for both the whole and a part of a company's business it is not the Panel's intention to require separate reports in respect of each forecast and that a report on the forecast for the whole of the business would be sufficient.

Profit "projections", where a company calculates the possible future profits which could arise under certain circumstances, were not allowed under the previous Code Rules. The Rules were revised to clarify that, if during an offer period a profit forecast for a future financial year is published or repeated, the document or announcement must include a corresponding profit forecast for the current and each intervening financial year(s). The reporting requirements concerning profit forecasts will then apply to each statement for a financial year ending 15 months or less from the date on which the forecast is first published.

8.1.3 The Code

In common with the UK Listing Authority Listing Rules (the UKLA Rules) and the Prospectus Directive, there is no requirement under the Code for a company to issue a profit forecast. The new Rules clarified that, if there is already a profit forecast on the public record before a bid is made, this will normally have to be repeated or, a revised forecast may be substituted. In the event that the Board does not wish to repeat the previously published statement the Code clarifies that it can either include in the announcement or document a statement that the previous forecast is no longer valid and an explanation as to why this is the case, or can amend the previous statement to produce a new forecast. At the outset, an adviser should invariably check whether or not its client has a forecast on the record. Particular areas to note relate to trading statements and cross-border transactions for territories where it is common practice to provide earnings guidance in communications with the markets. If a forecast is issued for the first time during an offer period (or in an announcement which commences an offer period), or an existing forecast is revised, this will need to be reported on by the company's reporting accountants and the financial advisor. If any document or announcement published by a company included a profit forecast, any subsequent document published by that party in connection with the offer must, unless superseded by a revised forecast included in the document, include a statement by the directors reaffirming the profit forecast. Where reports were obtained in respect of the original profit forecast, the document must include a statement that the reporting accountant and financial advisor have confirmed that their reports continue to apply.

It is very easy to get a forecast wrong and thus a forecast is prepared with scrupulous care and objectivity by the directors, who have sole responsibility for it.

8.1.4 Exceptions

There are certain exceptions to the requirement for a profit forecast to be reported on, set out in the Rules, which also make it clear that advisors should consult with the Panel over the application of these exemptions.

In particular, the changes to the Code introduced a new concept of "Ordinary course profit forecasts". These are defined in the Rules as a profit forecast published by either the target or bidder in accordance with its established practice and as part of the ordinary course of its communications with its shareholders and the market. Since this change to the Rules there have been few examples and so it is not yet clear how this concept will be implemented, in particular how long does it take for a practice to become "ordinary course". The Code specifically requires advisors to consult the Panel if they consider that a profit forecast should be treated as ordinary course, since the Panel has retained the right to require such forecasts to be reported on.

The Rules now provide the following exceptions from the requirement for a profit forecast to be reported on:

(a) here an "ordinary course profit forecast" was made prior to an approach regarding a possible offer;
(b) here an 'ordinary course profit forecast' is issued during an offer period and the other party to the offer agrees to the exception; and
(c) Where the forecast is for a period ending more than 15 months after the date on which the forecast is made.

In such circumstances the directors of the company making the forecast would be required to:

(a) Confirm in the offer document or offeree board circular that the forecast remains valid and has been prepared on a basis consistent with the company's accounting policies and includes the assumptions on which the forecast is based; or, if the forecast is made before commencement of the offer period
(b) Include a statement that the forecast is no longer valid, with an explanation of why that is the case.

It is worth noting, that if an "ordinary course profit forecast" is revised or amended during the course of the offer period then this would be regarded by the Panel as a new forecast which would need to be reported on by independent accountants and financial advisers.

The Rules also provide the following exceptions from the requirement for a profit forecast to be reported on:

(a) Where a profit forecast states a maximum figure for the likely level of profits for a particular period (a profit ceiling); and

(b)   In the case of an offeror, where the consideration securities will not represent a material proportion of its enlarged share capital or, alternatively, a material proportion of the value of the offer.

Each of these exceptions is only available with the specific approval of the Panel. It is also worth noting that the exceptions set out above do not apply where the offer is a management buy-out.

8.1.5   The forecast

The principal assumptions on which the forecast is based must be stated and should provide useful information as to the forecast's reasonableness and reliability. The forecast must, in certain circumstances, be reviewed and reported on by both the reporting accountants and the financial advisers. These reports need to be included in the offer or defence document and also in any announcement of the transaction, if that is made earlier.

Once a forecast has been made, its continuing validity must usually be confirmed in each subsequent document that is issued, so as to make sure that any significant changes are notified to shareholders.

The degree of risk of getting a forecast wrong increases with the length of time that is forecast ahead. For this reason, it is relatively unusual for a forecast to extend beyond the current financial year, particularly if the current year is not well advanced.

Whether a forecast can actually be reported on at all can depend upon the nature of the business. It is much easier to forecast the results of a business such as an aircraft manufacturer (with its long order books) than it is for a high street retailer where a week of seasonal trading can result in a significant range of possible financial results. In the financial services industry, the results of a life assurance company are so highly dependent upon its annual actuarial evaluation carried out at the end of the financial year that any forecast issued prior to that exercise carries a very significant degree of uncertainty.

In contrast, regulated industries such as the water industry have tended to be a stable and predictable business which can be forecast some way ahead.

It is not uncommon for a profit forecast to be revised upwards during the offer period. This is perfectly permissible and in theory would seem logical, because as time passes, the company would become increasingly certain about its actual profitability, and there is less need to provide a contingency for unexpected developments. In practice, however, whilst such a revision sets a higher future earnings figure, it leaves the company open to the potential criticism of manipulating its financial reporting. The revision of a profit forecast during an offer period may also result in the disapplication of a waiver from requiring reports from reporting accountants and the financial advisor that may have been given by the Panel on an original forecast.

In making a profit forecast the directors must ensure that it is:

- understandable: it must not be presented in such a way that it so complex that it cannot be readily understood;
- reliable: it must be supported by thorough analysis and represent factual strategies, plans and risk analysis; and
- comparable: it should be capable of comparison with information included in the historical financial information.

When making a profit forecast, directors should also have regard to the Guidance on Prospective Financial Information, published by the Institute of Chartered Accountants of England and Wales in 2003. The overriding principle of prospective financial information (PFI) is that it should be useful in the context of the judgements made.

8.1.6 Format of the forecast

There are no Rules concerning the format in which the profit forecast must be made. Indeed the forecast need not even mention a number. A statement that profits will be higher than last year or that the result will be breakeven, are both fully acceptable ways of making a forecast.

Whilst the directors and their advisers would often feel that to give a range of profits might be the most realistic approach, in practice a single figure is usually given, qualified by the words "not less than", "of the order of", or "approximately". These phrases have tended to be interpreted in subtly differing ways, with "not less than" meaning that one might actually expect to exceed the stated number by a small amount, perhaps a few percentage points. "Of the order of" might imply that one would expect the result to be a few percentage points either side of the stated figure. However, this form of disclosure is a lot less attractive than "not less than" as it implies much less certainty in the minds of the directors about the robustness of its forecast.

It is worth noting that the more precise or comprehensive the forecast, the greater the amount of work required by the company and its advisers. The directors may find that they have to balance their preference for more detailed information, for example profit by division or country, against the downside risk of any published element of the forecast not being achieved. In such circumstances, it would be expected that each published element of the forecast would require the same degree of rigorous analysis (and prudence) as that which would be applied to a total number.

If there is anything out of the ordinary which means it is not possible simply to tax-effect the pre-tax figure to arrive at earnings, the abnormal items, such as unusual tax charges, must also be given.

8.1.7 *The assumptions underlying the forecast*

It is a protection for shareholders that the principal assumptions upon which the forecast is based have to be published. In practice, however, it is unusual for many of the assumptions to be particularly interesting or informative in relation to the specific circumstances of the company. For example, they will almost invariably refer to there being no change in exchange rates or in the current rate of inflation.

Assumptions must identify clearly those factors that are within the directors' control and those that are not. Thus, an assumption that a new product will be launched would not be in the directors' control if the launch was subject to approval by a regulatory authority, but its introduction would be within the directors' control if there were no authorisations still awaited.

The directors have sole responsibility for the assumptions in the forecast, although in practice they often need substantial advice and guidance from their reporting accountants and financial advisers in formulating and wording the assumptions. The directors of a substantial, multi-location group would typically need more assistance, given the range and complexity of factors potentially affecting such a group's results.

In order to arrive at the directors' best estimate of the likely results, assumptions must clearly be realistic, and the directors cannot cover themselves by making an assumption on something which may well be wrong—for example, assuming that the company will not suffer a strike when in fact one is threatened would not be allowable.

There are certain assumptions that are not generally considered acceptable. For example, an assumption which in effect says nothing more than "we assume the forecast will be achieved" is not permitted. An example of this would be the assumption that "sales will be in accordance with budget". This is meaningless for the shareholders who do not know how demanding the budget is, and therefore are none the wiser regarding the preparation of the forecast. An assumption that is allowed would be, for example, "market demand will continue in line with recent trends and seasonal patterns". In this example, market demand is an uncertainty beyond the company's control.

That latter assumption is an example of what assumptions are supposed to be, that is, useful to shareholders in helping them to form a view as to the reasonableness and reliability of the forecast.

Published assumptions tend to be quite standard, but there are often one or two that are specific to a particular industry. One example was stated by Devenish in its defence against Boddington in 1991 in assuming that there would be no abnormal weather conditions—this being relevant because the level of beer sales is so highly dependent upon the weather. Predictably, Boddington referred to it as more a weather forecast than a profit forecast! A forecast by Manweb a few years ago assumed that weather conditions would be in line with the experience of the last 30 years.

There is a second level of assumptions which are always in existence but are not published and these could be described as the detailed working assumptions. These will be reviewed by the reporting accountants and financial advisers and discussed with the company in the same way as the published assumptions. It is important that such assumptions are identified because some could be critical to the achievement of the forecast and hence require careful consideration.

8.1.8 Responsibility

The Code is quite clear about who is responsible for making a profit forecast. Sole responsibility for a forecast lies with the directors. The reason for this is entirely logical. The people in the best position to determine the likely profits, and to take account of all relevant factors, and to know about current problems which could affect profits, are the directors. Having sole responsibility focuses the directors' minds and is designed to ensure that the directors do not either merely rely on their staff to produce the numbers without reviewing the outcome or wholly rely on their professional advisers. It is, after all, the forecast made by the directors.

This does not mean that the financial advisers and reporting accountants have no responsibilities. They are expected to carry out their duties with appropriate care and skill so as to express an opinion on the forecast. Indeed, failure to do so could involve legal liability.

One principal way in which the directors are able to demonstrate that they have taken due care in compiling the forecast is to commission a commentary "long-form" report from the reporting accountants, which will then be discussed with the directors. Such a report is of particular use to non-executive directors or directors who are executives of particular divisions or subsidiaries but who nevertheless have to take responsibility for the forecast as a whole. It is also an important benefit to the financial advisers in meeting its own responsibilities in relation to the forecasts.

Having discussed the long-form report with the reporting accountants and the financial advisers, the directors often refine or amend their forecast in the light of the matters which have been raised. Such a revision sometimes involves either taking a different view on a particular item in the forecast or, more typically, including a contingency element which the directors decide is necessary to take account of the various uncertainties which inevitably exist in a forecast. One thing that experience suggests is that if anything is not going to go as expected in a forecast, it is far more likely to have an adverse effect on profits than a positive one.

Forecasts are often put together and reviewed in a very short period of time to meet the requirements of the Code timetable. A company may not have adequate resources to do all the work necessary and so it is sometimes the case that external accountants provide assistance in elements of the preparation of a profit forecast. However, such work must be appropriate and clearly distinguished from the reporting work; an auditor's independence would be impaired if it both prepared a forecast and then had to report on it in public. Moreover, only the directors and staff of the company have sufficient detailed knowledge of the company's affairs to prepare a forecast of the required quality.

8.1.9 Preparation of a long-form report

There are a number of key matters that would typically be investigated by the reporting accountants and reported in the long-form report in order to satisfy themselves on a forecast. Normally a review would address the following:

1. how much of the forecast profit has already been achieved according to the company's management accounts;
2. how reliable those management accounts have been in the past, or if certain items typically needed adjusting, for example, the stock figure which was always found to be incorrect when the stock was actually counted;
3. whether the same accounting policies had been followed as in the past—it would be inappropriate for the forecast to assume plant and machinery was written off over 20 years when in last year's audited accounts it was written off over 15;
4. commentary on the assumptions and a comment if the reporting accountant believes any assumptions to be unrealistic;
5. an explanation of how the forecast had been prepared. The reliability of the forecast, and thus the extent to which there should be a contingency provision, will depend upon whether such a forecast had been done in exactly the same way many times before or whether it was a rushed, one-off exercise using short-cut methods;
6. the accuracy of previous forecasts, as a prudent contingency would be required where there is evidence of major errors in forecasting in the past;

7.   a comparison of the figures included in the forecast with those of equivalent periods in previous years with explanations for the changes; and

8.   the analysis of the sensitivity of profits to changes in the assumptions. Such an analysis is key, for example, if sales are two per cent less than budget, how much might this affect profits?

The forecast will have been based upon information available at the time it was prepared. After the main review work has been completed and immediately prior to issue of the forecast, further information may become available, and this should be compared with that used in the preparation of the forecast to ensure it is consistent.

The same updating exercise will be required when any subsequent documents are issued to shareholders by the company since the validity of the forecast has to be reconfirmed by the directors, and in addition, the reporting accountants and financial advisers have to confirm that they have no objection to their published reports continuing to apply. In the current economic environment where uncertainty is increased, this process of keeping current is likely to be a more extensive exercise than in more benign economic climates.

Although the directors have sole responsibility for the forecast, the financial adviser is required to discuss the forecast with the company and report that it has satisfied itself that the forecast is being made by the directors with due care and consideration.

The way in which the financial adviser satisfies its obligation to comment on whether the forecast has been prepared with due care and consideration will differ depending upon the investment bank. The extent of the bank's work will depend upon the approach of the bank involved, the firm of reporting accountants involved, the difficulty of the industry in terms of forecasting, and the extent to which the bank knows the client.

The reporting accountants have their explicit responsibility under the Code to examine the accounting policies and calculations and to report on them in the relevant documents issued by the company. In accordance with the Standard (SIR 3000) issued by the Auditing Practices Board, the reporting accountant will report that "the forecast has been properly compiled on the basis of the assumptions made by the Directors" and "the basis of accounting used is consistent with the accounting policies of the company".

At first sight such a report might appear to be very limited in scope. After all, if the forecast adds up and there is no distortion arising because different accounting policies have been used, then the job might appear to be done. However, whilst there is no overt statement about the assumptions, reporting accountants should not allow an assumption to be published which appears to be unrealistic and there is a general expectation that, if a firm of accountants reports on a profit forecast, it implies a reliability which goes beyond this restricted form of wording. The reporting accountants effectively have to satisfy themselves that the profit forecast on which they are reporting has been made by the directors with proper care and consideration, taking into account all relevant factors, and that the forecast is credible.

It is perhaps of interest to note that the United Kingdom is very different from the United States environment as regards profit forecasts. In the United Kingdom, it is recognised that forecasts depend upon subjective judgements and are subject to inherent uncertainties. Consequently although reporting accountants are not able to verify profit forecasts (a misconception, at times, of the press and others), they are nevertheless able to express an opinion thereon. In the United States, no doubt influenced by the litigious environment, profit forecasts are not part of takeover defences and, despite "safe harbour" Rules in certain circumstances, auditors or reporting accountants do not issue reports on them in the same way.

8.1.10   Conclusion

A forecast of profits is an extremely important piece of information for an investor during a takeover. Forecasts often result in an increased offer being made by the bidder. They sometimes persuade shareholders not to accept an offer. Where forecasts prove to be wrong, particularly when the actual result is less than the forecast, this can cause loss to investors and is clearly a serious matter. Whilst the Code is designed to minimise the risk of a forecast not being met, this can and does on occasion happen, either because of circumstances which could not reasonably have been envisaged when the forecast was drawn up, or because a forecast was not drawn up with requisite care and the review process was inadequate.

The Panel does investigate situations where forecasts have not been met to see whether there has been a breach of the Code. Whilst there have not been any completed legal cases in the United Kingdom, some legal actions have been mounted against financial advisers and reporting accountants which have reached a compromise settlement. However, until a case is actually completed in court, there will remain some doubt regarding the precise responsibilities of directors, financial advisers and reporting accountants in this area.

It is, of course, open to question whether the increasingly litigious environment in the United Kingdom, combined with a legal system that can still make accountants liable for 100 per cent of a claim (irrespective of what proportion they were actually responsible for), will lead us down the US route and result in profit forecasts not being made and much less information on the future being provided to shareholders during takeovers.

8.2 Quantified financial benefits statements

8.2.1 Introduction

During the Granada takeover of Forte in 1996, Granada published a circular which included a statement that the ongoing profit of Forte could be improved by over £100 million under Granada's ownership. At the time, no specific Rule in the Code governed such a statement although it was subject to the general standards of care. The Code was amended in 1997 by Rule 19.1 to cover "merger benefits" and "earnings enhancement statements" (i.e. a statement that an acquisition will enhance the acquirer's earnings per share) published during the course of a takeover. The Code was further amended in July 2013, introducing a new definition "quantified financial benefits statements", covering "merger benefits" and "earning enhancement statements" as well as extending the Code requirements to cost savings statements made by target companies.

8.2.2 The Code

The Rules concerning quantified financial benefits statements were moved to Rule 28 so as to be together with the Rules concerning profit forecasts. These statements are required to be reported on if such enhancement depends in whole or in part on material merger benefits or if cost saving measures are published for the first time (or previously announced cost savings restated) during an offer period. Merger benefits and earnings enhancement statements are now regularly seen in supporting the rationale for merger-style transactions and in bid defence documents published by target companies subject to a hostile takeover.

Rule 19.1 was originally introduced in order to ensure that there is a high standard of rigour underlying any statements that offeror companies make during the course of an offer. Rule 28.6 specifically covers disclosure requirements for quantified financial benefits, and requires sufficient disclosure to enable target companies to identify weaknesses in the proposed level of benefits being put in front of shareholders or support cost savings the target company expects to achieve if the takeover does not proceed. The Rule requires disclosure of the bases of belief underlying the directors' statement, an analysis of the constituent elements of the estimate, and a base figure for comparison.

The new Rules extended the requirement for public reporting from the accountants and financial advisers, to include all quantified financial benefit statements made during an offer period by either the bidder or the target. Previously reporting was only required in connection with a hostile offer. It is therefore likely that this change in the rules will result in an increase in the number of public reports required from reporting accountants and financial advisors for inclusion in offer and defence documents.

Where a target company has published cost savings measures prior to the receipt of an offer such a statement is not subject to the reporting requirements of Rule 28, however if the Board make any amendments to the statement during the offer period the revised cost savings will be treated as a financial benefits statement and Rule 28 will apply. As with most of the rules, a company and its advisors are encouraged to speak to the Panel in the event that a Company has or is intending to issue a cost saving statement whilst also considering an offer.

Reporting accountants and financial advisers are required to report independently whether a quantified financial benefits statement has been "properly compiled on the basis stated" and made with "due care and consideration" respectively.

The work involved in order for the directors to be satisfied that it is appropriate to make such a statement and for the accountants and financial advisors to report on it should not be underestimated. The bid for Abbey National by Lloyds Bank involved highly detailed assumptions regarding the statement being published by Lloyds, all of which would have needed careful consideration by the directors.

As with profit forecasts, if any document or announcement published by a company included a quantified financial benefits statement, any subsequent document published by that party in connection with the offer must, unless superseded by a revised benefits statement included in the document, include a statement by the directors reaffirming the quantified financial benefits statement. Where reports were obtained in respect of the original quantified financial benefits statement, the document must include a statement that the reporting accountant and financial advisor have confirmed that their reports continue to apply.

Parties wishing to make quantified financial benefit statements which are not intended to be interpreted as profit forecasts should include an explicit and prominent disclaimer to the effect that such statements should not be interpreted to mean that earnings per share will necessarily be greater than in the preceding year. If, based on such a statement, a reader is able to calculate or infer the prospective profits of the enlarged group or at least determine a floor or ceiling for such profits, the statement will be subject to the Rules governing profit forecasts. Parties to a takeover who are in doubt as to the interpretation of such a statement are encouraged to consult the Panel in advance.

Consistent with the approach taken for Profit Forecasts, most Boards request a long form style report from the reporting accountants to provide the Board with detailed diligence upon the approach taken by management in the preparation of the quantified financial benefits statement and the underlying assumptions used.

8.2.3 Conclusion

Whilst the new Rules did not change the extent of the Board's responsibility for quantified merger benefit statements, they previously had and retain sole responsible for such statements, the rules significantly increased the number of circumstances requiring reporting by accountants and financial advisors. It will be interesting to see whether this new reporting requirement has any effect on the number of quantified financial benefits statements made in future by companies as part of an offer process.

8.3 Asset valuations

Asset valuations are very similar to profit forecasts as far as the Code is concerned. Valuations are used, principally by a target company, to defend against an offer or to argue for a higher price, based upon furnishing information to shareholders about the asset value of the company. The Code, through Rule 29, ensures that such information is given only where it is properly supported by a report from an independent valuer unconnected with the parties to the transaction.

During the Granada bid for Forte, Forte used a number of defences including a valuation of their hotels—this resulted in a revalued net assets per share of 334 pence, which can be compared to Granada's initial lower offer of 323 pence, and their final offer of 373 pence per share.

The Takeover Panel published a consultation paper in March 2010 (PCP 2010/1) which proposed amendments to the Code which would have an impact upon the reporting on asset valuations. These mainly involved the provision of certain exemptions from requiring the asset valuation to be reported on. The consultation period however closed in May 2010 and any changes have been deferred to a subsequent consultation paper. Consequently the current Rules still continue to apply.

8.3.1 *Valuations and offers*

Valuations given in connection with an offer typically apply to companies whose share prices tend to be influenced by asset values as opposed to profits, and good examples of this are oil exploration companies and property companies. But any kind of asset valuation is covered by the Code. For example, there have been a number of cases in recent years where valuations of pension fund surpluses have been given.

The Code requires a valuation to be supported by an opinion from an appropriately qualified valuer, which in the United Kingdom is likely to be a member of the Royal Institution of Chartered Surveyors (RICS), or the Institute of Revenues Rating and Valuation (IRRV). In addition, the valuer must have sufficient current knowledge of the asset being valued, together with the skills and understanding necessary to make the valuation.

A requirement was introduced in 1998 dealing with valuations of the other parties' assets. The bidder or target can only publish a valuation of the other parties' assets if a valuation is unqualified and up to appropriate standards. In exceptional cases, it is permitted for one party to comment on the others' valuation. The interpretation of this part of the Rule by the Panel leads to an interesting consequence: until one party has issued a formal valuation during the offer, the Panel does not allow the other party to refer to an old valuation. Accordingly, a bidder is unlikely to be able to comment on the trend in net assets per share shown by a target's financial statements until an up-to-date valuation has been issued by the target. The Panel needs to be consulted on this area in advance.

Whereas if a profit forecast is "on the record" it has to be reaffirmed, withdrawn or amended and reported on, an asset valuation has to be reported on only if it is made in connection with an offer. So, for example, the directors' estimates of asset values, which are frequently included in audited accounts, can be reproduced in offer or defence documents when setting out statements of assets, and need not be supported by an independent valuer, provided the asset values are not a particularly significant factor and are not given undue promi-nence.

8.3.2   *Basis of valuation*

Clearly, a valuation is of little use to shareholders or any other party unless the basis of that valuation is set out clearly.

The appropriate basis of a valuation depends on the type of asset, for example properties in use by a company should be valued at open market value for existing use, whereas investment properties should be valued at open market value. The detailed requirements are set out in the Code.

Furthermore, the valuation of land, buildings and plant must be made in accordance with the Appraisal and Valuation Standards issued by RICS. A point of detail came up in the Bilton defence in 1998 concerning whether or not the valuation should be gross or net of purchasers' costs. Normal practice is for it to be net of purchasers' costs, although Rule 29 is not explicit on this point.

The Panel may, in certain circumstances, permit the provision of information additional to the basic valuation. For example, in the hostile offer for Wolverhampton & Dudley Breweries, a valuation report was also prepared based upon the value of the pubs if sold as one block rather than individually. In addition, in the hostile offer for Blue Circle a "calculation of worth" valuation was presented to illustrate the potential develop-ment value of certain properties which would not be reflected in the open market values. However, the Panel should be consulted in advance in such circumstances and may require additional disclosures if an alternative valuation is to be used.

Where there is a material tax liability which would arise on sale of the asset, this should be disclosed. There are also detailed disclosures required for land with development potential including the costs of development and an estimated value once development has been completed, together with confir-mation of whether planning consent has been obtained and the nature of any conditions to consent which might affect value.

8.3.3 Exceptions

There is one exception to the Rule that a valuation must be fully supported by a report. Where the target company has a large number of properties—perhaps a retailer with hundreds of high street shops, or a house builder with many half-built houses—the Panel is sometimes prepared to allow a valuation of a representative sample by the professional valuer which is then extrapolated by the directors to give a value for the portfolio as a whole. This is not because the costs of a full valuation would be prohibitive, but rather that the time required to carry out a valuation is not available.

Any valuation must state the effective date at which the assets were valued, which is particularly relevant in times of rapidly changing property prices. It is possible to use a valuation that is not current but, since the valuer must state that he is satisfied that a valuation at the current date would not be materially different, it must effectively be up to date before it can be published.

Chapter 9

Application of the Market Abuse Regime to Takeovers

Mark Bardell

Partner

Herbert Smith Freehills LLP

9.1   Introduction

It is a stated purpose of the Code to provide an orderly framework within which takeovers are to be conducted and that it is designed to promote, in conjunction with other regulatory regimes, the integrity of the financial markets (see 1.1 above and paragraph 2(a) of the Introduction to the Code). Indeed, the fourth of the six General Principles of the Code specifically provides that: "False Markets must not be created in the securities of the offeree company, of the offeror company or of any other company concerned by the bid in such a way that the rise or fall of the prices of the securities becomes artificial and the normal functioning of the markets is distorted".

The market abuse regime is designed to ensure the integrity of financial markets and promote investor confidence. The Government's stated purpose in introducing the regime was so "the [Financial Services Authority, the Financial Conduct Authority's predecessor] will be able to impose a fine on any person or firm, whether regulated or not, who engages in [market] abuse".

Even at the high level of the stated purposes of the Code and the market abuse regime, the potential for significant overlap is apparent. However, the rules of the Code and the provisions of the market abuse regime have not been designed to fit together as one coherent regulatory regime. This is apparent from the facts that: compliance with the Code will not in itself ensure compliance with the market abuse regime (for example an offeror acquiring an interest in shares in compliance with the Rules of the Code regarding share buying—see 3 above—while in possession of inside information disclosed to it during a due diligence exercise will likely constitute market abuse—see 9.3 below); and compliance with the market abuse regime will not in itself ensure compliance with the Code (for example a director of an offeror company who has recommended that shareholders reject an unannounced and public offer who wishes to sell shares in the offeree company while not in possession of inside information may only do so with the consent of the Panel after giving sufficient public notice of their intentions together with an appropriate explanation—see Note 5 on Rules 4.1 and 4.2).

Accordingly, it is essential for practitioners in this area to be aware of the provisions of the market abuse regime as well as the rules of the Code and to consider each separately.

The market abuse regime, set out in ss.118 to 137 (Pt VIII) of the Financial Services and Markets Act 2000 (the FSMA), is a civil regime under which the regulator, the Financial Conduct Authority (the FCA) (the successor since April 1, 2013 to the Financial Services Authority—the FSA) can take disciplinary or enforcement action against a person who commits market abuse or who requires or encourages another to engage in behaviour which, if engaged in by the first person, would have amounted to market abuse. Market abuse is behaviour which relates to, or has an impact on, investments traded on a market and consists of, broadly two limbs, misuse of information (including insider dealing) or market manipulation (see 9.3 below). The FCA's extensive powers are described further in 9.4 below.

The market abuse regime sits alongside the criminal offences relating to insider dealing (contained in the Criminal Justice

Act 1993) and market manipulation (now contained in ss.89 and 90 of the Financial Services Act 2012). It also applies in addition to relevant regulatory requirements of the FCA, the specified markets and the Code. There are some important areas of overlap between the jurisdiction of the FCA and that of the Panel in the context of transactions governed by the Code. Accordingly, the purpose of this Chapter is to:

1. set out some background to the market abuse regime;
2. provide an overview of the definition of market abuse;
3. describe the FCA's powers; and
4. explain how the regime impacts on takeovers in practice.

9.2 Background to the market abuse regime

The market abuse regime was introduced in the UK relatively recently in historic terms, in 2001 under the FSMA, to supplement the existing criminal offence of insider dealing under the Criminal Justice Act 1993. The regime created (and not without controversy) what is often referred to as a "civil offence", it was not, and still is not, a criminal offence. As such, there is a lower standard of proof required for the FCA to enforce, the FCA determines whether an offence has been committed rather than a court or jury and an offence can be committed by any legal person (including a body corporate) rather than just by an individual.

Another important aspect of the market abuse regime is that the FCA is required under s.119 of the FSMA to publish the Code of Market Conduct (the COMC) to give guidance on whether behaviour amounts to market abuse. Where the COMC provides that something is not market abuse, that is conclusive of the matter. Where it indicates that something may be market abuse, that is evidential only.

With effect from 2005, this UK regime was amended when the EU Market Abuse Directive (2003/6) was implemented. The original UK offences of market abuse were however retained with their original broader scope, in addition to the new offences introduced into FSMA as a result of MAD, subject to a "sunset" clause (see s.118(9) FSMA) giving them effect until 30 June 2008. The Treasury subsequently extended the sunset clause pending completion of the European review of MAD, until December 31, 2014. On April 14, 2014 the European Council approved a new Market Abuse Regulation (the MAR) and a new criminal sanctions directive (the CSMAD), Member States will have until July 3, 2016 (i.e. 24 months) to adopt these measures into national law following publication of these measures in the Official Journal in mid 2014. The Treasury has already indicated an intention to opt out of CSMAD because the United Kingdom has a criminal offence of insider dealing under the Criminal Justice Act 1993 which is broader than CSMAD. Much of the detail of the new regime is still unclear as most of the key areas of the MAR are to be supplemented by detailed technical standards to be prepared by the European Securities and Markets Authority (ESMA), for approval by the EU Commission. However, it is clear already that the new regime will impact takeovers and current practice, as the MAR narrows certain takeover related exemptions in certain respects, for example by providing that inside information obtained during the conduct of the takeover or merger (such as during due diligence) may only be used if that information has been made public (or ceased to be inside information) by the time the merger is approved or the time of acceptance of the offer by target shareholders. The choice of a regulation rather than a directive could be taken as a signal of the European Commission's desire for greater uniformity which raises doubts over the continued role of the FCA's COMC.

In contrast to the increased uniformity and rigidity under pan-European legislation of the market abuse regime, the Panel has always sought to preserve its exclusive jurisdiction over and flexible approach to matters relating to takeovers because it is only too well aware of the tactical opportunities which overlapping regulatory jurisdictions can provide and the risk of allegations of market abuse being used tactically to deter or delay takeovers. Accordingly, when the FSMA was originally being consulted on and debated, the Panel wanted the Government to make two amendments relating to market abuse in the context of takeovers. The first of these—the "safe harbour" amendment—was designed to ensure that where a person, in the opinion of the Panel, complied with relevant provisions of the City Code that person did not commit market abuse. The second—the "gatekeeper" amendment—was designed to ensure that no disciplinary or enforcement action could be taken in respect of market abuse committed during the course of a takeover except at the request of the Panel. Both were supported by the Opposition and the safe harbour amendment was briefly included in a late version of the Bill when the Government was defeated on the point in the House of Lords.

The Treasury offered a rival, and from the point of view of takeover regulation, a less satisfactory version of the safe harbour amendment in the form of what is now s.120 of the FSMA.

This provides:

"(1) The [FCA] may include in [the COMC] provision to the effect that in its opinion behaviour conforming with the City Code:
(a) does not amount to market abuse;
(b) does not amount to market abuse in specified circumstances; or
(c) does not amount to market abuse if engaged in by a specified description of person."

This is set out in the COMC in MAR 1.10.4 – 5C which provides a table of specific provisions in the Code and to the extent that such a provision expressly requires or permits particular behaviour, then that behaviour will not constitute market abuse (provided that it also conforms with the General Principles of the Code). The effect of section 120 of the FSMA and the COMC regime is that it is for the FCA (not the Panel) to determine, in the context of the market abuse regime, whether behaviour complies with the Code. This raises the possibility of different interpretations by the two different regulators because it is not open to the FCA simply to adopt the Panel's views. This would amount to an unlawful fettering of the FCA's discretion, which would open the possibility of a successful judicial review. Further, section 120 is not as flexible as the Panel's original safe harbour amendment was. Paragraph 2(c) of the Introduction to the Code provides that the Takeover Panel may derogate or grant a waiver to a person from the application of a Rule of the Code (provided, in the case of a transaction and Rule subject to the requirements of the Takeover Directive, that its General Principles are respected) in the circumstances set out in the Rule or in other circumstances if it considers that the Rule in question would operate unduly harshly or in an unnecessarily restrictive or burdensome, or otherwise inappropriate, manner. It is common for the Panel to do this in practice. Where it does so in relation to a Rule to which the FCA has given a safe harbour in the COMC (see 9.5 below), the person benefiting from the modification or relaxation will not fall within the safe harbour.

The FCA has made clear in the Decision Procedure and Penalties Manual that it is for the FCA to determine whether behaviour complies with the Code, but that it will attach considerable weight to the views of the Panel in interpreting and applying it (DEPP 6.2.23G).

The Government did not include any provisions in the FSMA dealing with the interaction between the Code and the enforcement by the FCA of the market abuse regime. This was left to the FCA and the Panel to agree between themselves and consequently, in reaching such agreement, the FCA must avoid fettering its discretion unlawfully because to do so would potentially expose it to a successful judicial review application. Their operating arrangements are summarised in 9.5 below.

9.3 Market abuse explained

Market abuse is defined in s.118 of the FSMA as behaviour by any person:

1.   which occurs in relation to qualifying investments admitted to trading on a prescribed market (or in respect of which a request for admission has been made). The FSMA 2000 (Prescribed Markets and Qualifying Investments) Order 2001 (SI 2001/996) (as amended) prescribes the qualifying investments and relevant markets for this purpose. Depending on which kind of behaviour is relevant, the legislation has different scope tests:

     (a)   the retained provisions of the original market abuse regime, i.e. those referred to in 2.(c), (g) and (h) (so far as relevant) below, cover any investments admitted to trading on any market established under the rules of a UK recognised investment exchange (RIE). This part of the regime therefore covers investments relevant under the Code such as shares admitted to trading on the London Stock Exchange or on AIM, or on ICAP Securities and Derivatives Exchange Ltd., the other RIE on which shares are traded. In the remainder of this Chapter, these prescribed markets are referred to as "domestic markets". The legislation also provides that behaviour which occurs in relation to certain investments, such as derivatives (whether or not traded on a specified market) based on appropriately admitted qualifying investments ("relevant products"), is treated as occurring in relation to the qualifying investments themselves;

     (b)   the other provisions of the market abuse regime cover all investments admitted to trading on a domestic market or a "regulated market" established or operating in any other EU state. In the remainder of this Chapter, these prescribed markets are referred to as "EU markets". In addition, the kinds of behaviour described in 2.(a) and (b) amount to market abuse where they occur in relation to a "related investment" i.e. an investment whose price or value depends upon an instrument admitted to trading on an EU market; and

2.   which meets any of the following descriptions:

(a) an insider deals, or attempts to deal, in a qualifying investment or a related investment on the basis of inside information (known as "insider dealing");

(b) an insider discloses inside information otherwise than in the proper course of his employment, profession or duties (known as "improper disclosure");

(c) the behaviour does not fall in (a) or (b) and is based on information which is not generally available to those using the market in question but which, if available to a regular user of that market, would be likely to be regarded by him as relevant when deciding the terms on which transactions in qualifying investments should be effected ("relevant information"). The behaviour must also be likely to be regarded by a regular user of the market in question as a failure on the part of the person or persons concerned to observe the standard of behaviour reasonably expected of a person in his or their position in relation to the market (known as "misuse of information");

(d) a person effects transactions or orders to trade which either give or are likely to give a false or misleading impression as to the supply of, or demand for, or as to the price of a qualifying investment or secure its price at an abnormal or artificial level (otherwise than for legitimate reasons and in accordance with accepted market practices on the relevant market) (known as "manipulating transactions");

(e) a person effects transactions or orders to trade which employ fictitious devices or any other form of deception or contrivance (known as "manipulating devices");

(f) a person disseminates information by any means which gives or is likely to give a false or misleading impression as to a qualifying investment, where that person knew or could reasonably be expected to have known this (known as "dissemination");

(g) the behaviour does not fall within any of (d) to (f) but is nevertheless likely to give a regular user of the market in question a false or misleading impression as to the supply of, or demand for, or as to the price or value of qualifying investments (known as "misleading behaviour") or to be regarded by a regular user of the market in question as behaviour which would, or would be likely to, distort the market in a qualifying investment. (known as "distortion"). In each case, the behaviour must also be likely to be regarded by a regular user of the market in question as a failure on the part of the person or persons concerned to observe the standard of behaviour reasonably expected of a person in his or their position in relation to the market; or

(h) requiring or encouraging behaviour falling within any of (a) to (g).

The provisions described in 2.(a) to (c) and, so far as relevant, (h) are referred to in this Chapter as the "misuse of information" limb and the remaining provisions as the "market manipulation" limb.

The territorial scope of the market abuse regime is very wide—it covers not only behaviour which occurs in the United Kingdom, but also any behaviour, anywhere in the world, which meets the requirements of 1. and 2. above in relation to a domestic market. Therefore any behaviour, wherever it occurs in the world, which relates to offeree securities or derivatives will potentially fall within the regime in cases where those offeree securities or derivatives fulfil those requirements. Behaviour occurring in an EU Member State other than the United Kingdom but related to investments admitted to trading on a regulated market based in the United Kingdom may therefore amount to market abuse both in the United Kingdom and in the jurisdiction in which it occurs.

As regards behaviour within 2.(c) or (g), a "regular user" is a reasonable person who regularly deals on the market in investments of the kind in question. It is because of this role that, in very broad terms, compliance with existing legal and regulatory requirements, accepted market practice and exchange rules will generally be sufficient to avoid committing market abuse under these provisions. It should be only rarely that the regular user would consider that complying with accepted market practice is an unacceptable standard. However, although accepted market practice will in general not amount to market abuse, there is no complete safe harbour in this respect and it is open to the FCA to decide that certain accepted market practices do nevertheless constitute market abuse.

In contrast, behaviour within 2.(d), the MAD offence of manipulating transactions, is exempted where it is carried out for legitimate reasons and in conformity with "accepted market practices" as formally recognised by the FCA. This test is rather different from the regular user test because the relevant competent authority (rather than a hypothetical market user) will have to accept the practices in question. The FCA does not currently recognise any "accepted market practices" in UK markets.

The misuse of information limb covers similar ground to the criminal insider dealing legislation. However, it covers a much wider range of behaviour because it is not limited to disclosure, procuring, encouraging or dealing. Accordingly, for example, seeking irrevocables is within the market abuse regime but outside the criminal insider dealing legislation (although, the COMC states that seeking irrevocables in the context of a public takeover bid or merger for the purpose of gaining control does not itself amount to market abuse (MAR 1.3.17C)). Behaviour such as underwriting also falls within the scope of the misuse of information limb because the regime starts to apply as soon as an application for admission is made.

There are significant differences between the misuse of information limb and the criminal insider dealing legislation in other areas. For example, the definition of market abuse does not generally require that a person knew that information was inside information or relevant information. Further, in Consultation Paper 59 (on the COMC) the FCA's predecessor, the FSA, also indicated that the defences of "no expectation of profit" and "no prejudice through inequality of information" which are available under the criminal insider dealing legislation are not relevant in the context of market abuse. Each of these can play an important role in takeovers.

Instead, the COMC includes (in MAR 1.3.17C) a specific takeover-related safe harbour contemplated in the Directive, which provides that:

> "behaviour, based on inside information relating to another company, in the context of a public takeover bid or merger for the purpose of gaining control of that company or proposing a merger with that company, does not of itself [breach the dealing prohibitions]."

This covers seeking irrevocable undertakings or expressions of support, making arrangements in relation to offering securities as consideration and making arrangements to offer cash consideration. It covers the actual making of a takeover offer but arguably does not cover stakebuilding when in possession of inside information acquired during due diligence. (A potential bidder also risks committing the criminal offence of insider dealing in such circumstances). Nor does this safe harbour apply where a transaction is entered into on the basis of inside information concerning a proposed bid that provides merely an economic exposure (MAR 1.3.2E). This is to be contrasted with the Panel's historic approach to Rule 4.1 which has been to permit transactions which merely provide an economic exposure. The COMC defence also applies, with appropriate modifications, to behaviour within 2.(c).

The market manipulation limb covers broadly similar ground to the criminal regime now set out in ss.89 to 91 of the Financial Services Act 2012, but it is more extensive in some ways, in particular because it does not require such a strong mental element.

The market abuse regime does not require a person to be of a particular state of mind. In the light of the European Court of Justice decision in *Spector Photo Group NV v CBFA* (C-45/08) [2009] E.C.R. I-12073, the FCA guidance in COMC which had suggested that a person would only be dealing "on the basis of" inside information if that information were the reason for, or a material influence on, his decision to deal, has been deleted. However, the FCA is not able to exercise most of its powers against a person who can show that he reasonably believed that he was neither committing market abuse nor requiring or encouraging another to do so. Nor can it exercise these powers against a person who took all reasonable precautions and exercised all due diligence to avoid committing market abuse or requiring or encouraging another. These partial defences are likely to make guidance from the FCA and legal advice particularly important precautions in cases which are not straightforward. It will also be relevant whether a person has followed internal consultation and escalation procedures or sought guidance from other relevant regulators (e.g. the Panel).

9.4 Relevant powers of the Financial Conduct Authority

The FCA has power to impose an unlimited fine on a person who commits market abuse or censure him publicly. Section 124 of the FSMA requires the FCA to publish a statement of policy on the imposition of penalties and the amount of those penalties. This statement must also cover the circumstances relevant to a determination of whether a person can avail himself of the reasonable belief or all reasonable precautions defences described above. The Decision Procedure and Penalties Manual contains a non-exhaustive list of factors that the FCA considers relevant in deciding whether to take action, which includes:

1. the nature and seriousness of the behaviour, including whether it was deliberate or reckless, its duration and frequency, its impact on the market and others (including any financial impact) and whether any benefit was gained or loss avoided;
2. the behaviour of the person in question after the breach, including whether he co-operated with the FCA or the

Panel in any investigations, whether he took any steps to address the market abuse and how promptly and whether he complied with any regulatory rulings;
3. the sophistication of the market in question;
4. the ability of another regulator to address the matter—this factor is obviously very important in the context of takeovers;
5. consistency;
6. the impact any penalty may have on the interests of the market or any consumers—it is specifically made clear that the FCA recognises that it may not be in the interests of consumers to impose a penalty where this may impact on the timing or outcome of a takeover bid; and
7. the previous disciplinary record of the person whose behaviour is at issue.

The FCA has indicated that the factors relevant to the form of the penalty (fine or censure) include:

1. whether the behaviour is serious and the abuser has made money or avoided a loss—all of these factors make a fine more likely;
2. whether the person in question fully co-operates with the FCA and takes remedial steps—either of these factors makes a public censure more likely;
3. consistency; and
4. whether or not deterrence may be effectively achieved by a public censure.

The FCA's policy regarding the amount of any fine is based on the principles of disgorgement (ensuring a person does not profit by his breach), discipline (the offender should be penalised) and deterrence (the person and others should be deterred from committing similar breaches in future). These principles are incorporated into a five-step framework as follows:

Step 1: the removal of any financial benefit derived directly from the breach;

Step 2: the determination of a figure to reflect the seriousness of the breach;

Step 3: an adjustment to the Step 2 figure to take account of any aggravating and mitigating circumstances;

Step 4: an upwards adjustment made to the Step 3 figure, where appropriate, to ensure that the penalty has an appropriate deterrent effect; and

Step 5: if applicable, a settlement discount will be applied. This discount does not apply to disgorgement of any financial benefit derived directly from the breach.

The FCA also has power to apply to court to obtain an injunction restraining market abuse or requiring remedial steps to be taken. A court to which an application of this kind is made may, if so requested by the FCA, impose a penalty of the kind described above. The FCA has given guidance in the Enforcement Guide on factors likely to be relevant to an exercise of its power to seek injunctions. These include:

1. the nature and seriousness of the misconduct, including its impact on the market and the extent and nature of any financial impact on market users;
2. whether the conduct has ceased and the interests of consumers are adequately protected;
3. whether remedial steps are possible;
4. whether there is a danger of assets being dissipated;
5. the costs to the FCA compared with the likely resulting benefits;
6. the disciplinary record and compliance history of the person in question; and
7. whether another regulator can address the matter.

An example of the sort of remedial step that could be ordered is the correction of a misleading statement. It is unclear whether the injunctive power is wide enough to order the "freezing" of a takeover offer.

The FCA can also apply to court for restitutionary orders or order them on its own initiative where profits have accrued to the person who has committed market abuse or another has suffered loss as a result of it. In contrast to the position regarding injunctions, the reasonable belief and all reasonable precautions defences are available in respect of such orders. The Enforcement Guide includes guidance on the exercise of these powers. Relevant factors include:

1. whether identifiable persons have suffered quantifiable losses and their number and the extent of any loss;
2. the costs to the FCA compared with the likely resulting benefits;
3. the availability of other forms of redress (for example through rulings of the Panel);
4. whether those who have suffered can bring civil proceedings themselves;
5. the conduct of those who have suffered loss; and
6. the context, in particular whether the exercise of such powers might affect the timetable or outcome of any bid.

These disciplinary and restitutionary powers, but not the injunctive powers, are available in relation to a person who requires or encourages another to engage in behaviour which, if engaged in by the first person, would have amounted to market abuse.

In some areas the FCA's powers extend beyond the Panel's powers. It is also easy to see how the exercise of FCA powers could interfere with a bid timetable or affect the outcome of a bid.

9.5   Impact on takeovers in practice

9.5.1   Overlap

As mentioned above, given the overlap it is essential for practitioners in this area to be aware of the provisions of the market abuse regime as well as the Rules of the Code. The remainder of this Chapter considers the overlap in practice across the two limbs of market abuse described above, namely misuse of information and market manipulation.

9.5.1.1 *The misuse of information limb*

Historically, insider dealing in a takeover context was policed by the Panel. Over the years, responsibility has moved to the London Stock Exchange and the Treasury. The City Code does still include a Rule relating to insider dealing (Rule 4.1) which broadly prohibits any dealings in offeree shares, in related derivatives and, except where the proposed offer is not price-sensitive in relation to such securities, in offeror shares before the announcement of a bid by any person, other than the bidder, in possession of price-sensitive information concerning the bid. In practice, however, almost all cases within Rule 4.1 also involve insider dealing and are passed on by the Panel. The FCA will, however, consult the Panel if it thinks its proposed action in respect of an insider dealing matter may have an impact in relation to the takeover bid.

On a separate point as mentioned above (see 9.3 above) the Panel's approach to trading for pure economic exposure is different (permissive) for the purposes of Rule 4.1 whereas the FCA's approach as set out in the COMC is that amounts to insider dealing.

Another area where the FCA has proven to be less permissive than the Panel is making third parties insiders. Take for example shareholders made insiders or counterparties to negotiations made insiders regarding an approach regarding a possible takeover offer. The Panel's practice is to allow selective disclosure to a limited number of persons (see Practice Statement 20), whereas the decisions of the FCA in *FSA v Einhorn and Greenlight Capital Inc* (January 2012) and *FSA v Ian Hannan* (February 2012), demonstrate that the FCA consider it to be important to follow a proper process both to make persons insiders and to ensure the information remains confidential even where selective disclosure is permitted.

9.5.1.2   The market manipulation limb

There is overlap in relation to market manipulation limb two main areas:

1.   the making of disclosures, announcements, communications and releases of information; and
2.   the sale of offeree securities by the offeror or its concert parties, which is permitted by the City Code in very limited circumstances (Rule 4.2).

As regards the first of these, the timing, dissemination or availability, content or standard of care requirements of the Code (as set out in specified rules) are given a safe harbour in the COMC (as set out in the table in MAR 1.10.4C referred to above) so that it cannot be argued, for example, that announcements ought to have been made earlier or a different standard of care observed in order to avoid market abuse. Rule 4.2 also has a safe harbour in the COMC. In each case, the safe harbour does not apply to the extent the behaviour in question breaches a General Principle of the Code relevant to the Rule in question.

Accordingly, a person who complies with the relevant Code provisions will also have a safe harbour under the market abuse regime. As mentioned above, there is theoretical scope for regulatory disagreement here, which parties to a bid might seek to exploit, in that it is the FCA's view on whether the Code has been complied with which is relevant for safe harbour purposes. However, it is to be expected that in practice the Panel and the FCA will manage their relationship so as to minimise the possibility of their reaching different views.

How about Code provisions which do not benefit from safe harbour status? The COMC states (by way of guidance, rather than safe harbour):

"There are no rules in the Takeover Code, which permit or require a person to behave in a way which amounts to market abuse (MAR 1.10.3G)."

435

Therefore a person who complies with the Code should avoid committing market abuse. However, this is not a complete safe harbour: first because it is guidance; and secondly because the person will need to demonstrate that action fell within the Rules of the Code whereas in practice most actions involve a combination of matters within and without the Code.

What then about a person who breaches the Code? It seems clear that not every breach of the Code will amount to market abuse. For example, the FCA is understood to be of the view that shareholder abuse (i.e. failure to treat shareholders equally) with which a significant part of the City Code is concerned is not market abuse. There are also a number of other rules in relation to which it is hard to believe that breach would amount to market abuse—for example Rules 10, 12 and 13 which require the inclusion of certain conditions to an offer and prohibit others. Even a breach of one of the rules of the Code given a safe harbour may not amount to market abuse, depending on the precise circumstances.

9.5.2 *Operating together in practice*

Where a Code breach is potentially also market abuse, the FCA will not necessarily get involved. As Sir Howard Davies, the then Chairman of the FSA, made clear in June 2000:

> "We fully share the objective of ensuring that the FSA is not unhelpfully dragged into takeover battles, with damaging consequences for the way in which takeovers are handled in London... We believe that outcome can be achieved... by means of good cooperation between the FSA and the Panel."

The Decision Procedure and Penalties Manual and the Enforcement Guide give details on how the FCA and the Takeover Panel will interact.

First, the FCA will always refer to the Panel and give due weight to its views. It will also consult the Panel before exercising its powers if it considers that the exercise may affect the timetable or outcome of a takeover offer. It will expect parties to exhaust procedures for complaint available under the Code.

Secondly, the FCA will not, save in exceptional circumstances, take action in respect of behaviour to which the Code is relevant before the conclusion of procedures available under the Code or exercise its powers during the currency of a takeover offer.

The principal circumstances (other than misuse of information cases—see 9.5.1.1 above) in which the FCA is likely to consider exercising its market abuse related powers are stated to be:

1. where the FCA's approach in previous similar cases (whether or not in a bid context) suggests that a financial penalty should be imposed;
2. where the Panel requests the FCA to consider the exercise of its powers;
3. where the market abuse extends to securities or a class of securities which may be outside the Panel's jurisdiction;
4. where the market abuse threatens or threatened the stability of the financial system.

Intervention by the FCA in relation to Code governed matters is likely to be a rare event and it is likely to be very unusual for this intervention to be contemporaneous. However, as mentioned above, the FCA is unable to fetter its discretion. Accordingly, while it is open to the FCA to adopt policy statements of the kind described above, in order to avoid successful judicial review, it will need to consider, in each individual case, whether it is appropriate to follow its policy in the circumstances or whether the case in question is one which merits its intervention. This is where the scope for tactical attempts to involve the FCA lies, although the FCA should be able to minimise the benefits to a person of doing so by being very fast on its feet.

Further, parties to bids may well have observed close liaison between the Panel and the FCA in the past. Where appropriate, the Panel and the FCA are likely to organise and run simultaneous and co-operative decision-making processes to minimise disruption to the takeover timetable and the possibility of parties to a bid playing them off against one another.

Although the jurisdictional overlap does provide some scope for litigation in takeovers, in practice it has not emerged to date. Further, assuming the Panel and the FCA continue a close and constructive working relationship the scope appears limited. Indeed the back-up of the wide-ranging powers that the FCA has in respect of market abuse (in particular, the power to fine) provides useful additional support for the Panel. The fact that the FCA clearly attaches importance (in the context of its decision on whether to impose a penalty in respect of market abuse) to co-operation with regulators and to the swift taking of appropriate action should also assist the Panel as it is likely to provide an additional incentive to remedy or compensate for market abuse and to do so quickly.

Index

All indexing is to heading number

439

447

statements of interest by potential
competing bidders, 2.6.6

"Whitewash procedure"
mandatory offers, 4.2.3.1